Latino Religions and Civic Activism in the United States

Latino Religions and Civic Activism in the United States

Edited by

GASTÓN ESPINOSA
VIRGILIO ELIZONDO
JESSE MIRANDA

OXFORD
UNIVERSITY PRESS
2005

OXFORD
UNIVERSITY PRESS

Oxford University Press, Inc., publishes works that further
Oxford University's objective of excellence
in research, scholarship, and education.

Oxford New York
Auckland Cape Town Dar es Salaam Hong Kong Karachi
Kuala Lumpur Madrid Melbourne Mexico City Nairobi
New Delhi Shanghai Taipei Toronto

With offices in
Argentina Austria Brazil Chile Czech Republic France Greece
Guatemala Hungary Italy Japan Poland Portugal Singapore
South Korea Switzerland Thailand Turkey Ukraine Vietnam

Published by Oxford University Press, Inc.
198 Madison Avenue, New York, New York 10016

www.oup.com

Library of Congress Cataloging-in-Publication Data
Latino religions and civic activism in the United States / edited by Gastón Espinosa,
Virgilio Elizondo, and Jesse Miranda.
p. cm.
Includes bibliographical references and index.
ISBN-13 978-0-19-516227-1; 978-0-19-516228-8 (pbk.)
ISBN 0-19-516227-7; 0-19-516228-5 (pbk.)
1. Hispanic Americans—Religion. 2. Religion and sociology—United States.
I. Espinosa, Gastón. II. Elizondo, Virgilio P. III. Miranda, Jesse.
BR563 .H57L38 2005
261.8'089'68073—dc22 2004008801

9 8 7 6 5 4 3 2 1

Printed in the United States of America
on acid-free paper

This book is dedicated to the thousands of women and men who have taken their faith to the streets in order to create a better society

Preface

This book is the first in a series of anthologies, monographs, and reports that seek to create a critical discourse on Latino religions and politics in the United States. Although there is a growing literature on black, Native American, and Euro-American religions and politics, almost nothing has been published on the influence of religion on political and civic engagement in the Latino community. Many people outside of the Latino community are surprised to hear that César Chávez's and Reies López Tijerina's struggles were deeply influenced by their Catholic and Pentecostal backgrounds. Still others are surprised to find that Latino religious symbols, leaders, organizations, and movements provided the critical ideological, rhetorical, and moral platform for many Latino demands for political, civic, and social justice. This anthology uncovers and explores some of these efforts over the past 150 years. We hope that it will lay the historical foundation and context for a forthcoming similar volume that will explore the contemporary developments in Latino religions and politics.

These essays were commissioned by the directors and project manager of the Hispanic Churches in American Public Life (HCAPL) research project—Jesse Miranda, Virglio Elizondo, and Gastón Espinosa. Early drafts of some of them were presented at the HCAPL conference at the University of California, Santa Barbara. This was the first major conference on Latino religions and faith-based civic activism in the United States and was funded under a $1.3 million grant from The Pew Charitable Trusts. We use "civic" as an umbrella term that also includes social and political activities. In addition to Pew, the HCAPL project was sponsored by the Alianza de Ministerios Evangélicos Nacionales (AMEN) and the Mexican American Cultural Center (MACC). The HCAPL project sought to examine the impact of religion on political and civic engagement in the Latino community in the United States and Puerto Rico. It was ecumenical and nonsectarian in nature and was one the largest studies of its kind.

We thank Luís Lugo, Kimon Sargeant, and The Pew Charitable Trusts for their generous financial support. We also thank Elizabeth-Conde Frazier, María Elena González, Edwin I. Hernández, Allen Hertzke, Dean Hoge, David C. Leege, Daisy L. Machado, Donald E. Miller, Harry Pachon, Samuel Pagán, Milagros Peña, and Wade Clark Roof for serving on our advisory board. We also thank the Tomás Rivera Policy Institute (TRPI) for their partnership and supervision of the national surveys and community profiles. In addition, we thank the Mexican American Cultural Center, the Department of Religious Studies at the University of California, Santa Barbara, the Department of Religious Studies at Westmont College, the Department of Religious Studies at Northwestern University, President Murray Dempster at Vanguard University, and Claremont McKenna College for their support in hosting HCAPL conferences and for providing office space or technical support in the preparation of this manuscript. Special thanks are in order for Cynthia Read, Theo Calderara, Linda Donnelly, and others at Oxford University Press for moving a long and complex book through the editorial and production process with a gracious spirit.

Last but not least, we thank Michelle Unzueta, Antonio Pravia, Anita González, Janie Dillard, Karen Tarbell, Victor Mendez, Ada Argueta, Jon Greene, Debbie Flores, Karen Doehner, Saskia van Gendt, Melissa Abad, Alea Huggins, Charles Geraci, Dorothy Delaney, and our subcontractors and student assistants for their excellent work. Perhaps most important, we thank our family, friends, and community, without whose support and patience this book would have never been completed.

Contents

Contributors

Paul Barton is assistant professor of Hispanic studies at the Episcopal Theological Seminary of the Southwest in Austin, Texas. He teaches and writes on the history of U.S. Latino/a Christianity and North American Christianity. His forthcoming book is entitled *Negotiating Two Worlds: A History of Hispanic Protestants in Texas.*

Rudiger V. Busto is assistant professor of religious studies at the University of California, Santa Barbara. His research interests are on Latinos, Asian Americans, and race and religion. He is currently finishing a book on Reies López Tijerina.

Socorro Castañeda-Liles is a doctoral candidate in sociology at the University of California, Santa Barbara. Her areas of research are sociology of religion, sociology of knowledge, women studies, and Chicana/o studies. She is a UC MEXUS Dissertation Fellow and Louisville Institute Honorary Dissertation Fellow.

Miguel A. De La Torre is associate professor of religion at Hope College, where he teaches ethics, theology, and religious studies. He is the author of *The Quest for the Cuban Christ: A Historical Search*; *Santería: The Beliefs and Rituals of a Growing Religion in America*; and *La Lucha for Cuba: Religion and Politics on the Streets of Miami.*

Jill DeTemple is a doctoral candidate in religious studies at the University of North Carolina at Chapel Hill. Her research interests lie in faith-based organizations, ethnography, and Latin American religions. She is currently writing her dissertation, "Building Faith: Evangelical Development Organizations and Identity in Highland Ecuador."

Virgilio Elizondo is visiting professor of Latino religions and culture at the University of Notre Dame and is co-principal investigator of the Hispanic Churches in American Public Life study. He has written or edited nine books, including *The Future Is Mestizo; Christianity and Culture; Guadalupe: Mother of the New Creation;* and (along with Gastón Espinosa and Jesse Miranda) the forthcoming *Latino Religions and Politics in American Public Life.*

Gastón Espinosa is assistant professor of religious studies at Claremont McKenna College and past project manager of the Hispanic Churches in American Public Life research project. He writes on American and Latino religions, politics, and pop culture. He is coauthoring the forthcoming *Latino Religions and Politics in American Public Life* and is writing *Brown Moses: Francisco Olazábal and Latino Pentecostal Charisma, Power and Faith Healing in the U.S. Borderlands.*

María Cristina García is associate professor of history at Cornell University. She is the author of *Havana USA: Cuban Exiles and Cuban Americans in South Florida, 1959–1994* and is currently working on a book on Central American immigration.

Mario T. García is professor of history and Chicano studies at the University of California, Santa Barbara. He is the author of *Desert Immigrants: The Mexicans of El Paso, 1880–1920; Mexican Americans: Leadership Ideology and Identity, 1930–1960;* and *Memories of Chicano History: The Life and Narrative of Bert Corona.* He is presently working on the role of Mexican American activism in the Catholic Church.

Luís D. León is visiting professor of ethnic studies at the University of California, Berkeley. He is the author of *La Llorona's Children: Religion, Life, and Death in the United States–Mexican Borderlands* and an upcoming book on César Chávez.

Stephen R. Lloyd-Moffett is a doctoral candidate in religious studies at the University of California, Santa Barbara. His research focuses on alternative Christianities, especially the ascetic and mystical traditions.

Timothy Matovina is associate professor of theology and director of the Cushwa Center for the Study of American Catholicism at the University of Notre Dame. He is the author of *Tejano Religion and Ethnicity* and coeditor of *Horizons of the Sacred: Mexican Traditions in U.S. Catholicism.*

Lester McGrath-Andino is professor of church history at the Evangelical Seminary of Puerto Rico. An advocate of social justice, he writes on church history, politics, and social activism. He is the author of *Un Ministerio Transformador; El Seminario Evangélico de Puerto Rico* and *Que Vadis, Vieques? Etica Social, Política, y Eeumenismo.*

Lara Medina is associate professor of Chicano and Chicana studies at California State University, Northridge, and writes on Chicana/Latino history, religion, feminism, and social activism.

Jesse Miranda is distinguished professor of religion and director of the Center for Urban and Latino Leadership at Vanguard University and co-principal investigator of the Hispanic Churches in American Public Life study. In addition to this present volume, he has authored *The Christian Church in Ministry* and *Liderazgo y Amistad*. He is also coauthoring the forthcoming *Latino Religions and Politics in American Public Life*.

Alberto López Pulido is director and associate professor of ethnic studies and sociology at the University of San Diego and writes about the relationship between race, religion, and community. He is author of *The Sacred World of the Penitentes*.

Daniel Ramírez is assistant professor of religious studies at Arizona State University, where he teaches courses on borderlands religions, migration, religion, culture, and music.

Elizabeth D. Ríos is a doctoral candidate at Nova Southeastern University. She is an ordained Assemblies of God minister, vice president of operations at the Latino Pastoral Action Center (LPAC) in New York City, and founder of the Center for Emerging Female Leadership in New York City.

Santos C. Vega is Professor Emeritus at Arizona State University and of the ASU Hispanic Research Center. His publications include various essays on U.S. Latinos in books, encyclopedias, and other scholarly venues.

Richard L. Wood is associate professor of sociology at the University of New Mexico and writes on the role of religion in civil society. He is author of *Faith in Action: Religion, Race, and Democratic Organizing in America*.

Latino Religions and Civic Activism in the United States

Introduction: U.S. Latino Religions and Faith-Based Political, Civic, and Social Action

Gastón Espinosa, Virgilio Elizondo, and Jesse Miranda

The Catholic Church refused to promote social action and limited itself to meeting the minimal spiritual needs of the people. . . . [It] was a missionary group that, by its silence, tacitly supported the oppressive conditions under which Chicanos had to live and work. . . . Protestant churches . . . were not interested in . . . championing rights or promoting brotherhood.

—Rodolfo Acuña, *Occupied America*, 1972

I don't think I could base my will to struggle on cold economics or some political doctrine. I don't think that there would be enough to sustain me. For me the base must be faith.

—César Chávez, cited in Jacques Levy, *César Chávez: Autobiography of La Causa*

The criticisms of Rodolfo Acuña and others like him have helped shape a generation of Chicano and Latino scholarship on Latino religions and politics. They have also contributed to the long-standing perception that religion has not had an important role in Latino political, civic, and social action. This perception, along with the growing disenchantment with organized religion and a growing interest in Marxist and socialist teachings during the countercultural movement of the 1960s and 1970s, prompted many Latino scholars to focus their scholarship on more overtly political and community-oriented areas of research like education, political science, sociology, and history.

Acuña's comments, however, appear at first to stand in sharp contrast to those of other Latino leaders like César Chávez, who said that his faith was the basis for his political activism. In fact, people are often surprised to see how crucial religious faith was to Chávez's struggle for social justice. Although Chávez is often compared to Martin Luther King Jr., until Frederick John Dalton's *The Moral Vision of César Chávez* (Maryknoll, New York: Orbis Books, 2003), the role that his faith and the Catholic Church played in his struggles have been largely overlooked. This is due in part to a lack of understanding of the internal dynamics that shaped his life and in part to a latent anti-institutional Catholicism and ambiguity about the role of religion in American society. Indeed, Americans are much more comfortable hearing about Chávez the political activist than about Chávez the religious mystic or charismatic prophet. As Steven Lloyd-Moffett shows in chapter 2 in this book, this largely secular image of him has been perpetuated by American society and the academy, which has stripped his activism of its deeply spiritual moorings. Indeed, in the twelve biographies about Chávez prior to Dalton's, not a single chapter solely examines the impact of his faith on his political, civic, or social action. This is remarkable given his deep faith convictions.

This largely secular interpretation of Chávez is being challenged by a growing number of young Latino and Anglo-American scholars who are exploring the religious factor in Chávez's activism. The struggle over the role of religion and faith-based action is not limited to Chávez. In fact, little has been written about the impact of religion on political, civic, and social action in the Latino community.[1] Indeed, in the many books on Latino history and political movements prior to 1975, religion and faith-informed activism almost appear to be irrelevant. The role that religion plays in Latino history, politics, and society is often relegated to a footnote or to several pages. When references are made, they are often negative or cited to support some other overarching theory or thesis.[2] This is true not only in the fields of American and Latino religions but also in political science, sociology, and Chicano and Latino studies. A student could rightly walk away from most courses in these fields wondering why religion has not had a more prominent role in the face of more than a century and a half of discrimination, suffering, and marginalization.

The lack of attention to Latino faith-based action stands in sharp contrast to the literature on African American political activism. Taylor Branch's *Parting the Waters: America in the King Years, 1954–63*; Juan Williams's *Eyes on the Prize: America's Civil Rights Years, 1954–1965*; Juan Williams and Quinton Hosford Dixie's *This Far by Faith: Stories from the African American Religious Experience*; Fredrick Harris's *Something Within: Religion in African-American Political Activism*; R. Drew Smith's *New Day Begun: African American Churches and Civic Culture in Post–Civil Rights America*, and many other books—all document the profound influence that religious values, symbols, rhetoric, leaders, and churches had on the African American civil rights movement.

This book spotlights the importance of religion in the Latino community and seeks to help fill this long-standing gap in the literature. These essays demonstrate that although Acuña was partially correct when he inferred that some Latino churches, denominations, and religious leaders did support the status quo in American society, we would add that many Latino clergy and laity also drew on their popular faith traditions and expressions to fight for political and civil rights and social justice. These essays contest, challenge, and revise the ostensibly "secular" narrative of Latino history, politics, and civil rights struggles by exploring the various ways religious ideology, institutions, leaders, and symbols have shaped the lives of prominent Latino leaders and movements.

The purpose of this book is to initiate a critical discussion about the impact of Latino religions on political, civic, and social action in the United States. It is also meant to lay the historical foundation and context for the next volume on Latino religions and politics in American public life. The second book will reveal the findings from the Hispanic Churches in American Public Life (HCAPL) research project. This three-year study was funded by a $1.3 million grant from The Pew Charitable Trusts. Through it, we surveyed and interviewed 3,000 Latinos across the United States and Puerto Rico. HCAPL fielded two surveys, including the largest Hispanic-framed bilingual survey (n = 2,310) on Latino religions and politics in U.S. history.[3] It is our hope that our work will invite and stimulate interest in the emerging field of Latino religions and politics. We also hope it will refine currently accepted ideas on the impact of religion in American public life. Finally, we trust it will prompt religious and civic leaders to recognize the importance of Latino religions as an important factor in the American public square.

The findings in this book suggest that Latino religious ideology, institutions, leaders, and symbols have played a crucial role in Latino political, civic, and social action in the United States. In fact, the evidence in this volume suggests that they have served as the ideological glue for some of the most important struggles in the Latino community over the past 150 years.

The papers and authors in this volume represent a cross-section of American society and the Latino community, although a majority of the chapters were written by and about Latinos of Mexican, Puerto Rican, Cuban, and Central American descent. The first chapters of this book focus largely on the Mexican American experience because it is the largest and oldest Latino subculture in the continental United States and because mass immigration of Puerto Ricans, Cubans, and Central and South Americans did not begin in earnest until 1917, the 1960s, and the 1980s, respectively. All of these essays examine the influence of religious ideology, clergy, lay leaders, organizations, centers, and controversies on political, civic, and social engagement among Latinos in the United States and Puerto Rico. The essays cover the period from 1848 to 2004 and spotlight the struggles in the Southwest, New York City, Miami, rural America, and Puerto Rico. Although a majority of the chapters deal with Catholicism, we have also included essays on Mainline, Evangelical, and Pentecostal Protestantism. And at least two essays touch briefly on Santería, Mormanism, and the Jehovah's Witnesses.

Despite our effort to be inclusive, it was impossible to cover all twenty-two

Latino nationality groups, regions, denominations, and religious traditions in the United States. In an effort to address the lack of attention to Evangelical Protestantism and women, we commissioned work on Reies López Tijerina, the Central American Sanctuary movement, and Puerto Rican Pentecostal women and faith-based organizations in New York City. We had a very difficult time finding women to contribute to the volume. Seven women declined invitations to submit essays due to prior commitments, lack of time, or lack of expertise on the intersection of religion and politics among Latinos. Most of these seventeen essays focus on various forms of Catholic- or Protestant-inspired political, civic, and social engagement because most of the social movements, leaders, and forms of activism were shaped primarily by these traditions. This fact, along with the reality that 93 percent of the Latino community self-identifies with the Christian religion and only 1 percent self-identify with a world religion, has also indirectly shaped the volume's final outcome. In 2004, 70 percent (28 million) of all Latinos are Roman Catholic and 23 percent are Protestant or Other Christian (9.1 million). Of the latter, 8 million are Protestant, and 88 percent (7 million) either attend an Evangelical denomination or self-identify as a "born-again" Christian. Furthermore, 64 percent (5.1 million) of all Latino Protestants are Pentecostal or Charismatic.[4] There are now more Latino Protestants in the United States than either Jews, Muslims, or Episcopalians. These factors, along with time and budget constraints and volume size, prevented us from including more essays. However, our goal is not to produce the largest, most comprehensive, or most definitive work on U.S. Latino religions and political, civic, and social action. Rather, our goal is much more modest: we simply want these essays to help stimulate and guide the emerging field of Latino religions and politics in the United States. It is in this spirit that we offer up this volume as a launching point for further research.

Despite its limitations, this volume is the first of its kind to explore under one cover the impact of religion on political, civic, and social engagement in the lives and work of famous Latino leaders and movements like Padre Antonio José Martínez, César Chávez, Reies López Tijerina, Jorge Lara-Braud, Tomás Atencio, Leo Nieto, Rosa Marta Zaraté, Aimee García Cortese, Leoncia Rosado Rousseau (Mama Leo), Juan Romero, Virgilio Elizondo, PADRES, Las Hermanas, faith-based community organizing, the Sanctuary movement, the Vieques controversy, the Elián González controversy, and many other important personalities, controversies, groups, and topics. Finally, some of these essays touch on the important contributions of Protestants, Pentecostals, women, and faith-based organizations and other groups that often are overlooked in most discussions on the subject.

We have divided the book into two sections. The first ten chapters look at the impact of religion on political, civic, and social engagement in past historical struggles; the next seven chapters explore contemporary struggles that recently took place in the United States and Puerto Rico. This is followed by our conclusion, which summarizes the key findings, areas for further research, and practical recommendations to chart a new course for the future.

In chapter 1, Timothy Matovina explores the various ways Latinos drew on their Catholic faith and popular traditions to resist the discriminatory treatment they faced after the U.S.–Mexico War and the Treaty of Guadalupe Hidalgo in 1848 ceded the Southwest to the United States. Although in theory the treaty promised Latinos the same rights and privileges as all other citizens, in practice Latinos were forced to live in segregated communities, had to attend segregated schools, and were discriminated against.[5] Matovina points out that this kind of shoddy treatment took place outside and inside of the Catholic Church. Matovina further explores the various struggles of indigenous (born and raised in the area) native-born priests like Antonio José Martínez, who resisted discrimination by Anglo-American public and church officials. He demonstrates the vital role that Latino clergy and popular Catholic traditions had in political, civic, and social action in the Southwest. He also shows the various ways Latinos used popular religious traditions as a resource to engage in civic and social action. This offers a valuable corrective to studies that ignore the impact of religion and popular religiosity or confine it to the "domestic sphere."

Clergy were often crucial in Latino action because they served as public leaders and advocates. Clergy-based activism was indirectly chipped away at in the late nineteenth and early twentieth centuries by the Anglo-American Catholic hierarchy, which replaced most of the indigenous native-born Latino priests and bishops with French bishops and priests in New Mexico and Irish in California.[6] This muted and slowed (although it did not silence) the level of Latino faith-based political, civic, and social action in the early twentieth century and unintentionally left the Latino community vulnerable to exploitation, abuse, and discrimination.

The transformation of the native priesthood and the move away from National Catholic Parishes could not have taken place at a worse time. The growth of the U.S.-built railroads in Mexico, along with employment opportunities after 1880, prompted hundreds of thousands of Mexicans to migrate to the United States. The Catholic Church was soon faced with a shortage of priests. A second wave of migrants flooded across the border as the Mexican Revolution (1910–1917) ripped through that country. Between 1880 and 1930, more than 1 million Mexicans migrated to the United States. The positive side to this development was that a large number of Mexican priests and nuns also fled into the country, and they augmented the Anglo-American Catholic Church's ministry to Mexicans.[7]

Not everyone was pleased by the massive influx of Mexican immigrants. In an effort to control Mexican immigration, the U.S. government set up the Border Patrol in 1925 and laid out strict immigration requirements. Nativism, the Ku Klux Klan, white supremacy, and segregation made life difficult for many Mexican Americans living in the Southwest. The Great Depression fed this nativism, and the American government deported or repatriated more than 500,000 Mexicans back to Mexico in the early 1930s, many with children who were born and raised in the United States. This, along with the end of the Mexican Revolution, prompted many Mexican clergy and sisters to return to Mexico. This left the U.S. Catholic Church bereft of their assistance.

The winds of fortune changed during World War II, which created a labor shortage in the United States as men marched off to war. The U.S. government signed an agreement with the Mexican government to import Mexican laborers, or *braceros*. This new agreement was called the Bracero Program (1942–1964). It allowed 250,000 Mexicans into the United States to work on farms, ranches, mines, and railroads. After the war came to an end, however, agribusinesses requested that the braceros be allowed to stay. This request was granted, and now many braceros began to bring their families with them into the country.[8]

The need for Mexican labor curtailed during a recession after the Korean War (1950–1953). Although some braceros were sent back to Mexico, many decided to return or remain in the United States illegally in order to provide for their families. The U.S. government responded by launching Operation Wetback in 1954, which led to the repatriation of more than 1 million undocumented immigrants to Mexico. After the Bracero Program came to an end in 1964, undocumented immigration into the United States soared, as thousands of former braceros now wanted to continue working here. Many became naturalized citizens and continued working in the agriculture industry as farm laborers, albeit under shabby conditions. Since that time, the Latino population in the United States has grown from 9.1 million in 1970 to 22.4 million in 1990 to 40 million in 2004, sixty-five percent of whom are of Mexican ancestry.

During the early twentieth century, the institutional Catholic Church did not have a vibrant national ministry to migrant farmworkers. There were exceptions. One such exception was the Mission Band, which was made up of four priests who traveled up and down central California ministering to thousands of migrant farmworkers between 1949 and 1962. One of the leaders, Father Donald McDonnell, influenced a young and little-known Mexican American Community Service Organization (CSO) leader named César Chávez.[9]

César Chávez is the most famous Latino figure in U.S. history. He indirectly stepped into the gap left by the Mission Band and other civil rights advocacy groups silenced by Cold War patriotism and the growing conflict in Vietnam. Like Father Martínez in New Mexico, Chávez drew inner strength and resolve from his Catholic faith and its popular traditions, symbols, and rhetoric. As Stephen Lloyd-Moffett points out in chapter 2, Chávez was inspired by Mahatma Gandhi, Martin Luther King Jr., and the civil rights movement. Chávez's fasts and pilgrimage from Delano to Sacramento were shaped by his reported deep mystical experiences with God. Lloyd-Moffett argues that we do not hear more about the spiritual dimension of Chávez's activism because the liberal intelligentsia have deliberately secularized his image to suit their own political and ideological goals.

In chapter 3, Luís León challenges this portrayal and, instead, posits that Chávez quite intentionally manipulated, invented, and recast religious symbols to further his political and social aims. This is not to say that Chávez took a utilitarian view of religion. To the contrary, he was a deeply spiritual person whose long fasts, prayer vigils, and pilgrimages were as sincere as they were powerful. However, his religious identity was much more complex and riddled with more ambiguity than most realize. In many respects, Chávez functioned like a Weberian prophet who was able to "infuse" an ostensibly secular political struggle with ultimate value and sacred meaning.

The work of nonviolent activists like Chávez stood in sharp contrast to the barn-burning style of former Pentecostal evangelist Reies López Tijerina. Tijerina was to Chávez what Malcolm X was to Martin Luther King. As a radical cultural nationalist, Tijerina saw himself as God's anointed to fight on behalf of the land grants "swindled" away from New Mexicans after the United States–Mexico War of 1848. He saw his activism in the tradition of the Gorras Blancas (White Caps) of the 1880s and 1890s. The Gorras Blancas were bands of hooded nighttime riders who descended on Anglo ranchers, tearing down fences and derailing trains. They hoped that this would scare off Anglo land developers and railroad companies.[10]

Taking a different strategy at first, Rudy Busto, in chapter 4, points out that Tijerina claimed that the Spanish Laws of the Indies, which granted in perpetuity Spain's right to determine the land grants, were still valid. Busto argues that Tijerina believed that these laws superseded Anglo-American jurisprudence because the Laws of the Indies were conferred by the Pope, God's representative on earth, and were thus binding in heaven as well as on earth. He came to this conclusion because of his magical-literalist interpretation of the Bible, which he learned from the Pentecostal movement. After his more traditional strategies did not work, he adopted more radical tactics like his armed takeover of the Tierra Amarilla courthouse and occupation of Kit Carson National Forest. Tijerina's tactics did not attract a large number of followers, and he was largely unsuccessful in his struggle. Busto notes that there is no room for radical activists like Tijerina in Robert Bellah's notion of American civil religion, precisely because of his Pentecostal magical-realist reading of the Bible. However, his struggle inspired other Chicano cultural nationalists like Rodolfo (aka "Corky") González to argue that, since the Southwest was the mythical homeland (or Aztlán) of the Aztecs, Mexicans had every right to return to the Southwest.[11]

Chávez's work, along with that of other Mexican American activists such as Tijerina, González, José Angel Gutiérrez, and thousands of Chicano/a students, helped give birth to the larger Mexican American civil rights movement and the smaller Chicano student movement in the Southwest. The boundaries between these two movements were very fluid and porous. These movements were most active between 1965 and 1975. They fought against discrimination and for self-respect and self-determination against Anglo-American prejudice and injustice.[12]

A growing number of Chicano priests picked up the ideals and goals of Chávez and the Chicano movement. After 1971 they also became increasingly influenced by the work of Gustavo Gutiérrez's liberation theology. Gutiérrez's theological work complemented the largely secular Chicano movement, especially at Catholic colleges and universities. Liberation theology's emphasis on liberation, economic justice, consciousness raising, and defending the rights of the poor resonated with Chicano activists and priests alike. It became the glue that tied the goals of the Chicano movement to the struggle for social justice for many Catholic and Protestant activists.

These intellectual ideologies coalesced among a growing number of Chicano priests who believed it was imperative that they become more politically, civically, and socially involved on behalf of the Latino community. Rather than take the route of the fiery Tijerina and González, both of whom were also theologically suspect in the minds of some since they came from Protestant backgrounds, many opted to follow the confrontational and yet nonviolent path to social justice laid out by Chávez. In 1969, fifty priests met in San Antonio and organized PADRES. In chapter 5, Mario T. García points out that PADRES activists like Father Juan Romero, Father Luis Quihuis, and Father Virgilio Elizondo functioned as "community priests." They differed from the French "worker priests" of post–World War II Europe primarily because they did not work or live alongside the workers. Instead, community priests fight primarily for civil rights in society and social justice and reform within the Catholic Church.

Inspired by the work of PADRES, the Chicano movement, and the feminist movement, a group of Chicana/Latina nuns met under the leadership of Sister Gregoria Ortega and Sister Gloria Gallardo to form Las Hermanas in 1971. They labored under the slogan of "Prayer and Action." Lara Medina points out in chapter 6 that, like PADRES, Las Hermanas sought the integration of spirituality and social action. Their ranks grew rapidly and shaped a number of key Catholic leaders such as Rosa Martha Zaraté, Tess Browne, and María Antonietta Berriozábal. Las Hermanas has since served as a springboard for hundreds of women religious and laity seeking a realized model of social spirituality.

It was precisely this kind of social spirituality that led to the founding of the Mexican American Cultural Center (MACC) in San Antonio in 1972. In chapter 7, Socorro Castañeda Liles argues that MACC provided Mexican Americans with agency and voice through historical retrieval. Like PADRES, MACC was inspired by Chávez, the Chicano movement, the civil rights movement, and liberation theology. Its cofounder, Virgilio Elizondo, actively sought to bridge the chasm that so often separated spirituality and social action in American Catholicism. Although founded by men, MACC has been run primarily by Catholic women and thus represents another example of the important ways that women continue to shape Latino/a social engagement in the United States.

The work of Chávez, Tijerina, PADRES, Las Hermanas, and other Chicano civil rights and liberation movements inspired Latino Protestants to become more politically, civically, and socially engaged. In chapter 8, Paul Barton notes that Latino Mainline Protestants not only followed Chávez in the 1960s and 1970s but even joined him on the picket lines in California and Texas. Latino United Methodists, Presbyterians (PCUSA), and Baptists took their experiences on the front lines into their Anglo-American denominations, where they fought for respect, autonomy, self-determination, and political empowerment.[13] Barton suggests that their activism challenged the largely "Evangelical" approach to social justice that dominated the traditions at that time. Their calls for justice coalesced nicely with those in the larger African American civil rights movement. As a result, Latino activists were relatively successful—not only in awakening the conscience of their white brethren but also in gaining valuable leadership skills that would one day serve them well as leaders in their respective traditions. In an interesting if not ironic twist of events, yesterday's Latino faith-based radicals became tomorrow's bishops and district superintendents in many Mainline Protestant denominations.

Latino Protestant and Catholic clergy fought for social justice in politics and in the church, as well as in the community. Many became actively involved with faith-based organizing in the early 1970s. In chapter 9, Richard Wood notes that, unlike other forms of political, civic, and social action, faith-based organizing cuts across religious, country-of-origin, language, and immigration lines. Today an estimated 3,300 congregations (20%, or 660, of them Hispanic) participate in faith-based organizing. Latino clergy have been actively involved with faith-based organizations because they are practical and local ways to fight for better housing, public schools, economic development, policing, health care, and recreational programs for youth.[14]

This ecumenical spirit of cooperation between Catholics and Protestants was also evident in the Sanctuary movement. María Cristina García points out in chapter 10 that in the 1980s faith-based organizations and more than 200 churches and several synagogues across the United States provided sanctuary or refuge to tens of thousands of political refugees from Guatemala, El Salvador, and Nicaragua who fled across the U.S.–Mexico border. Viewing themselves as the new Underground Railroad, Sanctuary movement leaders provided support and assistance to these immigrants in direct violation of the U.S. government. This movement laid the foundation for a revival of the Sanctuary movement in the Southwest in the late 1990s.[15]

Although most of the churches that took part in the Sanctuary movement were Mainline Protestant or Catholic, Daniel Ramírez points out in chapter 11 that Pentecostal churches not only provided succor to Central American immigrants seeking sanctuary in the 1980s but even welcomed them into their ministerial ranks. This challenges the traditional view of Pentecostal faith-based action and forces scholars to expand their understanding of Latino political, civic, and social engagement. Ramírez argues that Pentecostal and Evangelical churches serve as "micro public squares and transnational spaces" where people are constantly engaging in transgressive political behavior. As Espinosa has pointed out elsewhere, there is evidence to indicate that social action has been a part of Latino Pentecostal outreach ever since Susie Villa Valdez attended the Azusa Street Revival in Los Angeles around 1906 and sometime thereafter began work in the "slums" of Los Angeles and migrant labor camps throughout Southern California.[16]

Likewise, Elizabeth Ríos argues in chapter 12 that progressive Pentecostal women in New York City have been blending evangelism with social action for almost half a century. This trend is taking place primarily among second- and third-generation Pentecostals. Unlike their predecessors, who tended to limit "sin" to the individual, today's Pentecostals recognize structural sin and the need for both social and spiritual liberation. Scores of women and men like Rev. Leoncia Rosado Rosseau (aka "Mama Leo"), Rev. Aimee García Cortese, Rev. Ana Villafañe, Rev. Rosa Caraballo, Rev. Ray Rivera, and many other Pentecostal/Charismatics have been working in New York City *barrios* for spiritual and social justice for decades.[17] Their decision to blend evangelism and social work is not accidental. Although Latinos are now the largest minority group, they are also the most poverty stricken, the youngest, and the least educated of all American minority groups.[18]

Pushing the idea of reimagining social action further, Jill DeTemple, in chapter 13, suggests that we need to take our conceptualization of social action one step further. In her work on the Brazilian-based Pentecostal Universal Church of the Kingdom of God in Boston, she found that although they do not use the same social justice language found in Catholic and Mainline Protestant circles, in fact, Pentecostals do work to these ends. She carefully shows that a new model of social engagement should take into account the important impact that individual conversion and transformation has on community life. For poor and working-class Latinos, this is a much more practical, direct, and concrete way of changing society, she suggests. In this respect, spiritual liberation is directly tied to a new identity and the ability to overcome injustice, poverty, isolation, and disenfranchisement in their public lives. Thus, Pentecostalism empowers the individual to transform not only him- or herself but also society.

The fact that most Pentecostal churches and denominations produce native or indigenous leaders has been a key factor in their growth and in their ability to find creative ways to engage society. Alberto López Pulido and Santos C. Vega similarly argue in chapter 14 that indigenous leadership was a key reason that one African American Baptist Church in Phoenix was more socially active than a Latino Catholic parish. The African American civil rights struggle was successful largely because it had the support of many black churches, clergy, and denominations. Blacks did not have to go through the highly political process of seeking approval and support from white denominational leaders as do Latinos in the Catholic Church and in some Protestant traditions. However, Latinos do have leadership-forming events in indigenous practices like the Cursillo and the Encuentros.[19] National Latino parishes can also foster indigenous leadership training within the church that can serve as a springboard for future political, civic, and social action. There does seem to be truth to this argument, as elsewhere in the volume we have seen that Chávez, Ernie Cortés, Juan Romero, Virgilio Elizondo, and many others have participated in the Cursillo and in some of the Encuentros.

The problems facing Mexican American Catholics in the Southwest is not quite as sharply pronounced among Cubans in places like Miami because many priests also fled Cuba after Fidel Castro's Cuban Revolution in 1959. Because of Castro's avowed support of "Godless communism," Cubans have been more warmly aligned with the Christian church than have other Latino nationality groups. This was in large part due to the cooperation between Catholic and Protestant churches and the U.S. government during Operation Pedro Pan in Florida between 1961 and 1963, during which time over 14,000 Cuban children were smuggled out of Cuba and taken to the United States. President Dwight D. Eisenhower's administration worked with religious organizations to provide homes, counseling services, social services, and employment for Cuban children and adults fleeing Castro's 26th of July movement.[20] The close tie between religion and political activism is evident not only in Cuban faith-informed organizations like the Institute for Cuban Studies (1969) and the exilic Christian Democratic Party of Cuba (1991), but also in the Elián González controversy of the late 1990s and 2000.[21]

As Miguel De La Torre points out in chapter 15, Cuban Catholic priests and laity supported the efforts of Elián's uncle to gain custody of the child. Cubans flocked to Elián's uncle's home and drew on their faith to pray, protest, and demonstrate against President Bill Clinton's administration and Attorney General Janet Reno, who wanted the child returned to Cuba. Many Cubans interpreted the conflict as a deeper struggle about their own meaning and existence. Some also laid aside their theological differences and united in all-night prayer vigils and fasts. Catholics, Protestants, and practitioners of Santería all saw the child as symbolic of the exilic Cuban struggle and thus prayed that he would be allowed to stay in the United States.

The struggle over Elián tapped into the collective identity of the exilic Cuban community much like the Vieques controversy did among Puerto Ricans in Puerto Rico. In chapter 16, Lester McGrath-Andino suggests that perhaps for the first time in the history of the island, Catholic, Mainline Protestants, and Pentecostals joined forces to shut down the U.S. Navy base on the island of Vieques, just off the coast of Puerto Rico. The crisis was initiated after a civilian worker named David Sanes was killed after two 500-pound bombs were accidentally dropped on his observation post. This led to the formation of the Ecumenical Coalition of Churches of Vieques and to acts of civil disobedience in more than a dozen "disobedience camps" around the base. This struggle drew support from Puerto Ricans living on the U.S. mainland, including Bronx Borough President Adolfo Carrión Jr., the son of Assemblies of God Spanish Eastern District Superintendent Adolfo Carrión Sr. The hotly contested struggle may serve as a blueprint for future forms of political, civic, and social activism.

The Vieques struggle brought to the fore long-standing frustrations with Anglo-American imperialism and colonialism, which began after Puerto Rico was ceded to the United States by Spain in the wake of the Spanish-American War of 1898.[22] It has remained a U.S. territory (some say "colony") ever since. Many Puerto Ricans on the island and in the United States believed that the U.S. government should not only shut down the naval base but leave the island altogether—something that has now happened. However, this sentiment has simmered down somewhat, and the vast majority of Puerto Rican islanders still want to maintain territorial status or statehood rather than political independence. Regardless, the Vieques struggle tapped into the long-standing frustration and sense of colonialism and marginalization experienced by many Latinos in the United States. In the final analysis, the struggle over the United Farm Workers union, land grants, Elián, and Vieques are symbolic of the long-term struggle for self-respect and self-determination of all U.S. Latinos.

Clergy and lay leaders were the key to the success in Vieques. This is perhaps one reason that Puerto Rican clergy have high levels of support throughout the island. In chapter 17, Gastón Espinosa describes a similar level of confidence in the United States. Drawing on the findings from the Hispanic Churches in American Public Life national (n = 2,060) and leadership (n = 436) surveys in 2000 and 2001, he found that Latino religious leaders, churches, and religious organizations are much more active in political, civic, and social action than hitherto believed. He believes that this is one reason for such widespread support from the general Latino population and civic leaders. Not only do four out of ten Latino congregations help in voter registration, but 62 percent of Latinos nationwide and over 70 percent of Latino civic leaders indicated that they want religious leaders to become more involved in educational, social, and political issues.

Although Latino churches are less active then their white counterparts on standard measures of social action, they were as active or more active than their black counterparts in select social activities. The degree of Latino faith-based action is shaped by key factors like immigration status, generation, income, education, and religious affiliation and participation. This helps explain why Latino Protestants are generally more likely than Catholics to attend churches that engage in political and social action. Espinosa also found that Latino clergy leaders are increasingly attracting the attention of American presidents and political leaders in both the Democratic and Republican parties, largely because each addresses issues that resonate with the Latino community. This has been most evident in President George W. Bush's attempt to garner Latino clergy support for his voucher and faith-based initiatives and 2000 and 2004 presidential election bids.

Although these seventeen studies only scratch the surface of more than 150 years of political, civic, and social activism in the Latino community, it is hoped that they will spur on a new generation of scholars to explore this vitally important topic. It is also hoped that this collection of essays will help scholars, teachers, clergy, activists, and laity chart new courses for the Latino community in the future. After all, it is only after also drinking from their own wells of history, faith, and culture that Latinos can find the inner strength, confidence, and passion to engage society and become active and responsible participants in American public life.

NOTES

1. Juan Gómez-Quiñones, *Chicano Politics: Reality and Promise, 1940–1990* (Albuquerque: University of New Mexico Press, 1990).

2. Rudy Acuña stated that the Catholic Church was an Anglo-American institution that failed Chicanos and taught Latinos "to be complacent in the face of exploita-

tion and discrimination." He also stated that the church abetted bigotry and tacitly supported "the oppressive conditions under which Chicanos had to live and work." Rodolfo Acuña, *Occupied America: The Chicano's Struggle toward Liberation* (San Francisco: Cranfield Press, 1972), 144, 147–149.

3. We surveyed 2,310 Latinos (2,060 in the US and 250 in Puerto Rico) in our national random sample survey, 434 Latino leaders in our civic survey, and 266 Latinos in our community profiles in eight urban and rural locations representing twenty-five different denominations. For more on the scope and methodology of the HCAPL study, see Gastón Espinosa, Virgilio Elizondo, and Jesse Miranda, *Hispanic Churches in American Public Life: Summary of Findings*, 2nd ed. (Notre Dame, IN: Institute for Latino Studies at the University of Notre Dame, 2003), 12–14.

4. Ibid., 14. These 2004 figures are based on projections from the original HCAPL national survey.

5. Manuel G. Gonzáles, *Mexicanos: A History of Mexicans in the United States* (Bloomington: Indiana University Press, 1999), 73–112.

6. Timothy Matovina and Gerald E. Poyo, eds. *¡Presente! U.S. Latino Catholics from Colonial Origins to the Present* (Maryknoll, NY: Orbis Books, 2000), 48–57.

7. See Mario T. García, *Desert Immigrants* (New Haven, CT: Yale University Press, 1980); George J. Sánchez, *Becoming Mexican American* (New York: Oxford University Press, 1993).

8. Gonzáles, *Mexicanos*, 170–175.

9. Moises Sandoval, *On the Move: A History of the Hispanic Church in the United States* (Maryknoll, NY: Orbis Books, 1991), 61.

10. Matovina and Poyo, *¡Presente!* 50; Acuña, *Occupied America*, 47–49, 70–74; F. Arturo Rosales, *Chicano! The History of the Mexican American Civil Rights Movement* (Houston: University of Houston Press, 1996), 311–312.

11. Gonzáles, *Mexicanos*, 204–205; Rosales, *Chicano!* 154–184.

12. For a discussion of the Chicano movement, see Rosales, *Chicano!* and Carlos Muñoz Jr., *Youth, Identity and Power: The Chicano Movement* (New York: Verso Books, 1992).

13. R. Douglas Brackenridge and Francisco O. García-Treto, *Iglesia Presbyteriana: A History of Presbyterians and Mexican Americans in the Southwest*, 2nd ed. (San Antonio, TX: Trinity University Press, 1987), 197–225; Justo L. González, ed., *Each in Our Own Tongue: A History of Hispanic United Methodism* (Nashville, TN: Abingdon Press, 1991), 58–64; David Maldonado Jr., ed., *Protestantes/Protestants: Hispanic Christianity within Mainline Traditions* (Nashville, TN: Abingdon Press, 1999), 190–193.

14. Gómez-Quiñones, *Chicano Politics*, 179–180.

15. Hilary Cunningham, *God and Caesar at the Rio Grande: Sanctuary and the Politics of Religion* (Minneapolis: University of Minnesota Press, 1995); Susan Bibler Coutin, *The Culture of Protest: Religious Activism and the U.S. Sanctuary Movement* (Boulder, CO: Westview Press, 1993); Ann Crittenden, *Sanctuary: A Story of American Conscience and the Law in Collision* (New York: Weidenfeld & Nicolson, 1988).

16. Gastón Espinosa, " 'Your Daughters Shall Prophesy': A History of Women in Ministry in the Latino Pentecostal Movement in the United States," in *Women and Twentieth-Century Protestantism*, ed. Margaret Lamberts Bendroth and Virginia Lieson Brereton (Urbana: University of Illinois Press, 2002), 25–48.

17. For a discussion of early Pentecostal social action, see Gastón Espinosa, "Borderland Religion: Los Angeles and the Origins of the Latino Pentecostal Movement in the U.S., Mexico and Puerto Rico, 1900–1945" (Ph.D. diss., University of California, Santa Barbara, 1999), 284–286.

18. Edwin I. Hernández, "Moving from the Cathedral to Storefront Churches: Understanding Religious Growth and Decline among Latino Protestants," in *Protestantes/Protestants: Hispanic Christianity within Mainline Traditions*, ed. David Maldonado Jr. (Nashville, TN: Abingdon Press, 1999), 21.

19. For a discussion about the origins and development of the Cursillo and the Encuentros, see Sandoval, *On the Move*, 79–86.

20. Victor Andres Triay, *Fleeing Castro: Operation Pedro Pan and the Cuban Children's Program* (Miami: University Press of Florida, 2002), xi, xiv, 12–18, 103; Sandoval, *On the Move*, 107.

21. Matovina and Poyo, *¡Presente!* 178–189.

22. Luís Martínez-Fernández, *Protestantism and Political Conflict in the Nineteenth-Century Hispanic Caribbean* (New Brunswick, NJ: Rutgers University Press, 2002).

PART I

Historical Struggles

1

Conquest, Faith, and Resistance in the Southwest

Timothy Matovina

In September 1854, a Mexican resident of San Antonio, Texas, reportedly entered a local Catholic Church and began to destroy the images of Jesus and the saints. After some Mexican women stopped his destructive spree, the man explained that "the Mexican Gods could neither eat, walk, or talk, and were no Gods at all, consequently he wanted to put them out of the way." He also added, "if the Mexicans had worshiped the true and only God, the 'gringos' could never have taken Texas."[1]

Like the enraged man in this account, scholars of the nineteenth-century Southwest tend to see religion, specifically Mexican Catholicism, as providing scant (if any) resources for the defense of a conquered people. In fact, various extant studies document the institutional Catholic Church's frequent neglect of Mexicans and Mexican Americans, as well as the attempts of some Catholic and Protestant leaders to use religion as a mechanism of social control among their Mexican co-religionists. To be sure, a growing number of scholars insist that the history of Mexicans incorporated into the United States during U.S. territorial expansion "is not solely a story of people victimized by oppression. It is much more the history of actors who have sought to take measures in their own behalf for the sake of a decent living." But despite the increased focus on Mexican-descent residents as historical actors, the role of religion as one of the "measures" they took "in their own behalf" continues to be a peripheral topic in many historical investigations. The few scholars who do address the role of nineteenth-century Mexican Catholicism typically confine its influence to a strictly "domestic" sphere that primarily provided Mexican-descent residents with the "security and strength to *control their own privacy* and reaffirm their cultural uniqueness" (emphasis added).[2]

In this essay I explore the public role of Mexican Catholicism in what is now the Southwest during the last half of the nineteenth century. More specifically, I examine the social activism and public ethnoreligious celebrations of "conquered" Mexican Catholics, whose legacy of faith, struggle, endurance, and resistance provides inspiration and guidance for contemporary Hispanic congregations and believers. During the turbulent half century following the 1848 U.S. takeover of Mexican territories extending from Texas to California, Catholicism buttressed the conquered Mexicans' spirited defense of their dignity and rights. To be sure, in a number of Catholic dioceses and parishes, activist Mexican Catholics defended themselves from the discriminatory attitudes, policies, and actions of newly arrived European clergy. Nonetheless, in their struggle to survive, endure, and resist the U.S. takeover of their homeland, Mexican-descent residents drew on the heritage and traditions of their Catholic ancestors, whom they proudly acknowledged as the first European settlers in the region. To understand the role of Catholicism in shaping the conquered Mexicans' struggle in U.S. society, it is first necessary to explore the wider context of U.S. conquest and Mexican residents' resistance to their subjugated status under a new regime.

U.S. Conquest

The conquest of the American Southwest began with the war between Texas and Mexico (1835–1836), which resulted in the establishment of an independent Texas Republic. Nine years later, the United States annexed Texas and provoked another war by building Fort Brown (present-day Brownsville, Texas) in disputed territory across the Rio Grande from Matamoros. The war between the United States and Mexico (1846–1848) resulted in Mexico's loss of nearly half its territory: the present-day states of Texas, Nevada, California, Utah, and parts of New Mexico, Arizona, Colorado, and Wyoming. In 1848, the Treaty of Guadalupe Hidalgo brought an official end to this war and, in addition to establishing new borders between the two nations, guaranteed the citizenship, property, and religious rights of Mexican citizens who chose to remain in the conquered territories. Six years later, the 1854 Gadsden Purchase or, as Mexicans call it, the Tratado de Mesilla (Treaty of Mesilla), completed the U.S. takeover of former Mexican territories. With the threat of another U.S. invasion as the backdrop for the transaction, U.S. negotiator James Gadsden "purchased" the southern sections of present-day Arizona and New Mexico for $10 million.[3]

Military defeat merely initiated the process of U.S. conquest and expansion. As new territories changed hands through victory in battle and subsequent treaty negotiations, law-enforcement personnel, judicial officials, and occupying troops imposed U.S. rule. At times, violence against Spanish-speaking citizens reached epidemic proportions, but the judicial system afforded little if any protection for them. Moreover, while the increased military presence provided some civilian jobs, it was also a visible symbol of the new regime that now ruled the conquered lands.[4]

Padre Antonio José Martínez, 1793–1867 (Courtesy Museum of New Mexico, Neg. No. 174508)

Anglo-American newcomers also consolidated the conquest by asserting their dominion over political and economic life. When Texas became a state in 1845, for example, Mexican San Antonians lost control of the city council their ancestors had established and led for more than a century; over the following century, they held less than 5 percent of city council posts. At the same time, after Texas statehood, citizens of Mexican heritage increasingly became a working underclass and lost most of their land holdings.[5]

Demographic shifts facilitated the diminishment of Mexican political and economic influence. Nowhere was this shift more dramatic than in California, where the Gold Rush altered the demographic profile almost overnight. Even southern California settlements relatively distant from the gold mines experienced a rapid influx of newcomers. Census figures for Santa Barbara indicate Spanish-surnamed residents accounted for two-thirds of the population in 1860; with the accelerated growth of Anglo-American and other city residents, by 1880 they scarcely numbered one-fourth of the town's population. Other communities experienced a more gradual demographic shift, such as Tucson, Arizona, where Mexican-descent residents remained the majority until the early twentieth century.[6]

Hispanic hegemony in religious life and public celebrations also dissipated as population growth among Anglo-Americans and other groups facilitated the formation of new congregations and public festivities. By 1890 in the formerly "Catholic" town of Los Angeles, for example, there were seventy-eight religious organizations, including groups such as Congregationalists, Jews, Buddhists, Baptists, Unitarians, and an African Methodist Episcopal congregation. In San Antonio, Anglo-Americans promoted the participation of Mexican-descent residents in the parades and ceremonies of newly organized "American holidays" like the Fourth of July. As one report of an 1851 celebration stated: "We have many foreigners among us who know nothing of our government, who have no national feeling in common with us. . . . Let us induce them to partake with us in our festivities, they will soon partake our feelings, and when so, they will be citizens indeed."[7]

Parishes and other elements of Catholic life were not immune to change during the turbulent period of transition following the U.S. conquest. Dioceses were established at places like Galveston (1847), Santa Fe (1853), San Francisco (1853), Denver (1887), and Tucson (1897). European clergy served in many areas of the Southwest, with the French predominating in Texas, New Mexico, and Arizona and the Irish in California. During the second half of the nineteenth century, episcopal appointments in the region reflected this same pattern (with the exception of Thaddeus Amat and Joseph Alemany, two Spaniards who served as bishops in California). Scores of women religious also crossed the Atlantic and began schools, hospitals, orphanages, and other apostolic work in the Southwest.[8]

Frequently, differences in culture and religious practice led newly arrived Catholic leaders to misunderstand and criticize their Mexican co-religionists. One French priest claimed that, among the Mexican-descent Catholics he encountered in Texas during the 1840s and 1850s, "the religion of the great majority is very superficial, the great truths of the faith are overlooked, and the most essential duties of a Christian are neglected." The first resident bishop of Los Angeles, Thaddeus Amat, oversaw the 1862 diocesan synod which forbade Mexican Catholic faith expressions like *Los Pastores* (a festive proclamation of the shepherds who worshiped the newborn infant Jesus), a prohibition promulgated in order to avoid "the scandal which arises from such plays." Amat and the synod fathers also decreed that public processions, funeral traditions, and religious feasts strictly adhere to the rubrics of the Roman Ritual. Thus they banned long-standing local practices like festive displays of devotion during public processions, interring corpses within church buildings, cannon salutes as a form of religious devotion, and the fiestas and entertainments that accompanied religious celebrations.[9]

To be sure, in some instances foreign clergy acclaimed the religious practices of Spanish-speaking Catholics and even initiated new religious traditions that resonated with Hispanic faithful. Bishop Jean Marie Odin, the first bishop of Texas, participated in Mexican religious feasts like local celebrations in honor of Our Lady of Guadalupe and spoke enthusiastically of the religious zeal demonstrated in these celebrations. Unlike Bishop Amat, San Francisco's first archbishop, Joseph Alemany, did not ban Hispanic religious feasts and practices and apparently enjoyed the confidence and respect of Spanish-speaking Catholics in his see. According to one newspaper report, in Ysleta, Texas (near El Paso) the ministry of Italian Jesuits resonated so strongly with the local populace that the new clergy were able to inaugurate an annual feast day celebration in honor of Our Lady of Mount Carmel. Celebrated in a festive Mexican style with colorful decorations, elaborate church services, outdoor processions, a marching band, bonfires, and fireworks, this feast day drew an enthusiastic response from Mexican Catholics in the local parish and throughout the surrounding area. Despite such examples of foreign clergy working in concert with local Mexican Catholic communities, however, criticism and conflict frequently marked the relations between established Hispanic Catholic communities and the Catholic religious leaders who arrived in the wake of U.S. conquest.[10]

While Catholic leaders were often harsh in their assessment of Mexican Catholicism, a number of Protestants were utterly condemnatory. Observing the vibrant public devotion for the 1847 feast of Our Lady of Guadalupe at Monterey, California, Reverend Walter Colton, a navy chaplain and minister in a Congregationalist tradition, mockingly quipped, "I wonder if Guadalupe knows or cares much about these exhibitions of devotional glee." Baptist minister Lewis Smith wrote from Santa Fe in 1853 that, along with various other rituals, on Good Friday "the farce of crucifying the Savior was enacted in the church." Undoubtedly the most renowned of the attacks on Hispanic traditions was directed at the brotherhoods of Los Hermanos de Nuestro Padre Jesús Nazareno (Brothers of Our Father Jesus the Nazarene), or *Penitentes*, in northern New Mexico and southern Colorado. Local residents frequently deemed outside observers of their rites "Penitente hunters" because of their intrusive presence and the sensationalistic reports they wrote about the brotherhoods' religious practices. Among the most notorious of these sensationalistic and ethnocentric reports was that of journalist Charles Lummis, who wrote a widely read 1893 book that described in detail the "barbarous rites" he observed among New Mexican Penitentes.[11]

Mexican Resistance

Conquered Mexicans resisted the U.S. takeover in various ways. Some offered military resistance to the foreign invaders. After the U.S. occupation of New Mexico, the 1847 Taos Rebellion resulted in the killing of territorial governor Charles Bent and at least fifteen other Anglo-Americans before it was suppressed. California defenders during the war between the United States and Mexico won battles in the Los Angeles area and at the hamlet of San Pasqual, although subsequently they came to terms peaceably when the larger and well-armed invasion force overwhelmed them. When New Mexican governor William Carr Lane sought to occupy Mexican territory in 1853 (land later ceded to the United States through the aforementioned Gadsden Purchase), Father Ramón Ortiz rode out from his El Paso parish to confront the governor. The curate then returned to El Paso and alerted local authorities, who mounted a force of 800 men to defend their borders.[12]

Even after the U.S. conquest of northern Mexico, armed resistance erupted in various locales. Contemporary Mexican Americans still acclaim Joaquín Murieta for his vigorous defense of his people and his family honor in California after the U.S. war with Mexico. In the decades following the Civil War, guerrilla leaders like Tiburcio Vásquez in California and Juan Cortina in Texas led retaliatory movements protesting the endemic violence and injustice their people suffered at the hands of Anglo-Americans. Although their adversaries labeled them outlaws and "bandidos," to this day many Californians and Texans of Mexican heritage consider them heroic defenders of a dominated people. Claiming the right of self-defense against Anglo-American oppression, Hispanic residents also took up arms during the 1877 El Paso Salt War and when Las Gorras Blancas (White Caps) sought to safeguard land claims in San Miguel County, New Mexico from 1889 to 1891.[13]

In other instances, Spanish-speaking residents defended their rights in the political arena. Native Texan José Antonio Navarro made various legislative attempts to protect the ancestral lands of Mexican Texans. While his fellow lawmakers did not enact any of his land claim proposals, at the 1845 Texas Constitutional Convention Navarro was able to prevent passage of an "odious" and "ridiculous" law that restricted suffrage to the "free white population." Like Navarro, native Californian Pablo de la Guerra futilely tried to protect the land claims of Mexican-descent residents in his state. In an often-quoted 1856 speech to fellow members of the state senate, he described Mexican Californians as "strangers in their own land" and testified that he had "seen seventy and sixty year olds cry like children because they had been uprooted from the lands of their fathers." He further claimed that their plight was caused in part by "a legislature hungry to take away from us our last penny simply because the [Anglo-American] squatters are more numerous than the native Californians."[14]

Spanish-speaking residents also founded mutual aid societies and other organizations to protect their rights and promote their common concerns. One such organization was La Alianza Hispano-Americana (Hispanic American Alliance). In 1894, organizers founded La Alianza in response to an anti-Hispanic threat at Tucson, Arizona. Within three years of its establishment, the local group expanded its vision and convened its first national convention. Like similar organizations created to promote change at the local, regional, and national levels, La Alianza is noteworthy for its advocacy of Hispanic causes such as political representation, labor organizing, participation in civic and economic life, and desegregation in schools and other public facilities.[15]

Yet another arena for resistance was the issue of language. In 1858, elected officials at San Antonio instituted a program of teacher certification for public schools, decreeing that public funds would be available solely for the salaries of certified teachers in schools where the principal language was English. José Ramos de Zúñiga, the editor of a local newspaper, *El Correo*, contested this law.

Ramos de Zúñiga contended that, when limited to speaking English in school, Spanish-speaking (and German-speaking) children ended up speaking neither language fluently. During the mid-1850s in Santa Barbara, California, where 60 percent of the 1,200 residents spoke only Spanish, Hispanic leaders overcame Anglo-American Protestant opposition and succeeded in retaining Spanish as the only language for public school instruction. Although the policy of monolingual Spanish instruction was short-lived, the civic activism of Spanish-speaking Santa Barbarans illustrates Mexican-descent residents' attempt to retain Spanish as a public language in the Southwest.[16]

At times, conflicts between Mexican Catholics and Catholic leaders resulted in public controversy and even open resistance. When his Franciscan superiors reassigned Father José González Rubio from Santa Barbara to Zacatecas, Mexico, in 1856, some 1,000 parishioners and other supporters "kidnapped" the popular cleric by blocking his entrance to the boat on which he was to depart! They then enlisted the support of Archbishop Joseph Alemany in San Francisco and remained firm in their resolve to keep their priest until his superiors changed his appointment and allowed him to stay. Similarly, in 1875 Bishop Dominic Manucy of Brownsville rejected a request that twenty-two exiled Mexican sisters reside in the area and serve Mexican-descent Catholics. Local Spanish-speaking Catholics were incensed at Bishop Manucy's decision, particularly since they offered to pay the living costs for the sisters. On the day the women religious were to board the train and depart from Brownsville, an angry crowd removed their train from its tracks and refused to let authorities replace it. In yet another instance of conflict, French priest Henri-Paul-Marie Le Guillou collected some $500 for a new altar shortly after his arrival at Taos, New Mexico, in November 1902. This costly acquisition and his reportedly disrespectful behavior toward his parishioners led to a movement for his removal. On March 3, 1904, more than 1,000 local residents held a mass meeting and signed resolutions for Le Guillou's removal. They then sent the resolutions to Archbishop Pierre Bourgade of Santa Fe and published them in three local newspapers. One month later, the prelate transferred Father Le Guillou to the archdiocese of Milwaukee.[17]

Catholic Heritage and Social Activism

In the process of defending their rights in both church and society, various residents of the former Mexican territories drew explicitly on their Mexican Catholic heritage. This strategy of acclaiming the Mexican Catholic heritage that preceded the U.S. takeover of conquered lands is illustrated in the well-known conflict between Father Antonio José Martínez, the leading figure among nineteenth-century New Mexican priests, and Frenchman Jean Baptiste Lamy, the first bishop (and later first archbishop) of Santa Fe. Upon his arrival at New Mexico in 1851, Lamy encountered Catholic communities with long-standing traditions and the largest group of local clergy in any of the conquered territories. Two decades earlier, Padre Martínez had advocated successfully for the abolition of tithing regulations in New Mexico, arguing that fiscal conditions in this frontier territory precluded the feasibility of this practice. Within three years of his arrival, Bishop Lamy suspended several New Mexican priests, reinstituted mandatory tithing, and decreed that heads of families who failed to tithe be denied the sacraments. Padre Martínez publicly protested the prelate's actions, even openly contesting Lamy's decisions in the secular press. The resulting controversy led to Martínez's eventual suspension and excommunication. In his response to Lamy after hearing of the bishop's decision to suspend him, Martínez protested that decision, as well as Lamy's lack of response to his previous missives and the suspensions of other New Mexican priests like Father José Manuel Gallegos and Father Juan Felipe Ortiz. He also called on Lamy to rescind his decree on mandatory tithing, arguing that this decree "goes against canon law," was at odds with Catholic practice in the region, and "harms the spiritual well-being of the faithful." Implicit in the statements of Padre Martínez was the contention that Lamy was an outsider who neither understood nor appreciated the Hispanic Catholic heritage that characterized the territory now under his jurisdiction. Although largely an ecclesiastical conflict, Martínez's public resistance to Lamy's decisions illuminate the priest's concern for preserving long-standing traditions and practices in New Mexico's religious and civic life.[18]

Spanish-speaking residents also drew on their Mexican Catholic heritage to defend themselves in the electoral politics of mid-1850s San Antonio. In 1854 the anti-Catholic, anti-immigrant Know Nothing Party achieved its first Texas victory in the San Antonio municipal elections, gaining control of the mayoral office and the city council. During the first weeks in office it repealed a law requiring the city secretary to translate ordinances and other matters into Spanish and banned the long-standing practice of Mexican fandangos (dances). In response to the Know Nothing threat, San Antonians of Mexican descent joined with the Democratic Party in a vigorous organizing effort for statewide elections the following year. On June 28, Mexican-descent leaders convened the first in a series of "Democratic Meetings of Mexican-Texan Citizens of Bexar County." They promulgated formal resolutions, declared their opposition to the Know Nothings, and accused the Know Nothings of condemning them to "political slavery" solely because they chose "to worship God according to the dictates of our conscience and the rituals of our ancestors." Claiming their status as native-born residents of Texas, they also contended that Know Nothings were immigrant "strangers to this land, with four years, or less, of residence in our state." Local leader José Antonio Navarro wrote an open letter to his fellow citizens of Mexican Texan heritage that was read publicly and subsequently published in both the English and Spanish press. Navarro reminded his hearers that his people's Hispanic-Mexican ancestors founded their city and built the parish of San Fernando in which they worshiped God. Citing Know Nothing anti-Catholic attitudes, he also proclaimed that "the Mexico-Texans are Catholics, and should be proud of the faith of their ancestors, and defend it inch by inch against such infamous aggressors." Democrats won the

1855 state elections, besting their Know Nothing opponents by almost three to one among Bexar County voters.[19]

Rafael Romero, a political leader and superintendent of schools from a prominent New Mexican family, made a similarly spirited defense in 1878. During that year, territorial governor Samuel B. Axtell blocked Jesuit attempts to establish the tax-exempt and degree-granting status of their new school in Las Vegas, New Mexico. Romero's public address during festivities for the close of the school's first academic year acclaimed his hearers as native New Mexicans whose "ancestors penetrated into these deserted and dangerous regions many years before the Mayflower floated over the dancing waves that washed Plymouth Rock." He went on to remind his audience that Jesus was also "tormented by a provincial governor," claiming that the oppressive actions of their current territorial governor were worse than the misdeeds of Pontius Pilate, whose sin, according to Romero, was one of omission rather than direct persecution of the innocent. Defending himself against possible retorts that he spoke too harshly, he went on to ask rhetorically: "Am I not a Catholic citizen of a Catholic land, New Mexico? And have I not, as a New Mexican Catholic, been grossly insulted by a pathetic public official? What does it mean when a man sent to be the governor of a Catholic land, in an official message directed to Catholic legislators and to our Catholic people, piles insult upon insult against a religious order of the Catholic Church?"[20]

In these and other instances, Hispanic residents sought to defend their political rights by identifying themselves as the descendants of Spanish-speaking Catholic ancestors who founded and developed their communities. Drawing on their preconquest heritage, they expressed the heightened religious and ethnic consciousness of native-born residents who retained legitimate claims for respect within their homeland. By asserting that Anglo-Americans and European clergy were immigrant newcomers to their region, they contrasted their own identity as the harbingers of Hispanic Catholic civilization with that of the newcomers who scorned their heritage and usurped their political rights. Thus, rhetorically, they reversed their antagonists' claims that Mexican Catholics were "foreigners" and religiously and culturally depraved. In the process they expressed an identity as Catholics whose preconquest heritage merited their ethnic, religious, and political legitimization.

Mexican Catholic Traditions as Symbolic Resistance

Even more conspicuously and consistently, local communities in conquered territories asserted their Mexican Catholic heritage in the public spaces of civic life through their long-standing rituals and devotions. From Texas to California, various Mexican Catholic communities continued to enthusiastically celebrate established local traditions such as pilgrimages, Our Lady of Guadalupe, Los Pastores, Holy Week, Corpus Christi, and established patronal feast days.[21] The persistence of established religious traditions is particularly striking in light of

Catholic and Protestant leaders' attempts to ban, replace, and condemn these traditions. In the face of such efforts, as well as military conquest and occupation, indiscriminate violence and lawlessness, political and economic displacement, rapid demographic change, the erosion of cultural hegemony, and the appointment of Catholic leaders from foreign lands, Spanish-speaking Catholic feasts and devotions had a heightened significance. These religious traditions provided an ongoing means of public communal expressions, affirmation, and resistance to Anglo-American and other newcomers who criticized or attempted to suppress Mexican-descent residents' ethnoreligious heritage. Undoubtedly, fear and anger at their subjugation intensified religious fervor among some devotees.

The most renowned lay group that served as the protectors of treasured local traditions was the aforementioned Penitentes of northern New Mexico and southern Colorado. Penitente brotherhoods evolved in towns and villages well before the U.S. takeover of the area. Their most noticeable function was to commemorate Christ's passion and death during Lent and, in particular, during Holy Week, although they also provided community leadership and fostered social integration. Organized as separate local entities, Penitente brotherhoods had a leader named the Hermano Mayor (literally, older brother) and a *morada* (literally, habitation) or chapter house where they held meetings and religious devotions. Despite the sharp criticism they often received from outsiders and Santa Fe archdiocesan officials attempts' to suppress the brotherhoods and their ritual and devotional practices, to this day the Penitentes (and their female collaborators) continue providing leadership for prayer and social life in numerous local communities.[22]

In more urban areas, activist Mexican lay women and men continued traditional feast days and faith statements in Catholic parishes like Tucson's San Agustín and San Antonio's San Fernando. For example, the memoirs of nineteenth-century Tucson resident Federico José María Ronstadt state that "the annual feast of St. Agustín . . . started on the 28th of August and lasted for a month." Similarly, in the decades following their political separation from Mexico, San Fernando parishioners organized public rituals and festivities for Our Lady of Guadalupe, Christmas, San Fernando, San Antonio, San Juan, San Pedro, and other feasts. Most conspicuous among these rites was the annual Guadalupe feast, which the parish community celebrated in the Mexican way of a colorful outdoor procession with flowers, candles, elaborate decorations adorning the Guadalupe image and their parish church, gun and canon salutes, extended ringing of the church bells, and large crowds for services conducted in Spanish. As nineteenth-century parishioner Enrique Esparza proudly recollected toward the end of his life: "We had many saint days. Then we would visit with relatives and friends . . . [and] join in the fiesta around San Fernando."[23]

Newcomers like Protestants, Anglo-Americans, and, as previously mentioned, the Catholic clergy participated in the rituals and devotions of Spanish-speaking Catholics. Besides the aforementioned examples from Texas and San Francisco, European priests at places like Los Angeles, Tucson, and Santa Rita,

Texas, participated in the religious traditions of their Mexican Catholic counterparts. An 1861 Anglo-American visitor to Santa Barbara marveled that, during the Holy Week services he attended, the predominantly Mexican-descent congregation was joined by Native American, North American, Irish, German, French, and Italian worshipers. He concluded that "no place but California can produce such [diverse] groups." Both at Santa Barbara and Tucson, even Chinese immigrants reportedly attended Mexican Catholic celebrations. The presence of newcomers at these Hispanic celebrations illustrates Mexican Catholic attempts to prolong local traditions and even incorporate these newcomers into their expressions of religious and communal identity. Consciously or unconsciously, European clergy, Anglos, Protestants, and other newcomers bolstered ethnoreligious celebrations that helped reinforce public demonstrations of Mexican Catholic traditions and a collective identity that predated the U.S. conquest.[24]

Once other groups were sufficient in number to form their own congregations and social circles, however, their participation in Hispanic Catholic faith traditions frequently abated. With the emergence of religious pluralism and the organization of diverse public celebrations, particularly U.S. holidays like the Fourth of July, the hegemony of Mexican faith expressions and festivities diminished. As various scholars have pointed out in studies of "ethnicity," in addition to elements of perceived group commonalty such as language, customs, behavior patterns, religion, and political and economic interests, interaction with other groups also shapes ethnic identity. Such interaction enables a group to overcome "pluralistic ignorance" and become aware of their own tradition as distinct from other traditions. This awareness is accentuated when prejudice, conflict, and an imbalance in the distribution of power characterizes the contact between groups.[25] Thus while Mexican Catholic rituals, devotions, and festivities were an identifying mark of towns and local communities in the years prior to the U.S. takeover, afterward they increasingly differentiated Hispanics from other groups that settled in the occupied territories. The rise of religious and cultural pluralism in conquered lands enhanced the perception that Mexican Catholic faith expressions were a distinguishing characteristic of their ethnicity and group identity.

Women frequently played a key leadership role in public worship and devotion. At Santa Rita, Texas, and Conejos, Colorado, young women served in public processions as the immediate attendants for the image of Our Lady of Guadalupe, the principal ritual object in annual Guadalupe feast-day celebrations. Young women occupied similar places of prominence in processions at Los Angeles for the feasts of the Assumption and of Corpus Christi, as well as for the Our Lady of Mount Carmel procession at Ysleta, Texas. Even when male Penitentes provided significant leadership for communal worship, as in Arroyo Hondo, New Mexico, women played vital roles in local traditions like the annual procession for the feast of St. John the Baptist. The contribution of women in preparing and enacting public religious traditions illuminates what sociologist Ana María Díaz-Stevens calls the "matriarchal core" of Latino Catholicism—that is, women's exercise of autonomous authority in communal devotions, despite the patriarchy of institutional Catholicism and Latin American societies. Significantly, Mexican-descent women extended their domestic efforts to preserve familial heritage and devotion into a role of community leadership that shaped Mexican Catholics' public ritual expressions in the wider civic society.[26]

To be sure, some communities in the Southwest struggled for their very survival; in the process, their observance of long-standing traditions often abated or even ceased. At Santa Barbara, during the latter decades of the nineteenth century, many traditions and customs were necessarily modified in order to survive, with some cultural activities disappearing altogether. Mexican Catholic communities in places like Nacogdoches, Texas, suffered a similar fate. Nonetheless, as Bishop Henry Granjon of Tucson noted in 1902 during his first pastoral visit to Las Cruces, New Mexico, many Mexican-descent Catholics in the Southwest "continue[d] to observe their own traditions and customs as they did before the annexation of their lands by the American Union." Among these traditions and customs was *compadrazgo* (literally, godparentage), the network of relationships among families that is created through sponsorship in sacramental celebrations. According to Bishop Granjon, in the Southwest "these multiple attachments, mostly between families, maintain the unity of the Mexican population and permit them to resist, to a certain extent, the invasions of the Anglo-Saxon race."[27] The leadership initiatives of Mexican Catholics enabled a number of local populations to adapt and continue their treasured expressions of faith. In the wake of the expansionist U.S. takeover, the perpetuation of these ritual and devotional traditions enabled many Mexican-descent Catholics to defend their dignity, fortify their resistance to the effects of conquest, express their own ethnic legitimization, and endure as ethnoreligious communities. Often spilling out into town streets and plazas, ritual and devotional traditions were the primary means through which these Mexican Catholics expressed their collective identity in the public spaces of municipal life.

Conclusion

The significant impact of Mexican Catholicism on conquered Mexicans' political and civic engagement raises questions that are beyond the scope of this brief essay. How did the nineteenth-century activism of Mexican Catholics in the Southwest influence later Latina and Latino activist efforts in that region and beyond? Did women's leadership in public ritual and devotion, which contrasted sharply with their subordinate position in political and civic life, help those women or their female descendants demand greater parity in the wider society? In what ways did the strategies Mexican Catholics employed during ecclesiastical conflicts—such as collective protest, nonviolent resistance, enlisting the support of key allies, and direct confrontation—enable Mexican-descent residents to hone their capacity for political activism? Did Mexican Catholic traditions, while serving as a symbolic force of resistance to

Anglo-American domination, simultaneously function as a sacred justification for existing social hierarchies within Mexican communities themselves? Under what conditions can ritual and devotion function more as symbolic resistance than as a means of social control? How can future studies on churches and American public life incorporate and examine more profoundly the insight that Latino (and other) public ritual is an often overlooked but vital means of civic engagement in our pluralistic society?

Despite these unanswered questions, this chapter demonstrates that Mexican Catholics' heritage and religious traditions provided crucial resources for political and civic activism in the decades following the U.S. takeover of northern Mexico. The essay illuminates the first instances of Hispanics engaging religion as a resource for civic participation in the United States and offers a valuable corrective to historical studies that ignore the role of Hispanic religion or confine it to the domestic sphere. Other essays in this volume (e.g., León, García, Medina, Barton) show that more contemporary Hispanic leaders have greatly expanded their initiatives to increase church involvement in social concerns. Influenced by the reforms of Vatican II, the inspiration of Latin American liberation theology, and the increased activism in all areas of life during the 1960s, Latina and Latino leaders have founded organizations such as PADRES, Las Hermanas, the Mexican American Cultural Center, and numerous faith-based community organizations. As Hispanic organizations and leaders continue to emerge and struggle for greater church involvement in the political and civic arenas, the social activism of nineteenth-century Mexican Catholics offers a vital legacy that can animate and inform current efforts to transform the churches and help them play a more prophetic role in American public life.

NOTES

1. Timothy Matovina, *Tejano Religion and Ethnicity: San Antonio, 1821–1860* (Austin: University of Texas Press, 1995), 91.

2. Arnoldo De León, *The Tejano Community, 1836–1900* (Albuquerque: University of New Mexico Press, 1982; reprint 1997), 153, 203 (quotations). The historiography of nineteenth-century Mexicans and religion is too vast for a comprehensive review in this essay. For more general works, see, for example, Julian Samora and Patricia Vandel Simon, *A History of the Mexican-American People*, rev. ed. (Notre Dame, IN: University of Notre Dame Press, 1993), 223–234; Moises Sandoval, *On the Move: A History of the Hispanic Church in the United States* (Maryknoll, NY: Orbis Books, 1990), 25–40; Moises Sandoval, ed., *Fronteras: A History of the Latin American Church in the USA since 1513* (San Antonio, TX: Mexican American Cultural Center Press, 1983), 143–221; Timothy Matovina and Gerald E. Poyo, eds., *¡Presente! U.S. Latino Catholics from Colonial Origins to the Present* (Maryknoll, NY: Orbis Books, 2000), 44–89. *¡Presente!* is a collection of primary source documents with introductions by Matovina and Poyo. For regional and local studies with a particular focus on religion, see, for example, Michael E. Engh, *Frontier Faiths: Church, Temple, and Synagogue in Los Angeles, 1846–1888* (Albuquerque: University of New Mexico Press, 1992); David Maldonado Jr., ed., *Protestantes/Protestants: Hispanic Christianity within Mainline Traditions* (Nashville, TN: Abingdon Press, 1999); Matovina, *Tejano Religion and Ethnicity*; Robert E.

Wright, "Popular and Official Religiosity: A Theoretical Analysis and a Case Study of Laredo–Nuevo Laredo, 1755–1857" (Ph.D. diss., Graduate Theological Union, Berkeley, CA, 1992); Susan M. Yohn, *A Contest of Faiths: Missionary Women and Pluralism in the American Southwest* (Ithaca, NY: Cornell University Press, 1995).

3. Richard Griswold del Castillo, *The Treaty of Guadalupe Hidalgo: A Legacy of Conflict* (Norman: University of Oklahoma Press, 1990); Rodolfo Acuña, *Occupied America: A History of Chicanos* (New York: Harper & Row, 1988), 84–86.

4. Acuña, *Occupied America*, esp. 33–34, 65–68, 118–121.

5. De León, *Tejano Community*, 23–112; Thomas D. Hall, *Social Change in the Southwest, 1350–1880* (Lawrence: University Press of Kansas, 1989), 204–236; Timothy Matovina, "Guadalupan Devotion in a Borderlands Community," *Journal of Hispanic/Latino Theology* 4 (August 1996): 10–18.

6. Albert Camarillo, *Chicanos in a Changing Society: From Mexican Pueblos to American Barrios in Santa Barbara and Southern California, 1848–1930* (Cambridge: Harvard University Press, 1979), 117; Thomas E. Sheridan, *Los Tucsonenses: The Mexican Community in Tucson, 1854–1941* (Tucson: University of Arizona Press, 1986), 3, 259–262.

7. Engh, *Frontier Faiths*, 189–190; Matovina, *Tejano Religion and Ethnicity*, 53–54 (quotation).

8. Sandoval, *On the Move*, 30–36.

9. Matovina, *Tejano Religion and Ethnicity*, 67 (first quotation); Michael E. Engh, "From *Frontera* Faith to Roman Rubrics: Altering Hispanic Religious Customs in Los Angeles, 1855–1880," *U.S. Catholic Historian* 12 (Fall 1994): 92 (second quotation), 90–95.

10. Matovina, *Tejano Religion and Ethnicity*, 43–44; Jeffrey M. Burns, "The Mexican Catholic Community in California," in *Mexican Americans and the Catholic Church, 1900–1965*, ed. Jay P. Dolan and Gilberto M. Hinojosa (Notre Dame, IN: University of Notre Dame Press, 1994), 134–135; Engh, "From *Frontera* Faith to Roman Rubrics," 95–97; article, *El Paso Herald* 19 July, 1882, cited in Matovina and Poyo, *¡Presente!*, 78–80.

11. Walter Colton, *Three Years in California* (Stanford, CA: Stanford University Press, 1949), 224; Thomas J. Steele, ed., *New Mexican Spanish Religious Oratory, 1800–1900* (Albuquerque: University of New Mexico Press, 1997), 94; Charles F. Lummis, *The Land of Poco Tiempo* (New York: C. Scribner's Sons, 1893), 79–108.

12. Juan Romero, "Begetting the Mexican American: Padre Martínez and the 1847 Rebellion," in *Seeds of Struggle/Harvest of Faith: The Papers of the Archdiocese of Santa Fe Catholic Cuarto Centennial Conference on the History of the Church in New Mexico*, ed. Thomas J. Steele, Paul Rhetts, and Barbe Awalt (Albuquerque: LPD Press, 1998), 345–371; Leonard Pitt, *The Decline of the Californios: A Social History of the Spanish-Speaking Californians, 1846–1890* (Berkeley: University of California Press, 1966), 33–35; Mary D. Taylor, "Cura de la Frontera, Ramón Ortiz," *U.S. Catholic Historian* 9 (Winter/Spring 1990): 78–79.

13. Zaragosa Vargas, ed., *Major Problems in Mexican American History* (Boston: Houghton Mifflin, 1999), 143–146, 182; Acuña, *Occupied America*, 43–49, 70–74, 124–125.

14. José Antonio Navarro, *Defending Mexican Valor in Texas: José Antonio Navarro's Historical Writings, 1853–1857*, ed. David R. McDonald and Timothy Matovina (Austin: State House, 1995), 19–20; "Pablo de la Guerra, Speech to the California Legislature," in *El Grito: A Journal of Contemporary Mexican-American Thought* 5 (Fall 1971): 19–20.

15. Acuña, *Occupied America*, 96–97, 294–295.

16. Matovina, *Tejano Religion and Ethnicity*, 55; Pitt, *Decline of the Californios*, 226.

17. Michael Charles Neri, *Hispanic Catholicism in Transitional California: The Life of José González Rubio, O.F.M. (1804–1875)* (Berkeley, CA: Academy of American Franciscan History, 1997), 69–72; José Roberto Juárez, "La iglesia Católica y el Chicano en sud Texas, 1836–1911," *Aztlán* 4 (Fall 1973): 230–232; Enrique R. Lamadrid and Thomas J. Steele SJ, "Indigenous Voice in Nuevomexicano Anti-clerical Satire: Humor, Rumor, and Marginalia from the 'Mano Fashico' Numskulis to the 'Anti-cristo' of Taos," *Catholic Southwest: A Journal of History and Culture* 9 (1998): 64–74.

18. Antonio José Martínez to Jean Baptiste Lamy, April 13, 1857, Archive Collection AASF Loose Documents, Diocesan, 1857, no. 16, Archives of the Archdiocese of Santa Fe (quotations); Juan Romero and Moises Sandoval, *Reluctant Dawn: Historia del Padre A. J. Martínez, Cura de Taos* (San Antonio, TX: Mexican American Cultural Center Press, 1976). Quotations are my translation of the cited text.

19. Matovina, *Tejano Religion and Ethnicity*, 70–74; Navarro, *Defending Mexican Valor in Texas*, 21.

20. Steele, *New Mexican Spanish Religious Oratory*, 148–159.

21. Matovina and Poyo, *¡Presente!*, 44–89.

22. J. Manuel Espinosa, "The Origins of the Penitentes of New Mexico: Separating Fact from Fiction," *Catholic Historical Review* 79 (July 1993): 454–477; Alberto López Pulido, *The Sacred World of the Penitentes* (Washington, DC: Smithsonian Institution Press, 2000).

23. "Memoirs of Federico José María Ronstadt," as cited in Matovina and Poyo, *¡Presente!*, 77 (first quotation); Matovina, *Tejano Religion and Ethnicity*, 43–45, 52–53, 64–68; "Esparza, the Boy of the Alamo, Remembers," in *Rise of the Lone Star: A Story of Texas Told by Its Pioneers*, ed. Howard R. Driggs and Sarah S. King (New York: Frederick A. Stokes, 1936), 219 (second quotation).

24. Matovina and Poyo, *¡Presente!*, 58–89; William H. Brewer, *Up and Down California in 1860–1864: The Journal of William H. Brewer, Professor of Agriculture in the Sheffield Scientific School from 1864 to 1903*, ed. Francis P. Farquhar (Berkeley: University of California Press, 1966), 69–70 (quotation).

25. Robert Wuthnow, Martin E. Marty, Philip Gleason, and Deborah Dash Moore, "Sources of Personal Identity: Religion, Ethnicity, and the American Cultural Situation," *Religion and American Culture: A Journal of Interpretation* 2 (Winter 1992): 9 (quotation). For a fuller treatment and more extensive bibliographic overview on the formation of ethnic identities in pluralistic societies, see Matovina, *Tejano Religion and Ethnicity*, 3–5, 49–93.

26. Matovina and Poyo, *¡Presente!*, 65–85; Ana María Díaz-Stevens, "The Saving Grace: The Matriarchal Core of Latino Catholicism," *Latino Studies Journal* 4 (September 1993): 60–78.

27. Camarillo, *Chicanos in a Changing Society*, 65; Timothy Matovina, "Lay Initiatives in Worship on the Texas *Frontera*, 1830–1860," *U.S. Catholic Historian* 12 (Fall 1994): 108–111; Henry Granjon, *Along the Rio Grande: A Pastoral Visit to Southwest New Mexico in 1902*, ed. Michael Romero Taylor, trans. Mary W. de López (Albuquerque: University of New Mexico Press, 1986), 39.

2

The Mysticism and Social Action of César Chávez

Stephen R. Lloyd-Moffett

César Chávez is both the most celebrated Latino in American history and one of the most recognizable social activists of the modern era. Before and especially since his death in 1993, a battle has emerged to define his legacy. The image that has emerged and come to dominate the public discourse is erroneous and unbalanced. He has been championed as a social and political activist driven by a secular ideology of justice and nonviolence. Yet, contrary to common historical record, it was his *personal spirituality* and not a secularized "ideology" that informed his activism. A careful reading of the historical sources, particularly the words of Chávez himself, reveals that he routinely had direct, extraordinary, and profound encounters with God during his extended fasts. These mystical experiences grounded, directed, and infused his program of social reform by serving as the basis for his decisions. Engaging these mystical encounters and understanding their place within Chávez's mission is the critical ingredient to understanding his place in history.

Seeking to co-opt Chávez and his cause, those who defined his early legacy—the liberal intelligentsia and Chicano activists—embarked on a conscious, consistent, and comprehensive agenda to secularize Chávez and substitute their own values for his stated motivations. In the process, they erased the spiritual basis of his public record, thereby creating the "Christ-less" Chávez of popular perception. By eviscerating the spiritual core of the most famous Latino civil activist, they also perpetuated the widespread notion of a breech between religion and social engagement in the Latino culture. Yet, as some have begun to recognize, Chávez stands firmly within a long-standing tradition in the Latino Catholic heritage of mystic reformers whose extraordinary experiences with God led to a heightened vision of humanity, which was enacted through their life mission. To date, the widespread recognition of Chávez within this tradition has not occurred because of a perceived opposition between mysticism and civic engagement that proves ultimately misguided. As a result, the legacy of Chávez needs balancing. He is a social activist but not *only* a social activist. Rather, he is a unique breed of social reformer whose basis for action is derived from his mystical encounters with God.

Traditionally, the aims of Catholic mysticism have been considered opposed to civic engagement. Mysticism is "other-worldly," while civic engagement is decidedly "this-worldly." Due in large part to a misguided concentration on the mystical experience itself, a presentation as such represents a false dichotomy: mysticism is not *necessarily* opposed to civil activism; on the contrary, once understood as a social construction, mysticism is revealed to be by nature a form of *social protest.* To recognize this fundamental congruency of mysticism and civil action, one must closely examine the role of mysticism within the social realm.

The "mystic" is a common figure within the form of Catholicism that most Latinos practice. Yet, in scholarship and popular culture, mystics are a curious and often misconstrued group. Who is a mystic? Like the man who proclaims himself the humblest man in the world, a mystic who calls himself a mystic is hardly ever a mystic. Rather, mystics come to be known as such only because other people start referring to them as "mystics;" mystics, then, are simultaneously constructed by society.[1] Yet, unlike saints in the Catholic Church, there is neither an accepted process for recognition of mystics nor formal canonization; rather, it is the parish priests, scholars, and, particularly, common believers who identify mystics.

How are mystics recognized? In the most basic terms, a "mystic" is one whom the people consider to have "mystical experiences." As Bernard McGinn[2] and earlier Joseph Maréchal[3] argued, since mystical experiences vary widely in content, context, and medium, one must consider mystical experiences as *any experience of God which is perceived by others to be direct or extraordinary.*[4] A mystical experience must be radically different from the "common" religious experience, whatever that might be.

As Gershom Scholem, Steven Katz, and Bernard McGinn have reminded us, the outside observer has no access to the mystical experience itself.[5] Those who proclaim another a mystic *infer* a mystical prerequisite. Therefore, despite the monocular focus of scholars on the "mystical experience," mystics are *never* identified by the experience alone—neither its proclivity nor proximity; rather, the critical element is the imprint of the mystical experience on the life of the candidate. The mystical experience must be made concrete through some form of action that others recognize. In this way, the mark of the mystic is the active living-out of the "other-worldly" experience within the social world in which the mystic finds himself or herself.[6]

This understanding of mysticism has profound importance for the relationship of mysticism to civil engagement. The mystical experience that is enacted by the mystic is always understood relative to the socioreligious envi-

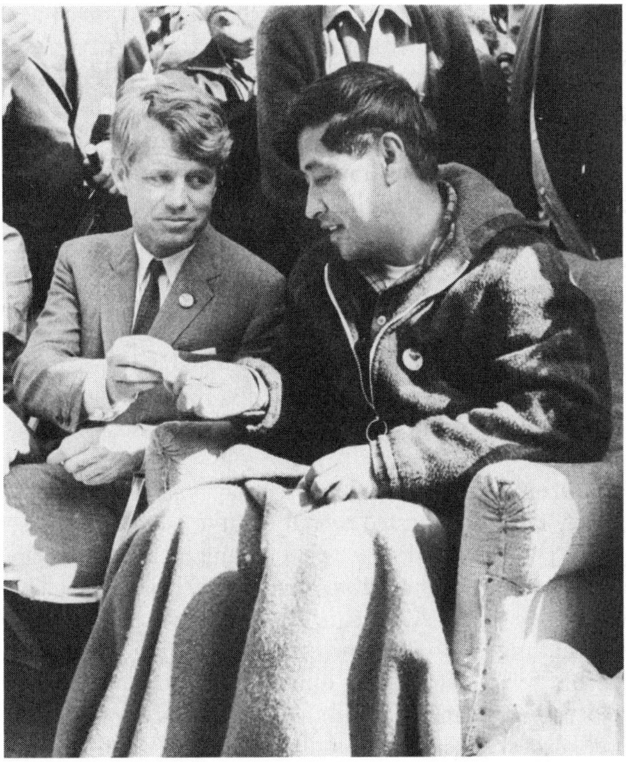

César Chávez breaks fast with Robert Kennedy in Delano, California, in 1968 (Courtesy of the Walter P. Reuther Library, Wayne State University)

ronment in which it is inscribed. As William James[7] and Gershom Scholem[8] remind us, the message of the mystical experience must represent a heightened version of the existing spiritual mandates of the socioreligious environments to which the mystic belongs, but nonetheless must be consistent with them.[9] As such, the extraordinary encounter with God always yields a call that questions the existing status of the world and presents a higher vision from God to which the Christian community should aim. By implication, then, the mystic's visions criticize the status quo. Thus, *the idea of the mystic is always linked with the call for change, reform, and reformation.* The mystic is a social reformer.[10]

In the Catholic heritage in which much of the Latino culture is embedded, there is a tradition of Catholic mystical reformers who translate their "higher view of reality" gained through their mystical experiences into an active, social transformation. It is no coincidence that many of the great mystics—including Ignatius of Loyola, Francis of Assisi, Theresa of Avila, and Hildegard of Bingen—were also active reformers. While the religious and social climate has radically changed, Chávez stands within this line, which does not only refuse to oppose religion and social engagement but actually merges the two. As will be demonstrated, Chávez translated his direct, extraordinary encounters with God achieved during his frequent extended fasts into active reform.

Throughout his life, Chávez was a devout Catholic. He spent usually an hour a day in prayer and attended mass almost daily.[11] Elements of his Catholic faith were standard practices of union activities: masses on the picket lines, prayers before meetings, and pilgrimages led under the banner of Our Lady of Guadalupe. During moments of crisis, however, Chávez consistently turned to the particular mystical vehicle of fasting. He made all of his major decisions while engaged in extended fasts. These periods of fasting propelled Chávez to direct and extra-ordinary encounters with God—mystical experiences—which he employed as the basis for his major decisions about the life of the union. Thus, one can make a direct link between his mystical experiences and his program for social reform. This link is evident throughout the historical sources.

While concerning himself with the everyday business of running a union, Chávez routinely fasted. He fasted "about eight to twelve days every forty-five to sixty days . . . [and] every day between midnight and noon the following day."[12] As a result, his state of mind was continually being shaped by his fasting experience. This is acutely evident in his three public fasts, which came at extremely critical times in his life and the life of his union.[13] For example, the conditions of his 1968 fast were so dire that he even questioned his will to continue.[14] For the popular press and many scholars, the extended fasts were assumed to be protest fasts: hunger strikes to call attention to a specific injustice,[15] but Chávez consistently and categorically stated otherwise.[16] His goal was not to incite change in others—which would be consistent for a protest fast—but a personal spiritual transformation.[17] Chávez explained this spiritual goal explicitly in a letter to the National Council of Churches during his 1968 fast: "My fast is informed by my religious faith and by my deep roots in the church. It is not intended as a pressure on anyone but only as an expression of my own deep feelings and my own need to do penance and to be in prayer."[18] By fasting, he was not "demanding something" but "giving" of himself under God.[19]

For Chávez, extreme fasting was a personal spiritual exercise. He stated that his fasts were "a very personal form of self-testing and prayer"[20] and were primarily "a very personal spiritual thing."[21] Thus, the goal was internal transformation. He stated, "The fast was first and foremost directed at myself. It was something I felt compelled to do to purify my own body, mind, and soul."[22] Thus, his motivations were personal, not social, and he sought to make this explicit to the public. An open letter issued by the United Farm Workers Organizing Committee at the time of his 1968 fast states, "César Chávez is engaged in a prolonged religious fast which is first and foremost a deeply personal act of penance and hope."[23] He was hoping for a profound spiritual encounter with God that would transform how he viewed the world.

The design of his fast followed a classical mystic model for preparing for a spiritual encounter with God. Chávez felt called by God to fast. He describes this dynamic in regard to his 1988 fast: "A powerful urge has been raging within me for several months," one that he could no longer resist and that led him to fast.[24] Fasting was the medium through which he discovered authentic existence. He once revealed, "I can't live without fasting anymore."[25] Next, he surrounded himself in an environment conducive to a profound religious experience. In the 1968 fast, he transformed a small storage room in a service station into his "monastic cell."[26] He surrounded himself with simple, religious paraphernalia such as a crucifix and images of the saints and the Virgin of Guadalupe. Like many of the medieval female mystics, he was sustained solely by the Eucharist.[27]

In time, he began to receive spiritual gifts and a wholly new perspective. He claims to have developed extrasensory hearing capabilities.[28] Chávez often spoke of his enhanced powers of the mind gained through fasting: "After seven days it was like going into a different dimension. I began to see things in a different perspective, to retain a lot more, to develop tremendous powers of concentration."[29] Finally, he was granted a fearless and unifying vision of the world. He said, "Once I am on a fast, I am on a different level. Patience is infinite. . . . Maybe what happens is you go on a fast, and get feelings so great you're not even afraid of death."[30]

Like many traditional mystics, Chávez found this experience ultimately ineffable. Commenting about his 1968 fast, Chávez told his biographer Levy, "There is . . . there is a force there. I don't quite know what it is."[31] Furthermore, he received this reward of fasting—a higher vision of reality—*every* time he fasted. Chávez stated:

> About the third or fourth day—and this has happened to me every time I've fasted—it's like all of a sudden you're up at a high altitude, and you clear your ears; in the same way, my mind clears, it is open to everything. After a long conversation, for example, I could repeat word for word what had been said. That's one of the sensations of the fast; it's beautiful. And usually I can't concentrate on music very well, but in the fast, I could see the whole orchestra and everything, that music was so clear.[32]

Given the frequency of his fasting, this perception must have become common to his everyday mindframe. Most importantly for this study, he received a new and higher vision of the world through these experiences by which to make decisions about his life and union. He explained:

> You are able to see things in a different light—see other people and yourself in a different light . . . it is easier to find solutions and be able to detach yourself much, much more completely . . . vastly more profound and yet more removed. . . . You speak then from that experience of fasting while you are fasting . . . you are really talking about nonviolence in a different light, in a different authority, with a lot of authority.[33]

> There haven't been in the last four or five years any major decisions that I didn't make while I was fasting. I wouldn't unless it was an emergency, but I would prepare for it by going into a fast and then look at it from that perspective, which is a completely different matter—fasting—I doubt if you can make mistakes when you are fasting. I really seriously doubt it because you are able to look at things in a very special way. You are ready to look at them when you are in a different mental and physical plane.[34]

On this "different plane," Chávez directed the critical movements of his social activism. His program of social change was guided by his encounters with God. In this process, he was directly placing his faith at the base of his social action. He seems aware of this dynamic when discussing prayer, which with penance was one of his two stated goals of fasting: "Prayer is for you, for one's self. . . . Your prayer then translates into action and determination and faith."[35] It is this "translation" of his mystical encounters into action that places him squarely within the mystical-reformer heritage of the Catholic tradition.

Chávez's own recognition of his place within this tradition is evident in the public speeches he gives following his fasts. They are decidedly religious in tone, content, and style. He speaks with the moral authority of a prophet, denouncing the kingdom of this world and proclaiming a new one under God. One should note the numerous biblical allusions—especially self-crucifixion in selfless love for others—in his 1968 speech:

> Our struggle is not easy. Those who oppose our cause are rich and powerful, and they have many allies in high places. We are poor. Our allies are few. But we have something the rich do not own. We have our own bodies and spirits and the justice of our cause as our weapons. When we are really honest with ourselves we must admit that our lives are all that really belong to us. So it is how we use our lives that determine what kind of men we are. It is my deepest belief that only by giving our lives do we find life. I am convinced that the truest act of courage, the strongest act of manliness is to sacrifice ourselves for others in a totally non-violent struggle for justice. To be a man is to suffer for others. God help us to be men![36]

This imagery could not be lost on the audience as they faced his emaciated body. Chávez was the one who suffered for his people; he sacrificed *his* body so that his people would live. The transparent reference to the mystic's goal of *imitatio Christi* (imitation of Christ) appears likewise in his 1972 public pronouncement: "The greatest tragedy is not to live and die, as we all must. The greatest tragedy is for a person to live and die without knowing the satisfaction of giving life for others."[37] Perhaps consciously linking himself to prophetic tradition of the church, he harkens to the prophet Micah to conclude his first major speech after breaking his fast in 1988: "What does the Lord require of you, but to do justice, to love kindness, and to walk humbly with your God."[38]

By the words and imagery Chávez chose to employ, he transmitted the character of his experience of God to the people around him. He proclaimed God's message for civic engagement and thus united the two realms in a manner unique in America.

The people around Chávez also seemed to instinctively place him within the tradition of the Catholic mystic-reformer by responding to him in a manner consistent with how generations of Christians have treated their holy mystics. Although it angered some of his followers, most felt impelled to visit, which took the form of a pilgrimage. Twenty thousand farm workers came to him during his 1968 fast, many of whom crawled on their knees from the highway to his cell, like the penitent to a holy man.[39] Some saw it as a Second Coming and they brought him crucifixes, kept constant vigil, and fought merely to touch him.[40] Masses were said nightly in vestments cut from his symbolic flag. Like pilgrims for generations, those who saw him came away altered. His primary biographer, Jacques Levy, observes, "there is a strength of spirit emanating from him that obviously touches those who see him."[41] When he had to go to Bakersfield to have a court date during his fast, over 1,000 farmworkers and priests sang and prayed on their knees around the courthouse. In short, his followers acted in the same spirit as generations of Christian communities have reacted toward a living mystic.

Despite Chávez's claims to the contrary, the analysis of fasts by the mass media has been primarily defined in terms of the labor struggle; they have been seen as calculated hunger strikes aimed to raise public opinion.[42] This "Godless" portrayal of his motivations for fasting is part of a much broader secularization of Chávez's persona within popular history. Sanitized of all religious referent, Chávez becomes a modern humanist, driven by philosophical ideals of justice and nonviolence. The diffusion of this caricature is widespread and ingrained.

The evidence for this secular vision of Chávez's victory is overwhelming. Of the twelve full-length biographies of Chávez, not a single chapter is devoted to the role his personal spirituality had on his social action. When works do directly address the role of his Christianity, it is usually the political role of the church that is discussed, and not the role of Chávez's personal faith in promoting his vision.[43] Occasionally, the texts will mention that he was a "deeply religious man" or "devoutly religious" or had "deep religious conviction" or "an unadulterated belief in God," or some like phrase, but such statements are always so embedded within the texts as to present the appearance that his faith was merely incidental to his actions.[44] The foundational relationship between his personal faith and action has never been explored.

Likewise, the mediums through which the legacy of Chávez will be transmitted to future generations all consistently disregard or downplay his spiritual basis. Of the seven major encyclopedias on the market today, none mention his faith as a motivation for social action.[45] Further, only the *New Encyclopaedia Britannica* gives *any* mention to his faith or spirituality and then only to show the negative impact it had later in his life.[46] Of the five major biographical dictionaries and biographical encyclopedias, all are likewise silent about his faith.[47] Oddly, this is also accurate in regards to books dedicated to Hispanic and Latino-American biographies.[48] Even a popular book that names Chávez the most influential Hispanic American in history fails to devote a word to his faith and claims priests taught him only labor history.[49] Similarly, the three lengthy Web sites dedicated to Chávez's life[50] and the one mural[51] do not record the impact of his faith on his action. This poverty of attention to his spiritual basis is especially acute in the numerous books written for teens and children.[52] Although most of these biographies note the faith of his mother and the role the church played in initially drawing him to organizing, his personal spirituality all but disappears when the texts move to his period of active reform.[53] In regard to his fasts, most authors categorize it as a hunger strike and record any religious meaning in secondary remarks that ultimately prove only to debase it. For example, one author qualifies his description by stating, "He did not deny the religious basis of his *hunger strike*."[54] Therefore, the electronic and textual mediums that will transmit Chávez's legacy erase his spiritual basis from the historical record and perpetuate a stereotype of a split between faith and action for Latino civic leaders.

With Chávez becoming part of the mandatory curriculum in some states, school lesson plans and curriculum become especially critical to the definition of his legacy.[55] Yet, it is here where the most thorough denial of his spirituality is discovered. None of the publicly available lesson plans of which I am aware treats the impact of his faith on his social activism;[56] rather, most programs actively coat his spirituality in secularized terms. Therefore, his spiritual fasts come to be defined, in one program, as "a peaceful way to protest by not eating food for a period of time" rather than personal spiritual exercise based in his Catholic faith tradition.[57] It is this completely secularized image of Chávez that is poised to become his legacy.

The secularization project was initially engineered by two separate groups—the liberal intelligentsia and Chicano activists—which sought to mold Chávez in variant forms. The liberal intelligentsia saw in Chávez a minority leader who shared their goals of social justice and who had gained the moral capital from his people to enact their vision. They sought to co-opt Chávez and his cause. Yet, their humanist basis for social justice was largely incommensurate with that of Chávez's religious basis.[58] So, when they wrote their highly influential early biographies, they framed the story and stressed the elements that coincided with their ideological vision. This meant that Chávez was a "guerrilla leader" engaged in a "power struggle" and "social revolution."[59] His life work was "conflict organizing."[60] In this way, they created a symbol out of Chávez that matched their own secular ideology. Richard Griswold del Castillo and Richard A. García capture this dynamic: "In a world in revolt, the liberal intelligentsia—in search of a hero, of a myth, of a soul—performed the necessary textual transfiguration. . . . Chávez had central private beliefs, but the old-style liberals created his public person."[61] Applying their secular matrix, the liberal intelligentsia created a motivation for Chávez that was devoid of any religious referent. Their Chávez was motivated by a drive for justice; his demand for nonviolence was a mere "pragmatic position."[62] Ultimately, his success was due to his "personal magnetism."[63] Chávez's encounters with God, which were so instrumental in shaping his action, were curiously forgotten.

The Chicano activists saw in Chávez a figure that united their race and had widespread support in the larger culture. Like the liberal intelligentsia, when the leaders of the Chicano movement recognized that their goals were incommensurate with those of Chávez, they "read their own desires, goals, and ideology into the Chávez leadership."[64] They created a Chávez that could fit within their model. For them, he was not motivated by a social ideology for justice or by a desire for nonviolence, but by a Chicano manifesto to liberate his people. Thus, Rodolfo Acuña in *Occupied America* presents Chávez as a social revolutionary and the essence of *La Raza*.[65] Likewise, Ignacio M. García[66] and Matt Meier and Feliciano Ribera[67] in their popular texts on the Chicano movement link Chávez to other "radical leaders" in the Chicano movement. In this way, his religious basis was sanitized and Chávez became another tool by which the Chicano activists sought their goals.

Both the Chicano activists and the liberal intelligentsia ascribed to Chávez their motivation in order to capitalize on his public goodwill. As a result, they erased his religious core from the historical record and substituted humanist political and social philosophies. By taking the most famous Latino civic activist and erasing all signs of his faith, they also unknowingly contributed to the impression that Latino civil action is divorced from religious belief. They created a paradigm that is firmly entrenched in the public perception of the Latino community.

One must recall that the American public warmly received this secularized Chávez, for the image of Chávez shaped by the liberal agenda was the *only* image to which most Anglo-Americans were exposed.[68] Their secularized Chávez *is* the Chávez that many in America came to respect. How popular would Chávez have been if his deep religious convictions and routine encounters with God were exposed and widely reported? Rather, it seems that the resultant image of a humanist and peaceful Che Guevara was seen as more palatable to the American public than a radically political St. Francis of Assisi. Few recognize how contrary this secularized portrayal is to how Chávez saw himself and the decision process he used to guide his social action as was presented above.

In transforming Chávez from a man driven by a personal spiritual encounter with God into a social activist driven by a secular ideology, the liberal intelligentsia and Chicano activists had ample material with which to work. Chávez often used phrases and imagery that lent themselves toward secular interpretation if left unbalanced by his Christian foundation; he repeatedly speaks of "justice" and "social revolution" and "liberation." But what does he mean when he uses these politically charged words? Here it is critical to place his statements within the profoundly Christian context in which he lived, but rarely spoke publicly about.[69] By his own self-conception, he sought to apply "the teaching of Christ." "I think," he confided, "you need very little else to make things work."[70] Thus, his "social revolution" was not conceived in the same terms as Peter Matthiessen's or Corky González's. As John C. Hammerback and Richard J. Jensen note, Chávez's "social revolution" is a "revolution of the mind and heart, not of economics."[71] Likewise, social justice for Chávez was not a cold economic equality but, rather, had its basis in his Christian faith and God. Chávez states, "The only justice is Christ—God's justice."[72] Similarly, his strong adherence to nonviolence was not based on abstract philosophical principles but came "from my own religion, from Christ's message."[73] Thus, when analyzing his rhetoric, it is paramount to place it within the context of his mystical experiences which grounded them. Without this lens—which none of the early interpreters shared—Chávez could easily be construed within purely secular terms.

However, Chávez was forthright in his response to those who secularized his motivation for action. Chávez states, "I was convinced [that my ideology was] . . . very Christian. That's my interpretation. I don't think it was so much political or economic."[74] Rather, he told others that he was motivated by his "faith in God and our choice to follow His son."[75] A purely secular ideology was ultimately unsatisfying to Chávez. He states, "Today I don't think I could base my will to struggle on cold economics or some political doctrine. I don't think there would be enough to sustain me. For me the base must be faith."[76] For Chávez, the connection to God was clear and direct; he saw himself doing "Christ's work on earth" and carrying out God's will.[77] Chávez describes it as "a fire—a consuming, nagging everyday and every-moment demand of my soul to just do it. It's difficult to explain. I like to think it's the good Spirit asking me to do it."[78] Furthermore, he was cognizant of the dangers of divorcing his politics from his spirituality. He said in a 1969 interview, "I don't think we can find total happiness in a purely economic struggle, regardless of how many benefits we may get. Not that these aren't important—I'd be the first to say they are important—but I think that if we divorce the struggle from religion we would not be totally happy, even though we may make great gains."[79] Despite his plea, this divorce of Chávez's spirituality from his social activism is the distinctive mark of the biographies written about him except for the recent biography written by Frederick John Dalton, *The Moral Vision of César Chávez* (Maryknoll, NY: Orbis Books, 2003). The image is firmly entrenched, and the stereotype of a chasm between civic engagement and religion is maintained.

Two separate clusters of individuals—academics and devout Latino-Catholic believers—have begun recently to recognize his spiritual basis of his social action and locate Chávez broadly within the mystical-reformer sphere. Historically, scholars have avoided Chávez's relationship to religion. Although there are more than 235 books and articles published about Chávez, a definitive spiritual biography has yet to be written. Three works have dealt narrowly with his social ethics, while a fourth focuses on his relationship and struggle with the California Migrant Ministry.[80] While unquestionably directed at his relationship with religion, these works do not confront the foundational mystical experiences that undergird his social action. They are examinations of his actions in light of the church's philosophy and ethics rather than probes into the basis for his action. As a result, his personal experiences with God are normally marginalized, hovering largely in the shadows of their analysis.

The move to reappraise Chávez began with Griswold del Castillo and Garcia's 1995 groundbreaking analysis of the "spirit" of Chávez. While their postmodern formulation of Chávez as a man "with an indefinable essence"[81] leads to a mixed view of the influence of religion, it is the first book to consider the role of religion in formulating his worldview.[82] John C. Hammerback and Richard J. Jensen's 1998 study of the rhetorical strategies of Chávez is the first examination to make Chávez's beliefs central to his motivation; they write that "at the base of his pyramid of reasoning lay his belief in God."[83] Yet his religion is more often depicted as a cold Millennialism by the authors rather than the daily living encounter with God that Chávez describes. For Hammerback and Jensen's Chávez, it is hard to see God's role beyond planning to lift Chávez and his union to victory.[84] By authentically engaging Chávez's religion, however, both of these studies issued an implicit call to explore the relationship between his civic engagement and spirituality. Most recently, this call has been reiterated forcefully by the Latino theologian, scholar, and priest Virgilio Elizondo,[85] who has spearheaded a revival of interest in Chávez's spirituality and the role of the mystic reformer in contemporary settings.

Beyond the academic world, the second major stimulus for looking at Chávez's mystic grounding derives from devout Latino Catholics who supported Chávez during his life. At St. Gregory's Episcopal Church in San Francisco, an icon is being created of him among the saints of the century. At the Mary Immaculate Catholic Church in Pacoima, in the San Fernando Valley, a vigil is held for Chávez each year; people are asked to fast beforehand, and prayers are conducted throughout the night. Yet, most characteristic of this movement is the popular piety and simple devotion shown to Chávez in the numerous vigils that occur around the anniversary of his death. To many within the Latino community, he is a contemporary savior figure. Griswold del Castillo and García capture this sentiment in a description of a meeting with Chávez that they attended toward the end of his life. They conclude:

> Chávez gave them solace in a world where they often felt alienated and powerless. . . . They were constructing a new spiritual reality around a man who, for the most part, just listened. Nobody said so, but many perceived Chávez as a spiritual rather than a political leader—a savior in their midst.[86]

Though unarticulated, these Latinos are placing Chávez within a tradition of mystic reformers and recognizing the spiritual foundation of his mission. They are placing their faith in him not as a political leader but as one who speaks from God. As Carlos Piar has argued, such reaching out to one's local spiritual heroes for personal guidance is a characteristic feature of Latino Catholicism. In Piar's article, James Joseph is quoted as saying the following:

> To be Catholic in the United States means to be affiliated with the church, to belong to its associations, and to be identified with its

> structures. In Latin America, the religious practice is marked by the quality of *personalismo*, the pattern of close intimate personal relationships that is characteristic of Spanish cultures everywhere. Individuals perceive their religious life as a network of personal relationships with the saints, the Blessed Virgin, or various manifestations of the church made flesh and blood.[87]

For many within the Latino community, Chávez is their political and spiritual hero; he is their "manifestation of the church made flesh and blood." As such, he is venerated not as a social activist but as a socially minded Messiah who operated under God. As a result, the perennial divide between civic engagement and religion seems largely absent in the popular devotion to Chávez. His supporters refuse to accept the sanitized image of him that is so firmly entrenched in American culture. As this "popular" Latino religiosity becomes more and more a part of the American scene in the coming decades, the Chávez of the farm workers will increasingly be opposed to that of the popular media. In the process, the unspoken myth that Latino religion has had little influence on civic engagement will inevitably be challenged. Thus, the battle to understand the relationship of religion to civil action in the Latino community will likely be waged through the legacy of Chávez. The question is what image of Chávez will remain standing to be engraved in the history books.

If Chávez had lived 500 years ago, he would have been readily identified as a mystic reformer. The fact that our contemporary society does not recognize him as such speaks to the values and biases of our cultural environment. Our modern society is uncomfortable with the confluence of religion and social action. America may want a social and political Messiah, but only a Messiah without any obviously religious traits. In the process of secularizing Chávez, his biographers transposed this stark division unnaturally to Chávez, and the American public embraced this divided Chávez. For Chávez, however, the two realms were fused.[88] It was his direct encounters with God that drove his action, and his political realities drove him increasingly toward God. Yet, at the center of his life were the direct experiences of God that he gained while fasting. It is through this prism that all his other actions must be understood. These encounters infused the core of his being and motivated his every action. Because of this, generations past would have termed Chávez a religious mystic with particularly far-ranging reach. Today, Chávez is a secular sociopolitical activist whose spiritual life has been intently buried. It is our task as scholars to resurrect that burial and reassess Chávez's central role in the Hispanic churches in American public life. In this process, scholars will gain a deeper appreciation for the role of religion in civic engagement as they meet the burgeoning surge of pious Catholic believers who are uplifting Chávez as a saint and, indeed, a mystic.

NOTES

1. See "Mystique," *Encyclopaedia Universalis* (Paris: Encyclopedia Universalis de France, 1965).

2. Bernard McGinn, *The Foundations of Mysticism: Origins to the Fifth Century* (New York: Crossroad, 1997), xix.

3. Joseph Maréchal writes that mysticism consists of "a religious experience which is esteemed as superior to the normal: more direct, more intimate or more rare," cited in ibid., 300.

4. Two considerations must be stated. First, the visions of Hildegard of Bingen, the stigmata of Francis of Assisi, and the rapture of Theresa of Avila are all considered mystical experiences, but they vary in nearly every other dimension. Thus, it is not the particular mystical "vehicle" that is important but the character of the encounter with God. Second, what constitutes an "extra-ordinary experience of God" varies widely by context and is thus a relativistic concept. Someone speaking in tongues may be engaged in a mystical experience in a Catholic liturgy while be perfectly normal at a charismatic or Pentecostal Church. Herein lies the difference between a mystic and a merely spiritual or devout person: if one follows normal procedures of a religious tradition and receives expected results (whatever they may be), then one may be termed "devout" or "spiritual," but not a mystic.

5. Gershom Scholem, *Major Trends in Jewish Mysticism* (New York: Schocken, 1961); Steven Katz, *Mysticism and Philosophical Analysis* (New York: Oxford University Press, 1978); McGinn, *Foundations of Mysticism,* xiv.

6. For many "traditional" mystics, their social environment was ecclesial to a degree that is unfamiliar in the modern world. Their mystical experience often involved church activities, and the "living-out" of their mystical experience was often directed at the church institution itself.

7. See William James, *The Varieties of Religious Experience* (New York: Simon & Schuster, 1997), 300.

8. See Gershom Scholem, *On the Kabbalah and Its Symbolism* (New York: Schocken, 1961), 7.

9. If the mystic "vision" is not extraordinary, then it is not mystical; if it is inconsistent with the socioreligious environment, it is heretical. In this way the category of "mystics" becomes intimately tied to the category of "prophet." While all mystics are somehow prophets, not all prophets are necessarily mystics. A prophet, at least in theory, can denounce the status quo without an extraordinary experience of God, while a mystic cannot, by definition, do so.

10. Not all social reformers are mystics. Only those whose vision derives from an extra-ordinary and direct encounter with God qualify as mystics.

11. According to Pat Henning, as quoted in Arthur Jones, "Millions Reaped What César Chávez Sowed," *National Catholic Reporter* (May 7, 1993): 7.

12. Paul Anthony Hribar, "The Social Fasts of César Chávez" (Ph.D. diss., University of Southern California, 1978), 332. See also Susan Ferriss and Ricardo Sandoval, *The Fight in the Fields: Casar Cháver and the Farmworkers' Movement* (New York: Harcourt Brace, 1997), 254. Additionally, he confided to Matthiessen that he often fasted without people knowing. Peter Matthiessen, *Sal Si Puedes: César Chávez and the New American Revolution* (New York: Random House, 1969), 139–140.

13. February–March 1968, amidst the strike and boycott of Giumarra Corporation; May 1974, while lobbying for a law in Arizona guaranteeing farm worker elections; July–August 1988, while battling for pesticide reduction.

14. Chávez wrote in his journal, "It's very tough. I don't know if I can continue." Quoted in Ferriss and Sandoval, *Fight in the Fields,* 140.

15. See *Cambridge Dictionary of American Biography,* ed. John S. Bowman (Cambridge: Cambridge University Press, 1995), 129; *Encyclopedia Americana, 2000;* "Grapes of Wrath," *Economist* (August 20, 1998): 25.

16. The one exception was his 1970 fast in response to the Teamsters' insurgence. This self-proclaimed "protest fast" was a failure at every level, in Chávez's own opinion. See Jacques E. Levy, *César Chávez: Autobiography of La Causa* (New York: Norton, 1975), 340.

17. "Now this is a fast which means that I'm not doing it to put pressure on anybody. . . . This is not a hunger strike." Chávez in Levy, *César Chávez,* 274. Referring to his 1968 fast, Chávez states, "It was not a hunger strike because its purpose was not strategic; it was an act of prayer and love." Matthiessen, *Sal Si Puedes,* 180.

18. César Chávez, "Letter to the National Council of Churches," February 20 1968, reprinted in Winthrop Yinger, *César Chávez: Rhetoric of Nonviolence* (Hicksville, NY: Exposition Press, 1975), 108.

19. Hribar, "Social Fasts," 372.

20. César Chávez, "Non-Violence Still Works," *Look* (April 1, 1969): 52.

21. Levy, *César Chávez,* 465.

22. César Chávez, "Address by César Chávez, President United Farm Workers of America, AFL-CIO," Pacific Lutheran University, Tacoma, Washington, March 1989. Available at www.ufw.org/fast.html.

23. United Farm Workers Organizing Committee, "Statement of the Fast for Non-Violence," February 25, 1968.

24. John C. Hammerback and Richard J. Jensen, *The Rhetorical Career of César Chávez* (College Station: Texas A&M University Press, 1998), 186.

25. Hribar, "Social Fasts," 378.

26. Richard Griswold del Castillo and Richard A. García, *César Chávez: A Triumph of Spirit* (Norman: University of Oklahoma Press, 1995), 85.

27. Levy, *César Chávez,* 464; Hribar, "Social Fasts," 264.

28. He reportedly heard music from across the street through almost soundproof concrete walls to the amazement of all those around him. Matthiessen, *Sal Si Puedes,* 187–188.

29. Levy, "César Chávez," 276.

30. Ibid., 350.

31. Ibid.

32. Matthiessen, *Sal Si Puedes,* 187.

33. Hribar, "Social Fasts," 368–369.

34. Ibid., 379.

35. John Dear, "César Chávez on Voting in the Marketplace," *Pax Christi USA* (Winter 1992): 21.

36. Levy, *César Chávez,* 286.

37. Ibid., 465.

38. Chávez, "Address."

39. Dunne, *Delano: Revised and Updated* (New York: Farrar, Straus Giroux, 1971), 185.

40. Ibid.

41. Levy, *César Chávez,* 465.

42. For example, a recent article in the *San Diego Union Tribune* states without qualification that the "labor leader" César Chávez went on a twenty-five-day "hunger

strike" in 1968. Steve Schmidt "3 decades after Chávez hungerstrike, UFW wages old battles," November 8, 1998: A-1.

43. For example, Dunne has a whole chapter devoted to the clergy's role but nothing on how Christianity shaped Chávez.

44. Respectively: Jean Maddern Pitrone, *Chávez: Man of the Migrants* (New York: Pyramid Books, 1972), 83; Jan Young, *The Migrant Workers and César Chávez* (New York: Julian Messner, 1977), 126; Ronald B. Taylor, *Chávez and the Farm Workers* (Boston: Beacon Press, 1975), 213; Griswold del Castillo and García, *César Chávez*, xiv.

45. See "Chávez, César" in *The New Encyclopaedia Britannica*, 1998; *The World Book Encyclopedia*, 1999; *Merit Students Encyclopedia*, 1989; *Collier's Encyclopedia*, 1994; *Academic American Encyclopedia, 1992; Encyclopedia Americana, 2000; Encarta*, 2000.

46. *New Encyclopaedia Britannica*, 143.

47. See "Chávez, César" in *American National Biography*, 1999; *Encyclopedia of American Biography*, 1996; *Cambridge Dictionary of American Biography*, 1995; *Merriam-Webster's Biographical Dictionary*, 1995; *Encyclopedia of World Biography*, 2nd ed.

48. See Matt S. Meier, Conchita Franco Serri, and Richard García, *Notable Latino Americans: A Biographical Dictionary* (Westport, CT: Greenwood Press, 1997); Matt S. Meier, *Mexican-American Biographies: A Historical Dictionary 1836–1987* (New York: Greenwood Press, 1988).

49. Himilce Novas, *The Hispanic 100: A Ranking of Latino Men and Woman Who Have Most Influenced American Thought and Culture* (New York: Citadel Press, 1995), 4.

50. See http://thecity.slsu.edu/~ccipp/cesar_chavez/cesarbio3-12.html; http://clnet.ucr.edu/research/chavez/bio; http://www.ufw.org/cecstory.html.

51. The only completed mural dedicated to Chávez alone is at Santa Ana College; it contains no religious symbols.

52. Bruce Conord, *César Chávez: Union Leader* (Broomall, PA: Chelsea House, 1992); David R. Collins, *Farmworker's Friend: The Story of César Chávez* (Carolrhoda Books, 1996); Mark Falstein, *César Chávez* (Paramus, NJ: Globe Feron, 1994); Doreen Gonzáles, *César Chávez: Leader for Migrant Farm Workers* (Springfield, NJ: Enslow Publishers, 1996); David Goodwin, *César Chávez: Hope for the People* (New York: Fawcett Coumbine, 1991); Burnham Holmes, *César Chávez: Farm Worker Activist* (Austin, TX: Raintree Steck Vaugn, 1994); Naurice Roberts, *César Chávez and La Causa* (Chicago: Children's Press, 1986); Consuelo Rodríguez, *César Chávez* (Broomall, PA: Chelsea House, 1991); James Terzian and Kathryn Cramer, *Mighty Hard Road: The Story of César Chávez* (Garden City, NY: Doubleday, 1970); Florance White, *César Chávez, Man of Courage* (Champaign, IL: Garrard, 1973). The most balanced presentation is by Rodríguez.

53. Frequent religious symbols are often noted with regard to the march/pilgrimage to Sacramento, but their use is not connected to Chávez's personal faith in any way.

54. Goodwin, *César Chávez*, 13; emphasis added. Holmes also writes, "Perhaps there was also an element of self-sacrifice in César Chávez." (*César Chávez*, 78).

55. In California, beginning in the school year 2000–2001, students celebrate March 31 as "César Chávez Day." The bill signed by Governor Gray Davis on August 19, 2000, requires that students take an hour on the morning of the holiday learning about Chávez and his "legacy of nonviolence and social justice" and then spend the afternoon in some form of social service.

56. See www.lessonplanspage.com/SSLAMDCesarChavez24.htm; http://teach1.com/teachthenews/lessonplan/lessonplan_arch/lessonplan_19990921.html; http://mhcalifornia.com/socialstudies/lesses/ca4410-4.html; http://tlc.ai.org/lessons/chavezlp.htm.

57. See www.lessonplanspage.com/SSLAMDCesarChavez24.htm.

58. The two major early and influential biographies by Levy and Matthiessen were written by established liberal authors intimately connected with the wider liberal ideology. Similarly, the other major early works—those by Nelson, Day, Dunne, Taylor, Kushner, London and Anderson, Young, and Horowitz—were all written by individuals with social rather than religious objectives.

59. For example, see Taylor, *Chávez and Farm Workers,* 181–182. Levy's "autobiography" of Chávez—which is the single most influential book—was instigated as an attempt to record the struggles of the union against the powerful agribusiness. Levy, *César Chávez,* xv. Similarly, the very title of Matthiessen's book—*Sal Si Puedes: César Chávez and the New American Revolution*—relays his political agenda.

60. Taylor, *Chávez and Farm Workers,* 85.

61. Griswold del Castillo and García, *César Chávez,* 114, 115.

62. Taylor, *Chávez and Farm Workers,* 139.

63. Eugene Nelson, *Huelga* (Delano, CA: Farm Workers Press, 1966), 51.

64. Griswold del Castillo and García, *César Chávez,* 152. It is important to note that Corky González's Crusade for Justice in Colorado, José Angel Gutiérrez's Raza Unida Party, and Reies López Tijerina all grounded their movements primarily in racial not religious terms.

65. Rodolfo Acuña, *Occupied America: A History of Chicanos* (New York: Harper & Row, 1988).

66. Ignacio M. García, *Chicanismo: The Forging of a Militant Ethos among Mexican-Americans* (Tuscon: University of Arizona Press, 1997).

67. Matt S. Meier and Feliciano Ribera, *The Chicanos: A History of Mexican-Americans* (New York: Hill & Wang, 1972).

68. This is true to a lesser extent for the influence of radical Chicanos on the Latino population.

69. He admittedly had a hard time conveying such ideas to "agnostic friends," as he referred to them. See Chávez's discussion in Hribar, "Social Fasts," 370–371.

70. Hammerback and Jensen, *Rhetorical Career,* 82.

71. Ibid., 37–38.

72. Dear, "Voting," 21.

73. Hribar, "Social Fasts," 377.

74. Griswold del Castillo and García, *César Chávez,* 111.

75. Hammerback and Jensen, *Rhetorical Career,* 153. When challenged by an interviewer who asked if he was a communist, Chávez responded, "No, I am not a communist. . . . I'm saying this because I am a Christian and I'm proud of that." Dorothy Day, *Forty Acres: César Chávez and the Farm Workers* (New York: Praeger, 1971), 67.

76. Levy, *César Chávez,* 27.

77. César Chávez, "Love Thy Neighbor," *U.S. Catholic* 50:10 (October 1985): 38. See also Hammerback and Jensen, *Rhetorical Career,* 99.

78. Chávez, as cited in Frederick John Dalton, "The Moral Vision of César E. Chávez: An Examination of His Public Life from an Ethical Perspective" (Ph.D. diss., Graduate Theological Union, University of California, Berkeley, 1998), 353.

79. César Chávez, "Our Best Hope," *Engage* 2: (November 11, 1969) 5.

80. Carlos R. Piar, "César Chávez and La Causa: Toward an Hispanic Christian

Social Ethic," *Annual of the Society of Christian Ethics,* Harlan Beckley, ed. (Georgetown Univ. Press, 1996), 103–120; Donovan O. Roberts, "Theory and Practice in the Life of César Chávez: Implications of a Social Ethic" (Ph.D. diss., Boston University, 1979); Dalton, "Moral Vision"; Jennifer Reed-Bouley, "Guiding Moral Action: A Study of the United Farm Workers' Use of Catholic Social Teaching and Religious Symbols" (Ph.D. diss., Loyola University, Chicago, 1998); Patricia Hoffman, *The Ministry of the Dispossessed* (Los Angeles: Wallace Press, 1987). None of these works has received widespread attention.

81. Griswold del Castillo and García, *César Chávez,* 179; Reed-Bouley, "Guiding Moral Action"; Dalton, "Moral Vision."

82. Ultimately, this approach is unsatisfactory, with the authors concluding that an interesting "philosophical Christian humanism" constitutes *one face* of Chávez that rightly balances a primary political motivation.

83. Hammerback and Jensen, *Rhetorical Career,* 82.

84. See ibid., 139–141, 190, and numerous other references.

85. This occurred in a graduate seminar in Catholic Mysticism offered at the University of California at Santa Barbara in 1999, in which I was a participant.

86. Griswold del Castillo and García, *César Chávez,* 140.

87. James A. Joseph, *Remaking America* (San Francisco: Jossey-Bass, 1995), 186–187, as cited in Piar, "Chávez and La Causa," 105.

88. "If I'm going to save my soul, it's going to be through the struggle for social justice," Chávez in Levy, *César Chávez,* 276.

3

César Chávez and Mexican American Civil Religion

Luís D. León

We need a cultural revolution. And we need a cultural revolution among ourselves not only in art but also in the realm of the spirit.
—César Chávez, cited in Richard Griswald del Castillo and Richard A. García, *Cesar Chavez: A Triumph of Spirit*, 1995

César Estrada Chávez (1927–1993), founder of the United Farm Workers Union (UFW) and civil rights activist, lived what is perhaps the most public of all Latino lives in the United States. He is the most celebrated Latino in U.S. history. In the year 2000, Governor Gray Davis declared Chávez's birthday an official state holiday in California. At his funeral in 1993, President Bill Clinton declared Chávez an "authentic hero," and Latino California senator Art Torres called Chávez "our Gandhi," our "Martin Luther King Jr."

Overall, César Chávez occupies a complex historical and mythological place for people of Latino origin in the United States.[1] During his lifetime, Chávez's work on behalf of farmworkers inspired many Chicanos and Chicanas to struggle for civil rights. As a political leader and a catalyst for the Mexican American civil rights movement, Chávez's legacy is well documented, but Chávez's role as a distinctively *religious* leader has remained largely unexplored and not fully understood. "In the course of this movement," argues Chicano poet Gary Soto, "César became—whether he accepted this status or not—a spiritual leader for all Chicanos [Mexican Americans]."[2] Certainly, he articulated and emphasized the distinctly moral, spiritual, and ultimately universally human aspects that were central to his unionization of California Farm Workers. These religious dimensions of his work unfolded around the doctrines of self-sacrifice for social justice.

My fascination for Chávez and this project began while growing up in California's East Bay Area. During the early 1970s, the exploits of Chávez and the farmworkers were central to the political discourse of California, as well as to the public mythology of the nation. To many, Chávez was reputed to be a rabble-rouser, an anti-American labor agitator who upset the delicate illusion of an avowedly liberal democracy espousing justice and equality for all. But for many Latinos and Latinas, Chávez was a dignified public presence who embodied the hopes and dreams of the perennially marginalized—those who were erased from the chart of civil rights, which appeared to follow a black and white divide exclusively. Chávez seemed to speak for "us," the muted voices of the American democratic chorus sang.

As a young boy I followed Chávez's life with awe for what I felt were my personal connections to him: when he was a young boy, my father worked in California's agricultural fields; Chávez's parents immigrated from Mexico to work in agribusiness. And even as suburban Latinos, to my family and me Chávez was a hero. I remember my mother's profound disappointment when California's ballot initiative, Proposition 14—designed to support farmworkers—was rejected by California voters in 1976. Even though she was a Puerto Rican and liberal Protestant, my mother also felt personally connected to the Chávez movement: Chávez's charisma extended well beyond the boundaries of Mexican and Latino Catholics, but created extensive ranks of passionate supporters from all walks of life who believed in the basic dignity of the human person.

In what follows, I outline the background and formative moments of Chávez's life. I turn next to a discussion of Chávez's organizing career in the agricultural fields of California, Texas, and Arizona, which leads to an elaboration of his ethics and religious views. Chávez preached a gospel of self-sacrifice, nonviolence, and social justice, worked ecumenically with both Catholic and Protestant clerics, and deftly created and manipulated religious symbols to enlist the ultimate loyalties of the multitudes—including the rich and powerful in this country and in Latin America.

I am currently writing a manuscript on Chávez that examines his role as a distinctively religious or prophetic leader. My research emphasizes Chávez's powerful relationship to the political spirituality of Gandhi and to the religiosity of nonviolence. Central also to my research is Chávez's creation of a public political space for Mexicanos and other Latinos in the United States by holding America to its promises of justice and equality. America's deepest values and commitments, those that underpin democracy and unfold policy, are held as religious doctrines for our nation with the soul of a church. In the eighteenth century, French philosopher Jean-Jacques Rosseau theorized that, in the absence of an official alliance between church and state, the nation state would need to develop a religious dimension that conferred ultimate legitimacy upon the union and could implicitly perform the other functions of a national church; this he called civil religion. With this in mind, Chávez deftly navigated the moral terrain of American public life and waxed critical in his role of Mexican American prophet. Chávez's intellect and scholarly acumen have often

United Farm Workers pilgrimage from Delano to Sacramento, California, in 1966 (Courtesy of the Walter P. Reuther Library, Wayne State University)

been overlooked or dismissed altogether by his biographers. The larger project from which the following is drawn compares Chávez to Martin Luther King Jr. and begins from the premise of Chávez as organic intellectual, brilliant in his complexity: not a "simple" man. However, I wish to distinguish my writing from recent publications on the religious dimensions of Chávez.

My manuscript (in progress) on Chávez and the UFW is organized around a focus on Chávez's body as an allegory of the passion of Christ: (A) Spirit: The Prophetic Voice; (B) Flesh: Part I—The Crucified Body; Part II—The Religion of the UFW; (C) The Penitential Body: Sin and Salvation in the Farm Worker's Movement; (D) The Fragmented Body: Gender/Sexuality, Nationalism, and Class; (E) The Resurrection: The Death and Afterlife of César Chávez; Conclusion: Religion and Political Discourse in Delano and Beyond.[3] My genealogy of Chávez pieces together his legacy as a prophetic figure and suggests something about the tensions and religious hybridity that are characteristic not only of Chávez's movement but also of other borderland political movements.

The legacy of Chávez as a labor leader and Chicano activist is constituted by erasures and misperceptions of his deliberately spiritual qualities. The nascent and emergent discourse on his religious impulse does not fully fathom its complexity and depth. This conversation has been limited by Christian theology which unfolds on stark orthodox divisions of the phenomenal world: religious/secular; spiritual/political; saint/sinner. Generally, this literature bifurcates the religious and political into two discrete realms of Chávez that informed one another: his spiritual life inspiring his political work.[4] Overlooked in these writings is the way he integrated religion and politics, so that the religious or symbolic order is more than a crumbling veneer masking real economic and political relations. Rather, in the words of one Islamic theorist: "The symbolic is not a residual dimension of purportedly real politics. The symbolic is real politics, articulated in a special and often powerful way."[5] Chávez was symbolic of a religious bricoleur, powerfully adept at inventing, recasting, and ordering religious and cultural symbols and infusing political struggles with ultimate value or sacred meanings. I argue that Chávez's life follows the classical patterns of the "hero's return," or the narrative of the classic heroic figure who leaves his home to mature and return as prophet, warrior, and hero.[6]

Background and Socialization

César Chávez was born on March 31, 1927, near Yuma, Arizona. His parents, immigrants from Mexico, owned a small grocery store and other businesses in a Latino and Indian barrio. The Depression, racism, and corrupt legal practices resulted in the loss of the Chávez businesses, and the family moved onto a farm owned by César's grandmother, Mamá Tella. It was there, surrounded by elder family members, that César came to learn the ethics that became the foundation of his public activism through *consejos* and *dichos* (proverbial advice and sayings). Mama Tella's stories would focus particularly on the heroes of the Mexican Revolution. His mother pledged never to turn away someone in need, and many homeless would gather at the Chávez house every night to receive food and shelter from César's mother—and most of these homeless were white. "I didn't realize the wisdom in her words," Chávez reflects, "but it has been proven to me so many times since."[7] Another narrative told of his family's influence was the legacy of the Mexican Revolution, wherein common folks rose up to depose a corrupt Mexican dictator and to change an exploitative social system.

César's formal education was marred by xenophobia, from both teachers and students (e.g., he was punished for speaking Spanish). In 1942 César's father was permanently injured in an automobile accident, and after completing the eighth grade, César left school to work full time to help his family financially.

Once again, racism and corrupt legal practices resulted in the loss of the Chávez farm, and the family moved to California's Central Valley in search of agricultural labor work. The majority of farmworkers were Mexican Americans, the next largest group Filipinos, with a smaller presence of Puerto Ricans, all of whom lived and worked with few rights and protections: they were literally at the mercy of the farm owners. One Central Valley police officer explained the situation as follows: "We protect our farmers here in Kern County. They are our best people. They are always with us. They keep the country going. . . .

But the Mexicans are trash. They have no standard of living. We herd them like pigs."[8]

Indeed, farmworkers were an easily exploitable population, especially since a de facto Jim Crow style of segregation barred Latinos from many jobs during the 1940s, 1950s, and even into the 1960s. It was common to read signs in business windows across California and the Southwest that read: "No Mexicans or dogs." As a result, workers traveled hundreds of miles up and down California's Central Valley earning barely enough money for basic supplies. During their first winter in California, the Chávez family lived in a tent that was soggy from rain and fog. Their situation did not improve much once they moved into one of the many labor camps owned by the growers. The camp manager or contractor would deduct the workers' rent from their pay at exorbitant rates, and contractors also ran company stores that charged much inflated prices for basic supplies. Workers had to plead for their pay, and they were commonly paid late or underpaid. In fact, the evils of the labor system were multiple: contractors would overrecruit workers and lower the announced wage; they would make deductions for social security and not report them; occasionally workers would have to buy their jobs; and it was also common for contractors to demand sexual favors from female workers. In addition, growers used toxic pesticides on the crops, resulting in alarming rates of cancer and birth defects among farmworkers.

In the fields, workers spent long hours under a blazing sun performing monotonous and backbreaking work without rest or proper equipment. Contractors often did not provide water for the workers. But the most difficult part of this task was working with the short-handled hoe, which required workers to stoop over and contort their bodies unnaturally to perform their task. Chávez described this work as follows: "I would chop out a space with the short handled hoe in the right hand while I felt with my left to pull out all but one plant as I made the next chop. There was a rhythm, it went very fast . . . it's like being nailed to a cross."[9] Chávez's union contracts prohibited the use of the short-handled hoe, and as a tribute, one of the tools was placed on his coffin as a sign of his achievement.

In 1944, at age 17, Chávez joined the U.S. Navy. It was during his travels with the Navy that he discovered another world, one in which many kinds of people were exploited and oppressed. After the navy, Chávez married Helen Fabela, and by 1958 they had eight children. The family moved to San Jose, California, where César got a job in a lumber mill. They lived in a Mexican neighborhood called *Sal Si Puedes*—"get out if you can." It was in San Jose that Chávez met Father Donald McDonnell, a Roman Catholic priest who was attempting to start a parish in Sal Si Puedes. At McDonnell's urging, Chávez read the papal encyclicals on labor, and books on St. Francis of Assisi, as well as Louis Fischer's *Life of Gandhi*. He often repeated the wisdom of St. Francis of Assisi, "You can't really feel the pain of the poor unless you are one of them."

Soon, as a result of his work with McDonnell and Saul Alinsky's Industrial Areas Foundation, Chávez began organizing farm workers. In 1965 the union executed its first strike. Union demonstrators were met with violence both from goons hired by the growers and from the police. But Chávez held firmly to his belief in nonviolence. In 1968 he held the first of his many public fasts, in the hopes of rededicating his movement to the principles of nonviolence. Dr. Martin Luther King Jr. sent a telegram encouraging Chávez.

Spirit: The Prophetic Voice

In February 1968, César Chávez's body was ravaged from starvation and on the verge of collapse. Chávez had gone twenty-five days without food. His only sustenance during this time was water and the body of Christ: Chávez went to mass and took communion every day during this initial fast. He only broke the fast when he felt it successful and at the urging of his family and advisors, including his medical doctor. From the back of a flatbed truck, a mass was said in the Delano fields among the farm workers. There Chávez literally broke bread—eating the bread directly from the hand of the young senator and presidential candidate from Massachusetts, Robert Kennedy. After Chávez ate, a statement was read aloud, Chávez being too weak to read it himself. His words emerged as if they were a new revelation from God—a revelation that sacrifice, justice, and social change were central to the Christianity of the farmworkers. These subsequently provided an ethical basis for the UFW:

> Our struggle is not easy. Those who oppose our cause are rich and powerful, and they have many allies in high places. We are poor. Our allies are few. But we have something the rich do not own. We have our own bodies and spirits and the justice of our cause as weapons. . . . We must admit that our lives are all that really belong to us. So it is my deepest belief that only by giving our lives do we find life. I am convinced that the truest act of courage, the strongest act of [humanity] is to sacrifice ourselves for others in a totally nonviolent struggle for justice. To be [human] is to suffer for others. God help us to be [human]![10]

During this initial fast, Chávez cloistered himself in a small "cell" at Forty Acres, which was subsequently transformed into a pilgrimage site. One eyewitness recalls:

> I visited the forty acres on several occasions during the fast. It was both a fascinating and awesome spectacle to view. By the second week of the fast a sprawling tent city had sprung up around the little service station at the forty acres. Farm workers from all over California came to live in the tents and to share in the event . . . the deliberate pace, the quiet voices, the huddled figures, the sharing of food and drink—all these gave the impression of serious religious vigil.[11]

Reportedly, Chávez received a revelation from God while on his twenty-five-day long "spiritual fast." He spoke this message in March of 1968, at the

Second Annual Mexican-American Conference in Sacramento where he read a paper entitled, "The Mexican-American and the Church." The paper was subsequently published in the Chicano journal, *El Quinto Sol* the following summer (1968). In the paper, he admonished Chicanos to access the power of "the whole Church," defining it as

> an ecumenical body spread around the world, and not just its particular form in a parish in a local community. The church we are talking about is a tremendously powerful institution in our society, and in the world. That Church is one form of the Presence of God on Earth, and so naturally it is powerful. It is powerful by definition. It is a powerful moral and spiritual force which cannot be ignored by any movement.

There was a pragmatics to his theology, a preferential option for the poor. "Furthermore, it [the Church] is an organization with tremendous wealth. Since the Church is to be servant to the poor, it is *our* fault if that wealth is not channeled to help the poor in our world."[12]

Indeed, Chávez's prophetic message resounded meaningfully in the ears of many beyond Delano, inspiring the formation of a Chicano activist political Catholic group in East Los Angeles who called themselves Católicos Por La Raza (CPLR). CPLR gained fame in Los Angeles for holding a disruptive protest outside of the newly erected St. Basil's Cathedral on fashionable Wilshire Boulevard in Los Angeles on Christmas Eve, 1969. CPLR'S first newsletter quoted directly from Chávez's paper. Ricardo Cruz, founder of CPLR, traveled to Salinas to organize workers. There he met Chávez, and before leaving, "Cruz promised Chávez he would see what he could do to get Church support."[13]

After Chávez's 1968 public fast, during which he wrote his earliest published work, Chávez explained the fast in a letter to the National Council of Churches as follows: "My fast is informed by my religious faith and by my deep roots in the church. It is not intended as a pressure on anyone but only as an expression of my own deep feelings and my own need to do penance and to be in prayer."[14] Chávez makes a distinction here between his "religious faith" and his "deep roots in the church." There was probably never a better opportunity than this letter for Chávez to declare a Catholic or otherwise institutional commitment. Also key to understanding Chávez is his call to enlist the Catholic Church in his struggle: it was not a call to become Catholic, to submit to the will of the church, or to obey Catholic teachings. Chávez's fast was not a public declaration of his Catholic devotion but, rather, a siren to enlist the support of an institutional ally.

Many people misunderstood (and continue to misunderstand) Chávez's actions. Dolores Huerta, who became a spokesperson for Chávez, explains:

> A lot of people thought César was trying to play God, that this guy really was trying to pull a saintly act. Poor César! They just couldn't accept it for what it was. I know it is hard for people who are not Mexican to understand, but this is a part of the Mexican culture—

> the penance, the whole idea of suffering for something, of self-inflicted punishment. It's a tradition of very long standing. In fact, César has often mentioned in speeches that we will not win through violence, we will win through fasting and prayer.[15]

Huerta's attribution of penance to Mexican culture, rather than to Mexican Catholicism, speaks powerfully of Chávez's commitments and of how Chávez needs to be understood.

La Causa: Justice, Nonviolence, and Mexicanidad

That the UFW emerged as a religion sui generis, or on its own terms—no doubt a variation of Christianity—become all the more clear in one of the foundational texts of the UFW: "The Plan of Delano," written by Luís Valdéz—and signed by the farmworkers—on the occasion of the UFW "pilgrimage/march" from Delano to the State Capital on March 16, 1966. The pilgrimage was scheduled to take place during Holy Week and to end on Easter Sunday. Each night the twenty-five-day peregrination culminated with "spirited" ceremonies of singing, dancing, speeches, and a dramatic reading of the plan, creating a collective effervescence. The plan of Delano was inspired by Emiliano's Zapata's *Plan de Ayala*. In it, printed first in both English and Spanish, Valdéz articulates the doctrine of penance under the title, "Pilgrimage, Penitence, and Revolution," which was also the title of their famous pilgrimage to Sacramento.

"The Penance we accept symbolizes the suffering we shall have in order to bring justice to these same towns, to this same valley," claims the plan. "The Pilgrimage we make symbolizes the long historical road we have traveled in this valley alone, and the long road we have yet to travel, with much penance, in order to bring about the Revolution we need."[16] The plan of Delano articulates many of the foundational teachings of the UFW; in a sense, it inscribes modes of sin and modes of salvation into the farm worker's movement. The plan begins by declaring that it is a "Plan of liberation." It continues:

> We, the undersigned, gathered in Pilgrimage to the capital of the State in Sacramento in penance for all the failings of Farm Workers as free and sovereign men, do solemnly declare before the civilized world which judges our actions, and before the nation to which we belong, the propositions we have formulated to end the injustice that oppresses us.

The pilgrimage was led by a priest in full collar and, perhaps more significantly, a flag of La Virgen de Guadalupe. The plan explains, "We seek, and have, the support of the Church in what we do. At the head of the pilgrimage we carry La Virgen de Guadalupe because she is ours, all ours, Patroness of the Mexican people." But even while the pilgrims carried Guadalupe, they made it clear that the march was of an independent religious mind:

> We also carry the Sacred Cross and the Star of David because we are not sectarians, and because we ask the help and prayers of all religions. All men are brothers, sons of the same God; that is why we say to all men of good will, in the words of Pope Leo XIII, "Everyone's first duty is to protect the workers from the greed of speculators who use human beings as instruments to provide themselves with money. It is neither just nor human to oppress men with excessive work to the point where their minds become enfeebled and their bodies worn out." God shall not abandon us.

Political action was not only *inspired* or *informed* by mystical or religious faith: for the UFW, political revolt was a sacred action itself.

Salvation for the farmworkers meant, specifically, growers signing union contracts that would improve working and living conditions for farmworkers, but the vision of Chávez and the UFW extended far beyond. This doctrine emphasized suffering—*penance*—and sacrifice; nonviolence was also a way of salvation for the farmworkers, and there was also a sacred tie to the land, *la tierra*. According to the plan: "It is clearly evident that our path travels through a valley well known to all Mexican farm workers. We know all of these towns . . . because along this very same road, in this very same valley, the Mexican race has sacrificed itself for the last hundred years. Our sweat and our blood have fallen on this land to make other men rich. This Pilgrimage is a witness to the suffering we have seen for generations." The emphasis on land continues Emilano Zapata's southern agrarian Mexican revolutionary movement (1910–1917). The UFW often symbolized their sacred union with images of Zapata.

Here the religion of the farmworkers is delineated around the twin mandates of justice and land, underpinned by the primary imperative of sacrificial love. According to Chávez:

> Love is the most important ingredient in nonviolent work—love the opponent—but we really haven't learned yet how to love the growers. I think we've learned how not to hate them, and maybe love comes in stages. If we're full of hatred, we can't really do our work. Hatred saps all that strength and energy we need to plan. Of course, we can learn how to love the growers more easily after they sign contracts.[17]

The clause "after they sign contracts" signifies the collusion of spiritual and worldly goals. Especially distinctive about Chávez's religious movement was its explicitly expressed political end—as opposed to the frequently implicit political ends of formal religious institutions.

In short, the UFW wove a religious matrix that decentered institutional authority, and poetically centered the authority of revolution. They developed their own image and discourse of the sacred, based on justice, sacrifice, land, and love. A 1969 statement of Chávez's sums up his goals for the farmworkers in a mythical narrative that recalls the Exodus of the Hebrews from Egypt:

> We have been farm workers for hundreds of years and pioneers for seven. Mexicans, Filipinos, Africans and others, our ancestors were among those who founded this land and tamed its natural wilderness. But we are still pilgrims on this land, and we are pioneers who blaze a trail out of the wilderness of hunger and deprivation that we have suffered even as our ancestors did. We are conscious today of the significance of our present quest. If this road we chart leads to the rights and reforms we demand, if it leads to just wages, humane working conditions, protection from the misuse of pesticides, and to the fundamental right of collective bargaining, if it changes the social order that relegates us to the bottom of society, then in our wake will follow thousands of American farm workers. Our example will make them free.[18]

Resurrection

The funeral of César Chávez was a momentous event in itself. Sixty thousand people converged on Delano to march in the hot May sun. Mourners carried images of Chávez, symbols of the United Farm Workers, and banners of La Virgen de Guadalupe. Among the speakers at the ceremony were Edward James Olmos, Jesse Jackson, Dolores Huerta, Joseph Kennedy, and John Kennedy Jr. There, at Forty Acres, Chávez was enshrined. President Clinton sent a telegram to the funeral, naming him an "authentic hero."

Today, religious shrines across California and the Southwest are dedicated to César Chávez. *Corridos* and stories possessing mythological qualities ring forcefully in the ears of millions, buttressing the heroic and sacred image of Chávez. These narratives about him ascribe themes of death and resurrection to his life, adding even greater power and meaning to the mythology of his legacy. No other Mexican American has reached the iconographic status of César Chávez, who has become, in effect, a community (or "folk") saint.

In closing, I want to highlight Chávez's social vision. He was once asked what kind of government he would like to see in this country. His response was that he did not advocate any particular organization or ideology but felt that

> so long as the smaller groups do not have the same rights and the same protection as others—I don't care what you call it Capitalism or Communism—it is not going to work. Somehow, the guys in power have to be reached by counter power, or through change in their hearts and minds.[19]

NOTES

1. I use the terms "Mexican American" and "Chicano" interchangeably. "Latino" here refers to people of Latin American descent, including Mexicans and Mexican Americans. There is no universally accepted way to denote Mexicans in North America, and all terms are problematic. My choices reflect the desire to be situated within an existing and emergent body of Chicano studies scholarship.

2. Gary Soto, preface, *The Fight in the Fields: César Chávez and the Farmworkers Movement*, ed. Susan Ferris and Ricardo Sandoval (New York: Harcourt Brace, 1997), xvi.

3. Luís D. León, *César Chávez and the Religion of Revolution: Toward a Genealogy of Borderlands Political Movements* (Berkeley: University of California Press, forthcoming).

4. See Stephen R. Lloyd-Moffett, "César Chávez as Mystic," paper delivered to the American Academy of Religion, regional meeting (March 14, 2000), Azusa Pacific, Azusa California; also Alan J. Watt, "The Religious Dimensions of the Farm Worker Movement" (Ph.D. diss., Vanderbilt University, 1999); and Jennifer Reed-Bouley, "Guiding Moral Action: A Study of the United Farm Workers' Use of Catholic Social Teaching and Religious Symbols" (Ph.D. diss., Loyola University, Chicago, 1998). Llolyd-Moffett's essay is a hagiography based mostly on secondary sources. Watt's history of the UFW relies on an institutional definition of "religion" exclusively. Reed-Bouley's dissertation employs Clifford Geertz's notion of religious symbols enacting models "of" and "for" reality. None of these authors explores the "religious" or "sacred" dimension beyond institutionally controlled and invested definitions and therefore confirm a rigid orthodox view of the world by translating Chávez into the authorized idioms of the religious status quo: "Catholic saint" and Christian mystic.

5. Clive Kessler, *Islam and Politics in a Malay State* (Ithaca, NY: Cornell University Press), 244–245.

6. For an elaboration of "religious poetics," see Luis D. Leon, *La Llorona's Children: Religion, Life, and Death in the U.S.–Mexican Borderlands* (Berkeley: University of California Press, 2004). See James Clifford and George Marcu, eds., *Writing Culture: The Poetics and Politics of Ethnography* (Berkeley: University of California Press, 1986), and José Limón, *Dancing with the Devil: Society and Cultural Poetics in Mexican-American South Texas* (Madison: University of Wisconsin Press, 1994).

7. César Chávez, quoted in Jacques E. Levy, *César Chávez: Autobiography of La Causa* (New York: Norton, 1975).

8. Cited in Richard Griswold del Castillo and Richard A. García, *César Chávez: A Triumph of Spirit* (Norman: University of Oklahoma Press, 1995).

9. Ibid.

10. César Chávez, quoted in Levy, *César Chávez*, 286.

11. Jerry Cohen, quoted in Levy, *César Chávez*, 283.

12. César Chávez, "The Mexican American and the Church," *El Grito* 4 (Summer, 1968): 215–218, 215.

13. Alberto L. Pulido, "Are You an Emissary of Jesus Christ? Justice, the Catholic Church, and the Chicano Movement," *Explorationsin Ethnic Studies* 14 (January 1991): 30.

14. César Chávez, cited in Levy, *César Chávez*.

15. Dolores Huerta, quoted in Levy, *César Chávez*, 276.
16. From "The Plan of Delano" (n.p., n.d.).
17. Chávez, quoted in Levy, *César Chávez*, 196.
18. Ibid.
19. César Chávez, quoted in Griswold del Castillo and García, *César Chávez*, 150.

4

"In the Outer Boundaries": Pentecostalism, Politics, and Reies López Tijerina's Civic Activism

Rudiger V. Busto

In late October of 1966, a group of New Mexican Spanish Americans reclaimed 500,000 acres of the San Joaquín del Cañon del Río de Chama land grant. Under the leadership of land grant activist, Reies López Tijerina, this determined group calling themselves the Alianza Federal de Mercedes Reales (Federal Alliance of Land Grants), drove a caravan of some fifty cars into the land grant and proclaimed it the "Free City-State" Republic of San Joaquín del Río de Chama. Unfortunately for them, this sizable tract of pristine pine forest was also known as the Kit Carson National Forest, and the center of the new republic happened to sit in the Echo Amphitheater campground. When a pair of U.S. forest rangers attempted to collect the entrance fees to the campground, they were summarily "arrested" by the Aliancistas and then tried for trespassing and being a public nuisance. They were found guilty by the ad hoc San Joaquín court, fined $500, and handed down a suspended sentence. After celebrating their victory for having regained the old Spanish land grant, the Alianza camped for a few days, but eventually the last remaining citizens of the Free Republic were thrown out by federal officials holding restraining orders.[1]

The 1966 occupation of the Echo Amphitheater campground was the first public event that drew Tijerina into the national spotlight. The ensuing confusion and struggle over the ownership of the San Joaquín grant eventually lead to the Tierra Amarilla County courthouse raid—the 1967 landmark event in Chicano history for which Tijerina is most widely known. What is less understood about Tijerina's land grant activism, however, is the religious motivation that led him to direct civil disobedience and outright aggression. This essay examines the roots of Tijerina's land grant activism in light of his Pentecostal training, his experience with "sacred" texts, and his eventual return to Roman Catholicism. I examine the singular quality of Tijerina's religious vision and underscore two (obvious, but worthy of further scrutiny) points: (1) that Tijerina's remarkable religious commitment had a profound influence on his civic activism and (2) that it is precisely his intense and "magical-literalist" religious worldview that relegates him an outsider to the pantheon of heroic ethnic religious leadership in American public life.

Magical-Literal Realms

In one of the accounts of his extraordinary life, Reies Tijerina, described his early religious life as existing "in the outer boundaries of the religious world."[2] Trained at the Assemblies of God Latin American Bible Institute (LABI) in Saspamco, Texas, Tijerina's entry into Pentecostal Bible education has influenced every major event of his life to date. As a teenager and migrant farmworker, Tijerina had turned away from the familial Roman Catholicism he had learned at his mother's knee and was converted through the evangelizing efforts of a Mexican-American Baptist missionary worker. The young Tijerina eagerly embraced his "born-again" life with all of the hope and energy that accompanies the young adult convert's new life in Jesus. He was baptized in the cleansing waters of a local river as a public profession of his faith. But rather than choose the fellowship of the Baptist tradition, he elected to follow the flames of the Pentecostal fire that was sweeping through many Latino communities in the first half of the twentieth century.

Referring to his conversion to evangelical Christianity and his affiliation with Pentecostalism as the "outer boundaries of the religious world," Tijerina is well aware of the sociological and economic factors that structure religious affiliation. "The center of religion" he observed,

> was like the Islamic world, the Catholic world. They had powers! The Protestants [were young and small], a hundred, or two hundred years old. . . . So I was in the outer boundaries of the religious world. And I grabbed onto [Pentecostalism] because that's where I was! I was very poor. I was brought up a migrant. So that was the best I had at that time. But that was good enough to lead me and move me on to my life, my dreams.[3]

Echoing Niebuhr's comment that "the sect has ever been the child of an outcast minority," here is Tijerina's self-understanding of his sociological marginality in the United States—as a migrant farmworker, as a Mexican American, as uneducated, as Pentecostal.[4] Tijerina studied for three years at the LABI (1944–1946) but was expelled for allegedly transgressing a prohibition against unchaperoned friendships with female students. From the sources, we know that he was a "sincere" student but was described by the school's director as "fa-

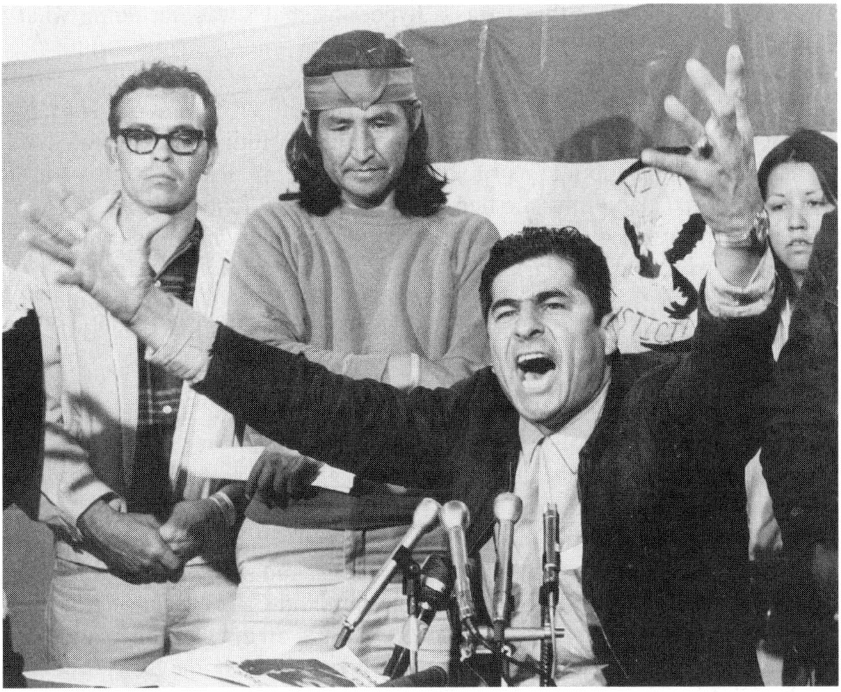

Reies López Tijerina speaking on behalf of the land grant struggle in New Mexico ca. 1967, others not identified (Courtesy of the Karl Kernberger Collection, Center for Southwest Research, University of New Mexico)

natical, more peculiar in his thoughts . . . he was not orthodox."[5] The extent to which Tijerina was "fanatical" after his expulsion from the Bible Institute in 1946 is evidenced in both his writing and his ministry.

Tijerina spent almost a decade preaching and traveling around the country as an unaffiliated, nondenominational evangelist. Although he started his career with the imprimatur of the Assemblies of God, by 1950 he was on his own preaching a stern, moralistic version of the gospel. Wandering the entire length of the country accompanied by his wife, Maria, and their first child, Tijerina honed his fiery rhetorical skills in front of small, poor congregations, perfecting a style of delivery that later electrified and ignited his Chicano audiences.

Sometime in the early 1950s, Tijerina developed the sense that God had called him for a particular task for which he was as yet unworthy or unprepared. In an effort to prove his faith, he gave away his material possessions on at least three occasions—only to reap the wrath of his wife who was growing weary of their poverty. "We didn't have much, a radio, some chairs, but I gave it, you know, to the poor" he recalled; "Because I kept on having a struggle with my conscience, my soul. I was not satisfied, I was always finding that the Bible rebuked me. I found . . . that I was a hypocrite, that I was not doing what I could do."[6]

Convinced that God would show him the way, Tijerina decided to coax God's counsel through asceticism. Simply, he would wait upon the Lord. Determined to "seek the light, a better opening" for his ministry, he retreated into a small cave in the mountains of southern California near where his travels had taken him. Cushioning the hard rock floor of the dusty grotto with cotton batting from a car seat, he covered the small opening with brush, burrowed in, and waited in the still darkness. "I had it in my mind that it had to be so that I couldn't turn back, that I wouldn't get out of there unless I could find something better. And if I died, I wanted it to be where they wouldn't find me," he recalled:

> I don't know how long I was there . . . but it was some days, and I had great illuminations. I found that there were not so many religions as they had taught me in Bible School, there was just the two strong powers of good and evil. I saw that those of different religions were all the same, they all wanted new automobiles, they were all full of pride and coveted the same things, and so I learned that there was no difference between Protestant and Catholic after all. Being subject to certain pressures, they would all act the same. And so I went back to my wife with *a new interpretation for the Bible, just literally, the way it was,* and I started out preaching again.[7]

Note the last phrase here: "a new interpretation for the Bible, just literally, the way it was." We can detect here the impact of his Bible Institute training. His conclusion that he had discovered a "new" interpretation of scripture "just literally, the way it was" turned out to be the standard literal, "common sense" reading of scripture in the American evangelical tradition.[8] And certainly, when one reads Tijerina's writing, his ample use of Christian scripture and his "literalist" interpretation positions him directly within the Anglo-American evangelical tradition.

But observe the difference between Tijerina's method of achieving his "new" interpretation and the American evangelical tradition. There is something medieval, almost Byzantine, in his ascetic, hermit's search for mystical illumination which comes, however, not out of the historical traditions of the church but directly from the Bible: from the example of the prophet Elijah in I Kings 19:9–18.[9] Fleeing the wrath of Queen Jezebel, the prophet took refuge in a cave when "the word of the Lord came to him, and he said unto him, 'What doest thou here, Elijah?' " (v.9 KJV). Speaking words Tijerina surely must have taken as his own, Elijah replied: "I have been very jealous for the lord God of hosts: for the children of Israel have forsaken thy covenant, thrown down thine altars, and slain thy prophets, with the sword: and I even I only, am left; and they seek my life, to take it away" (I Kings 19:10 KJV).

This voice of the solitary, zealous, and misunderstood rugged prophet of God is precisely the one Tijerina identified as his own. We find Tijerina's close attention to biblical example, as well as appeals to divine judgment, and a thinly veiled apocalypticism throughout his writing. It appears in his collection of sermons published around the time of his illuminations articulated in perfect Reina-de Valera Spanish—the florid, baroque language of the seventeenth-century Spanish translation of the Bible.[10] It provides the forensic basis for his political pamphleteering on the land grant issue,[11] authorizes the anger in his dark memoir,[12] and supports the speculations in his recent (unpublished) writing that explores the genealogy and fate of Spanish-speaking New World inhabitants.[13]

What is unusual in Tijerina's reading of the Bible goes beyond the evangelical literalism he learned as a Bible student. Because he enacts the text in his life—he literally "performs" I Kings 19—his version of evangelicalism can only be describe as "magical-literalist."[14] That is to say, in his commitment to the Bible as God's word, he moves beyond the Anglo-American view of the Bible (as one that diminishes and limits the "magical" aspects of the text to history or allegory) and recaptures from his early Pentecostalism the power and promises of God's miraculous work in the everyday life of his elect. But far beyond the miracles of the Pentecostal faith healer, or the sign of "speaking in tongues," both of which occur in the context of religious ritual, Tijerina's magical literalism accepts the overlapping of sacred and profane worlds. For him, the world contains much more than can be normally perceived. Conventional reality is replaced by a lush existence layered with signs and symbols—a world that Cuban novelist Alejo Carpentier referred to as *lo real maravilloso* (the marvelously real).[15] Coupled with the magical realism of the Mexican worldview, where the Virgin Mary appears to those in need and where the hoot of an owl portends imminent death, Tijerina's magical-literal reading of the Bible provides a framework and set of passwords for reading an enchanted universe. For him, engaging the Bible is not so much about the act of interpretation as it is how the Bible literally opens the door to miracles and "magic." This magical, marvelous universe, however, is ordered and commanded by the just and exacting God of Protestant fundamentalism. Importantly, unlike the literal reading of the Bible by evangelicals, where the truths of God's word are nevertheless guided by a distinct hermeneutic tradition and canons of theology, Tijerina's solitary reading of scripture leaves him open to the suggestions, typologies, and miracles in the text. Unfettered by the limits of someone else's theology, the magical realms of the Bible extend into the present time and space.

Tijerina's Bible training tied him close to the text, and in so doing provided him with the models of prophetic leadership he has always aspired to attain. It has opened up the entire universe as a "text" to be gleaned for deeper and apocalyptic knowledge. So it is that Tijerina "reads" God's hand in the timing of world events; in cryptic, symbolic messages brought to him in dreams; and in the unfolding knowledge about the destiny of his people. So it is that Tijerina turns to and reiterates Elijah's example to discover what God intends for him. His magical literalism serves as an entry point for the sacred. And like the prophet Elijah and all hermits in the history of Christianity, Tijerina's withdrawal into his cave affirmed what Timothy Ware notes is the role of the hermit:

to serve as a "counterbalance" to the ossified institutions and complacency of established Christianity. The hermit's work and presence, Ware concludes, serves the "prophetic and eschatological role in the life of the church, reminding us that the Kingdom of God is not of this world."[16]

Influence of Religious Life on Civic Activism

Into the new millennium Tijerina continues to organize his life around a framework constructed from his religious education and his itinerant ministry. His careful attention to sacred scripture and his willingness to reenact the text provides him with a blueprint and examples of divinely sanctioned direct action for his political work. We are now prepared to see that Tijerina's prosecution of the New Mexican land grant struggle is based on his "magical literalist" hermeneutic: Spanish land grant deeds that prove ownership legitimate his retaking of those lands; U.S. Constitutional guarantees of equal justice animate his entry into the court system; medieval Spanish colonial administrative texts provide him with the key to unlocking the truths of Mexican-American sacred genealogy.

There is, however, one more turn in Tijerina's religious life that is relevant for understanding his politics. In 1963 Tijerina returned to Roman Catholicism. In his early investigations of New Mexican land grant history, Tijerina had come across the *Recopilación de leyes de los reinos de las Indias* (*Laws of the Indies*), a massive compendium of Spanish texts governing Spain's New World colonies. He believed these *Laws of the Indies,* which had administered every detail of New World colonial life, took precedence over U.S. Federal law. Arguing for the legitimacy of the statutes contained in these volumes became central to Tijerina's case against the federal government in the land grant issue.[17] Impressed by the scope of the *Laws,* and comfortable with the familiar "biblical" Spanish of the documents, he soon came to see that the authority of this text came not just from its antiquity but from its origins: the Spanish Catholic monarchy. Given the Spanish Crown's complete identification with Catholicism at the time the *Laws of the Indies* were compiled, their authority, argued Tijerina, was as good as Papal edict.[18] The Catholic Church, he concluded, must remain the ultimate earthly authority in the land grant issue. "We cannot challenge the authority vested in the priesthood by Christ," he argues:

> Christ told Peter whatever you bind on earth shall be bound in heaven. Pope Alexander VI, by his authority, made the title of America for Spain. That is holding; that is binding. It was the Pope's authority. Nobody had given the Anglos any right in America. None whatsoever. They built [their claim to America] themselves. They built their rights by dropping out of the [Catholic] church and creating a new religious authority.[19]

Eventually, Tijerina came to believe that if he was to legitimately deploy the *Laws of the Indies* in his political work, he had to gain access to its authority by making a personal commitment to it. This required him to rejoin the corporate, divinely authorized body of the Universal Church. Tijerina's decision to rejoin the Catholic Church was, in no small measure, also motivated by his work among New Mexican Hispano Catholic communities and out of respect for the secretive *Penitente* brotherhood that assisted his earliest political efforts.[20] The power of the text for Tijerina is clear. Despite all of his Pentecostal training and prejudice against Roman Catholicism in his ministry, Tijerina's reading of the *Laws of the Indies* convinced him to submit to the authority vested in the Catholic tradition. Once reconnected to the Universal Church, he laid claim to and harnessed the power of these ancient sacred books. Though now Roman Catholic by affiliation, Tijerina's religious faith nevertheless continues to operate on the "magical-literalist" level forged out of his extraordinary magical life revealed to him through books. Accusations that Tijerina returned to Catholicism simply because his followers and supporters were Catholic misunderstand the seriousness of Tijerina's commitment to sacred texts.

By the time Tijerina and the Alianza moved to occupy the Echo Amphitheater in 1966, he had completed his religious transformation from Pentecostalism back to Roman Catholicism. Reclaiming the San Joaquín del Cañon del Río de Chama land grant, we can now understand, was a religious and political design driven by appeals to ancient models of prophetic, institutional, and legal authority.

Beyond the Outer Boundaries of American Civil Religion

By all accounts, Tijerina's place in the American religious landscape remains terra incognita. His distinctive, singular religious worldview and colorful life locate him alongside other dynamic religious leaders and "prophets" in American religion. Given such an unorthodox religious life and the limited success of his political work, it comes as no surprise that Tijerina remains at the "outer boundaries" of normative religious and political life in the United States. These common religious and political values constitute what Robert Bellah popularized as "American Civil Religion" in 1967 (the same year that Tijerina and the Alianza shot up the Tierra Amarilla County courthouse).[21]

Bellah's articulation of American Civil Religion describes the nation's understanding of itself as bound up in preserving classical, republican virtues of citizenship coupled with the American people's covenantal relationship with the God of ancient Israel. As Americans, we are inheritors of the freedoms granted by religious choice and the Enlightenment liberal celebration of individualism. Simultaneous with these freedoms are the negative freedoms required by the social contract and the awesome responsibilities as a "chosen" nation in the world. This delicate balance between freedom and responsibility, Bellah observes, is nevertheless more ideal then actual reality.

For Bellah, the true test of whether the United States lives up to its ideals is in the treatment of ethnic minorities. The calamitous offenses against Native Americans provides the nation with its first breach of the national covenant—

what Bellah refers to as the "primal crime on which American society is based."[22] The civil war over the issue of African slavery subsequently pushed the nation to the brink of dissolution.[23] Leaders from minority communities, especially those who have a bridging capacity between race groups, play a pivotal part in deciding the fate of the American people in times of national crisis. And among these leaders, it is the religious leader who serves the most crucial function to the nation by providing "an essential mediation between the ethnic group and the larger culture of the modern world. [Because] not only does religion often preserve the deepest symbols of ethnic identity, it also exerts a pull away from ethnic particularity to that which is morally and religiously universal."[24] What Bellah is suggesting here is that the ideals and values that constitute civil religion also set a standard for judging ethnic minority religious and political leadership.

However, religious and ethnic leaders—the "brightest and most creative" intellectuals—he notes, tend to get "absorbed" into the larger body, "so as to deprive the communal groups of their natural leaders." Bellah's view is that the only truly effective ethnic religious leaders are those capable of speaking to the larger whole of U.S society, and who, in so doing, invigorate and renew a "public theology" that expresses the universality of American Civil Religion's highest aspirations.[25] For Bellah, César Chávez and Martin Luther King Jr., as prophets of public theology, are such bridging ethnic leaders whose movements worked "to make America more fully realize its professed values."[26] This translation from the particular struggle of minority communities to the common good explains the public and political successes of minority religious leaders such as King and Chávez. In contrast, minority religious leaders like Elijah Muhammad, Louis Farrakhan, and Reies Tijerina, move oppositionally: from the universality of religious traditions, these leaders refashion their particular religious faiths to suit the particularity of racially defined groups.

There is no room for Tijerina in Bellah's conception of American civil religion. Unlike Chávez, whose careful orchestration of vernacular Mexican Catholic symbols and ritual action overlapped with the larger American meanings of religious sacrifice and sainthood, Tijerina's singular magical-literalist approach to similar issues of justice and equality keep him from approaching the status of either Chávez or King. The animating impulse behind Tijerina's political activism, although originating in the obvious illegality of land theft in New Mexico, lacks the civil religious appeal of Chávez's righteous anger, enacted in his twenty-five-day fast, and the moral authority of King's Selma-to-Montgomery march. Believing that the weight of ancient religious models of authority, international law, and U.S. legal precedence on the land issue granted him legal and moral high ground in his activism, Tijerina's idiosyncratic voice and role in social justice issues can never attain public appeal, precisely because his reading of these texts are too evangelical and are read with the force of "obvious truth for anyone who open[s] their eyes."[27]

Unlike King and Chávez whose otherwise "radical" messages were delivered in ways digestible for politically liberals, the raw evangelical quality and presentation of Tijerina's politics never captured the hearts of many outside the Chicano community. The differences between Chávez and Tijerina can also be measured in their relationship to the symbols and motifs of American civil religion. In a hopeful and constructive essay, Spencer Bennett argues that Chávez's genius was his ability to introduce elements of Mexican culture into the American civil religion.[28] Chávez's use of the Virgin of Guadalupe symbol in his political work, Bennett suggests, complements the Anglo-American inventory of American civil religious images and themes. Bennett's description of the Virgin of Guadalupe as feminine, passive, brown, tied to the natural world, and the protector of the poor and victimized, and revealed through "mystic vision," is in marked contrast to the American civil religious themes and patterns of masculinity, expansion, triumphalism, truth revealed through texts, and a "Jehovah of Battles." He writes: "Chavez points to a recognizable and cherished symbol of past [Mexican] tradition and future hope in the Virgin. All of his followers may not be devout Catholics but the cultural implications and the political meaning of the Guadalupe become clear as he rehearses her epic [in his political activism]."[29] Bennett's argument notwithstanding, his description of Guadalupe is less revealing about the Virgin than it is a reflection of how the majority of Americans view "good" Mexican Americans and their politics. Contrast this view of Mexican American politics with the assertive, vocal, and even violent, confrontational style of Tijerina and his organization, and it is clear why Bellah and Spencer prefer minority leaders who do not threaten or disrupt the hegemony of a "common" (read: assimilationist) set of public values. The irony here is that while Chávez's Roman Catholic–based political movement was capable of galvanizing wide support, Tijerina was fully invested in the very symbols and motifs of a Protestant American civil religion: a god of justice, the sanctity of the founding documents, the transformative effect of the frontier, and an appeal to the ideals of justice and equality. Thus given what we know of Tijerina's unorthodox religious world, his essentially legal and canonical affiliation with Roman Catholicism, and especially his fundamentalist presentation of politics, he can only ever remain in the "outer boundaries" of ethnic religious leadership in American public life.

There is an epilogue to what occurred at the Echo Amphitheater campground in 1966. Despite repeated defeats in the courts and his disappearance from the public eye in the 1970s, Tijerina eventually returned to the San Joaquín land grant. Into the 1990s, Tijerina and his followers were living within the boundaries of the Republic of San Joaquín del Río de Chama. The Republic does not appear on any official government maps, but its boundaries and its civil administration are nevertheless sanctioned by a land grant deed whose authority rests in the hands of God's earthly authority, the church. In the overlapping sacred and profane worlds of Reies Tijerina's magical literalism, the Republic of San Joaquín exists because the text says it does.

NOTES

1. Peter Nabokov, *Tijerina and the Courthouse Raid* (Albuquerque: University of New Mexico Press, 1969), 51–54; *United States v. Tijerina*, 407 F2d 349 (1969).

2. Interview with Reies López Tijerina, Coyote, New Mexico (April 2, 1990).

3. Quoted in Rudy V. Busto, *King Tiger: The Religious Vision of Reies López Tijerina* (University of New Mexico, forthcoming).

4. H. Richard Niebuhr, *The Social Sources of Denominationalism* (New York: Henry Holt, 1929), 19.

5. Kenzy Savage, quoted in Robert Gardner, *¡Grito!: Reies Tijerina and the New Mexico Land Grant War of 1967* (Indianapolis: Bobbs-Merrill, 1970), 38–39.

6. Gardner, *¡Grito!*, 39; Nabokov, *Tijerina and the Courthouse Raid*, 200.

7. Gardner, *¡Grito!*, 39. Italics in original.

8. George Marsden, *Fundamentalism and American Culture: The Shaping of Twentieth-Century Evangelicalism, 1870–1925* (New York: Oxford University Press, 1980), 55–62.

9. Other passages where caves are used as sites of refuge and communication with God include Genesis 19:30; Joshua 10:16; I Samuel 22:1,2; I Kings 18:4, 13; Judges 6:2; Psalms 57:1, 2; Jeremiah 9:2; and Hebrews 11:38.

10. For example: "I know the evil that these words will bring upon myself from the church; I am aware of the tempest these words will cause in the hearts of those who deceive the people. Yet, what dishonor can I bring to the church? Are not her very own sons those who bring dishonor, not only to the churches, but even unto their homes? Where is the son who in these days obeys the Lord?" "El malo en la silla del bueno," Reies López Tijerina *¿Hallará Fe en la Tierra . . . ?* (n.p, 1954?), 53.

11. "Therefore, every person has a vested interest in seeing to it that not only his but his neighbor's property is being adequately protected, so that the thieves will not inherit the earth." Reies López Tijerina, "The Spanish Land Grant Question Examined" (Albuquerque: Alianza Federal de Pueblos Libres, 1966).

12. "My advice for the people is to search for and demand leaders that are children of the earth, wise in the laws and values of the land, powerful in the knowledge of the earth. In the end, ideologies and politics are superfluous. Particularly in these times, when politics and politicians have become so perverted they have no solutions. The people had lost faith in their political representatives and in a matter of days would be vomited out." Reies López Tijerina, *Mi lucha por la tierra* (Mexico: Fondo de Cultura Económica, 1978), 417. Note the allusion to Revelation 3:16 here.

13. Telephone conversation with Reies López Tijerina, Albuquerque, New Mexico (July 13, 2000).

14. I am reworking the film/literary phrase "magical realism," following Naomi Lindstrom's definition that emphasizes "an equal acceptance of the ordinary and the extraordinary" and the fusing of "(1) lyrical and, at times, fantastic writing with (2) an examination of the character of human existence and (3) an implicit criticism of society, particularly the elite." In addition, Tijerina's memoir exemplifies the magical-realist "characteristic attitude of narrators toward the subject matter: they frequently appear to accept events contrary to the usual operating laws of the universe as natural, even unremarkable. Though the tellers of astonishing tales, they themselves express little or no surprise." Naomi Lindstrom, "Magical Realism," *Twentieth-Century Spanish American Fiction* (Austin: University of Texas Press, 1994).

15. Alejo Carpentier, *Viaje a la semilla* (Havana: Ucar García y Cía, 1944). According to Richard Young: "In general terms, the concept of the marvelous implies a sense of wonder produced by unusual, unexpected, or improbable phenomena. It may occur naturally, may be the result of deliberate manipulation of reality or its perception by the artist, or may be produced by magic or supernatural intentions. In any case, it provokes the presence of something different from the normal." Richard A.

Young, *Carpentier: El Reino de Este Mundo* (London: Gran & Cutler, 1983), 35–36. In Tijerina's case, the centrality of the Bible in the ordering of the "magical" in the world requires the alteration of these original concepts. See also Donald Shaw's discussion of the distinctions between magical realism and the marvelous real in *Alejo Carpentier* (Boston: Twayne, 1985), 15–34.

16. Timothy Ware, *The Orthodox Church* (New York: Penguin, 1963), 45.

17. Tijerina is particularly drawn to Books 4 and 6, which deal with New World discovery and the disposition of indigenous peoples.

18. William A. Christian Jr. observes that "the [Spanish] monarchy in the fifteenth century had become identified with Catholicism. In the century before 1575 it had established the Inquisition, expelled the Jews, forced Moors to convert, had its political actions ratified by Rome with the Bulls of the Crusade, sent ships that defeated the Turks at Lepanto, and attempted to police the heretics of the Low Countries." Christian, *Local Religion in Sixteenth-Century Spain* (Princeton: Princeton University Press, 1981), 154.

19. Quoted in Andrés Guerrero, *Chicano Theology* (Maryknoll, NY: Orbis Books, 1987), 87.

20. Busto, *King Tiger*, chapter 1.

21. Robert N. Bellah, "Civil Religion in America," *Daedalus* (Winter 1967): 1–21.

22. Robert N. Bellah, *The Broken Covenant: American Civil Religion in Time of Trial* (Chicago: University of Chicago Press, [1975] 1992), 37.

23. Bellah, *Broken Covenant*, 99–111. In his discussion of racially ethnic groups, Bellah, to his credit, understood the how and why of "ethnic separation," particularly of Blacks and Chicanos in the 1970s; but he nevertheless stuck to his position as a liberal cultural pluralist.

24. He continues: "That particular ethnic groups are linked in larger religious groups, Catholic, Jewish, and Protestant, and that the religious groups share certain common symbols is undoubtedly an important element in whatever cultural unity and universality exists in America But unfortunately, not only the Protestant tradition but the Catholic and Jewish traditions have undergone severe attrition in America and in their present form it is doubtful whether they can provide the basis for a genuine cultural renewal." Bellah, *Broken Covenant*, 108.

25. Bellah adopts Martin Marty's term here to describe public elaborations of national religious symbols. *Broken Covenant*, 178.

26. See Clayborne Carson's discussion of King's ability to transcend racial boundaries in "Martin Luther King, Jr., and the African-American Social Gospel," in *African-American Religion: Interpretive Essays in History and Culture*, ed. Timothy E. Fulop and Albert J. Raboteau (New York: Routledge, 1997), 341–362. *Broken Covenant*, 179.

27. Tijerina, "The Spanish Land Grant Question Examined."

28. Spencer Bennett, "Civil Religion in a New Context: The Mexican-American Faith of César Chávez" in *Religion and Political Power*, ed. Gustavo Benavides and M. W. Daly (Albany: State University of New York, 1989), 151–166.

29. Ibid., 153, 159.

5

PADRES: Latino Community Priests and Social Action

Mario T. García

In my work in Chicano history, one of the key themes that I have stressed concerns the role of leadership.[1] For the most part, this has involved political and community leadership. However, in my recent work on Chicano Catholic history, I have been impressed with another form.[2] This is the leadership, both spiritual and temporal, of Chicano Catholic priests. It seems to me that one of the key issues overlooked in Chicano history, as well in contemporary Chicano studies, is the major part that many Chicano priests have played and continue to play in their communities. This gap also reflects the lack of emphasis by scholars on the contributions of Catholic parishes in providing both organization and a sense of community among Chicano Catholics, and here I am using the term Chicano in a generic sense, including both Mexican Americans and Mexican nationals.

As leaders, some Chicano priests represent a version of the "worker priests" that surfaced in post–World War II Western Europe, principally in France. Reacting to the devastation, dislocation, and class unrest unleashed by the war, these priests left the safety of their churches and took the church directly to the workers. Laboring in factories and industries, worker priests immersed themselves into working-class life and culture as a way of promoting Catholic social doctrine. At first supported by the French church hierarchy, many of the worker-priests left their parishes and secured employment in factories as a way of associating with the workers. They no longer lived in their more comfortable rectories, but in poor working-class quarters. Some emerged as trade union leaders and merged their faith with socialist beliefs. As worker-priests became more militant and public, the church by the 1950s withdrew its support and brought an end to this experiment.[3]

Despite the short life of the worker-priest movement, I am struck by the leadership they provided to their communities and how in these pre–Vatican II years they were already redefining "church" as "people." By the same token, some Chicano priests in our time, and probably earlier as well, represent a modified version of worker-priests. By this I mean not that they are to be found working in factories but that, like their French counterparts, they are taking and have taken the church beyond its institutionalized structure to the people themselves. Through their community leadership they have sought not only to redefine the church but also to assist in the empowerment of the Chicano community in the United States. As such, they represent what I call "community priests." To an extent, of course, all Catholic priests are community priests in that they engage with their parish communities. The distinction I would make is that for some Catholic priests community primarily means ministering to the spiritual needs of their members within the institutionalized boundaries of their churches. By contrast, "community priests" in my definition are those priests, of whatever ethnic background, who see their spiritual ministry as also involving being part of community struggles in areas such as civil rights, workers' rights, community empowerment, and community identity and self-respect. Community priests are both inside and outside the institutional church, but it is a separation that they do not make. Reflecting Vatican II influences, as well as those of liberation theology, community priests are redefining the meaning of church and the role of the clergy.

Community priests, however, must be distinguished from worker-priests in that community priests maintain their foothold in their parishes and rectories rather than apart from them. As a rule, they do not work primarily with labor unions, as did the worker-priests. Instead, community priests engage in a variety of community movements comprised for the most part of working-class Latinos who are not usually members of labor unions. In addition, community priests have not embraced the more radical socialist leanings of the French worker-priests but, instead, have reemphasized Catholic social doctrine, as well as civil and human rights principles. Finally, community priests, because of their more moderate politics, have had the support of church leaders for their work.

Still, despite the more moderate or liberal veneer associated with community priests, they share with worker-priests the deep belief that the church cannot stand aside while its people face exploitation and discrimination. As Chicanos, the community priests identify with their ethnic community and with its suffering. Community priests are distinguished not only by taking the church to the people but also by transforming the American church by bringing the people—Latinos—into the church and Latinizing the church. This Latinization is forcing the church to become even more public in addressing the needs of its growing Chicano and Latino working-class members. In this process, the community priests are examples of the Catholic Church's direct intervention into the public sphere and its relationship to the modern world.

This essay looks at different examples of Chicano community priests based on oral histories with three Chicano priests.[4] They include Father Juan Romero,

Father Juan Romero, Dolores Huerta, César Chávez, and Father Adolfo Perez Esquivel striking against Red Coach Lettuce on behalf of the United Farm Workers Union in the 1970s (Courtesy of Father Juan Romero)

a diocesan priest in Los Angeles; Father Luis Quihuis, a Jesuit in Santa Barbara; and Father Virgil Elizondo, a diocesan priest in San Antonio. These three versions of community priests involve, in turn, three models of community priests: (1) the community activist, (2) the community organizer, and (3) the cultural worker. These categories are only of significance for an analysis of the concept of community priests and are not meant to be reductionist. All three priests in one way or another provide leadership in each category. The distinctions are only meant to stress a particular emphasis that characterizes the work of each of them.

Community Activist

Juan Romero is the former pastor of St. Clement's Church in Santa Monica, but he possesses a long personal involvement in the Chicano community. Born in New Mexico during the Great Depression, Romero has always appreciated his family roots in that state. He is particularly proud of his family connections with Padre José Antonio Martínez, the nineteenth-century *nuevomexicano* priest who provided leadership to the Hispano community against the threats posed by the new Anglo-American order following the U.S.–Mexico war. This included challenging the likewise new Catholic Church led by French-born Archbishop Jean Baptiste Lamy, who was fictionally immortalized by Willa Cather in her classic southwestern novel *Death Comes for the Archbishop*. Like many other Mexican Americans, Romero and his family migrated to California in order to find work when he was still a young boy. Settling in East Los Angeles, his father, an accountant, found employment with the newly established aviation industry at the time World War II broke out.

Raised in a very religious family and attending Catholic school in East Los Angeles, at a very early age Romero felt that he possessed a vocation to the priesthood. He pursued it and entered the local seminary after elementary school. He studied at the minor seminary in Los Angeles and at the newly opened St. John's major seminary in Camarillo. While there, Romero displayed his leadership skills and his interest and passion for civil rights and social justice. He also knew that he wanted to work in the Chicano community and helped organize a Spanish-language radio program, "La Voz Guadalupana," which included religious issues such as the lives of the saints. Situated in a farming community, St. John's was also in close proximity to *bracero* camps peopled by the Mexican contract workers who had been entering the country under the World War II labor agreement between the United States and Mexico. Romero, along with other seminarians, visited the camps and met with the workers, and he assisted at the masses at the camps said by the priests from the seminary.

After his ordination in 1964, Father Juan was first assigned to St. Francis' Church in East Los Angeles. Two years later, he was sent to Our Lady of Guadalupe in Santa Barbara. Here he participated in some of the first *cursillos*, or lay retreats, aimed at promoting religious leadership among Chicano Catholic men. It was at this time that he also developed an interest and association with César Chávez, himself a cursillista. He was invited along with other priests to San Jose to attend a meeting concerning the church's relationship with Spanish-speaking laity. Chávez addressed the priests and noted that while many Protestant ministers especially through the Protestant-led Migrant Ministry were supporting the farmworkers' cause, very few Catholic priests were involved, even though the majority of farmworkers were Catholics. This impressed Father Juan, who vowed to himself to be one of those committed priests. It was as if the spiritual power of César Chávez had spoken directly to him. "This was the first time I had met César," Romero later wrote, "and [I] was greatly impressed with his style, firmness, soft-spoken manner, and the way he very directly challenged church people to be present in the struggle of the farm worker." He was particularly struck by Chávez's wholeness as a person and his spirituality: "[He possessed an] integratedness, a beautiful combination of toughness and gentleness, the best qualities of masculinity and femininity, and his deep spirituality, which some people thought was contrived but I was close enough to see that it really was religious, a conviction of a faithful person."[5]

Six months later, Father Juan again met Chávez in 1968 in Santa Barbara at the Franciscan seminary where he was recuperating from his twenty-five-day fast. "He has undertaken this fast," he noted, "as a sacred discipline for himself, to affirm his own commitment to nonviolence, and to be an example to his fellow *campesinos*. It was by no means a show, but a genuinely religious act."[6] Shortly thereafter, Romero deepened his involvement with the farmworkers' cause when he attended a talk by the Rev. Wayne C. Hartmire, a Protestant minister and one of the leaders of the Migrant Ministry. Hartmire likened those ministers who were working with the union to the famous worker-priests of Europe. Romero had read about the worker-priests in the seminary, but he now recognized how he could emulate them by working with the farmworkers. "I thought how ironic it was that priest-workers in the United States," he reflected, "were neither priests in our usual understanding nor were they even Catholics. They were Protestant ministers who took seriously the challenge of the Gospel, and patterned much of their own life and ministry after the 'noble experiment' of the priest-worker movement."[7] Romero joined those ranks.

Beginning in Santa Barbara, Father Juan commenced a three-decade period of involvement with and support of the farmworkers. In each of his parishes, he organized support for the strike and both the grape and lettuce boycotts. Along with other priests and sisters, in 1973 he was arrested outside Fresno when they joined striking workers in challenging restrictions on picketing activities. Romero and the others challenged the morality of the injunction through civil disobedience. A total of sixty clergy and religious leaders were arrested, men and women, Catholic and Protestants, and held for almost two weeks until released. Of this confrontation, Romero wrote:

> When I joined the picket line on the morning of August 2, the line captains were very careful that we remain on public (state) property—from telephone post to telephone post outward toward the street—and that we not trespass the private property of the grower. The line itself was well ordered and disciplined, although noisy: *Huelga*! [strike] *Vengan compañeros*! (join us comrades) *Esquiroles*! (scabs) *Chávez sí*, Teamsters no! The point of the pickets and gathering was precisely to challenge the injunction which was calculated to diminish the effectiveness of the strike. Shortly after we arrived, two large gray line busses, empty except for the driver, came and waited. A Spanish-surnamed sheriff's officer said he spoke in the name of the people of California, and through his efficient mobile loudspeaker system informed us that we were "An unlawful assembly!" One of my fellow inmates, a young Chicano who would like to study law, had a penal code book with him. In the evening upon the visit of the UFW lawyer he showed the definition of "unlawful assembly" which included "riot" and other things which did not apply. The le-

> gal system can be effectively used to thwart the organizing efforts of the farm workers by hampering their right to free assembly and free speech through this kind of illegal, immoral and unconstitutional injunction. By 9 o'clock that morning, most of us were arrested, and by 11 o'clock were booked and jailed. Our stay was unexpectedly prolonged for almost two weeks, which became a time of prayer and literal fasting for many of us in order to cast out demons of injustice and oppression which are still the lot of many migrant farm workers in our land.[8]

This commitment to supporting the farmworkers regrettably also involved Father Juan and the organization of the liturgy or ritual of César Chávez's funeral in 1993.

Using Chávez as his model of faith and social commitment, Romero in the late 1960s participated in drug rehabilitation programs for *pintos* (Chicanos in prison). Moreover, having participated in small anti-Vietnam war protests while at Santa Barbara in the mid-1960s, Romero helped organize other Chicano priests and some members of his then Orange County congregation to participate in the National Chicano Anti-War Moratorium of August 29, 1970. He had met with Rosalío Muñoz, one of the key organizers of the moratorium, who had requested Chicano priests to join what proved to be a historic protest by about 20,000 people. Following the police riot that disrupted the proceedings and the killing of Ruben Salazar, veteran *Los Angeles Times* reporter and KMEX news director, Romero within a few days arranged for a press conference featuring Bishop Patricio Flores of San Antonio in order to protest the destructive actions of the Los Angeles county sheriffs and the death of Salazar.

Father Juan's community activism was furthered after the formation of PADRES October 5–7, 1969. A grouping of Chicano priests that Romero helped to organize, PADRES aimed to foster change within the Catholic Church by increasing the role of Chicanos and empowering the Chicano Catholic community. From 1972 to 1975, Romero served as executive director of the new organization. One of his key leadership roles was the establishment of what was called the Mobile Team Ministry in connection with the Mexican American Cultural Center in San Antonio. Influenced by the writings and work on literacy and consciousness of Paulo Freire in Brazil and by the developing theology of liberation in Latin America, the Mobile Team Ministry was a traveling contingent of certain PADRES members, along with religious sisters and some lay people, including some Protestant ministers who attempted to raise the critical consciousness of poor and disenfranchised Chicanos in different parts of the Southwest. They also promoted civic involvement to deal with issues of discrimination and social justice. Voter registration drives formed part of the agenda, and the ministry organized workshops for anywhere from thirty to fifty people at each location. Romero and his colleagues stressed Freire's concept of *conciencia crítica*, which Father Juan noted was not just consciousness raising but mobilizing people to take action. Of the Mobile Team Ministry, Romero later wrote:

> They perceived as one of the main tasks to be accomplished the development of what Paulo Freire has term[ed] the conciencia crítica. The critical consciousness enables one to clearly recognize her/his own oppressive reality with a certain hope and ability to change it in conjunction with efforts of others. This kind of consciousness leads to action based on human (cultural) and Christian (Gospel) values which influence our lives and destiny.[9]

Besides Freire's influence, the ministry also employed from liberation theology the concept of *comunidades eclesiales de base* (base communities), which involved biblical reflections on particular social problems but also with the intent to act on these reflections. Here, Father Juan likewise employed St. Thomas Aquinas's call to "observe, judge, and act."[10]

Although the Mobile Team Ministry was effective up to a point, it was limited with respect to personnel and resources. As a result, Romero and PADRES made arrangements with the Saul Alinsky–led Industrial Areas Foundation in Chicago to advance and revise the concept of the base communities (comunidades de base) by establishing more extensive and permanent organizations centered around parishes. The first successful effort was COPS, or Communities Organized for Public Service in San Antonio, which was formed in the mid-1970s. While not, strictly speaking, a base community (which tends to focus more on smaller biblical study groups), COPS reflected the comunidades' stress on linking reflection with action. Romero was not directly involved in the formation of COPS, but he was with its Los Angeles counterpart UNO (United Neighborhoods Organization). After his stint with PADRES, he returned to Los Angeles to his old family church, St. Alphonse, on the eastside. There with Alinsky people such as Ernie Cortés, Romero was one of several priests in East Los Angeles who brought together eighteen parishes to form UNO. Each parish put together councils composed of priests, sisters, and lay people. They identified issues held in common by all parishes. As Romero notes, the trick was to go beyond recognizing problems and instead to focus on issues. A problem, according to him, is something that nobody can do anything about unless it is first analyzed and dissected. At this point, it moves from being a problem to becoming an issue or issues that "you attach a name to it and a place." Issues, Romero contends, are winnable. He further adds that issues correspond "to a real and unselfish *self-interest* of the person. It is thus able to move him or her, together with others, into focused action to deal with that situation."[11]

As base communities, UNO and the different parish councils identified specific community issues that would lead to community action and, at the same time, to the development of local organic leadership. Through parish meetings, personal interviews, and house meetings, issues were brought forth, and, through collective action and pressures on elected officials, new leadership surfaced. It was clearly a way of refocusing the meaning of "church." One of the first successful issues that UNO confronted was the excessive auto insurance rates in East Los Angeles. Through organization and consistent pressure on county supervisors, UNO succeeded in reducing rates. Other similar local issues were subsequently pursued by the parish-based organization. These included the construction of new street and traffic lights in the barrio.[12]

The successes of both COPS and UNO helped to raise political consciousness and led to the empowerment of the Chicano communities in both San Antonio and Los Angeles. At the same time, it created a different perception of the church by laypeople involved. Rather than seeing the church as only a religious institution, the laity began to recognize it as a leadership force in the community itself. And rather than seeing priests as aloof religious figures, they began to see figures such as Father Juan as key community leaders. Of this profound changes in perceptions, Romero comments:

> It is my opinion that in San Antonio and in East Los Angeles, Mexican Americans certainly see the Church as much more than a place to pray, or the priest as merely a person who celebrates Mass and baptizes children. Because of the local churches' involvement in the real concerns of its people, the Church and its ministers would be easily perceived as closely connected to the people. This has been achieved through the community organizing experience which has been solidly based in the institution of the various local churches or congregations of the predominantly Mexican American communities.[13]

Since 1976 and the formation of UNO, Romero has continued to be active in the community, including in the 1980s supporting the Sanctuary movement for Central American refugees. Today, as pastor of his Santa Monica church, Father Juan continues his active involvement with the life and issues affecting his parishioners. He remains an example of a Chicano community priest.

Community Organizer

Father Luis Quihuis is the associate pastor of Our Lady of Sorrows church in downtown Santa Barbara. He was born in 1951 in Phoenix to a strongly religious family and one which was college educated on both sides. He attended Catholic schools through high school. But the foundational source of his moral socialization came from his parents and grandparents. His family stressed social justice issues and helping those less fortunate. "We were raised traditional Catholics with strong Catholic values," he notes, "but more importantly it kind of forced us to get actively involved in justice related issues, working always on behalf of the downtrodden and poor."[14] In addition to these values, he recalls that his father was active in local Mexican American politics and was a member of several community organizations. At the dinner table, issues of justice and politics were not uncommon. Religious and political discourse and practice were carried out in an ethnic context so that the Quihuis children grew up with a sense of pride of being Mexicanos.

This family socialization was buttressed by Quihuis's Catholic education. Attention to the African American civil rights movement led by Martin Luther King and discussions about the Vietnam War were part of classroom learning. He recalls that his father admired King and was against the war.

Since elementary school, Quihuis believed that he had a vocation in the church, but at the same time he wanted to experience more of life before making a final decision. After high school graduation, he enrolled at Arizona State University (ASU) in order to be close to his family even though he had been accepted into more prestigious schools. At ASU, he majored in business with the intent of becoming a stockbroker when he didn't think about his vocation. As an undergraduate student, the young Luis displayed the leadership talents that would characterize his later religious and community life. He was active in student politics, including participation in Chicano student activities—especially in organizing cultural events around Cinco de Mayo and Día de los Muertos. As a strong and practicing Catholic, he also joined the Newman Club, the campus Catholic student organization. It was at the Newman Center in the early 1970s that he first learned about liberation theology. It was also at ASU that, like Father Juan, he had an impressionable encounter with César Chávez. Chávez was in Phoenix in 1972 to promote the lettuce strike and to get people to stop buying lettuce, especially from Safeway. To this end, Chávez was engaged in one of his periodic fasts. Along with many other Mexican Americans, Quihuis visited with Chávez and expressed his support. Again like Juan Romero, what impressed Quihuis the most about the farm labor leader was his deep spirituality and how this seemed to guide and support his politics. "Anybody can have a social movement or a justice movement and may not produce faith," he recalls about this encounter, "but if it's based on faith . . . it will endure forever."[15] The concept of a faith-based movement such as César Chávez's would remain a model for Quihuis.

Following his graduation from ASU in 1973, Quihuis still felt that he had a church vocation, but he was not ready to pursue it. Instead, he was fortunate to be hired as assistant to the speaker of the Arizona House of Representatives. He was responsible for upgrading and modernizing the legislative process and the reorganization of state agencies so that they could be more effective and efficient in delivering human services. This brought him at age twenty-three significant fortune and power. When hired, he was making close to $70,000 which, according to him, would be equivalent today to more than double that amount. In his administrative capacity, he focused on social legislation such as health care, which was consistent with his interests and religious and social values. He remained in this position from 1974 to 1982.

Despite his good fortune, and maybe because of it, Quihuis never lost sight of his vocation. Finally, after a retreat at the famous Trappist monastery in Gethesemani, Kentucky, made famous by Thomas Merton, at age thirty-one he decided to enter the Jesuit order. He gave up his savings and possessions, except for some artwork, to family and others. As a Jesuit novitiate, Quihuis was pleased that, besides his studies, he was able to continue to pursue his interests in community and social issues. He worked with the poor in Los

Angeles, Orange County, and the Imperial Valley. He returned to work with the sick and dying in Phoenix. As part of his theological studies, he went to Spain where he furthered his interest in liberation theology after meeting Gustavo Gutiérrez, the leading liberationist theologian, as well as other Latin American theologians. This interest was later expanded when he traveled to Brazil for additional training. There he participated in the base communities movement and met and studied with Dom Helder Camara, Brazil's leading liberationist.

Following his return from Spain to the United States and before being formally ordained, Quihuis was dispatched in the mid-1980s by the Jesuits to be their chief lobbyist in Washington, D.C. Here he concentrated on faith and justice issues. He was part of the religious coalition that opposed the Supreme Court nomination by the Reagan administration of Robert Bork, a staunchly conservative jurist with little record of being sensitive to civil rights issues. The nomination was defeated. He also helped forge the successful religious organization opposed to reintroducing funding to the Nicaraguan Contras, the right-wing military forces supported by Reagan in order to topple the Sandinista revolutionary government. While in Washington, he likewise worked on Hispanic issues within the church hierarchy, especially on the U.S. Bishops Hispanic Pastoral Plan with Pablo Sedillo.

Skillful in organizing based on his own personal talents and his prior legislative experiences, Father Luis after his ordination in the early 1990s was assigned to the University of San Francisco (USF), the Jesuit institution. He was specifically asked by the president of the university to organize and launch a new outreach initiative into the Latino community of San Francisco. Father Luis eagerly accepted. In the following nine years, Father Luis would become an example of the concept of a community priest and, more directly, of a priest community organizer.

Named the Martyrs of El Salvador Project after the six Jesuits and two laypersons killed by the military in El Salvador during that country's recent civil war, the El Salvador Project represented USF's effort to take the university to the Latino community. "It was an exercise in the university recapturing part of its motto [as a university]," Father Luis explains; "so we were moving back into the community."[16] Based on the model of the comunidades de base and Paulo Friere's concept of *educación popular*, the idea was to develop initiative and leadership out of the community rather than having the university go in and do everything. "It was not the university of the ivory tower coming down with all the answers to tell the people what their problems and needs were," explains Quihuis.[17] Focusing on the Mission District, the main Latino area of San Francisco, and centering activities at St. Peter's, the largest Catholic church in the Mission, the project first organized community meetings to identify issues. A community board composed of recognized community leaders, parents, community groups, and youth, both men and women, was formed, and regular general community meetings were held at St. Peter's.

After a series of gatherings, various key issues were identified, with the top ones being education and health. On education, Father Luis, with the assistance of Sister Ignatius of the Sacred Heart of Mary order, first started a tutoring program at the church with USF students serving as the tutors and as teacher's aides. In addition, he got the School of Education at the university involved by working with the teachers from St. Peter's parochial school to assist them in new pedagogy and curriculum approaches. Soon progress among the Latino children became visible. Moreover, scholarship programs to USF for Latinos, as well as recruitment to the university, were commenced.

On health issues, the project responded to the lack of school nurses in both the parochial and public schools in the Mission by having student nurses from the School of Nursing volunteer at the schools. Health records for the children were updated, and nutritional classes for both parents and students were started. Eye exams and hearing tests were administered to the children. Health fairs for the community were organized. Assistance was given to register those qualified for Medi-Cal, especially the young. Medical assistance, referrals, and counseling were made available to Latinos with AIDS. Finally, a clinic serving both children and families was opened at St. Peter's, with the assistance of some of the city's physicians and the student nurses. It was free and opened to the public. Undocumented Latino immigrants flocked to the clinic during the tense period generated by Proposition 187 in 1994 when Latinos believed that public clinics and hospitals would now inquire about one's legal status. On health issues, Father Luis was assisted by Sister Briou Kelber of the Sisters of Mercy.

Because of immigrant bashing connected to Proposition 187, the project also began free legal services. For example, law students from USF volunteered to accompany individuals and families to hospitals and clinics to make sure that they were not harassed about their status. Moreover, they provided legal counseling on immigration issues, including sponsoring citizenship classes. To help on household budgets and income taxes, business students at USF were organized by Father Luis to provide assistance in completing income tax forms.

Growing gang warfare in the Mission was allayed by the project sponsoring afternoon programs for kids, as well as counseling parents and meeting with gang members. Father Luis and his assistants in particular concentrated on getting mothers involved in the anti-gang effort. Mothers began to walk the streets in the afternoons and evenings to prevent gang violence. "If the mothers are out in the streets," Father Luis stresses, "you're not gonna have the gang members doing drive-by shootings."[18] According to him, this plan worked. In addition, issues of police abuse especially against Latino youth were addressed by organizing community meetings with police officials, including Father Luis's direct appeals on some occasions to Mayor Willie Brown. Moreover, seminars on street law were put together to inform people about their civil rights.

Part of the effort to self-empower the Latino community involved transforming people's attitudes about community and themselves. Family attitudes and behavior that led to spousal and child abuse were addressed by forming parental meetings to discuss such issues. To ensure that parents attended, both mothers and fathers, these meetings were mandatory for families receiving project services.

Cultural and religious traditions were not avoided by the project. It helped organize popular religious activities, especially around the feast day of Our Lady of Guadalupe, Día de los Muertos, and the feast day of Santa Cecilia the patron of musicians when Father Luis blessed mariachi and other musical groups. Mother's Day and Cinco de Mayo were additional community celebrations sponsored by the project.

Finally, community meetings held twice a month specifically addressed various injustices concerning labor practices, housing, educational issues, and the lack of health insurance in the Latino community. These meetings were conducted in Spanish with English translation provided. In addition, Father Luis kept in further contact with the community by just walking around the Mission talking to people. "I knew everything that was going on in the community," he recalls; "I was taking time talking to *abuelitos* [grandparents] and . . . the people of the barrio."[19]

For nine years Father Luis worked in the Mission District. While his leadership was crucial to the success of the El Salvador project, it was not indispensable and it was not intended to be so. The development of local leadership was to ensure the continuity of the project with or without Father Luis. Recognizing this and wanting to return to parish work, he left in 1999 and was assigned to Santa Barbara. At Our Lady of Sorrows he has successfully duplicated some of the programs of the El Salvador project. As he looks back on those nine years, Father Luis believes that the combination of faith and community work, examples he took from César Chávez, proved to be highly successful. "I think that the model that best sums it up," he notes of the project, "was something that the ancient Greeks wrote many years ago which was the theme of the project and that was 'to tame the savageness of man while making gentle the life of the world.' "[20] From a theological perspective, he further adds: "It was very simple. It was helping to promote faith and justice."[21] And from a political and sociological angle, Father Luis concludes that his role as a community organizer and that of the church-based project reveals the importance of Catholic parishes and priests in the development of organization and a sense of civic community for Latinos. Secular political organizers need to be cognizant of this and at their risk shun the churches and parishes as natural organizing centers. Here is where the people are both citizens and immigrants. "What it tells us about organizing," Father Luis concludes, "is . . . that politicians need to listen . . . to . . . the needs of the people by working more closely with pastors, regardless of what religious denomination because they [the pastors] have the pulse of the people."[22]

Cultural Worker

Virgilio Elizondo is the best-recognized theologian of Chicano religion. At the same time, he is an example of a community priest. In his case, he is what I call a "cultural worker." Like both Romero and Quihuis, Elizondo's proclivity to serve others was part of his early socialization. Born in San Antonio in 1935, Elizondo grew up in the predominant Mexican westside. His parents were both immigrants from Mexico—his father working class and his mother from the upper class of Mexico City. Thanks to advice from Jewish American acquaintances, his father bought property in the barrio and started a family grocery store. Elizondo recalls that his own ecumenism stems from this help offered to his father. "So that became part of my sense of humanism later on," he notes, "that it was thanks to the Jewish people of San Antonio that my dad got going."[23]

Like Romero and Quihuis, Elizondo grew up in a very religious household although, as he observes, his family was not "churchy." This meant that, due to the family business, his parents did not have time to participate in many organized church groups. The young Virgilio was sent to Catholic elementary schools although not to high school. Instead, he attended the Peacock Military Academy where his sense of discipline was reinforced. Images of the Sacred Heart and of Our Lady of Guadalupe were permanent icons within the home. Religious feast days such as that of Guadalupe, Good Friday, and Ash Wednesday represented particularly impressive events, and some, such as that of Guadalupe, he remembers "were like carnival days."[24]

Growing up in the westside also meant that Elizondo was very much aware of his ethnic roots. Mexican culture surrounded him, reinforced by his parents and the speaking of Spanish at home. His father did have time to participate in Mexican American community activities, including being a member of several organizations such as the League of United Latin American Citizens (LULAC) and the Mexican Chamber of Commerce. Elizondo recalls at age ten helping his parents organize house bingo parties to raise money for the campaign of later congressman Henry B. González for city council. Elizondo's father would often remind Virgilio and his sister of their ethnic identity and how they needed to be proud of it—of "solidarity in nuestro pueblo."[25] Elizondo likewise grew up aware that Mexicans were subordinated and discriminated against in San Antonio. Unfortunately, in some cases this involved the Catholic Church. He recalls that in his parochial school, some of the nuns punished kids for speaking Spanish. They had to stand in front of the class and say, "I will never speak Spanish again in my life."[26]

Despite such discrimination, Elizondo grew up in a nurturing environment where religion and ethnicity complemented one another. Mexican popular religiosity, for example, was everywhere. This included *pastorelas* (the Shepherds' Play) and *posadas* (Mary and Joseph seeking shelter) during Christmas time. He remembers that people would purchase Mexican religious calendars from Jewish merchants, and then, in turn, they would get empty cigar boxes from his father's store. They would put the image of Our Lady of Guadalupe in the *cajita* (box). "They would take the cigar boxes and paint them real pretty con florecitos y todo," Elizondo notes, "and put the *santito* in there and you would have a nicho."[27] Moreover, irrespective of some of the nuns' prohibition of Spanish in school, the Spanish language was everywhere, including all of the Masses in the westside churches. "Once, I remember," Elizondo observes, "they put an English mass and people thought *que horror*, it was going to ruin the church with English."[28]

One of the key values stressed by his parents and which would come to characterize Elizondo's later life was that of service to others. He developed this very early on when he would work in his father's store and help the customers, especially the *viejitos* (the elderly).

Education was likewise emphasized and college promoted. Following his graduation from high school, he enrolled at St. Mary's University in San Antonio where other Mexican Americans of more middle-class backgrounds attended. Unlike Romero and Quihuis, Elizondo does not appear to have possessed an early sense of a vocation to the priesthood. This would develop more in college. At first, he was more interested in science and majored in chemistry. However, besides its academic programs, St. Mary's also encouraged social consciousness. He became more aware and sensitive to racism in San Antonio. He was particularly impressed with the leadership of Archbishop Robert Lucey, who for years had been a champion of Mexican American civil rights. Elizondo understood that he was privileged to be attending college, but that this also carried with it social responsibilities.

These changes in his life led Elizondo in his senior year to make the decision to become a priest. He felt that this was a way of fulfilling these obligations. "I felt that through the priesthood and the Church I could contribute in some way to the betterment of my people," he notes. "I didn't become a priest just to become a social activist. But, on the other hand, I saw that the Church had something to do to help the activists in what was necessary."[29] This sense of social commitment was furthered in his seminary studies on Catholic social doctrine.

Following his ordination in the mid-1960s and after his initial parish assignments, Elizondo matured in his social consciousness and in his development as a cultural worker within the church by his close association with Archbishop Lucey. The archbishop appointed the young priest to work on religious education and, in time, as director of religious education for the archdiocese. This appointment coincided with the conclusion of Vatican Council II, which significantly influenced the thinking and praxis of Elizondo, as did Romero and Quihuis. Father Virgil was particularly affected by the document on the church in the modern world, especially the idea of the church returning to its original source as a service to its people. He understood that this involved what he refers to as "collective charity," which is being involved with people and social justice. "That the basic identity of the Church is to be of service to the world," he stresses:

> That the Church doesn't exist for itself alone, but it exists to serve the world. So, therefore, the Church was the best Church when it didn't think as a Church, [but] when it was out organizing the day camps or was helping the peasants to set the water system, or

> feed[ing] the hungry, [or] give[ing] drink to the thirsty . . . so the Church was not called into existence for itself but to be of service. So the word "service" becomes the key word.[30]

Vatican II likewise impressed Elizondo with the concept of people as church. This was a concept that had been forgotten by the church and yet was crucial—"that the Church is fundamentally people, the people of God."[31]

Father Virgil's commitment to social justice issues was furthered when the archbishop invited him to accompany him to the conference in 1968 in Medellín, Colombia, where the bishops of Latin American met to discuss implementing the changes of Vatican II and what this meant for the Catholic Church in Latin America. Here Elizondo became acquainted with the beginning of liberation theology and met some of the early liberationists, such as Gustavo Gutiérrez. He was especially struck with the concept of "social sin" and the attention paid to the glaring class and social inequities in Latin America and "turning the Church inside out; instead of the Church siding with the rich, it's the poor that the Church sides with." Of this particular emphasis at Medellín, Elizondo adds:

> That was the thing at Medellín. Sin was always seen as personal, but to see that the whole structure could be a sinful structure and that the whole structure could be productive of certain circumstances, misery, poverty, and all that. I think that's what was radical at Medellín. To see how sin had become so engrained in the culture that the very culture would produce people who would exploit. So Medellín stressed that sin was not just personal, but that it's structural, and that part of the task of the Church is to denounce such evil and to provide new alternatives that people haven't thought about. So in that sense the Church begins unmasking the evil that's hidden behind the structure. Medellín for me was a great encounter with an aspect of Christianity that I had never suspected. I knew that the Church was involved in social justice concerning just wages, rights for workers, and all of that, but the question of what produces injustice was something new.[32]

Accepting liberation theology and including it as part of his religious education, Elizondo would expand it to incorporate issues of culture rather than just of class. His orientation toward culture as contested territory in the struggle for social justice first came from his own strong Mexican American cultural background. Vatican II enhanced this with its stress on inculturation and the need for the church in the modern world to recognize cultural and ethnic diversity in implementing the changes of the Council. This was particularly made evident to Father Virgil after a one-year stay at the East Asian Pastoral Institute in Manila, where he learned from Asian Catholic theologians an anthropological approach to Christianity. It reinforced for him the idea that the church was culture. As he would stress later in his own writings, Jesus had not only come into the world as a human but specifically as a Galilean and hence of a specific culture. "The basic principle in Christianity is when God became man," Elizondo stresses, "he didn't become any man—he became a Galilean. So therefore He affirms culture and it's through culture that He celebrates the presence of God."[33] "I was fascinated with their way of approaching this question," he concludes of his Manila experience, "but in some way I felt this was similar to the Chicano struggle in the Southwest where the Church didn't understand our perspective."[34]

Elizondo began to implement these ideas in the early 1970s after the formation of PADRES of which he was an early member. In 1972 the organization believed that it was important to establish a cultural training institute to prepare priests, sisters, and laypeople to work more effectively in the Chicano communities. They started the Mexican American Cultural Center, or MACC, in San Antonio and selected Elizondo as its director. For the next eleven years, Father Virgil would head this effort. The basic principles of MACC were, one, to further the process of inculturation with respect to Chicanos and the Church and, two, through the legitimization of Chicano culture to empower Chicanos in both sacred and secular terms. By recognizing and validating the Chicano experience, its history and culture, MACC as part of the Chicano movement would deal with the identity question among Chicanos and give them a sense of their own self-worth. Feeling good about themselves and being confident of themselves would empower Chicanos to make changes within the church and outside of it. Like other expressions of the Chicano movement, MACC recognized the importance of the cultural wars in the United States and staked out culture as its contribution to liberation theology. "That here [in the United States] [it] wasn't just the matter of economic poverty. . . . We were being denied the right to our own existence, to name ourselves. So that was a deeper type of poverty than just economic poverty—the poverty of non-being, the poverty of non-existence. And in that sense I think we were pushing further than in Latin America."[35]

MACC believed that if priests, sisters, and lay leaders, both Chicanos and Anglos, were going to work in Mexican American parishes, they had to prepare themselves as cultural workers by knowing and appreciating the history and culture of the people. By sponsoring cultural leadership, MACC indirectly would also be helping to create organic leadership in the barrios, as its disciples would assist in the empowerment of the communities.

In this effort, MACC, utilizing what Elizondo refers to as "religious imagination," organized institutes and classes on Chicano history and culture, Spanish-language classes, and religious courses where scriptures would be studied with a Chicano perspective. And through bringing together a variety of scholars, MACC began publishing various texts on Chicano religious culture.[36] As part of its program, the center hosted a variety of Chicano artists, musicians, poets, and writers. Through a re-study of the liturgy or ritual of the church, MACC promoted liturgical inculturation that integrated within barrio churches various Chicano religious traditions, customs, and music. These included renewed attention to feast days such as that of Guadalupe and Día de los Muertos. At the same time, MACC worked to stress the importance of Chicano popular religiosity in the form of home altars, popular devotions, *peregrinaciones* (popular pilgrimages), and other expressions of a people's faith. These manifestations were presented not as superstitions, in the way that some in the church did, but as legitimate expressions of the sacred. "This was a very legitimate expression of Christianity," Elizondo observes, "It was different from the U.S. Catholic Church but not inferior."[37]

In its leadership program, MACC stressed the importance of Chicano priests serving as community organizers. Working with PADRES and Archbishop Patricio Flores, MACC helped to organize COPS in San Antonio as an effective empowering community movement. MACC alumni, both Chicanos and Anglos, not only worked with COPS but also helped to organize similar base communities in South Texas, Los Angeles, and other locations.

As a cultural worker, Father Virgil further expanded his efforts when in 1983 he was appointed rector of San Fernando Cathedral in San Antonio. There, building on his work at MACC and earlier cultural activities at the cathedral by sympathetic Spanish priests, Elizondo showcased the cathedral as a model of inculturation and cultural empowerment. The liturgy was revised to incorporate a whole array of Chicano religious cultural traditions. It focused on Elizondo's concept of church as fiesta. "It was a liturgy with lots of mexicano things," he notes, "a lot of mariachi music and decorations and danzantes (dancers). So really a very fiesta Mass."[38] To increase the range of these changes, he initiated a television Mass each Sunday from the cathedral that was nationally broadcast. The centerpiece of this liturgical transformation focused on the Passion Play during *Semana Santa* (Holy Week). Earlier passion plays had been performed in the barrios, but Father Virgil believed that it would have an even greater impact if it moved downtown to use the cathedral as the crucifixion climax. It worked, and now each year thousands participate in the procession and ritual. Each Good Friday the downtown streets belong to the Mexicanos, many of them poor and immigrants. Such ritual is not only religiously empowering but socially and politically as well. Besides the liturgical changes, Father Virgil used his years as rector to help people in other ways. Medical programs were started, the homeless were given shelter, immigrants were provided assistance, and an ecumenical AIDS march was organized which has become an annual event. In addition, Elizondo used his visible position as rector to participate on various civic committees. In a short period of time, he had transformed San Fernando again as the center of Chicano Catholic life in San Antonio. "I think San Fernando became effectively the Latino cathedral of the United States," Father Virgil concludes.[39]

Through his work at MACC and San Fernando, as well as in his writings on Chicano theology which center on the important role of culture in Chicano religious life, Virgilio Elizondo exemplifies the concept of community priest, and, in particular, that of cultural worker.

Conclusion

Leadership can be defined in many ways. What I am proposing is that in the study of Chicano history and Chicano Studies, we expand that definition beyond the secular to include the religious. The example of Fathers Romero, Quihuis, and Elizondo suggest that some Catholic priests, as well as other religious figures, provide key leadership, not just in a spiritual sense but in a temporal one as well. The sacred and the secular are joined together in a very powerful way. In this sense, the earlier model of the worker-priests in France is reconfigured in the form of community priests. Through such leadership, churches and parishes become significant organizing centers. It is not only where many of the people are, but also where they are motivated by their faith. It is the faith communities, like the comunidades de base in Latin America, which perhaps serve as the model for sustained and permanent community organization in the struggles against injustice. Faith and social consciousness come together, as the example also of César Chávez reveals, to propel *la causa* (the struggle). As scholars, we need to rediscover and understand this tradition.

NOTES

1. See, for example, Mario T. García, *Mexican Americans: Leadership, Ideology and Identity* (New Haven, CT: Yale University Press, 1981); García, *Memories of Chicano History: The Life and Narrative of Bert Corona* (Berkeley: University of California Press, 1994); García, *The Making of a Mexican American Mayor: Raymond L. Telles of El Paso* (El Paso: Texas Western Press, 1998); García and Frances Esquibel Tywoniak, *Migrant Daughter: Coming of Age as a Mexican American Woman* (Berkeley: University of California Press, 2000); and García, *Luis Leal: An Auto/Biography* (Austin: University of Texas Press, 2000).

2. See, for example, Mario T. García, "Catholic Social Doctrine and Mexican American Political Thought," in *El Cuerpo de Cristo: The Hispanic Presence in the U.S. Catholic Church*, ed. Peter Casarella and Raul Gómez (New York: Crossroad Publishing, 1998), 292–311; and García, "Fray Angélico Chávez, Religiosity, and New Mexican Oppositional Historical Narrative," in *Fray Angélico Chávez: Poet, Priest, and Artist*, ed. Ellen McCracken (Albuquerque: University of New Mexico Press, 2000), 25–36.

3. See, for example, Oscar L. Arnal, *Priests in Working-Class Blue: The History of the Worker-Priests, 1943–1954* (New York: Paulist Press, 1986).

4. Oral history interviews: Father Juan Romero with Mario T. García (June 18, 1998, Los Angeles, and July 1, 1998, Santa Barbara). Father Luis Quihuis with Mario T. García (September 15, 1999; September 30, 1999; October 5, 1999; October 12, 1999; December 7, 1999; February 1, 2000; and March 28, 2000, all in Santa Barbara). Father Virgilio Elizondo with Mario T. García (February 10, 1997; February 13, 1997; February 20, 1997; April 21, 1998; May 11, 1998; and May 27, 1998 all conducted in Santa Barbara). All page numbers refer to transcripts. Transcripts of interviews are in possession of Mario T. García.

5. See Juan Romero, "Ministry to Farm Workers: Experiences in Advocacy," *Notre Dame Journal of Education* 5 (Summer 1974): 186–187.

6. Ibid., 187.
7. Ibid.
8. Ibid., 190.
9. Juan Romero, "Religiosidad Popular as Locus for Theological Reflection and Springboards for Pastoral Action," unpublished paper.
10. Interview with Romero (July 1, 1998), 8, 10.
11. Juan Romero, "Usefulness of Hispanic Survey to Ministers of the Southwest," unpublished paper.
12. See Peter Skerry, *Mexican Americans: The Ambivalent Minority* (New York: Free Press, 1993).
13. Romero, "Usefulness to Ministers of the Southwest," 5.
14. Interview with Quihuis (September 15, 1999), 14.
15. Ibid. (October 8, 1999), 24–25.
16. Ibid. (March, 28, 2000), 8.
17. Ibid. (February 1, 2000), 1
18. Ibid., 12.
19. Ibid. (March 28, 2000), 25.
20. Ibid., 16.
21. Ibid., 29.
22. Ibid., 31.
23. Interview with Elizondo (February 10, 1997), 1–2. For an introduction to Elizondo's work, see Timothy Matovina, ed., *Beyond Borders: Writings of Virgilio Elizondo and Friends* (Maryknoll, NY: Orbis Books, 2001).
24. Interview with Elizondo (February 10, 1997), 17.
25. Ibid., 24.
26. Ibid., 12.
27. Ibid., 2.
28. Ibid., 18.
29. Ibid. (February 13, 1997), 9.
30. Ibid. (Feb. 20, 1997), 11, 13.
31. Ibid.
32. Ibid. (April, 21, 1998), 1–2.
33. Ibid. (May 11, 1998), 15–17. Also, see Elizondo, *Galilean Journey: The Mexican-American Experience*, 2nd ed. (Maryknoll, NY: Orbis Books, 2000).
34. Interview with Elizondo (April 21, 1998), 3.
35. Ibid. (May 11, 1998), 22.
36. Ibid., 18.
37. Ibid., 17.
38. Ibid. (May 27, 1998), 8.
39. Ibid., 12

6

The Challenges and Consequences of Being Latina, Catholic, and Political

Lara Medina

The women I met in Las Hermanas gave me the language and the support to integrate my faith and my spirituality into my politics, which is the only way I survived.

—María Antonietta Berriozábal, city council member and mayoral and congressional candidate

Initially I saw Las Hermanas as too radical. Little by little I began to see they had something to say. . . . I learned about the exploitation of Mexican sisters, like myself.

—Rosa Martha Zárate, community organizer, singer, and composer

Las Hermanas nurtured me and kept me going . . . because they were so rooted in the people's struggle. Also seeing the tremendous faith of the farmworkers helped me reclaim the faith that I inherited. At times I have wanted to walk away . . . but there are too many people who have paid the price for me to be here.

—Tess Browne, community activist and previous staff member of the National Farm Worker Ministry and the Peace and Justice Center

María Antonietta Berriozábal, native of San Antonio, Texas; Rosa Martha Zárate, of San Bernardino, California; and Tess Browne, of Boston, Massachusetts—all three see themselves as catalysts of change in their communities. Their involvement with Las Hermanas, a thirty-four-year-old national religious-political feminist organization of Chicana/Latina Catholics, influenced their profound commitment to community, justice, and faith. Whether in electoral politics, community organizing, or farm labor representation, these women understand their work as service to their communities. A service grounded in their faith: faith in a God that seeks political, social, and ecclesiastical justice.

The paths of these women crossed in Las Hermanas, an "official" yet autonomous Catholic organization historically concerned about social justice and empowerment for grassroot Latinas.[1] Their association with Las Hermanas proved transformative. Zárate and Browne were among the founding members, and Berriozábal was introduced to the organization in 1985. Berriozábal's involvement in electoral politics found spiritual nourishment in Las Hermanas, Zárate's introduction to community activism in the United States occurred through the organization, and Browne received support for her work with the United Farm Workers from Las Hermanas. The interweaving of faith and politics in Las Hermanas helped to strengthen these women for long-term commitments to civic engagement. The women of Las Hermanas defy longstanding stereotypes of Catholic women as apolitical passive bearers of their faith. Influenced by the renewal of Vatican II, American Catholic feminism, the black and Chicano civil rights movements, and Latin American liberation theology, Las Hermanas organized to fight the overt discrimination within the church *and* society toward Chicano and other Spanish-speaking communities.

In this essay I provide a brief overview of the sociohistorical context from which Las Hermanas emerged; then I present snapshot profiles of Zárate, Browne, and Berriozábal. These brief descriptions of their extensive work provide windows into the effect that Las Hermanas has had on Latina Catholic political activism. I argue that the autonomous space created by Las Hermanas and its integration of spirituality and social activism influenced and strengthened these women in their involvement in civic affairs. No other Latina Catholic organization exists that serves this purpose.

In chapter 8 in this volume, Paul Barton discusses the mobilizing of Chicano Methodist clergy and laity in the 1970s around farm labor activism. My research provides an important parallel to the mobilizing of Chicano/a Catholic clergy and nuns during this same time period. Both Protestant and Catholic religious leaders attempted to bridge the ministry of their churches with the social needs of their people.

Las Hermanas first organized in 1971 in Houston, Texas, when fifty primarily Chicana women religious and nuns met to discuss how they might better serve the needs of Spanish-speaking Catholics in the United States. Gregoria Ortega, a Victoryknoll Sister, and Gloria Gallardo, a member of the Sisters of the Holy Ghost, organized the event. Sister Ortega had been transferred out of the diocese of San Angeles, Texas, where she had supported student walkouts and opposed the severe physical abuse of Chicano/a students by their teachers. Sister Gallardo worked as a community organizer and Catholic catechist in Houston among Chicanos living with chronic unemployment, inadequate health care, and malnutrition. Together they decided to organize other Chicana sisters "who have tried to become more relevant to our people and because of this, find themselves in 'trouble' with either our own congregation

Las Hermanas members and supporters at the Third Hispanic Encuentro at the National Cathedral in Washington, D.C., in 1985 protest the vote to reject the full ministry of women in the Catholic Church (Courtesy of Las Hermanas)

or other members of the hierarchy."[2] A letter of invitation was sent to as many Mexican American sisters they could identify with the help of the Leadership Conference of Women Religious (LCWR).

The fifty Chicanas present at the first meeting joined religious life prior to Vatican II (1965) or shortly thereafter. They gathered with varying levels of political and ethnic consciousness. The majority of them shared the experience of being forced to deny their cultural heritage and language once they entered convent life. Many of them also felt angry and frustrated about being denied the opportunity to minister in their own ethnic communities. Sister Yolanda Tarango reflects on her experience:

> At that time you were supposed to leave behind your past as it was not desirable to work with one's people. I experienced much racism.

> . . . We were forbidden to speak Spanish even in hospitals, schools, not even to the janitors. . . . It was a violent tearing away from our pasts.[3]

The call to unite and the opportunity to "tell their stories" enabled the women to recognize the similarities, identify the elements of oppression, and "realize it was not just my order or my life but that we were in a widespread situation. In the coming together we raised each others' consciousness."[4] Despite the tremendous pain that many of the sisters had experienced in religious life, they understood their potential to affect change. Acknowledging their "unique resources as Spanish-speaking religious women," they dedicated their individual and collective purpose "to enable each other to work more effectively among and with the Spanish-speaking People of God in bringing about social justice *and* a truly Christian peace."[5] From its inception, members of Las Hermanas envisioned themselves as social activists.

Institutionalized patterns of discrimination within the church comprised only a portion of the women's concerns. In secular society, Mexican Americans and Puerto Ricans nationwide faced a higher proportion of unemployment and held the most unskilled and lowest paid jobs in the work force.[6] Farmworkers organizing under the leadership of César Chávez and Dolores Huerta needed the support of religious institutions. Drop-out rates for Mexican Americans averaged as high as 50 percent in parts of the Southwest. Mexican Americans were being recruited for the Vietnam War and dying overseas at a disproportionately higher rate than the rest of the population.[7] Historically, the Catholic Church had taken a paternalistic approach to these social concerns or chose to look the other way.

The emerging Chicano movement of the late 1960s and early 1970s responded to these injustices with a "politics of mass protest."[8] Fundamental to the movement was a quest for cultural identity, self-determination, and civil rights. Chicano/a activists challenged the Catholic Church with pleas for institutional support. The women gathering in Houston responded to the challenge to effectively serve their people.

Those present at the first meeting chose "Las Hermanas" as the organizational name. Their motto was "Unidas en accíon y oración" (United in action and prayer). The emphasis on prayer held a primary place for Sister Ortega. She explains, "We couldn't do anything without prayer. Without it we would be like empty tombs."[9] The importance of prayer combined with activism marked a characteristic that was distinct from other Chicana organizations forming in the 1970s.

The first three-day conference in Houston included the support of official representatives of the church hierarchy: a welcome by Bishop Morkovsky of the Galveston-Houston diocese, a keynote address by Bishop Patricio Flores, and an address of full support by Father Ralph Ruiz, the National Chairman of Padres Asociados para los Derechos Religiosos, Educatives y Sociales (PADRES).[10] A mariachi Mass, dancing, the showing of *Yo Soy Joaquín*, and a presentation on the Crusade for Justice by Sister Carmelita Espinoza provided a cultural and political perspective.[11] The presence of Chicano clergy reflects the mutual respect that both Ortega and Gallardo had for PADRES, who Gregoria credits as "inspiring" her to organize Chicana sisters. Understanding the importance of recognition from the hierarchy motivated them to invite the bishops. The inclusion of cultural and political programming indicates that Las Hermanas saw itself as a part of the Chicano movement fighting for civil rights.

The women chose four specific projects to achieve their goal of service for social justice. First, ministry teams comprised of two to five "intercommunity specialists" in the fields of education, health, social work, and religious education would travel to Chicano communities then underserved by the church. Second, "sensitizing teams" would educate religious congregations on the cultural and social realities of Spanish-speaking communities. Third, a religious formation center would offer young Chicanas their basic formation in preparation for religious life. Fourth, an information clearinghouse would foster a communication network among the members for political conscientization, leadership development, employment opportunities, support, and collaboration. These projects emphasized the multiple roles that the women envisioned for themselves: as ministers immersed in the social context of La Raza (people of Mexican and Latin American ancestry), as bridges between Spanish-speaking communities and Anglo ministers, as mentors to potential Chicana sisters, and as collaborators in political education and leadership development. With the election of three national officers, six consultants, and several state coordinators, and the filing of incorporation papers shortly after the first conference, Las Hermanas began its journey as the first national organization of Chicana Roman Catholic religious political activists. As the first national president pro tem, Sister Gallardo declared, "We are finally on our way to REAL ACTION! . . . Adelante con La Raza y su hermana en La Causa."[12]

State coordinators lost no time in recruiting potential members. By September a total of 900 Spanish-speaking sisters representing twenty-five states, as well as Mexico and parts of Latin America, had been contacted.[13] Sisters of Puerto Rican and Cuban descent also joined, broadening the diversity of membership. California, Texas, and Colorado held state conferences for the purpose of giving "LH wider and better exposure, to organize better in each state, and to become better acquainted with the local problems so that some action might be taken."[14] In the first newsletter, *Informes*, circulated on September 19, 1971, Sister Gallardo addressed the Conference of Major Superiors of Women Religious in Atlanta, Georgia. Describing her reception, Gallardo states, "*Hermanas, hemos ganado otra victoria*! [Sisters, we have won another victory!] I met most of your superiors and their response was the same—positive and enthusiastic and hopeful!"[15]

While the initial reaction to Las Hermanas was supportive, relationships often became strained as individual sisters challenged their religious communities on issues ranging from racial discrimination to support for farmworkers. According to *La Historia de Las Hermanas*, the "Leadership Conference of Women Religious (LCWR) feared that perhaps the organization of Las Hermanas would eventually become a separate Hispanic religious congregation, thus taking away from their constituency."[16] Sister Yolanda Tarango explains:

> For a few years some communities forbade their members from joining Las Hermanas. The implication was that when a sister went to the organization she became a rebel. She returned conscienticized and questioned every structure. . . . Some religious orders felt it wasn't good because Las Hermanas made them too radical.[17]

Despite the varying responses to the organization, membership increased. By the time of the next national conference eight months later on November 25–27, 1971, in Santa Fe, New Mexico, membership quadrupled with close to 200 sisters attending.[18] By 1975, lay women joined the organization—initially because some of the members were leaving religious life but wanted to maintain their involvement in Las Hermanas. Las Hermanas recognized the significant role of lay women in their work and in the life of the Catholic Church. Membership continued to increase, and by the early 1990s, approximately 700 women belonged to the organization with an average of 200 attending the *asembleas* (annual conferences). Membership currently averages approximately 200 and includes highly educated religious women, and a majority of middle- and working-class laity.[19] Their ethnic and class diversity has given Las Hermanas recognition as "the most creative and successful effort for solidarity in a diverse U.S. Latino reality."[20]

Between 1971 and 1980, Las Hermanas collaborated with PADRES, and collectively they influenced the policy decisions of major Catholic organizations such as the National Conference of Catholic Bishops/United States Catholic Conference (NCCB/USCC) and the Secretariat for Hispanic Affairs of the USCC. Their concerns addressed the institutional representation for the Spanish-speaking, culturally sensitive ministry programs and employment practices. Together they lobbied for the appointment of Chicano bishops and lay Chicano leadership, developed regional Latino pastoral offices, published a joint newsletter for three years, and developed plans for the first Chicano/Latino national pastoral institute, the Mexican American Cultural Center in San Antonio, Texas. The two organizations also helped plan the first and second national *encuentros* held in 1972 and 1977, which ultimately led to a National Pastoral Plan for Latino ministry in 1987.[21]

Of equal significance is the activism of Las Hermanas and PADRES in the civic arena. Members from both organizations participated in student protests for educational rights, the farmworker struggle for union representation, immigrant rights advocacy, Central America solidarity work, and widespread community organizing. Community-based organizations concerned with local empowerment such as Communities Organized for Public Service (COPS) in San Antonio, Texas, United Neighborhoods Organization (UNO), and El Paso Interfaith Service Organization (EPISO) all had representation from Las Hermanas and PADRES. Their activism represents the first time that a critical mass of Latina and Latino religious leaders systematically challenged civic institutions to address ethnic and class discrimination. PADRES and Las Hermanas played an instrumental role in mobilizing and supporting Catholic religious leaders in their efforts to meet the social needs of their ethnic communities. Their efforts clearly brought the Chicano movement into the religious arena and the Catholic Church into the Chicano movement.

By 1980, Las Hermanas decided to focus specifically on issues affecting grassroots Latinas, including moral authority, sexuality, domestic abuse, education, and women's ordination. Their decision to focus on women resulted from the difficulties and great tension in working in a "sanctified patriarchy" where "the power to govern . . . derives from Holy Orders, which is a sacrament reserved to men."[22] Difficulties also occurred between PADRES and Las Hermanas, as some members of PADRES ultimately found it difficult to accept women as mutual partners in leadership. Las Hermanas' conferences and newsletters continued to provide the space to address and collaborate on issues reaching beyond the boundaries of the institutional church. Their work stands in sharp contrast to the silence of the church hierarchy on matters of gender and politics. Las Hermanas provided the source of inspiration for the Latina Catholic theological understandings first published in Ada María Isasi-Díaz and Yolanda Tarango's *Hispanic Women: Prophetic Voice in the Church.*[23] Some members of Las Hermanas subsequently named themselves *mujeristas* and called their beliefs and praxis Mujerista theology in order to distinguish their concerns from a form of white feminism which is mainly concerned with gender oppression.[24] Mujeristas understand that the oppression of Latinas results from the intersection of gender, class, and race/ethnicity. A mujerista identity is nonstatic so that new understandings of oppression can be addressed. As a theology based on "reflective action that has as its goal—liberation," Mujerista theology reflects the engagement in political and religious issues held by Las Hermanas.[25]

Women attracted to Las Hermanas share a commitment to the empowerment of Latino communities, especially women. This "community-centered consciousness" reflects one of the basic characteristics of Chicana feminism, as it is believed that a people cannot be liberated if the women are not free from racism, sexism, and poverty.[26] Many of them also share certain life experiences: working-class origins, a Catholic school education, and varying degrees of oppression in the Roman Catholic Church. Following are three profiles of women initially drawn to Las Hermanas because of its integration of spirituality and social activism.

Rosa Martha Zárate emigrated from Mexico in 1966 as a member of the Sisters of the Blessed Sacrament religious community, which she describes as a "very conventional community." In fact, her community did not support the work of Las Hermanas. Zárate met Las Hermanas representatives in 1970 while her religious community developed a parish school in San Ysidro, California. She recalls:

> Representatives of Las Hermanas came to our community and invited us to a meeting because they wanted to inform us about the reality of our people, how many Mexicana sisters were restricted to

> being maids and dishwashers in seminaries and rectories. I knew that my community was teaching more children for less pay than the Irish sisters and the Italian priest was always scolding us. It was very humiliating.[27]

Initially Zárate thought Las Hermanas too radical as they were very outspoken, and they no longer wore religious habits. She shares, "But I felt ashamed for not responding to what they were asking." She soon joined them in challenging discrimination in and outside of the church. She continues:

> I began going to Las Hermanas meetings. It became a real struggle for me within my religious community. The other nuns became hostile towards me, as I did not remain quiet. They accused me of always being in the streets, of not being a woman of prayer. Finally they told me to change to a different community, leave the convent, or go back to Mexico. I did not want to do any of those choices.[28]

After negotiations between Bishop Gilbert Chávez of San Diego and her superiors, Zárate received permission to become the coordinator of the first Office of Religious Education for the Spanish Speaking in the San Diego diocese. As assistant to Bishop Chavéz, Zárate became the first Mexicana to fill such a position. Influenced by the teachings of liberation theology, Zárate began organizing *comunidades eclesiales de base* (church-based communities) (CEBs) with an emphasis on social analysis and a critical reading of the Bible to discern appropriate strategies for social change. Her superiors prohibited her from sharing her work with the other nuns as they feared the political implications of her work.

In 1974, Latinos comprised 52 percent of the San Diego diocese, then including San Diego, Imperial Valley, Riverside, and San Bernardino Counties. Zárate remembers, "I was working very hard, organizing the people. . . . All the leadership was emerging out of the *comunidades de base*."[29] By 1976 Zárate had organized twenty-seven CEBs throughout the diocese.

In 1978 when the San Bernardino diocese was established, Zárate became coordinator of the Department of Religious Education for the Spanish Speaking (DECH) along with Father Patricio Guillén, of PADRES. Under their leadership, DECH sought to address social injustice, as well as the spiritual needs of Latino Catholics. Zárate's many projects included a diocesan pastoral plan for Latino ministry and the development of the first national guidelines for the certification of Spanish-speaking catechists. By 1985, Zárate and Guillén had established five pastoral centers and forty-five *comunidades eclesiales de base* (CEBs) in the San Bernardino diocese involving families, businesses, and parishes.[30] Their focus consistently included social empowerment for impoverished Latino communities.

In 1986, both Zárate and Guillén were asked to leave DECH. Bishop Phillip Straling branded Zárate a "Marxist" and a "Communist."[31] Her teachings on liberation praxis proved too radical for superiors and many of her clerical peers. Bishop Straling asked for the dismissal of Sister Zárate and pressured

Father Guillén for a voluntary resignation. Zárate ultimately filed a civil law suit against the diocese and bishop charging wrongful termination and defamation of character.

Zárate lost her legal case in 1992, but she has not been deterred from direct involvement in community organizing. Since 1985, she has co-directed Librería del Pueblo, Inc., a nonprofit agency serving over 300,000 immigrants on citizenship matters. Believing that social and economic change is possible through collective action, she continues to establish small CBCs through the Calpulli Project, a network of economic cooperatives in San Bernardino County that emphasize economic self-empowerment and historical and cultural knowledge.[32] A legal clinic, an international sewing cooperative with the Zapatistas, and the first training program for Spanish-speaking day-care providers in San Bernardino County are among her ongoing projects. In a county where approximately 20 percent of Latinos live below the poverty level and public social services are limited, the Calpulli network provides a vision of hope for communities underserved by public resources.[33]

Zárate has extended her vision of international collective action by co-founding El Proyecto de la Red de Intercambio y Comercial Alternativa de Abya Yala (RICAA),[34] a network of fifteen native communities in San Bernardino, Central America, the Caribbean, and Mexico. RICAA focuses on the sustenance of Indigenous communities through alternative economic projects. Zárate helps to direct RICAA workshops in San Bernardino, and she travels frequently to Chiapas, Mexico, to assist six textile cooperatives operated by indigenous women and to participate in the Zapatista struggle as a civil rights observer.

Zárate is also an internationally recognized guitarist, composer, and singer of liberation music, or "La Nueva Canción."[35] Her revolutionary vision of the role of the church *in* society has not faded, despite the tremendous obstacles placed in her path by the institutional church. As she recently stated, "I see myself as a woman who has assumed her historical, cultural, and social responsibility. . . . I have faith in God and that I can change things."[36]

Tess Browne, a dynamic woman of African, Carib, Spanish, French, Irish, and English ancestry and originally from Trinidad, migrated to the United States at the age of twenty with a scholarship to the Franciscan College in Milwaukee. Her plans to become a medical doctor met interference as she struggled over a decision to enter the convent. Ultimately, she opted for religious life as she could "not ignore God's call."[37] She joined the Sisters of St. Francis and remained with them until 1991, when she transferred to the Sisters of Charity of Nazareth.

Browne first met Las Hermanas in 1971 and she quickly "got involved with them on the picket line for the UFW."[38] Support for farmworker rights consistently found a home with Las Hermanas. Exchange of information between regional representatives kept the membership abreast of rapid changes in the labor movement. Browne began attending regional meetings before she attended the Las Hermanas National Conference in 1977. In the mid-1970s, Browne began working full-time with the United Farm Workers (UFW), the

National Farm Worker Ministry, (NFWM), and the Peace and Justice Center in Milwaukee.

The organizing efforts of the UFW required a vast amount of people power, both volunteer and minimally paid staff. In the early 1970s as the UFW organized the boycott against nonunion table grapes, head lettuce, and Gallo wines, César Chávez reached out for support from religious groups. When the UFW closed their boycott office in Milwaukee in 1975 to reassign staff to the fields in California, Tess Browne was asked to work full-time as the boycott director for the state of Wisconsin through her position at the Justice and Peace Center (JPC) in Milwaukee. Funds from the Wisconsin Migrant Mission supported her boycott work at JPC, where she worked closely with the union in Chicago to "keep the boycott strong." She also traveled between the Midwest and California to make sure Proposition 14 got on the ballot in 1976.[39] As director of the Wisconsin boycott, she garnered the support of religious and secular groups, picketed, and faced her days in court as Gallo tried to get an injunction against picketing. As a citizen of Trinidad at the time, Tess risked her residency in the United States for farm labor justice.

After serving on the NFWM board from 1975 to 1978, Browne relocated to Texas, where she served as director of the National Farmworker Service Center in San Juan. Appointed in 1981 by the UFW as citizen advocates before the Texas legislature, Sister Browne and Sister Carol Ann Messina successfully lobbied for legislation to abolish *el cortito,* the short-handled hoe previously outlawed by California's State Supreme Court in 1975.[40] This twenty-four-inch-long farming tool required workers to stoop for numerous hours, causing debilitating back problems and premature arthritis. Browne reflected on the legislative battle, "We wanted workers' comp or unemployment comp to be the top priority. The workers said el cortito is the first priority, the right to stand upright, to work with dignity. That taught me much."[41] Browne who served as "a major force testifying at committee and House hearings on behalf of the workers" continues to serve on the board of NFWM.[42] After a 1997 board meeting, Browne "kicked off" a UFW statewide march and rally in Watsonville, California, in support of strawberry pickers. The march drew 30,000 people and reflects the resurgence of the UFW under the leadership of Arturo Rodríguez, Chávez's son-in-law.[43]

Besides her commitment to the farm labor movement, Browne helped to establish the Hidalgo County Women's Political Caucus in Texas, to educate grassroots women on electoral politics. Drawing on her extensive background in organizing, she is now completing a graduate degree in human services from the College of Public and Community Services at the University of Massachusetts at Boston.

María Antonietta Berriozábal provides another example of a Latina integrating her faith with her politics. Berriozábal came into contact with a Las Hermanas member, Sister María Carolina Flores, in 1985 when she was invited to Our Lady of the Lake University in San Antonio, Texas, to discuss the Catholic bishop's efforts to write a pastoral letter on women in the church. "That meeting was the first time that someone helped me make the connection between my church and my politics. I was very involved in my church and in my city, but the two worlds did not meet," she said.[44] As the first Latina to be elected to the San Antonio city council, Berriozábal had experienced her share of alienation. Berriozábal explains:

> I had been in politics for five years. It was very lonely, as the political system did not welcome my philosophy of service, of advocating for the vulnerable people. I kept losing my issues, but there was something inside, a faith that I was not wrong.[45]

Following her meeting with Sister Flores, Berriozábal met Sister Yolanda Tarango, also of Las Hermanas, through their mutual work for the homeless in San Antonio. Tarango then introduced her to another member, Ada María Isasi-Díaz. Berriozábal began attending Las Hermanas conferences where she met many other women, including Sister Rosa Martha Zárate and Sister Tess Browne. She describes the impression they made on her:

> I loved to listen to them talk. They gave me the "language" for my Chicanisma, for integrating my faith and my spirituality into my politics. They accompanied me in my journey as a politician. Through them I met other women. We prayed together. I don't see how any women can do what is needed without a support group of women.[46]

Growing up in San Antonio in a close-knit community, Berriozábal witnessed the hard labor of her parents and their profound commitment to justice. She came to know the Catholic social teachings not through attendance at church but learning in her home, through her parents and grandparents: "They taught me that there are basic things, like justice and respect. That we must practice being fair to people; that there are rich and poor and that is not good. The big teachings were at home."[47] Berriozábal took this sense of justice with her into her political career. Unwilling to engage in "back door politics," she mobilized Latino communities into neighborhood associations that approached the entire city council on significant issues, including surface water projects, tax abatement, zoning, nuclear waste storage, and tax revenue. She also appointed numerous Latinas to city boards and commissions and organized Hispanas Unidas, a nonprofit organization for the personal and community empowerment of Latinas. By the time of her second term, no other candidate ran against Berriozábal. "I was strong because I was connected to the community. They knew I was not alone."[48] Berriozábal's concerns focus clearly on the needs of the economically disadvantaged, the homeless, women, families, and AIDS victims. She speaks of her motivations: "I thought of politics as my ministry. It was my way of working out the gospel beliefs and working for justice, for my people, but particularly the poor."[49]

After five successful terms, Berriozábal ran for mayor in 1991 and won 47 percent of the vote. Although she failed to win the election, the near majority vote proved that many understood "another way of doing politics." For Berriozábal, this was a great affirmation as young politicians now tell her they want to "do it her way" with the people. Berriozábal did not accept losing the election as an obstacle, and in 1998 she campaigned for the Twentieth-District Congressional seat left vacant by Henry B. González. Her commitment and grassroots campaigning won her broadbased support from educators, entrepreneurs, health care workers, artists, and many others. She also won the honor of having a *corrido* written about her work by a San Antonio–based band, Grupo División. As historian, Antonio Castañeda stated "that a corrido was written about her is a clear sign of María's importance to the community."[50]

Despite Berriozábal's loss of the congressional election, her commitment to the community has not wavered. She provides consulting to several non-profit organizations, including the Esperanza Peace and Justice Center that serves poor women and working-class people through the arts. She sits on many educational boards and is a member of the Women Leadership Conference of the Americas in Washington, D.C., a group involved in inter-American dialogue. She continues to bridge spirituality and politics in her work. Berriozábal says, "I want to continue the double road that I began with Las Hermanas, the two worlds of faith and activism."[51]

Zárate, Browne, and Berriozábal's involvement with Las Hermanas in the 1970s and 1980s supported their faith and their politics, and in many ways it planted or nurtured the seeds for activism beyond the reach of the organization and their church. Their active involvement in Las Hermanas has subsided over the last several years, but the experience of mobilizing with other women remains central to their stories of civic engagement. As Mujeristas, *feministas*, or socially responsible women, Zárate, Browne, and Berriozábal offer a new understanding of Latina Catholic political participation.

NOTES

1. "Grassroot" refers to economically disadvantaged women.

2. Circular letter to prospective members from Sister Gloria Gallardo, S.H.G. (October 20, 1970).

3. Interview with Yolanda Tarango (August 2, 1998). San Antonio, TX. In possession of the author.

4. Interview with Tarango.

5. Sister Gloria Gráciella Gallardo, to Leadership Conference of Women Religious, 17 November 1971, Las Hermanas Collection, Box 4, Mexican American Studies Department. Our Lady of the Lake University, San Antonio, Texas. Emphasis added.

6. Nationwide, 20.4 percent of "families of Spanish heritage" headed by two parents lived below the poverty level in comparison to 8.6 percent of Euro-American families. *1970 Census of Population. General Social and Economic Characteristics, U.S. Summary.* PC(1)-C1.

7. Olga Rodríguez, ed. *The Politics of Chicano Liberation* (New York: Pathfinder, 1977).

8. "Politics of mass protest" refers to a stance of resistance and strategic community mobilization that demanded change of the status quo. See Carlos Muñoz Jr., *Youth, Identity, and Power: The Chicano Movement* (New York: Verso Books, 1989), 171.

9. Interview with Gregoria Ortega (April 21, 1997), Los Angeles. In possession of the author.

10. PADRES first met in October 1969 as an organization of Chicano clergy to address the pastoral and socioeconomic issues facing Mexican American and other Spanish-speaking Catholics.

11. *Yo Soy Joaquín* by Rodolfo "Corky" González is considered an epic poem reflecting the Chicano struggle for self-determination. The Crusade for Social Justice began in Denver, Colorado, in 1969 under the leadership of Corky González. Chicano youth and adults mobilized under a cultural nationalist agenda that influenced the ideology and politics of the Chicano movement.

12. The leadership structure would change to a national coordinating team in 1972.

13. *Informes* (19 September 1971): 2. *Informes* is the newsletter of Las Hermanas.

14. Ibid., 2.

15. Ibid., 4.

16. *La Historia de Las Hermanas* (n.p.: Privately printed, 1979), 25.

17. Interview with Tarango. San Antonio. In possession of the author.

18. While this conference was the second time that Las Hermanas gathered, more recent archival literature recognizes the Houston meeting as preparatory and the Santa Fe meeting as the first national conference.

19. The membership reflects the general reduction of women religious in the past thirty years.

20. Ana María Díaz-Stevens, "Latinas and the Church," in *Hispanic Catholic Culture in the U.S.: Issues and Concerns*, ed. Jay P. Dolan and Allan Figueroa Deck S.J. (Notre Dame, IN: University of Notre Dame, 1994), 268.

21. Although this national plan never received adequate funding from the National Catholic Conference of Bishops for implementation, it continues to represent the efforts of Latino clergy, sisters, and laity to shape their participation in the church.

22. Díaz-Stevens, "Latinas and the Church," 245.

23. Ada María Isasi-Díaz and Yolanda Tarango, *Hispanic Women: Prophetic Voice in the Church* (San Francisco: Harper & Row, 1988). Members of Las Hermanas were among the informants for this publication. Although not all members of Las Hermanas use the term *mujerista* for self-identification, many were instrumental in its formulations. Mujerista theology is further developed in Ada María Isasi-Díaz, *En la Lucha: Elaborating a Mujerista Theology* (Minneapolis, MN: Fortress, 1993).

24. Ada Maria Isasi-Díaz, "Roundtable Discussion: Mujeristas—Who We Are and What We Are About," *Journal of Feminist Studies in Religion* 8 (Spring 1992). See also a collection of articles on mujerista theology in Ada María Isasi-Díaz, *Mujerista Theology* (Maryknoll NY: Orbis Books, 1996).

25. Isasi-Díaz, "Roundtable Discussion," 108.

26. See Chapter 5 in Vicki Ruiz, *From out of the Shadows: Mexican Women in Twentieth-Century America* (New York: Oxford University Press, 1998), 105–126.

27. Interview with Rosa Martha Zárate (March 6, 1997). Los Angeles. In possession of the author.

28. Ibid.

29. Ibid.

30. "Hispanics Now 'Enter Desert, Hard Part of the Journey,' " *National Catholic Reporter* (September 5, 1985): 7; "Two Hispanic Centers Dedicated," *San Bernardino and Riverside Newsletter* (October 28, 1981): 6–7.

31. *Rosa Martha Zárate Plaintiff v. Roman Catholic Diocese of San Bernardino*, Case 244 193. Filed March 8, 1989, 7.

32. Lara Medina, "Calpulli: A Chicano Self-help Organization," *La Gente* (1990). See also Gilbert R. Cadena and Lara Medina, "Liberation Theology and Social Change: Chicanas and Chicanos in the Catholic Church," in *Chicanas and Chicanos in Contemporary Society*, ed. Roberto M. DeAnda (Needham Heights, MA: Allyn & Bacon, 2001), 106–108.

33. *1990 Census of Population and Housing Characteristics for Census Tracts and Block Numbering Areas Riverside–San Bernardino* (Washington, DC: U.S. Department of Commerce, 1993).

34. Project for the Exchange of Alternative Commerce in the Land of Our Ancestors (my translation).

35. "Nueva Canción," or new song, refers to music with social justice themes.

36. Interview with Rosa Martha Zárate (July 18, 2000).

37. Interview with Tess Browne (May 20, 1997), by Telephone, Boston. In possession of the author.

38. Ibid.

39. Ibid.

40. "Short Hoe Ban Victory for UFW," *McAllen (Texas) Monitor*, June 18, 1981: D-1; *NFWM: 75 Years of Farm Worker Ministry 1920–1995* (n.p.: Privately printed, 1995), 35. See also Susan Ferris and Ricardo Sandoval, *The Fight in the Fields: César Chávez and the Farmworkers' Movement* (New York: Harcourt Brace, 1997), 206–207.

41. *NFWM: 75 Years of Farm Worker Ministry*, 35.

42. "Short Hoe Ban Victory for UFW," sec. D-1; *NFWM: 75 Years of Farm Worker Ministry*, 35; Ferris and Sandoval, *Fight in the Fields*, 206–207.

43. March in Support of Farmworkers Draws Thousands," *San Francisco Chronicle*, (April 14, 1997): A-13; "Thousands Take Part in UFW March," *San Jose Mercury News* (April 14, 1997): A-1; "The UFW's Resurgence," *San Francisco Chronicle* (September 1, 1997): A-22.

44. Interview with María Antonietta Berriozábal (June 15, 2000). San Antonio, TX. In possession of the author.

45. Ibid.

46. Ibid.

47. Ibid.

48. Ibid. For an in-depth analysis of Berriozábal's political strategies, see Rodolfo Rosales, *The Illusion of Inclusion* (Austin: University of Texas Press, 2000).

49. Interview with Berriozábal.

50. "An Open Letter from María Antonietta Berriozábal," campaign pamphlet, María for Congress Campaign Headquarters, San Antonio, Texas.

51. Interview with Berriozábal.

7

Spiritual Affirmation and Empowerment: The Mexican American Cultural Center

Socorro Castañeda-Liles

This study of Mexican Americans demonstrates that, despite the structural problems of the U.S. Catholic Church, U.S. Latina/o Catholics find empowerment through spiritual affirmation. Latino/a practices of faith and the search for a respected space in the U.S. Catholic Church are transforming this social institution.[1]

This sociological analysis of the life histories of Mexican Americans uses religion as a theoretical lens. First, I sketch the social movements with ties to the Mexican American Cultural Center (MACC). Next, I address the reasons behind the founding of the cultural center and discuss women's contributions. Then I explore two ways through which Mexican American Catholics have exercised their voice and agency to claim a religious space in the U.S. Catholic Church from which social change is envisioned.[2] The first of these is through Virgilio Elizondo's Mexican American Catholic theological influence on MACC. I refer to this section as "affirmation through historical retrieval." I apply Antonio Gramsci's theory of organic versus traditional intellectuals to Elizondo. In the second section on symbolic capital, I use Pierre Bourdieu's theories of symbolic and social capital to explore three ways that Mexican American Catholicism challenges the exclusionary history of the religious institution.

I conducted the fieldwork for this study between September 1999 and April 2000 using a questionnaire tailored to fit the respondents' connection to MACC. It covered three broad areas: (1) the reasons behind the founding of MACC; (2) how symbolic capital is produced; and (3) Catholicism and ministry. Fourteen in-depth interviews were conducted: eight men and six women participated. Of these, four were priests, five were sisters, four were lay men, and one was a lay woman.[3]

Social Movements with Political and Religious Ties to MACC

United States, Latin America, and Europe

MACC has sociopolitical and religious ties to four social movements that took place during the 1960s: The Chicana/o movement, the United Farm Workers movement, Christian base communities, and the Second Vatican Council.

In the United States, the Chicana/o movement confronted the social institutions that marginalized and rejected them and their ways of knowing. Among the first institutions to be challenged was the educational system, and the movement quickly spread throughout college campuses of the Southwest. Young people of Mexican ancestry who called themselves "Chicanos" and "Chicanas" not only collectively fought for social justice but also reclaimed their Mexican pre-Columbian heritage. They insisted on being not just Mexican or merely wanting to assimilate to Euro-American ways but on being bicultural. At the same time, the United Farm Workers movement, spearheaded by César Chávez and Dolores Huerta, fought for the rights of farmworkers. Both of these movements demanded respect and opportunities for Chicanos, just as in other parts of the world other waves of resistance and calls for justice were forming, eventually influencing Latinas/os in the United States.[4]

> As Americanization of the church was increasing here [United States], a different understanding of the church's mission was developing in the rest of the world.[5]

Grassroots movements were spreading quickly throughout Latin America among the most economically marginalized of society. With clergy concentrating their efforts on the pastoral needs of people in urban areas, the rural poor were largely left with no religious leadership and support and so became agents of their own faith, forming Christian base communities (*comunidades de base*) throughout Latin America. These groups met to learn about the teachings of the Bible in the context of their everyday struggles for social justice and economic equity.[6]

Europe: Vatican II

In Europe, Vatican Council II (1962–1965) took place and challenged the missionary way the Catholic Church related to its members. The council reflected upon how the Catholic Church related to the laity and on the importance of culture. Many believed that if the church was indeed for the people, then it had to walk with them, starting from their unique cultural and sociohistorical locations. This also meant that the laity had the right and responsibility to take an active role within their own parishes.

Latin America after Vatican II

The bishops of Latin America felt that the needs of their people had to be discussed in light of Vatican II. CELAM (Episcopal Council of Latin America)

Unidentified Latina nuns joining the United Farm Workers in a nonviolent protest march in California (Courtesy of the Walter P. Reuther Library, Wayne State University)

met in Medellin, Colombia, in 1968 and later in Puebla, Mexico, where the bishops specifically addressed issues pertinent to the socioeconomic situation of Latin America, including poverty, violence, and education. As a result of these conferences, the preferential option for the poor became the priority of the Latin American Catholic Church, leading to the birth of liberation theology. Spearheaded by Gustavo Gutierréz, liberation theology became a new way of reading and interpreting the Bible that placed the struggles and reality of people at the center of biblical interpretation.[7]

The United States

In 1969 in the Southwest a group of Latino priests gathered and formed Padres Asociados para Derechos Religiosos, Educativos y Sociales (PADRES). PADRES stemmed from the commitment of a group of priests to support the efforts of the United Farm Workers movement. Founded by a group of priests that met to explore ways to support César Chávez in his struggle for farmworkers' rights, PADRES provided religious leadership and support to those involved in that movement.[8]

A year later the idea of an organization for women and women's ministry took shape through the efforts of Sister Gloria Gallardo of the Holy Spirit

Sisters and Sister Gregoria Ortega of Victory Knoll Sisters. Unlike PADRES, whose members were only Latino priests, Las Hermanas was a group of Latina and non-Latina religious sisters and lay women.[9] In April of 1971, Sister Gloria and Sister Gregoria gathered about fifty religious sisters in Houston, Texas. Their purpose was to work with the Spanish-speaking communities to promote respect and equality for all women in the church, lay and religious.[10]

Formation of the Mexican American Cultural Center

PADRES and Las Hermanas gained the respect of both the Mexican American community and the Catholic Church by relating to the concerns of Mexican Americans from within the official church.[11] PADRES and Las Hermanas had been in existence and working with the Mexican American community by the time the idea for a pastoral center emerged, and both were staunch supporters of it. Virgilio Elizondo is considered by many to be MACC's founder. His vision for a place where Mexican Americans could learn and explore their ways of knowing and practicing faith became MACC's central purpose.

The idea of a pastoral center emerged at the first National Retreat of PADRES in Santa Fe, New Mexico, in 1972. Reflecting on the place of Mexican Americans in the U.S. Catholic Church, these priests were particularly interested in finding means of moving Latina/o, particularly Mexican American, ways of knowing and practicing faith from the margins to the center of the U.S. Catholic Church.

In 1972, Father Tom Syte of San Angelo and Father Ron Anderson presented the idea of PADRES to the annual assembly of the Texas Catholic Conference in Austin. At the Assumption Seminary Library in San Antonio, Texas, the idea of a pastoral center became a reality and was named: the Mexican American Cultural Center. Bishop Patrick Flores, the head of MACC's board of directors, appointed Virgilio Elizondo as first director. MACC was housed in an unused building at the Assumption Seminary for one dollar rent per year, according to Elizondo. Under the leadership of Elizondo and through the dedicated work of PADRES, Las Hermanas, Sister Angela Erevia of the Missionary Catechists of the Divine Providence, Yolanda Tarango of the Sisters of Charity of the Incarnate Word and lay leaders like Ruben Alfaro and Leonard Anguiano, among others, MACC was founded.[12]

According to Elizondo, the first document about a possible pastoral center referred to the center as the "Hispanic Pastoral Center." However, there was only one non-Chicano member in PADRES, Anthony Stevens-Arroyo, a Puerto Rican. Stevens-Arroyo suggested that promoting the center as a place that addressed the pastoral and cultural needs of Hispanics was inadequate and "biased" since they were mostly Mexican Americans working in the Southwest: "You will be considered arrogant and lose credibility. Do something truly new and effective for your own people in your own geographic and historic region. If you succeed, you will render a great service to the rest of us."[13] Elizondo comments:

> He was truly prophetic! Precisely because we were so historically and geographically defined, so particular, we would, without ever claiming to be, become universal. In our own little story, others would discover their own story and the greater story of humanity.[14]

One of the reasons for the success of MACC is that it was geographically situated in a homogenous community and was initially operated by Mexican Americans. The strong presence of Mexican Americans in San Antonio and the Southwest in general became the ethnic support mechanism crucial in guaranteeing the survival and existence of MACC. The organization's ability to address and understand not only Mexican American but also Latino and non-Latino ways of knowing and practicing faith stems from a deep understanding of its own historic reality.

However, the question remains: Why a pastoral center? According to Sister Rosa María Icaza, Ruben Alfaro, Irma Mireles, and other respondents cited there was a need to create a place where Mexican Americans could come together to research from within their own geographic and historic reality who they were as bicultural people.[15]

MACC's development is complex. The cultural center is a product of the Southwest through the efforts of PADRES, Las Hermanas, Elizondo, and many lay leaders, yet its intellectual roots did not sprout only out of the Southwest. Scholars from Latin America and Europe also played a significant part in the formation of MACC's philosophy.

The influence of the East Asian Pastoral Institute on MACC came by way of people like Alfonso Nebraska, Teresita Nitoreah, José Calle, and Eves Raguin. They taught that faith is better understood when people let go of the things that comfort them in order to place themselves in the collective reality of others.

MACC was also influenced by European religious thinkers like Casiano Floristán, Luis Maldonado, Juan Mateos (editor of *La Nueva Biblia Española*), and Luis Alonso Schökel (vice-rector of the Pontifical Biblical Institute), Jacques Audinet, and Abel Pasquie. They contributed to the development of MACC by underscoring the necessity of understanding the Bible in light of the living faith of the people. First, the Bible must be understood from its own sociocultural and historical setting, and for this to happen creativity must be part of liturgical celebrations; second, this must be accompanied by the recognition of the spirituality of religious expressions and an analysis of the socioeconomic and political structures of people's lives.

From Latin America, MACC benefited from the expertise of people like Edgar Beltrán, José Marins,[16] Gustavo Gutierréz, Enrique Dussel, Francisco Aguilera, and Sister Carmen Aurora Gómez who emphasized, first, the need to work with people at the grassroots level, taking into account the social teachings of the church; second, the need to rewrite history from the perspective of the people whose voices had historically been ignored; and third, the need to understand all this within the complexity of *mestizaje*.[17] These intellectual regional, national, and international contributions are the three pillars on which MACC stands.

MACC is the first National Catholic Institute for Pastoral Leadership and Language Studies in the United States and also the first pastoral institute in the nation to receive initial accreditation by the U.S. Catholic Conference Commission on Certification and Accreditation.[18] Founded in the early 1970s to address the pastoral needs of Mexican Americans, MACC has since developed to be inclusive of Latinos of all nationalities. To this day, its strength lies in teaching and forming leaders from within the Mexican American experience.

Pilares de Nuestra Comunidad: Religious Women's Social Agency

Lay and religious women have played a fundamental part in bringing a blend of empowerment and faith to MACC's ethos of individual voices and a strong sense of community through shared authority.

Since its inception MACC has benefited from the talents and contributions of its co-founding organization—Las Hermanas. Lara Medina in her dissertation "Las Hermanas" shows how three members spearheaded the Mini-Pastoral Program, a program centered on Latina/o cultures, religious traditions, and social concerns.[19] Furthermore, between 1974 and 1976, Hermana Sylvia Sedillo directed and contributed to the development of MACC's Language Institute. Today, the Mini-Pastoral Program and the Language Institute continue to thrive and are two of three programs that received accreditation by the U.S. Catholic Conference, Commission of Certification and Accreditation.[20]

Like all institutions, the U.S. Catholic Church has been challenged by women's increasingly vocal assertion of their rights. MACC is no exception. Serving as cofounders, board members, and faculty, Las Hermanas contributed to the spiritual and consciousness development of MACC. Their feminist consciousness challenged ecclesiastical patriarchal conceptions of who is allowed to be a co-equal in the church. Las Hermanas faced gender discrimination at MACC, experiencing what Arlie Hochschild refers to as "the second shift,"[21] for besides their responsibilities as faculty, Las Hermanas were expected to "sign up for cooking duties."[22] Male students, most of whom were seminarians and priests, constantly questioned Las Hermanas' Catholic feminist agenda. Unfortunately, the continuous tension between Las Hermanas and conservative seminarians and priests led to the termination of some contracts of Las Hermanas members; others opted to leave the center.

However, the efforts of Las Hermanas for gender inclusion and equality at MACC were not in vain, for they laid the groundwork for women at MACC. In the mid-1990s, MACC faced a critical financial crisis that created the opportunity to demonstrate the significant contributions of women in the church.

By the mid-1990s, the old building that had housed the center for almost twenty-eight years was rapidly deteriorating. When Sister María Elena González, MACC's current president, took office in January 1994, most of the money was used to keep the building standing. Student enrollment was low. There was barely enough money for employee salaries and, consequently, staff morale was low. González approached her congregation, the Sisters of Mercy, and they lent her $150,000 dollars at no interest to help sustain MACC.

Once again, as in the 1970s, religious women's social agency made itself palpable in the social infrastructure of MACC. In August of 1994, González hired Sister Jane Hotstream of the Sisters of Mercy as development director, and later she appointed Rubén Escobedo as campaign committee chair. With the help of staff members and volunteers, they raised $6 million, exceeding their goal by $1 million. This money from religious communities, public and private organizations, and individual donations covered the $5-million-dollar payment for a new facility and left MACC with $1 million.

On April 9, 2000, the 50,000-square-foot complex opened its doors to the public. It is equipped with a language lab, small meeting rooms, a lecture hall, several classrooms, four dormitory buildings, a student lounge, an administrative building, a chapel, a bookstore/gift shop, and a shrine to Our Lady of Guadalupe.

The commitment of Las Hermanas and The Sisters of Mercy to establish, develop, and expand MACC demonstrates that Latinas in the church blend their self-determination for a respected space and *compromiso* (commitment) to the church with a deep sense of community. Las Hermanas and the Sisters of Mercy are examples of the critical role women's religious groups had and continue to have in the struggle for the ongoing creation of an inclusive church.

Affirmation through Historical Retrieval

The socioeconomic and political circumstances from which people theologize are crucial in understanding why Latino Popular Catholicism plays an important part in the lives of Latina/o Catholics.

In a society where Latinas/os and their cultural perceptions are constantly challenged, rejected, and caricatured, Catholic expressions of faith function as a collective self-affirming mechanism. For many Latina/o Catholics, the essence of life *en la frontera* (on the border) is rendered meaningful through religious cultural faith expressions.[23] Thus, in the reenactment of popular religious events across the nation, such as the apparitions of Our Lady of Guadalupe to Juan Diego, *Las Posadas,* and *El Viacrusis,* one sees how Latina/o Catholics give new meanings to these events to fit their sociopolitical situation.[24] For example, in my research in San Jose, California, I have seen how the posadas have been reinterpreted to mirror the contemporary situation of Latina/o immigrants who come to this country in search of a new home and an opportunity for a dignified life.

MACC gives Latinas/os a unique opportunity to find public affirmation for their particular Mexican American ways of knowing and practicing their faith. Gloria Anzaldúa argues that this life in the U.S.–Mexico border is often an experience of violence and fear, where one is pulled every which way, leaving one with a feeling of profound incertitude.[25] MACC offers affirmation for those who live out this difficult borderlands existence.

Amid such incertitude, Latinas/os influence and challenge U.S. religious institutions such as the Catholic Church, consequently revising Antonio Gramsci's theory of traditional versus organic intellectuals.

> Every "essential" social group which emerges into history out of the preceding economic structure has found (at least in all history up to the present) categories of intellectuals already in existence and which seem indeed to represent a historical continuity uninterrupted even by the most complicated and radical changes in political and social forms.[26]

For Gramsci, ecclesiastics are representative of the category of "traditional intellectuals" for they are "organically bound to the landed aristocracy." That is, these traditional intellectuals experience their uninterrupted historical continuity, special qualification, and "monopoly of a number of important services" such as "religious ideology, schools, education, morality, justice, charity, and good works."[27] However, if indeed in Gramscian thought church leaders are traditional intellectuals, then what issues arise when we apply his premise to the United States?

I propose that, given the historic marginalization of people of color in the United States, his conceptualization of ecclesiastics no longer holds true. Latina/o church leaders have been marginalized in U.S. society within their own religious institutions. Elizondo's example not only challenges Gramsci's notion of "ecclesiastics" but also calls for a broadening of Gramsci's theory of "organic intellectuals" to include the very ecclesiastics that he considers "traditional intellectuals."

For example, Elizondo's ability to ground theology in the past and everyday experience of Mexican Americans has led many to consider him the "Father of U.S. Catholic Theology." His social position as a Mexican American and a renowned theologian has been essential to the success of MACC and in helping Mexican American Catholics come to understand and appreciate their culture, struggle, and history.

Elizondo's unique standpoint makes him what Gramsci refers to as an "organic intellectual."[28] One of the attributes of an organic intellectual is the cyclical movement from the everyday struggles and life of people and community to the world of knowledge. Out of this experience, the intellectual generates new knowledge from the everyday life experiences of people. Roberto Piña says of Elizondo: "He knew that collectively as a people we needed to get that affirmation and that integrity . . . that we were good people. That we had a history, that we had maintained our faith in spite of the church. If anyone can speak about us, he can because he knows us."[29] Elizondo's ability to relate to the pain, joys and struggles of Mexican Americans stems from his personal experience growing up Mexican American in San Antonio, Texas, Piña said: "Father Elizondo wanted us to look at the genius of our parents that raised us on much lower than minimum wage, you know and that is what he affirmed in us first. He was the first person to help us."[30]

Elizondo's affirmation of Mexican Americans as "good people" was a common thread throughout my interviews when I asked about his influence on MACC and about Latina/o Catholicism in general. Respondents' comments that "MACC is about bringing back *la dignidad de nuestro pueblo*" (the sense of self-worth of our people) reflect Elizondo's influence. His life, work, and experience as a Mexican American priest revises Gramsci's intellectual understanding of ecclesiastics and modifies Gramsci's notion of organic intellectuals to include marginalized clergy.

Roberto Piña, a grassroots activist and faculty member at MACC, comments that "many [Mexican Americans] find that in their own families and communities they have practices of faith for which they could give no explanation. Nevertheless, through those expressions they have been able to maintain their faith."[31] Piña stated that many of the people that come to MACC come not fully understanding the history or reasons behind religious practices and found explanations at the center.

Paulo Freire's contention that individuals have the knowledge and ability to act as agents of social change[32] is borne out in Elizondo's life and theology which blends leadership, in the Gramscian tradition, and the Freirerian approach to consciousness. That is, his commitment to religion, faith, and social justice calls forth the spiritual self to embody affirmation and empowerment for social justice and change.

Building on the teachings of Elizondo, MACC adopted a Freireian approach to leadership formation by beginning with what the people already know and can relate to. The center became a space where Latina/o, particularly Mexican American values, traditions, and popular Catholic worldview are warmly affirmed and some Euro-American Catholic and cultural values are questioned.

Symbolic Capital

Through the Instituto de Liturgia Hispana, music production, and leadership training, MACC has been able to claim space in the U.S. Catholic Church through the production of "symbolic capital." As Pierre Bourdieu argues, symbols accrue value the more they are borrowed freely by others. The more the Catholic Church as a whole borrows Latina/o religious practices, the more value such practices gain.[33]

According to Arturo Pérez, through the efforts of Father John Gallen S.J. of the Center of Pastoral Liturgy of the University of Notre Dame, Indiana, and Pablo Sedillo of the Secretariat for Hispanic Affairs, Washington D.C., a meeting was held at MACC to explore the need for the liturgy to reflect the religious customs, language, and reality of Hispanics. This meeting led to the birth of the Instituto de Liturgia Hispana in 1979.[34] The institute engaged in the study, development, and promotion of the liturgical celebrations of Latinas/os in the United States. It emphasized the context of liturgical celebrations in the lives of the people and their ways of knowing and of practicing faith. My interviewees referred to the Instituto de Liturgia Hispana as a respected space, one where respect for culture in liturgy is shown.[35] This is demonstrated in placing culture at the center of liturgy by taking faith-oriented cultural expressions and incorporating them into religion and worship. To disseminate these ideas, the Instituto published guidelines for worship and material on the importance of popular religiosity among Latinas/os. Furthermore, a group of MACC faculty travels throughout the United States, Latin America, and Europe to give workshops on working with multicultural and diverse parish communities.

Today, according to Arturo Pérez, the Instituto has established an official relationship with the National Federation of Diocesan Liturgical Commissions. It has also assisted in the Spanish translation of official texts for the Bishops Committee on the Liturgy (BCL). In addition, Sister Rosa María Icaza, a faculty member at MACC and former president of the Insitituto, said that the Instituto de Liturgia Hispana has assisted in the liturgy preparation of national events sponsored by the church such as "Encuentro 2000."[36]

Affirmation through *Flor y Canto*

Carlos Rosas, one of the first Mexican American composers in the United States to gain fame and popularity in the United States, particularly in the Southwest, has strong ties to the Mexican American Cultural Center. It was through it that he changed his traditional way of doing liturgical music.

Rosas's education, training, and experience in liturgical music stemmed from the Latin polyphonic music style of the Middle Ages. He opposed the use of guitars, the accordion, and trumpets in church choirs arguing that "the church was not a *cantina* (bar)."[37] According to Rosas, he owes his conversion to Archbishop Flores of San Antonio, Texas.

In 1973 as part of the first anniversary celebration, MACC sponsored a choir contest. Rosas and his choir entered the contest, sure that they would win. To his surprise, they did not. Puzzled, he asked Archbishop Flores why not. Flores told Rosas that his choir sang beautifully but by not encouraging congregational participation, he did not follow the Vatican II guidelines for liturgical music. This conversation prompted Rosas to reflect differently on the meaning and purpose of liturgical music. Rosas's second encounter with MACC was during a mass at San Juan de Los Lagos Parish in San Antonio, Texas, where the director of MACC's print shop heard Rosas's choir. Amazed by the choir's songs, he asked Rosas who had written them. Fascinated by his music, he recruited Rosas to become director of MACC's music department.

That same year, Rosas began to publish. Rubén Alfaro, MACC's development director, helped Rosas produce his first songs, one of which was "Rosas del Tepeyac mass" in honor of Our Lady de Guadalupe. Shortly after its publication, it sold out and was reprinted. Later that year, Rosas published other songs in *Modern Liturgy*'s special issue on culture. Rosas, along with Father Robert Macker, published ten songs in Spanish that were later published under the tittle *Diez Cantos para la Misa* (Ten Songs for Mass). Rosas's music not only became popular in the U.S. Catholic Church but also in other religious traditions.

Rosas's song "Aleluya" became one of the most popular songs in the U.S. Spanish-speaking church. It soon transcended the Catholic tradition through its inclusion in several Protestant hymnals. The Methodists translated the song into English and published it in *The United Methodist Hymnal*. "Aleluya" was later included in the hymnals of the Baptists, Lutherans, and the Disciples of Christ, who also published three other songs by Rosas.[38]

Not everybody welcomed his songs. The song "El Profeta del Barrio" was banned in one parish in Texas because the priest thought the song "invited people to revolt and create disorder in the church."[39] For Rosas, songs are a form of theology: "Liturgical songs must reflect the struggles and the traditions of *el pueblo* (the people) even if they may make some clergy uncomfortable. Liturgical songs should be able to communicate and speak to the reality of el pueblo—*de corazón a corazón* (from heart to heart)."[40]

Leadership Training

The production of symbolic capital develops through a complex process. Leadership training as the third illustration of symbolic capital is one example. For Pierre Bourdieu, symbolic capital, besides the production of symbols, can also be "the acquisition of a reputation for competence and an image of respectability and honourability that are easily converted into political positions as a local or national *notable*."[41] According to Díaz-Stevens and Stevens-Arroyo, pastoral centers have a tendency to produce symbolic capital as opposed to social capital—the social networks necessary to bring about social change.[42] Some say that MACC primarily produces symbolic capital. But can it generate social capital?

According to Elizondo, "the founders [of MACC] knew that there was a need for more lay leaders in the church and in politics."[43] The center's alumni include bishops, superior generals, religious sisters, and lay people who, inspired by MACC, have pursued doctoral studies and become community leaders and university faculty. According to Moisés Sandoval, "in its first ten years 9,000 persons, half of them Anglo laypersons, clergy, and religious took short or long courses on Hispanic ministry."[44]

One question remains: Has MACC, through its theology, pastoral training, and leadership formation helped shape faith-based empowerment and leadership in parish communities? There are no documented case studies on the impact MACC has had on parish life, but my initial research in places like Sacred Heart Parish in San Jose, California, shows that, through the teachings of MACC, the church has taken an active role in the leadership formation of Latino/a Catholics.

In an interview, Monsignor Mateo Sheedy, the pastor of this parish, stated that leadership in liturgical music and ministry—particularly *el despertar de nuevo* (the reawakening)—as well as education, community outreach, and organizing are all equally essential in his pastoral and theological practices. Sheedy's efforts include the establishment of the annual Juan Diego full scholarship to Santa Clara University for a Latina/o student that demonstrates commitment to education and the Catholic Church. Other church-based community projects involve Sacred Heart Nativity School and a 147-unit affordable housing complex, both of which opened in 2001.[45]

Through the teachings of Elizondo and other faculty at MACC like Rosa María Icaza and visiting faculty like Gustavo Gutierréz and José Marins of Brazil, whose expertise includes the formation of Christian base communities, MACC has contributed to the shaping of his ministry. For Monsignor Sheedy, the parish must serve not only as a space in which the community can find spiritual comfort and nourishment but also as a place to train people to exercise their voice and agency on behalf of parish and civic life.[46] In these various ways, MACC's leadership formation demonstrates how symbolic capital, when applied to parish and civic life, generates social capital.

Conclusion

Organizations like the Mexican American Cultural Center have had tremendous influence on the Mexican American Catholic community. They have transformed pressures and tensions among conflicting social groups by calling marginalized people to claim who and what they are. Thus strengthened, their collective voice can penetrate institutionalized boundaries, and this often leads to social transformation. Elizondo, PADRES, Las Hermanas, and Catholic laity all helped give birth to a respected space that they could call their own, the Mexican American Cultural Center. MACC, like other grassroots organizations and people, has contributed significantly to the transformation of the U.S. Catholic Church and public life.

MACC's story demonstrates that political, cultural, and religious developments in the Mexican American and Latina/o communities generally do not operate in isolation, and that these intersections of religion and public life are far more complex and multifaceted. MACC challenges, revises, and complicates our understanding of the impact of religion on political and civic engagement in the Latina/o and particularly the Mexican American community. Through symbolic and social capital, MACC functions as a space where the social *hybridity* of faith, culture, and justice envisions social change. It encourages a union of spirituality and social change grounded in the daily lives of ordinary people informed by Latina/o Catholic values.

MACC's story also demonstrates that studies of U.S. Latinas/os must analyze how Latinas/os exercise their voices and sociopolitical agency to challenge religious structures at the everyday life level. Only then will we be able to recognize the social contributions religious Latinas/os have made and continue to make in the U.S. church and society.

NOTES

1. The respondents in my study identified themselves and their experiences as Mexican American and/or Hispanic. "Latina/o" here refers to all U.S-born individuals whose origin can be traced to Latin America, regardless of their political ideology. "Faith" refers to belief in God and the devotion and veneration of saints in the Catholic tradition. "Religious space" refers to the physical and sacred space where people can practice their faith from their own sociohistorical and cultural locations.

2. I define "voice" and "agency" as the desire and the action of a person or group of people to seek positive alternatives and make a positive change in their lives or community.

3. The inclusion of only one lay woman is a methodological problem that I will address in my later research. At the time of the interview, all the respondents resided in San Antonio, Texas, with the exception of one who resided in San Jose, California.

4. See also Rodolfo Acuña, *Occupied America: A History of Chicanos* (New York: Harper & Row, 1988); David G. Gutiérrez, *Walls and Mirrors: Mexican Americans, Mexican Immigrants, and the Politics of Ethnicity* (Berkeley: University of California Press, 1995).

5. Isidro Lucas, *The Browning of America: The Hispanic Revolution in the American Church* (Chicago: Fides/Claretian, 1981), 53.

6. An integrated race, class, and gender analysis of *comunidades eclesiales de base* is needed to thoroughly understand the complex social context behind the lack of response of the Catholic Church in the rural areas of Latin America that led to the formation of *comunidades.*

7. For further reading on the church in Latin America, see Enrique Dussel, *A History of the Church in Latin America: Colonialism to Liberation (1492–1979)* (Grand Rapids, MI: Eerdmans, 1981).

8. Lucas, *Browning of America,* 53; Ana María Díaz-Stevens and Anthony M. Stevens-Arroyo, *Recognizing the Latina/o Resurgence in U.S. Religion: The Emmaus Paradigm* (Boulder, CO: Westview Press, 1998).

9. For a thorough analysis on Las Hermanas, see Lara Medina, "Las Hermanas: Chicana/Latina Religious-Political Activism, 1971–1997" (Ph.D. diss., Claremont Graduate University, 1998).

10. See Díaz-Stevens and Stevens-Arroyo, *Recognizing Latina/o Resurgence*; Ana María Díaz-Stevens, "Latinas and the Church," in *Hispanic Catholic Culture in the U.S.: Issues and Concerns,* ed. Jay P. Dolan and Allan Figueroa Deck S.J. (Notre Dame, IN: University of Notre Dame Press, 1994); Virgilio Elizondo, "The Mexican American Cultural Center Story" *Listening: Journal of Religion and Culture* 32 (Fall 1997): 152–160; Medina, "Las Hermanas."

11. Díaz-Stevens, "Latinas and the Church."

12. Ibid.

13. Ibid., 154.

14. Ibid.

15. Taped interview with Rubén Alfaro, San Antonio, Texas (September 24, 1999); taped interview with Rosa María Icaza, San Antonio, Texas (September 21, 1999); taped interview with Irma Mireles, San Antonio, Texas (September 24, 1999).

16. José Marins and his team gave the first workshop on base communities at the Mexican American Cultural Center. See Elizondo, "Mexican American Cultural

Center Story." The following people also contributed to the Mexican American Cultural Center: Juan Alfaro, Rubén Alfaro, Leonard Anguiano, Bishop Joseph Bernardin, Margaret Brenan, Jesús Chavarria, Teresita Creighton, Monsignor Jack Egan, Angela Erevia, María Elena González (MACC's current president), Coreen Hart, Monsignor George Higgins, Angelica Inda, Jean Jadot, Margaret Kaferty, Archbishop Tom Kelly, Marcine Klem, John Linskens, Alan McCoy, Consuelo Pacheco, Ricardo Ramírez, Bishop James Rausch, Cardinal Ardnelo Rossi, Archbishop Sheen, Sister Philip Solis, Margaret Truitt, and Rosendo Urrabazo.

17. According to Elizondo in *The Future Is Mestizo: Life Where Cultures Meet* (Boulder: University Press of Colorado, 2000), *mestizaje* is "the process through which two totally different peoples mix biologically and culturally so that a new people begins to emerge."

18. Taped interview with Rudy Vela, San Antonio, Texas (September 22, 1999).

19. For a thorough analysis, see Medina, "Las Hermanas."

20. This accreditation means that the U.S. bishops recognize and confer the legitimacy of the program according to the Catholic Church.

21. Arlie Russell Hochschild, *The Second Shift* (New York: Avon, 1989).

22. Medina, "Las Hermanas," 277.

23. Orlando O. Espín, *The Faith of the People: Theological Reflections of Popular Catholicism* (Maryknoll, New York: Orbis Books, 1997).

24. *Las Posadas* is a nine-day Mexican Catholic religious ritual of prayer and festivity in memory of Mary and Joseph's pilgrimage from Nazareth to Bethlehem in search of shelter. *El Via Crucis,* a Mexican and Latin American Catholic popular religious tradition, is the reenactment of Jesus' journey to his crucifixion. For a further discussion on these and other Mexican Catholic rituals, see Virgilio P. Elizondo and Timothy Matovina, *Mestizo Worship: A Pastoral Approach to Liturgical Ministry* (Collegeville, MN: Liturgical Press, 1998); Virgilio P. Elizondo, *Christianity and Culture* (San Antonio, TX: Mexican American Cultural Center, 1999).

25. Gloria Anzaldúa, *Borderlands La Frontera: The New Mestiza* (San Francisco: Aunt Lute Books, 1999).

26. Antonio Gramsci, *An Antonio Gramsci Reader: Selected Writings, 1916–1935,* edited by David Forgacs (New York: Schocken Books, 1988), 259, 302.

27. Ibid., 302.

28. Ibid. See also Díaz-Stevens and Stevens-Arroyo, *Recognizing the Latina/o Resurgence*; Gramsci, *Reader*, 300–322.

29. Taped interview with Roberto Piña, San Antonio, Texas (September 23, 1999).

30. Ibid.

31. Ibid.

32. For further discussion on Freire's theory of empowerment, see Paulo Freire, *Pedagogy of the Oppressed,* translated by Myra Bergman Ramos (New York: Herder & Herder, 1970); Freire, *Letters to Cristina: Reflections on My Life and Work* (New York: Routledge, 1996).

33. Pierre Bourdieu, *Distinction: A Social Critique of the Judgment of Taste* (Cambridge: Harvard University Press, 1984). See also Díaz-Stevens and Stevens-Arroyo, *Recognizing Latina/o Resurgence.*

34. Taped interview with Rosa María Icaza, San Antonio, Texas (September 22, 1999).

35. Arturo J. Pérez "The History of Hispanic Liturgy since 1965," in *Hispanic*

Catholic Culture in the U.S.: Issues and Concerns, ed. Jay P. Dolan and Allan Figueroa Deck S.J. (Notre Dame, IN: University of Notre Dame Press, 1994), 360–408.

36. Encuentro 2000 (Encounter 2000), in Los Angeles, CA, was a multiethnic religious event that took place in July of 2000. It brought together different ethnic groups in parishes and dioceses to share their cultural diversity while affirming the values and teachings of the Catholic Church.

37. Taped interview with Carlos Rosas, San Antonio, Texas (September 22, 1999).

38. Some of his well-known songs include "*Rosas del Tepeyac*," "*Padre Nuestro*," "*De Donde Nace Una Flor*," and "*El Profeta del Barrio*."

39. Taped interview with Rosas.

40. Ibid.

41. Bourdieu, *Distinction*, 291.

42. Díaz-Stevens and Stevens-Arroyo, *Recognizing Latina/o Resurgence.*

43. Taped interview with Virgilio Elizondo, San Antonio, Texas (September 23, 1999).

44. Moises Sandoval, "The Organization of a Hispanic Church," in *Hispanic Catholic Culture in the US: Issue and Concerns*, ed. Jay P. Dolan and Allan Figueroa Deck, S.J. (Notre Dame: University of Notre Dame Press, 1994), 156.

45. For extended discussion on Sacred Heart Parish, see Socorro Castañeda, "El Catolicismo en la frontera: una fe perfumada de flor, canto y cambio social," in *El Mensajero de San Antonio* no. 7–8 (Padua, Italy: Prov. Pad. FMC, Messaggero di S. Antonio, Editrice) (July–August 1999): 10–11 (in Spanish).

46. Taped interview with Monsignor Mateo Sheedy, San Jose, California (December 7, 1999).

8

¡*Ya Basta!* Latino/a Protestant Activism in the Chicano/a and Farm Workers Movements

Paul Barton

In the 1960s and 1970s, an emerging Chicano/a social consciousness converged with the efforts of César Chávez to organize a farmworkers' labor union. The Chicano/a and farmworker movements challenged many Mexican American "mainline" Protestants throughout the southwestern United States to reconsider the beliefs and practices they had inherited from their Anglo-American missionaries. Until that time, Mexican American Protestants of the "mainline" traditions, also referred to as *los Protestantes* in this chapter, had adhered to an ideology inherited from their Anglo-American missionaries—the idea that social reform was primarily a matter of evangelizing individuals so they could become productive and moral citizens.[1] The Chicano/a and farmworker movements created a language of liberation that made the evangelical model of social reform seem out of touch with the Latino/a context in the Southwest.

This new language of liberation offered Mexican American Protestants a cultural and historical analysis to critique the racist elements of their Protestant tradition. As several Mexican American Protestants gained a new appreciation for *la causa*, they, in turn, joined the struggle of Chicanos/as for autonomy, self-determination, and economic and political empowerment. This cadre of Chicano/a Protestants served as a bridge between the politically active sector of the Mexican American community and their own ecclesial communities. They challenged the church to reconsider its purpose and mission in light of the suffering in its midst. While they sought to build bridges between their Latino/a Protestant church and the politically active Latino/a community, others within their ecclesial communities, Anglo-American and Mexican American, resisted this reorientation toward social involvement. Indeed, there was much tension between this small minority of Chicano/a activists and the majority of Latino/a Protestants, who were yet to be convinced of the appropriateness of the church's involvement in social justice.

This study of the variety of responses of los Protestantes in the U.S. Southwest to the Chicano/a and farm worker movements illuminates their role in the public arena during the last thirty-five years.[2] My aim in this essay is two-fold: (1) to highlight the catalytic ability of a cadre of Chicano/a "mainline" Protestant leaders to move their churches and ecclesial organizations to endorse and support the Chicano/a and farmworker movements in Texas from the 1960s until the early 1980s and (2) to examine the three basic responses of Latino/a Protestants to these social justice movements (solidarity, ambivalence and indifference, and opposition). As the Chicano/a Protestants led their church co-faithful into the public struggle of these popular movements, they caused a realignment of loyalties among a number of "mainline" Latino/a Protestants. Ethnic affiliation became as important to them as their denominational affiliation.[3] Additionally, they promoted a theological understanding of the Gospel that embraced the oppressed and viewed the kingdom of God as a goal to strive for in contemporary society.[4]

Edwin Sylvest accurately asserts that a large segment of the Latino/a Protestant church remained highly ambivalent about these movements.[5] However, such an assessment discounts the important contribution that a cadre of Mexican American "mainline" Protestants have made in the public arena. I focus on the catalytic role of a cadre of Protestant Chicanos/as who moved their churches and ecclesiastical organizations to endorse and support the Chicano/a and farm worker movements in Texas. As they cajoled their church co-faithful to identify with these popular movements, they promoted a realignment of loyalties among Mexican American "mainline" Protestants. Los Protestantes involved in the Chicano/a campaign for self-determination, racial justice, and cultural affirmation (*la causa*) began to value their ethnic identity as much as their denominational identity.

Chicano/a Protestants Involved in La Causa

Like their Latin American liberationist counterparts, a cadre of Mexican American religious elites sympathetic to the Chicano/a and farmworker movements exercised their intellectual and leadership abilities to leverage the resources of their church in support of the movement.[6] Among the United Methodists, the Texas Council of Churches employed the Reverend Leo Nieto, an elder in the Rio Grande Annual Conference from 1964 until 1969, to minister to migrant farmworkers in Texas.[7] In 1969 he received an appointment to coordinate the ethnic and language program of the United Methodist Church's Board of Missions. From that influential position, he was instrumental in obtaining the board's support for the Fund for Reconciliation project in the lower Río Grande Valley of Texas, an economic and political development project. Four Río Grande Annual Conference clergy—the Reverend Joel Martínez, Reverend Leo

Unidentified Latino Protestant engages in a prayer vigil to protest abuse of undocumented immigrants (Courtesy of Jimmy Dorantes/Latin Focus Photos)

Nieto, Reverend Isabel Gómez, and Reverend Arturo Fernández—provided logistical support for the farmworkers' historical march from San Juan in the lower Río Grande Valley to Austin, Texas, in 1966, to draw attention to their cause.[8] The Reverend James Navarro, a Hispanic Baptist pastor from Houston also helped coordinate the march. The Reverend Joél Martínez and Reverend Leo Nieto served on the board of directors of the National Farm Workers Ministry during the 1970s.[9]

A small number of United Methodist laypersons were also involved in the farmworkers' cause. Brothers Andy and Bobby Hernández of La Trinidad United Methodist Church in San Antonio, Texas, were active in these movements. As a youth, Bobby addressed the conference's youth assembly on the farmworkers' strikes and boycotts in 1974. He encouraged the youth to promote the boycott of California grapes and to picket stores that sold the grapes. The Reverend Andy Hernández was initiated into the Chicano movement as a youth, when he assisted in the city council campaign of Pete Torres, a Chicano activist, in San Antonio in 1967. The Reverend Hernández joined the Southwest Voter Registration Education Project following his college graduation in 1974 and eventually succeeded the director, Willie Velásquez, upon the latter's death. He and the staff of that organization conducted hundreds of voter registration campaigns throughout the Southwest and filed suit in several Texas counties for redress of discriminatory electoral policies.[10]

Mexican American United Methodists in southern California and Arizona responded to the neglect and alienation they had experienced since their conference, the Latin American Mission Conference, had been absorbed within the California-Arizona Conference in 1956. United Methodist clergy in the California-Arizona Conference organized the Latin American Methodist Action Group (LAMAG) in March 1968, with the future Bishop Elías Galván as the organization's first president. The Latin American Methodist Action Group became a significant caucus in that region, serving to address the pattern of neglect and paternalism toward Mexican Americans by their conference.[11] That same year, the Southern California–Arizona Conference's Ethnic Strategy Committee recognized that the conference's strategy of integration of ethnic minorities with the dominant Anglo-American population had failed. The report stated that "integration seen as Angloization is an outmoded concept among Mexican Americans and no longer can be tolerated by our Latin churches.' "[12] Félix Gutiérrez states this report "brought closure to the missionary mentality and its successor, integration through assimilation. Rather than accepting an Anglo model, the Hispanic leadership challenged the fundamental thinking of the church and called for others in the region to adapt to the Hispanic reality."[13]

A parallel cadre of Latino/a Presbyterians became involved in the Chicano/a and farmworker movements.[14] In New Mexico, Tomás Atencio, the son of a Presbyterian minister, cofounded with Facundo B. Valdéz, the Academia de la Nueva Raza, "a non-profit Corporation for Educational and Research purposes" in 1969.[15] The 1970 General Assembly of the United Presbyterian Church U.S.A. allocated $200,000 for the the Academia de la Nueva Raza and two other organizations involved in la causa, and committed itself to finding an additional $604,300 from outside sources.[16] In California, a group dedicated to representing the concerns of Mexican American Presbyterians, La Raza Churchmen, organized in the late 1960s. The Synod of Southern California officially recognized the association after La Raza Churchmen presented the synod with a list of *pronunciamientos* (pronouncements). The pronouncements reflected the prevailing sentiments among Chicanos/as—self-determination, inclusion in leadership positions, a priority placed on ministries to the Spanish-speaking, and an increased distribution of resources for the Mexican American community.[17]

Jorge Lara-Braud became a leading advocate of Mexican Americans within Presbyterian leadership circles. The writings and public speaking by Lara-Braud brought the concerns and needs of Latinos/as into the decision-making circles of the Presbyterian Church. He served as the first director of the Hispanic American Institute, a Presbyterian center established at Austin Presbyterian Theological Seminary in Austin, Texas, in 1966. Lara-Braud used his position to create links between Mexican Americans and the mainline Protestant church. He eloquently articulated the Chicano/a perspective before "mainline" Protestant leaders and readers in a position paper written for the Synod of Texas (U.S.) Program Coordinating Committee in 1967, titled "The Church's Partnership with Mexican Americans: A Proposal to Anglo Protestant Churchmen."[18] This widely circulated paper helped influence the 1966 General Assembly of the United Presbyterian Church U.S.A. to change its policies and strategies relating to Latinos/as. The General Assembly committed itself to greater inclusion of Latinos/as in the decision-making processes at all levels of the denomination, increasing the allocation of funding for Spanish-speaking ministries, evaluating existing Spanish-speaking ministries in judicatories throughout the denomination, and seeking funding from private and governmental agencies for projects that would improve the condition of Latinos/as.[19] Lara-Braud also influenced church leaders' viewpoints of Mexican Americans and other Latinos/as through a paper he wrote in 1969, titled "Hispanic-Americans and the Crisis in the Nation."[20]

The Reverend Lydia Hernández and the rest of her family worked for several years in the 1950s and 1960s with the farmworkers. Her entire family was employed with the Migrant Ministry Program, the predecessor of the National Farm Worker Ministry. At one point, her father, a Presbyterian minister, supported the farmworkers' campaign for higher wages in Wisconsin. The farmworkers asked the Reverend José Angel Hernández to give the opening prayer at their rally. Knowing that the local migrant ministry council was going to ask him to refrain from participating in the rally, he resigned his position and accompanied the farmworkers in their struggle. The Hernández family maintained a close relationship with César Chávez for several years. He had stayed in the homes of the Hernández family in Florida at various times while coordinating farmworker union activities there during 1973 and 1974.[21]

The Fund for Reconciliation

In the wake of the movement for equality among disenfranchised groups, the United Methodist Church realized it could no longer consider reforming society without addressing the gross inequalities that existed between Anglo-Americans and racial and ethnic minorities. The General Conference of the United Methodist Church responded to racial and ethnic minorities' demand for racial justice and equality with a $20 million "Fund for Reconciliation" in 1968. The overall aim of the fund was to work toward a reconciliation of racial and ethnic minorities with Anglo-Americans through the funding of projects that fostered the economic and social empowerment of underrepresented groups.[22]

Under the auspices of the denomination's Board of Missions, a task force, which included four members of the Río Grande Annual Conference, allocated all $100,000 reserved for their national constituency for empowerment projects among impoverished Mexicans and Mexican Americans in the lower Río Grande Valley of Texas.[23] Upon this recommendation, the Board of Missions established the Local Spanish Speaking Task Force in the lower Río Grande

Valley. This local task force consisted of four ministers of the Río Grande Annual Conference and four farmworkers (seven Latinos/as and one Anglo-American). The Local Spanish-speaking Task Force formulated the Valley Fund for Reconciliation Project in August 1969. The project began operating in 1970 and ended October 1, 1972.

Members of the local task force formulated a plan that they believed would most effectively meet the needs of the poor in the lower Río Grande Valley. The Valley Project helped fund an existing weekly radio program produced by Antonio (Tony) Orendain, a union organizer for the United Farm Workers Organizing Committee (UFWOC) in the Río Grande Valley. Through the radio program *La Voz del Campesino* (The Voice of the Farmworker), Orendain notified the Spanish-speaking population of the activities of the farmworkers' union-organizing committee and other organizations involved in community organizing. The Valley Project also funded at subsistence level seven volunteers who engaged in legal advocacy, social work, and community organizing. Two of the volunteers edited a biweekly newspaper—*¡Ya Mero!*—with a circulation of 5,500.[24]

The infusion of such a large amount of money for the political, economic, and social empowerment of Mexican Americans in the lower Río Grande Valley became the catalyst for an imbroglio between Anglo- and Mexican American United Methodists. Anglo-American United Methodists in the lower Río Grande Valley, who were accustomed to a patronage system based on race and class, had difficulty watching Mexican Americans administer a $100,000 program for the political, economic, and social empowerment of low-income Mexican Americans. Anglo-American resentment toward the project climaxed when one of the volunteers of the Fund for Reconciliation Valley Project, working out of a local United Methodist Community Center, became associated with a protest that ended in a police riot and the death of an innocent bystander in Pharr, Texas, in 1971.[25] Anglo-American laity became so outraged over this event and the transformation of welfare ministries into social action ministries that the area's bishop, Eugene Slater, convened a meeting in McAllen, Texas, on February 11, 1972, to hear their complaints. The meeting, consisting of a few hundred United Methodists from the Anglo-American dominant Southwest Texas Annual Conference, as well as members of the Río Grande Annual Conference, gave local United Methodists an opportunity to express their objections to the program.[26]

The conflict that arose between leaders of the Río Grande and Southwest Texas Annual Conferences crystallized the ethnic fault line between them. Anglo-American United Methodists of the Southwest Texas Annual Conference pressured the leaders of the Río Grande Annual Conference to either modify or terminate the Valley Project. It was intimated that, if the Río Grande Annual Conference wanted to continue receiving sizable mission-aid contributions from its sister Southwest Texas Annual Conference, it had "better not kill the goose that laid the golden egg." Such pressure was interpreted by the leaders of the Río Grande Annual Conference as a message to "keep the peace." The pressures that Río Grande Annual Conference leaders felt from their counterparts of the Southwest Texas Annual Conference revealed to Mexican American Methodists that constituencies within their own denomination were oblivious and somewhat blind to the continued exploitation and oppression of their Mexican American community.

The valley project had the opposite effect of its intentions: instead of creating reconciliation, it polarized Anglo- and Mexican American United Methodists in South Texas. By the time the Valley Project had ended, relations between Mexican and Anglo-American United Methodists were strained; each group mistrusted the other. Anglo-American United Methodists felt that their Mexican American co-faithful had manipulated the program and taken advantage of their good will, while Mexican Americans felt that the Anglo-Americans had attempted to impose their will on their activities. Mexican American United Methodist leaders of the Río Grande Annual Conference and Anglo-American United Methodist leaders of the Southwest Texas Annual Conference spent the next twenty years in a dance of interethnic and interconference relations, with neither partner willing to embrace the other.

Conference Deliberations on the Chicano/a Movement

In addition to the involvement of a cadre of young Chicano clergy and laity, the Río Grande Annual Conference struggled to consider its relationship to the Chicano/a and farmworker movements and its moral responsibility to its ethnic community. From the late 1960s until the mid-1970s, leaders of the conference recognized a prophetic dimension of their ministry. In their 1970 report to the annual conference, the district superintendents acknowledged the conference's past tendency to retreat from social issues. An excerpt of the report exhibits what Alfredo Náñez called "a message of confession":

> Again when our people have begun to demand justice, reciprocity and a share of the power in positions of decision-making which effect the general welfare and being denied this, have arisen with emotion and vehemence to demonstrate in favor of these rights, we have tended to withdraw, to criticize them from a distance and to assure our brethren of the majority we still love them. Our evangelical Methodist people need to rethink their theological basis. We need to remember that the Gospel calls us to love and to share the sufferings of those who are afflicted, defenseless, and victimized. We have the weighty obligation to hear their complaints, identify ourselves with their cause, remembering that we should put the weight of our influence on the side of justice and the right . . . and stop shielding ourselves behind our privileged status as we have so often done in the past.[27]

The concern for the plight of farmworkers and injustices experienced by Mexican Americans supplanted the traditional program of social reform in the Río Grande Annual Conference in the late 1960s and the early 1970s. The conference's Board of Christian Social Concerns, chaired by the Reverend Isabel Gómez, placed the farmworkers and ethnic and racial justice at the center of its agenda. This board and other Chicano clergy successfully lobbied the annual conference to endorse collective bargaining for the farmworkers and to pass resolutions that condemned injustices committed against Mexican Americans. From 1966 to 1972, the Río Grande Annual Conference passed several resolutions endorsing the right of the farmworkers for collective bargaining and their right for just wages and working conditions. The 1970 report of the conference Board of Christian Social Concerns echoed the superintendents' concern over the inattention the conference churches had paid to the "human problems" of Mexican Americans in the barrios.[28]

Involvement with the Industrial Areas Foundation

Following a lull in political activity in the late 1970s, the rise of the church-based community activism challenged the Mexican American church to engage in solidarity with the politically disenfranchised. The Industrial Areas Foundation (IAF), led by Ernesto Cortés Jr. in Texas, established church-based political organizations to empower the politically disenfranchised groups, especially Latinos/as. Many Mexican American Catholic parishes, and a handful of Mexican American Protestant Churches, supported this faith-based political movement. Two Mexican American United Methodist Churches (UMC) joined the grassroots faith-based political organizations in the 1980s. La Trinidad UMC in San Antonio, Texas, led by Dr. Daniel Z. Rodríguez, joined Metro Alliance in the mid-1980s. Bishop Minerva Carcaño, then pastor of El Redentor UMC in McAllen, Texas, from 1982 to 1986, led her church to join Valley Interfaith, an almost entirely Catholic-based grassroots political organization in the Río Grande Valley. When it joined Valley Interfaith in 1983, El Redentor UMC was the only Protestant church in the organization.

Carcaño paid a price for her participation in Valley Interfaith. Since Valley Interfaith held public officials accountable to voters who often suffered from lack of public services, the conservative Anglo-American leadership in the Río Grande Valley opposed the organization. At one point, Carcaño and her church came under fire from public leaders and the media because of their participation in Valley Interfaith. The local news media criticized Carcaño for her support of Valley Interfaith, and many of her clergy colleagues disapproved of her involvement with the organization.[29] Despite the pressure to disassociate itself from Valley Interfaith, El Redentor UMC maintained its membership in the organization until 1998.[30]

Ambivalence of Los Protestantes

While the Río Grande Annual Conference issued public resolutions in support of the farmworkers, the vast majority of its members remained ambivalent or indifferent to these social movements and refrained from direct involvement in the farmworkers' struggle. Latino/a Protestants generally remained ambivalent or indifferent about these justice movements for three basic reasons. First, their dependent relationship with Anglo-American denominational co-faithful constrained them from social action against the status quo. Second, they associated the farmworker movement with the Catholic Church. The strong anti-Catholic sentiments by Latino/a Protestants kept them from participating in events that had a strong Catholic presence or sanction. Third, they argued that social activism distracted them from evangelism, which they considered the primary purpose of the church's ministry.

Since many Mexican American Southern Baptist pastors in the Río Grande Valley were accountable to and financially dependent on the local Anglo-American Southern Baptist churches that sponsored their work, they lacked the independence to support the political and economic struggle of their people if they so desired. According to Martha Remy in "Protestant Churches and Mexican-Americans in South Texas," one reason Mexican American Southern Baptists in the lower Río Grande Valley did not participate in the farmworkers' march to Austin was because "the majority of the growers [in the valley] were Baptist."[31] Sylvest states that

> the deeply ambivalent response of Hispanic American Protestantism to the struggle of liberation as it developed during the 1960s and 1970s is not surprising. To embrace the farm workers' movement, for example, would often result in conflict between Anglo and Hispanic churches of the same denomination in the same town.[32]

Mexican American Southern Baptists and other Mexican American "mainline" Protestants also disassociated themselves with the farmworkers' struggle because the latter employed Catholic symbols in their public demonstrations. In the 1966 march from the lower Rio Grande Valley to Austin, Texas, the farmworkers carried the emblem of Nuestra Señora de Guadalupe (Our Lady of Guadalupe) at the front of the procession. The use of this image, the involvement of a few Catholic priests, and the farmworkers' overwhelming affiliation with the Catholic Church led the Mexican American Baptists, Presbyterians, and Methodists to perceive the march as a Catholic event.[33] Anti-Catholic sentiment remained strong enough to prevent the majority of Latino/a Protestants from participating in social causes that also had the support of the Catholic Church.

Many Mexican American "mainline" Protestants did not reject the Chicano/a and farmworker movements as much as regard them as peripheral to the mission of the church. The focus on evangelism as the primary purpose of the church made it difficult for many Mexican-American "mainline" Protestants to support social action on behalf of their disenfranchised ethnic community. Following the evangelical ecclesiology of their Protestant tradition, many Latino/a Protestants argued that the church needed to focus its energy on Jesus' commandment in Matthew 28:19: "Go therefore and make disciples of all nations, baptizing them in the name of the Father and of the Son and of the Holy Spirit."[34] The church's involvement in the Chicano/a and farmworkers' movements was seen as a distraction from the central work of the church. In the Río Grande Annual Conference, the traditional emphasis on evangelism competed with the new view of social engagement. Among Mexican American Southern Baptists, evangelism remained the central thrust of their mission and ministry.[35]

Opposition to the Chicano/a and Farmworker Movements

While a small group of Chicano/a Protestants pushed their churches to support these justice movements, another vocal group argued against such involvement. The more moderate opponents of the Chicano/a activists considered involvement with justice movements undignified. They had inherited from the Anglo-American missionaries the idea that the solution to one's socioeconomic deficiencies was to improve oneself, not criticize the social system. The moderate opponents of the Chicano/a Protestants had adopted the fundamental ideology that pervaded much of North American Protestant thought—the idea that God would bless those individuals who dedicated their lives to following Jesus Christ and thereby changed their lives to become productive citizens.

The more vociferous opponents of the Chicano/a activists considered these justice-oriented movements un-American. Perhaps as a legacy of the strong nationalist impulse following World War II, the McCarthy era, and the Cuban Revolution, activism on behalf of the poor was viewed as un-American. This sentiment was shared by the Reverend José Mendiola, the most outspoken critic of Chicano/a activists in the Río Grande Annual Conference. He wrote letters attacking the Chicano clergy. In a letter dated March 3, 1972, he attacked the Chicano clergy of the conference, but referred only to the name of the Reverend Roy Barton, who at the time was the conference's program director.[36] He juxtaposed Barton's allegedly anti-American sentiments with the evangelistic and patriotic attitude of another conference leader, the Reverend Roberto Escamilla. He wrote sarcastically, "If the Rev. Roy D. Barton is elected Bishop and I do not obtain this 'Chicano' philosophy, I may be without a job. So please help me get re-educated at once."[37]

Generational Differences in Attitudes toward the Chicano/a Movement

Mendiola's attacks on the Chicano clergy was a manifestation of the conservative worldview and ethos the veteran members of the conference had received from missionary-minded Protestantism. Indeed, the different responses to the political struggle being waged by Chicano/a activists reflected generational differences. Evidence of this generational division in approaches toward social ministry is found in a public confrontation between two groups at a national Spanish-speaking ecumenical meeting.

The Council on Hispanic American Ministries (COHAM), an established, Spanish-speaking national organization sponsored by the National Council of Churches, met in Miami, Florida, for four days in January 1972. During that period, a younger contingent of Latino/a national church leaders met separately to organize a new association that would focus on a ministry of liberation among the oppressed in the Latino/a communities. The Reverend Leo Nieto, a participant of the alternative meeting, wrote that the context for the separate meeting had been the death of a young woman on a nearby picket line. Nan Freeman, an eighteen-year-old college student, had been killed by a truck while picketing with farmworkers affiliated with César Chávez, at the Talisman Sugar company. Nieto and the other younger church leaders were frustrated that COHAM was holding seminars nearby, honoring its leaders, and celebrating its history without recognition of the tragedy of the young woman's death and the oppression related to it.[38]

On January 25, 1972, the group of twenty-five to forty church activists entered, unannounced, the banquet of COHAM to read their statement at the podium and to urge the members of COHAM to commit themselves to solidarity with the oppressed. The banquet participants rebuffed Nieto and his colleagues. The unexpected presence of these activists, as well as their desire to divert the intended focus of the celebration by reading a political statement in the middle of COHAM's banquet ceremonies, created such a commotion that the police were called to restore order. The young "churchmen" left the banquet hall without being heard by COHAM. The next morning they read the following statement at a press conference:

> We, a group of Christians committed to the cause of liberation of our oppressed Latin peoples, came before the COHAM banquet last night with the intention of reading a two-minute statement. Not only were we received with hostility and violence but were also denied the right to speak by people who call themselves Christians.
>
> In that statement we wished to warn the churches in general of the wrong direction that they have taken for many years in relation to the oppression of our people and invite them to join the picket line of the Talisman Sugar Company workers as their situation is a local manifestation of general oppression of all our people.[39]

The members of COHAM perceived the action of the church activists differently than the young church leaders. They viewed the young activists as interlopers in their proceedings. The members of COHAM produced their own statement following the banquet. They sent a communication to several denominations' mission agencies that employed several of the young churchmen denouncing their interference and asking them to investigate the church leaders' actions.[40]

Assessment of the Legacy of Chicano/a Protestants

The Chicano/a and farmworker movements created a turning point in the identity formation of some Mexican American "mainline" Protestants. As Chicano/a activists critiqued the practices and policies of institutions dominated by Anglo-Americans, they demonstrated that Mexican Americans could wrestle control of their destinies from oppressive institutions and acquire a greater level of self-determination. The ideas and actions of the Chicano/a activists and farmworkers led a number of Mexican American Protestants to reconsider their own loyalties. Through their involvement with these movements, the primary frame of reference for a minority of Latino/a Protestants shifted from their denomination to their ethnic community. This realignment of loyalties resulted from what Sylvest refers to as "the quickening of a church not defined by institutional affiliation or structures but by its identification with the struggles of the people."[41]

The Chicano/a church activists brought the concerns and ideals of the Chicano/a and farmworkers movements into their ecclesial organizations. Those Chicano/a Protestants who participated in these movements found the traditional activities of social reform unacceptable, for these efforts failed to address the endemic causes of oppression, poverty, racism, and discrimination. The Chicano/a Protestants reinterpreted the Christian Gospel in light of the context of these justice and cultural movements. They pushed their ecclesial communities to re-examine their purpose and mission and to respond tangibly to the suffering in their Mexican American communities. They also criticized the existing social structure, through which Anglo-Americans maintained domination over Mexican Americans. All of these efforts resulted in an attempt by the Chicano/a Protestants to reorient their church along a justice axis.

One lasting consequence of the activism of Mexican American "mainline" Protestants was the institutionalization of their leadership. Ironically, many of the younger clergy who protested against their denomination's paternalism and neglect became influential leaders in the denomination. The Reverend Elías Galván, the first president of LAMAG, was elected the first Hispanic bishop in the United Methodist Church in 1984. The Reverend Joel Martínez, who actively supported the farmworkers, was elected a United Methodist bishop in 1992. The Reverend Leo Nieto and the Reverend Arturo Fernández both became superintendents in western United Methodist conferences. Not only was the leadership institutionalized, but so were many of their goals and priorities.

As they obtained leadership positions in their denominations, the activist clergy were able to leverage the power of their denominations to support la causa. In 1988, when the Reverend Lydia Hernández served as a staff associate in the Racial Ethnic Ministry Unit of the Presbyterian Church (U.S.A.), that agency approved an $8,000 grant to the United Farm Workers of America, a farmworkers union in the Río Grande Valley of Texas.[42] Likewise, when the Reverend Leo Nieto moved from working directly with farmworkers in South

Texas to serving as the director of ethnic and language ministries in the United Methodist Church's Board of Missions, he shepherded the $100,000 grant to the Fund for Reconciliation within the board. Through the leadership of the Reverend Isabel Gómez, the associate general secretary of the United Methodist Church's General Commission on Religion and Race, the agency approved a $15,000 grant to support the farmworker's organizing activity in the Río Grande Valley of Texas.[43] These are a few examples of the ability of an elite group to leverage the power of their institutions to foster social change, first from outside their denominational structures and later from within.

Another lasting effect of the activism of the Chicano/a clergy was the establishment of Hispanic (or Latino/a) programs in seminaries and schools of theology. Seminarians at Perkins School of Theology in Dallas, Texas, highly influenced by the Chicano/a movement, had a crucial role in persuading their institution to establish the Mexican American Program.[44] Perkins established the Mexican American Program in 1974, with Roy D. Barton as the first director. McCormick Theological Seminary in Chicago established a similar Hispanic program. Several other seminaries in the "mainline" Protestant tradition established Hispanic centers in the 1970s and 1980s. These Hispanic centers were the long-term effects of the calls by the early Chicano/a clergy for greater participation in determining the mission of the church. It was from within these centers that the values of justice and cultural identity flourished in the aftermath of the heyday of the Chicano/a movement.

This historical sketch of Mexican Americans' involvement with the Chicano/a and farmworker movements, together with their varied responses to these movements, demonstrates a degree of complexity of "mainline" Latino/a Protestantism. Latino/a Protestants find themselves in a kind of Nepantla, torn between their loyalty to their Anglo-American Protestant denomination and their ethnic community.[45] The Chicano/a movement provided a language of liberation that allowed many among the younger generation of los Protestantes to articulate their faith, while asserting their cultural identity and placing a priority on racial and economic justice. Still, the majority of Mexican American "mainline" Protestants remained within the evangelical umbrella, in which social activism was perceived as tendentious to the church's mission. In the end, the conservative and traditional form of evangelical Protestantism prevented the Chicano/a movement from gaining a lasting foothold within grassroots Mexican American "mainline" Protestantism in the U.S. Southwest.

The form of Mexican American Methodists' social involvement in the Río Grande Annual Conference has changed in the last two decades. Following the heyday of the Chicano/a movement, the politically astute and assertive elites of the conference of the 1960s and 1970s gave way to a progressive and less confrontational leadership. Instead of working with the farmworkers and Chicano/a activists, Mexican American United Methodist leaders turned to church-based community services in the 1980s. Following the missionary tradition of their denominations, congregations opened day-care centers and food and clothing pantries; others offered services for the elderly and after-school programs. The most recent trend has been to address the health and medical needs of the barrio. Several churches in San Antonio and South Texas now operate church-based medical clinics and sponsor church-based community nursing. The emphasis on community services in recent years demonstrates that the "mainline" Latino/a Protestant church in the Southwest has remained domesticated; it has yet to address the underlying causes for the inequalities that remain among Latinos/as and the dominant society. Despite the domestication of social involvement in recent years, the examples of Mexican American "mainline" Protestant leaders in this chapter, as well as those mentioned in other chapters in this book, leave no doubt that the Latino/a "mainline" Protestant Church has produced individuals and groups who have made a public witness of their faith by accompanying their Chicano/a brothers and sisters in *la lucha* (the struggle) for a just society.

NOTES

1. Southern evangelicals typically asserted that society would be reformed as each individual converted to their Gospel. The West Texas Conference's Commission on Temperance and Social Service reported in 1919: " 'The unrest, turmoil and strife of the present day are symptoms of a 'social disorder,' which the church must face 'honestly and courageously.' In such a time, the 'first and greatest duty of the church' was a 'call to personal repentance and faith for both employer and employee, the capitalist and laborer.' 'No mere social program, however elaborate' could correct these evils.' " Walter N. Vernon, Robert W. Sledge, Robert C. Monk, and Norman W. Spellman, *The Methodist Excitement in Texas: A History* (Dallas: Texas United Methodist Historical Society/Bridwell Library, Southern Methodist University, 1984), 241. Quoting the *West Texas [Conference] Journal* (1919): 61–62.

2. For a history of the Latino/a church that encompasses the various groups under the Hispanic umbrella and is written from Latino/a perspectives, see Daniel R. Rodríguez and David Cortés-Fuentes, eds., *Hidden Stories: Unveiling the History of the Latino Church* (Decatur, GA: Asosiación Educación Teológica Hispana, 1994).

3. An accurate assessment of the number of "mainline" Latino/a Protestants is difficult to make because there were very likely clergy and laity who sympathized with and supported the Chicano/a and farmworker movements but did not leave a historical record of their activities. Historical materials suggest that there were a few dozen activist clergy and an equal amount of laity involved in political and social activism in the U.S. Southwest from the 1960s until the 1980s.

4. This chapter focuses on Mexican American United Methodists, especially the Río Grande Annual Conference, a primarily Mexican American United Methodist annual conference that overlaps with six other annual conferences in Texas and New Mexico. The chapter also studies Mexican American Presbyterians in the U.S. Southwest. Some attention is also given to Latino/a Southern Baptists.

5. Edwin Sylvest Jr., "Hispanic American Protestantism in the United States," in *Fronteras: A History of the Latin American Church in the USA since 1513*, ed. Moíses Sandoval (San Antonio, TX: Mexican American Cultural Center, 1983), 331.

6. Christian Smith, *The Emergence of Liberation Theology: Radical Religion and Social Movement Theory* (Chicago: University of Chicago Press, 1991), 53.

7. Nieto has written two articles on the relationship between the Chicano/a movement and the church: (1) Leo D. Nieto, "The Chicano Movement and the

Churches in the United States/El Movimiento Chicano y las Iglesias en Los Estados Unidos," *Perkins Journal* 29 (Fall 1975): (English) 32–41; (Spanish) 76–85. (2) Leo D. Nieto, "The Chicano Movement and the Gospel: Historical Accounts of a Protestant Pastor," in *Hidden Stories: Unveiling the History of the Latino Church,* ed. Daniel R. Rodríguez-Díaz and David Cortés-Fuentes (Decatur, GA: AETH, 1994), 143–157.

8. Telephone interview with Bishop Joél Martínez, by Paul Barton, Dallas, Texas (April 23, 1998).

9. For an overview of the history of Latino/a United Methodists, see Justo L. González, ed., *Each in Our Own Tongue: A History of Hispanic United Methodism* (Nashville, TN: Abingdon Press, 1991).

10. Telephone interview with the Reverend Andy Hernández, by Paul Barton, San Antonio, Texas (July 25, 2000).

11. Félix Gutiérrez, "The Western Jurisdiction," in *Each in Our Own Tongue,* ed. Justo L. González (Nashville, TN: Abingdon Press, 1991), 82.

12. Ibid., 82.

13. Ibid., 83.

14. With the exception of the section on the Reverend Lydia Hernández, the following section on Latino/a Presbyterians is distilled from Brackenridge and García-Treto, " 'God Does Not Speak Only English': Developments since 1960," in *Iglesia Presbiteriana: A History of Presbyterianism and Mexican-Americans in the Southwest,* Douglas Brackenridge and Francisco García-Treto (San Antonio, TX: Trinity University Press, 1987). The concluding chapter of the second edition, "A Vision of Partnership in Mission: Progress in the 1970s and 1980s," examines the progress made by Latino/a Presbyterians in the aftermath of the Chicano/a movement. These two chapters provide a thorough account of the efforts by Latino/a Presbyterians to cooperate with the Chicano/a and farmworker movements and to challenge their denominations to reconsider the nature of the relationship between the Presbyterian Church and the Latino/a community.

15. Brackenridge and García-Treto, *Iglesia Presbiteriana,* 221.

16. Ibid., 221–222.

17. Ibid., 217–218.

18. For a full treatment of this important paper, see ibid., 204–208.

19. Ibid., 208–209.

20. Jorge Lara-Braud, "Hispanic-Americans and the Crisis in the Nation," *Theology Today* 26 (1969): 334–338.

21. Telephone interview with the Reverend Lydia Hernández, by Paul Barton, Austin, Texas (January 14, 1998).

22. A desire for reconciliation between the Anglo-American dominant denominations and ethnic minority groups was prevalent throughout other "mainline" Protestant denominations in the late 1960s. The 1969 General Assembly of the United Presbyterian Church U.S.A. approved dramatic initiatives to respond to the calls by ethnic minorities for a reorientation of the church's policies and practices of ministry to ethnic minorities, including the support of the collective bargaining efforts of the farmworkers. Brackenridge and García-Treto, *Iglesia Presbiteriana,* 216.

23. The following were the members of the National Spanish-Speaking Task Force:

Tony Orendain—a union organizer for the United Farm Workers Organizing committee in San Juan Texas

Roberto Gómez—a member of the Río Grande Annual Conference and a seminary student at Perkins School of Theology, Dallas, Texas

Minnie Zuniga (now Minnie Trejo)—a college student, member of the Río Grande Annual Conference, from Floresville, Texas

Ernesto Cortés Jr.—a Catholic community organizer in San Antonio, employed by the Industrial Areas Foundation

The Reverend Alex Rodríguez—a United Methodist minister from Boston, Massachusetts

The Reverend Hector Navas—a United Methodist minister from Tampa, Florida

Trini Garza—a layman from Dallas; he was the chairperson of the Río Grande Annual Conference Council on Ministries

The Reverend Leo Nieto—a member of the Río Grande Annual Conference and staff on the National Division of the Board of Global Ministries

See "Additional Data: The Fund for Reconciliation Project," Eugene Slater—Personal Papers, Box 360, Item 16, "Valley Ministry. Fund for Reconciliation," Bridwell Library, Perkins School of Theology, Dallas, TX, 1.

24. Slater, "Additional Data," 1.

25. "Violence Rages for Four Hours," *The Monitor* (February 7, 1971), 1. See also David M. Fishlow, "Poncho Flores Is Dead," *The Texas Observer* 63, no. 4 (1971). "Poncho Flores Is Dead" was also published in *La Voz Chicano* 3, no. 2 (n.d.).

26. Lloyd Glover, "Methodists Hear Details on Church 'Reconciliation' Project in Valley," *Pharr News* (February 17, 1972), 1. Located in *Eugene Slater—Personal Papers*, Box 360, Item 42, "Fund for Reconciliation. Valley Meeting—McAllen, February 11, 1972."

27. Alfredo Náñez, *History of the Río Grande Conference of the United Methodist Church* (Dallas, TX: Bridwell Library, Southern Methodist University, 1980), 136. Quoting *Actas Oficiales de la Conferencia Anual Río Grande de la Iglesia Metodista Unida*, held in Kerrville, TX (June 5–9, 1970), 52 (trans. Alfredo Náñez).

28. *Actas Oficiales de la Conferencia Anual Río Grande de la Iglesia Metodista Unida*, held in Kerrville, TX, 1970, 79 (trans. mine).

29. Telephone interview with Bishop Minerva Carcaño, by Paul Barton, Austin, Texas (July 29, 2000).

30. The church's membership in Valley Interfaith was terminated unilaterally by a Pentecostal-style United Methodist pastor.

31. Martha Caroline Mitchell Remy, "Protestant Churches and Mexican-Americans in South Texas" (Ph.D. diss., University of Texas at Austin, 1971), 189.

32. Sylvest, "Hispanic American Protestantism in the United States," 329.

33. Telephone interview with the Reverend Rudy Sánchez, by Paul Barton, Dallas, Texas (May 8, 1998), 10.

34. *The Holy Bible Containing the Old and New Testaments with the Apocryphal/Deuterocanonical Books. Revised Standard Version* (London: Collins Publishers, c. 1989). Division of Christian Education of the National Council of the Churches of Christ in the United States of America (p. 32 in the New Testament section).

35. Interview with Sánchez, 10. Further research needs to be done to adequately treat the social involvement of Mexican American Southern Baptists. Joshua Grijalva's book focuses almost exclusively on the institutional and evangelistic history of Hispanic Southern Baptists in Texas. See Joshua Grijalva, *A History of Mexican Baptists in Texas 1881–1981: Comprising an Account of the Genesis, the Progress, and the Accomplishments of the People Called "Los Bautistas de Texas"* (Dallas: Office of Language Missions, Baptist General Convention of Texas, in cooperation with the Mexican Baptist Convention of Texas, 1982). See also Ernest E. Atkinson, "Hispanic Baptists in Texas:

A Glorious and Threatened History," *Apuntes: Reflexiones Teológicas desde el Márgen Hispano* 17, no. 2 (1997): 41–44.

36. For the sake of disclosure, Roy Barton is my father.

37. José G. Mendiola, "Letters from Mendiola to 'Dear Friend.' " March 3, 1972. Located in *Alfredo Náñez' Archives*, Bridwell Library. Box 2, Drawer 1, File: "Mendiola."

38. Leo D. Nieto, "Un martes inolvidable (otra versión)," *Texas Methodist—Río Grande Conference Edition* (March 10, 1972), 1.

39. "Activist Chicano Group Splits off from COHAM." *Texas Methodist—Southwest Texas Edition* (February 18, 1972), 3.

40. "COHAM celebra sus bodas diamantinas en Miami, Fla.," *Texas Methodist—Río Grande Conference Edition* (February 11, 1974), 1.

41. Sylvest, "Hispanic American Protestantism in the United States," 329.

42. Lydia Hernández, "Letter from the Reverend Lydia Hernández to Rebecca Flores Harrington," February 29, 1988. Located in the archives of the United Farm Workers of America, San Juan, TX.

43. The $15,000 grant financed the weekly radio program of Tony Orendain. It informed Spanish-speaking listeners of farmworkers' organizing activities and other political organizing work occurring in the Río Grande Valley of Texas.

44. Edwin E. Sylvest, "The Mexican-American Program: Twenty-five Years of History," *Apuntes: Reflexiones Teológicas desde el Márgen Hispano* 20, no. 2 (2000): 47–48.

45. Pat Mora, *Nepantla: Essays from the Land in the Middle* (Albuquerque: University of New Mexico Press, 1993), 5, 10.

9

Fe y Acción Social: Hispanic Churches in Faith-Based Community Organizing

Richard L. Wood

Off the radar of most political observers, a new form of political engagement has taken hold among Latinos across the United States in the last twenty years: what I will call "faith-based community organizing." Also called broad-based, congregation-based, and institutional organizing, it has become a potent force in organizing Hispanic urban residents to represent their interests in the public arena.[1] In the process, it has helped forge ties between Latinos, African Americans, and Anglos and helped to join Latinos across many divides—including those rooted in political views, country-of-origin, immigration status, language preference, and religious affiliation. Indeed, I argue that faith-based community organizing represents a crucial emerging form of Latino political engagement. Engaged in this work are churches made up primarily of Salvadoran immigrants in Los Angeles and Mexican immigrants in Oakland, California; suburban immigrant communities in Orange County and longtime Mexican American communities in San Diego and San Antonio; rural Mejicano communities in South Texas, Hispanos in New Mexico, and Puertorriqueños and Guatemaltecos in New England and Florida.

The success of faith-based community organizing in Hispanic churches may be due partly to the fact that contemporary statements of this work were first pioneered in Hispanic barrios in San Antonio, Texas, largely by Hispanic organizers, clergy, and nuns like Father Virgilio Elizondo, MACC, and Ernesto Cortés (see below). I argue in three parts for the democratic promise of this kind of political organizing by Hispanics. First, I describe faith-based community organizing generally, including its origins and contemporary contours. Second, I note current levels of Hispanic engagement in this work, both as participants and as professional staff. Third, I analyze the movement's future democratic potential for Latinos. I conclude by noting three kinds of challenges posed by this discussion: challenges to the literature on Hispanic civic engagement; challenges to the field of faith-based community organizing; and challenges to Hispanic youth and all those who work with them.

Faith-Based Community Organizing

Most grassroots "community organizing" efforts in America today trace their origins to the work of Saul Alinsky in Chicago, initially with white ethnic groups and later with African Americans.[2] Over the course of four decades, Alinsky and others spread his highly confrontational model of populist organizing to various cities around the country. Though much of this work was sponsored by churches, over time it lost most of its religious roots and became a kind of secular technique for cultivating power in poor communities; in some places, it also was implicated in efforts by white communities to exclude black homeowners. By the late 1970s, old-style Alinsky organizing had lost much of its influence, like most other grassroots democratic movements.

Meanwhile, a group of organizers, pastors, and religious sisters—many of them Hispanic—were adapting Alinsky's ideas for use in the politically marginalized and economically poor barrios of San Antonio, Texas. Beginning in the mid-1970s, the local organization known as Communities Organized for Public Service (COPS) transformed Alinsky's model by linking it much more intimately with the religious congregations and faith commitments of participants.[3] As a result of this innovative work, COPS generated far greater political participation among poor barrio residents than had existed previously, accumulated significant power as an organization (including substantial influence on the city's expenditure of federal block grant money by the 1980s), and deeply transformed formerly Anglo-controlled politics in San Antonio. These changes helped create the context in which Henry Cisneros would rise to become perhaps the most salient Hispanic political figure in the United States. It also became the foundational experience leading to the elaboration of the faith-based model of organizing analyzed here.

Though COPS' work to break open San Antonio's power structure generated significant conflict, its links to religious culture and accumulating organizational power and confidence gradually led COPS to become less one-dimensionally conflictive in its relations with political officials. The organization developed a sophisticated political capacity for contestation and compromise that has come to be the hallmark of the stronger versions of faith-based community organizing.[4]

Also in the mid-1970s, Alinsky's model both spread nationally and divided internally, eventually giving rise to four major faith-based community organizing networks: the descendant of Alinsky's own organization, the Industrial Areas Foundation (IAF; based in Chicago), of which COPS is a part; the Pacific

Faith-based San Diego Organizing Project leaders fight for better social and infrastructure services in the 1990s (Courtesy of Richard Wood)

Institute for Community Organization (PICO; Oakland, California); the Gamaliel Foundation (Chicago); and Direct Action, Research, and Training (Miami).[5] In addition, smaller regional networks exist in some areas. Each ultimately adopted some lessons from the COPS experience and elaborated its own version of the faith-based community organizing model. Though differing organizational cultures within the networks give them rather divergent internal tenors for participants, very similar organizing practices characterize their work.

Faith-based community organizing remains rather unknown in academic circles but today arguably represents the most widespread movement for social justice in the United States.[6] As of 1999, about 133 local or metropolitan area organizations existed, the large majority of these affiliated with one of the four networks. Some 3,300 congregations plus nearly 500 public schools, labor union locals, and other institutions are members of these organizations. Through them, faith-based community organizing touches the lives of perhaps 1.5 million members of religious congregations in all the major urban areas and many secondary cities around the United States.[7]

Each organization trains interfaith teams of leaders from local congregations to do research on issues and negotiate with political and economic elites. But the heart of the process involves "relational organizing"—building networks of residents concerned about a particular issue that affects them or their communities. These leaders work together to research that issue, define specific policies to address it, then turn out anywhere from several hundred to 6,000 participants in nonpartisan political actions at which political or corporate leaders are asked to commit to those policies. Through this process, the organizations gain civic power and negotiate leverage for local residents, thereby influencing government policy on a variety of issues that affect the quality of life of "working families," as they typically term their constituency. These issues include:

- Housing: In New York, the Nehemiah Project gained government funding for building homes for thousands of low- and middle-income families.
- Public schools: The San Diego Organizing Project worked with teachers to raise pay and reduce class sizes in public schools. The Oakland Community Organization worked with the local school board to create smaller schools-within-schools. The PICO California Project convinced the state to launch a statewide initiative promoting parental engagement in their children's schools and led a $190-million bond initiative for public school infrastructure. The Texas IAF led the Alliance Schools effort that transformed public education for low-income residents. All these benefited large numbers of Hispanic students.
- Economic development: In San Antonio, COPS led the launch of Project Quest, a job-training program for enabling workers from low-income families to gain access to better-paying jobs.
- Policing: The Oakland Community Organization worked with the local police department to establish and promote a "Beat Health" unit for shutting down drug houses, most in poor neighborhoods. This became a model program for police departments nationally.
- Health care: The PICO California Project is leading the struggle to expand health coverage for families of the "working poor"—those who make too much to qualify for Medicaid/MediCal, but whose jobs include no health coverage. This effort has already generated $50 million in new funding for the primary care clinics that are the front line of medical coverage for poor families.
- Recreational programs for youth: Local projects around the country have generated new recreational and after-school academic programs for children.

Typically, these organizations have only been capable of wielding influence on the level of citywide politics. Such local work remains the bread and butter of this kind of organizing, but, as reflected in this list, recently the most successful organizations have gained significant power at the level of state government. Examples of the latter include the PICO California Project, the Texas Industrial Areas Foundation, Gamaliel's regional work in the Midwest, the Greater Boston Interfaith Organization, Arizona Interfaith, Direct Action, Research, and Training (DART) statewide work in Florida, and PICO statewide work in Louisiana and Colorado. Very recently, at least one has launched a drive to shape policy at the national level (PICO's *New Voices* campaign).[8]

Faith-based community organizing thus represents a widespread movement to empower lower- and middle-class residents of American cities to gain greater influence over the political and economic decisions affecting their lives. But how significant is the Hispanic presence within this movement?

This question takes on greater urgency given the findings of a massive and influential assessment of the underpinnings of democratic life in the United States. In *Voice and Equality*, Sidney Verba et al. analyze how Americans influence the political process through both their financial contributions and acquisition of civic skills.[9] On both measures, Hispanics systematically fall behind other ethnic groups in their ability to influence the political process; as a result, they have less voice and also suffer greater inequality than other ethnic groups.

Current Hispanic Engagement in Faith-Based Community Organizing

Anecdotal reports of Hispanic engagement in this field vary from glowing accounts of a burgeoning movement in which Latinos play a predominant role to highly charged critiques that suggest minimal connection with Latino communities. These conflicting reports appear to be driven both by political biases and by regional variation. In different parts of the country, faith-based community organizing may be primarily rooted among African American churches, Hispanic churches, or white/Anglo churches—or they may be richly multiracial, multicultural, and multilingual. Good data from which to draw a reasonably objective picture of the field have been sadly lacking.

The Interfaith Funders study (Wood and Warren, "A Different Face") provides the best data available on Hispanic participation in faith-based community organizing. The key finding (for the purposes of this volume) is that about 20 percent of the 3,300 participating congregations are predominantly Hispanic—meaning that one out of five participating churches is more than half Latino. Extrapolating from this figure to individual participants is unreliable.[10] My observations suggest that a significant portion of Hispanic-majority churches are very large (often swollen by burgeoning immigrant communities); if that is so, the 20 percent figure may underestimate the presence of Latinos within faith-based community organizing.

The level of Hispanic involvement in faith-based community organizing varies widely from one region to another. The heaviest Hispanic presence (local organizations for which 30%–100% of their member institutions are more than half Hispanic) is found in Texas, California, Illinois (Chicago), Pennsylvania (Philadelphia), Arizona, New Mexico, and Colorado. Though no data exist on variable participation across different Hispanic populations, this listing strongly suggests that it is heaviest among Mexican American and Mexican immigrant populations (with Philadelphia being the only probable exception). Also, immigrant Hispanics participate to a significant degree: about one-third of the Hispanic-dominant institutions (mostly churches) involved in faith-based community organizing are made up mostly of immigrants.

The study also shows more than 16 percent of the approximately 550 professional organizers employed in faith-based community organizing to be Latino. These are relatively well-paid jobs, not based on the sacrificial wages paid in some sectors of grassroots civic engagement. Half of the Hispanic organizers are women—an important fact in a field historically dominated by men. However, Hispanics are underrepresented in high-level supervisory roles in the field. This may be changing: as the corps of professional organizers has diversified, more Hispanic organizers are gaining the experience to become supervisors and have, in fact, moved into supervisory positions in those parts of the country with heavy Hispanic involvement. Also, as discussed here, some of the most prominent and influential figures in the field are Hispanic.

For present purposes, I assume 20 percent to be our best estimate of Hispanic participation. This is greater than the average presence of Latinos in the total U.S. population (roughly 14%, 2003 U.S. Census Bureau) but may underrepresent the presence of Latinos in the core urban home turf of much of this kind of organizing. Thus, the best available data are ambiguous, and characterizations of the Hispanic influence on faith-based community organizing run the risk of being shaped more by the inclinations of the analyst than by real knowledge.

At risk of following into that trap, I offer my own interpretation of these data.[11] First, as noted, the level of Latino participation varies significantly from one location to another, reflecting both the level of Hispanic population in a given city and the effectiveness of outreach to that population. Second, at least in some places, Latino participation is extraordinarily high, either as a result of Latinos being the predominant force within a local organization or through strong Latino presence within a highly multiethnic organization. The IAF's Valley Interfaith project in South Texas and Gamaliel's project in the Pilsen neighborhood of Chicago represent the former case; examples of the latter include the IAF's Chicago project and PICO's Oakland project. In Oakland, for instance, at public actions with 2,000 or more attendees, participants are often evenly split between Hispanics, Anglos, and African Americans, with a smaller contingent of Asian immigrants. At a statewide action on health care for the working poor in May 2000, sponsored by the PICO California Project, the 3,000 participants present were likewise rather evenly split. Such large, multiracial gatherings are extraordinary in American public life. Organizations capable of putting them together gain significant political leverage.

Third, some skepticism is warranted in assessing claims of remarkable diversity in this field, as well as charges of racial or ethnic exclusion within it. Organizers in the field are competitive professionals and prone to making exaggerated claims, especially when under pressure to diversify their membership bases. Equally as significant, however, are the outsiders' charges of ethnic exclusion, which often appear to be motivated by resistance to the field's tendency to appeal to diverse ethnic groups on the basis of their religious ties and class interests rather than on the basis of ethnic identity.[12] Indeed, the internal culture of organizing tends to implicitly suppress identity-based political claims, due to its commitment to cross-racial organizing and coalition-formation. For those inclined more toward identity-based politics, this appears insufficiently "political" and "radical." Again, the best data on this question come from the Interfaith Funders study: 36 percent of member institutions are predominantly African American, 35 percent are predominantly Anglo, 21 percent are predominantly Hispanic, and more than 6 percent are interracial.

Fourth, it is important to note that faith-based community organizing does not line up easily with Democratic, Republican, or third-party politics. The fact that these organizations disproportionately engage working-class and lower-middle-class urban residents, often under the rubric of "representing working families," and sometimes seek government funding for programs to benefit those families, in some places appears to give them some affinity for Democratic Party policy positions. But this is not at all universal, and faith-based organizations have worked very collaboratively with politicians of both major parties, as well as with independent and minor-party representatives. In part, they are forced into an official nonpartisanship by their tax-exempt status as 501(c)3 or 501(c)4 organizations. Generally speaking, their nonpartisanship is not just a veneer. They tend to eschew partisan ties and actively seek links with figures who can exert political leadership on a given issue, regardless of party affiliation. This tendency distances them from those Latino leaders embedded in either party or opposed to any party linkages whatsoever.

Thus, Hispanics represent a numerical minority within the field of faith-based community organizing, but a minority with a significant profile—albeit with a political style rooted in religious faith that not all Latinos find appealing.

Hispanic Leadership in Faith-Based Community Organizing

The fairly strong presence of Hispanic churches is reflected, and in some cases amplified, by the prominent roles played by Latinos in this field. Whereas more traditional models of community organizing (including these networks in their prior work) have frequently been criticized for being rather the province of white men,[13] today all four networks have significant numbers of Latinos working as front-line professional organizers. Perhaps more significantly, Latinos hold positions of primary influence among the top-level directors within the field. Among the most important examples are Ernesto Cortés, head of the Southwest IAF, perhaps the best-known organizer in the country; José Carrasco, an academic with longtime ties to the PICO network who played a key role in its elaboration of its own distinctive version of faith-based community organizing, now a key visionary and intellectual advisor within the organization; Mary Gonzáles, the associate director and head of training for the Gamaliel Foundation; Juan Soto, a lead organizer for Gamaliel in Chicago; Denise Collazo, national PICO staff and former director of PICO's San Francisco organization; and a significant number of mid-level organizers and directors around the country.[14]

Faith-based community organizing also benefits from public support on the part of Latino religious leaders. Jaime Soto, the auxiliary bishop of the Roman Catholic Diocese of Orange County, is paradigmatic in this regard, but numerous other examples exist, at both the episcopal and local congregational levels. In addition, many pastors (both Hispanic and non-Hispanic, and including Roman Catholics, mainline Protestants, and evangelicals) involved in organizing traditions have previously been involved in either the United Farm Workers Organization or the Central American peace movement, or worked as missionaries in Latin America.

Finally, a significant number of the Anglo organizers involved in the field had previous experience in Latin America, through the Peace Corps, church work, or international exchange programs. Many are bilingual. Many thus reach out relatively effectively to immigrant Latino communities and help bring Hispanic cultural influences into the culture of organizing.

Religious Bases of Faith-Based Community Organizing

The primary institutional sponsors of faith-based community organizing are Catholic, moderate and liberal Protestant, and black Baptist and historically black congregations.[15] Two of the fastest-growing sectors of the U.S. religious world—suburban white evangelical churches and urban Pentecostal, evangelical, and "Holiness" churches (many that are Hispanic or black)—participate only in very small numbers. Since most Hispanics are Catholic, evangelical, or Pentecostal, these groups are of particular interest here.

The Catholic Church has a long-standing presence as a key sponsor of faith-based community organizing in urban areas throughout the United States. Indeed, the Catholic bishops have been primary funders of community organizing for several decades. Today, the national office of the Catholic Campaign for Human Development (CCHD) provides about 16 percent of the operating funds of faith-based community organizing.[16] The social teachings of the Catholic Church (see below) on a living wage, unionization, and other issues often form part of the lingua franca in the culture of organizing, and the clergy "up front" at political actions often include Catholic priests or bishops. Finally, about one-third of the professional organizers are themselves Catholic.

Currently under way is an effort to reach out to evangelical and Pentecostal pastors, under the aegis of Christians Supporting Community Organization (CSCO).[17] Should this effort prove effective, it will bring another important Hispanic constituency into the fold of faith-based community organizing—a constituency that is fast-growing, dynamic, and scripturally articulate. Should it fail, this constituency may be ripe for recruitment by other political movements, especially those placing more emphasis on moral issues and cultural conservatism.

Prospects for the Future

Given this analysis, what can we say about the future, particularly about the role of Hispanics in the field? Two sets of comments are relevant—one rooted in the characteristics of the Hispanic community, and one rooted in the current American political context.

Three characteristics of the U.S. Latino population make Latinos crucial in the future of faith-based community organizing. First, about 70 percent of U.S. Latinos are Catholic and, if trends continue, this affiliation will remain predominant for the foreseeable future, despite successful outreach to Latinos by other faith communities. Furthermore, although only one of many religious traditions represented in faith-based community organizing, the Catholic Church has the most salient role of any single religious institution in the field: bishops and pastors are frequent spokespersons at public events and provide a religious imprimatur to political actions, and the Catholic Campaign for Human Development has been a long-standing source of funding for these organizations.[18] Thus, as Catholics—both through their growing numerical preponderance in the U.S. Catholic Church and through their increasing leadership roles as bishops, priests, sisters, and lay leaders—Hispanics will exert real influence over an institution key to the field of faith-based community organizing.

Second, Hispanics break down the frequent standoff between African American and white sectors of American life. Where Hispanics exist in sufficient numbers to provide a significant counterweight to the black–white polemic in American political culture (sometimes articulated, more often existing under the surface), they introduce an element of dynamism into political calculations.

Third (and more speculatively), the frequent tension between Hispanic economic interests linked to the left end of the Democratic Party and social values linked to the Republican Party may bring pressure to bear in favor of continuing nonpartisanship as a political strategy within faith-based community organizing.[19] To the extent that nonpartisanship (or perhaps better, a kind of pan-partisanship) has been one key to the field's success, Hispanics may be able to parlay this pressure into growing influence.

Fourth, as noted, if Hispanics continue to be attracted to the Evangelical/Pentecostal/Holiness wing of American Christianity, with its historical legacy of involvement in social causes, cross-racial constituency, and resources for Bible-based discourse, they may emerge as a powerful voice within that movement. Combined with continuing income polarization in American society, Hispanics' overall low socioeconomic status, and the Bible's rich tradition of prophetic denunciation of inequality, this could lead Hispanics to reshape the contours of the Evangelical/Pentecostal movement and strengthen their hand as key leaders of faith-based community organizing.

Our current political context suggests further ways in which Hispanics will shape the future of this field. First, their growing numbers and strategic placement geographically will give Hispanics a weighty political profile for years to come.[20] On one hand, in the future they will be the determinative vote in California, with its huge congressional delegation, massive influence in the presidential electoral college, and weight in political fund-raising. At the same time, Hispanics are a key swing vote in other electorally influential states, including Texas, Florida, and Illinois, as well as smaller "battleground" states for presidential elections, such as New Mexico and Arizona. Together, these factors make Latinos crucial in the future of American politics—especially if the new immigrants can be successfully brought into the political process. Faith-based community organizing appears to be one of the most successful ways of doing this.

Second, continuing international economic integration, with both its positive and negative aspects, will gradually erode the boundaries between the United States and Mexico. One vision for the long-term development of this trend, most prominently being articulated by Mexican President Vicente Fox, involves the creation of a fully integrated, borderless North America. The full implications of such a move are vast, perhaps unforeseeable, and certainly beyond this analysis—but it would surely mean an exponential increase in Hispanic political influence and a whole new field of operations for faith-based community organizing. Similar dynamics may well develop as economic integration with the rest of Latin America also moves forward.

Lastly, I note that Latino religiosity has already had a profound influence on the rest of American religion. A few examples may suffice. The "option for the poor," originally articulated by the Latin American Catholic bishops, today shapes universal Catholic social doctrine in profound ways and is a key principle of the U.S. bishops' pastoral letter, *Economic Justice for All*. The current boom in Pentecostal Christianity in America draws both from the original Azusa Street Revival of a hundred years ago and from more recent Latin American Pentecostalism, with rich cross-fertilization between the two.[21] Latin American *mestizaje*, especially its Mexican version linked to the Virgin of Guadalupe, represents one religious approach to the emerging reality of multiculturalism in the United States. And the notion of a this-worldly spirituality linked intimately to religious faith but also to work for justice represents an important counterweight to the escapist and deracinated "spiritualities" so in vogue in American mainstream culture. In all these ways, but more importantly no doubt in a myriad of ways not foreseeable, Hispanic religiosity will shape the future of faith-based community organizing and American political culture.

Conclusion

This analysis of Hispanic engagement in faith-based community organizing suggests that scholars should adopt a broader lens than often used in studying Hispanic political engagement in the United States. Excellent studies exist of Hispanic electoral participation, including the work of Louis DeSipio (1996),

Harry Pachon (1992), F. Chris García (1988, 1997), and Christine Sierra (1985).[22] But electoral participation among Hispanics continues to be muted, primarily because many are not citizens and because those Hispanics eligible to vote do so at less than half the rate of Anglos.[23] Faith-based community organizing represents one crucial venue of political engagement by Hispanics, both important in its own right and as a point of entry for Hispanic electoral participation. We should thus broaden our lens to view Hispanic civic engagement beyond the bounds of politics narrowly conceived, to understand all those non-electoral activities that hold promise to increase Latino influence and thus make American life more fully democratic.[24]

Perhaps it is appropriate to conclude such an upbeat analysis with two strong caveats. This optimistic reading of the intersection of Hispanic faith and politics within faith-based community organizing assumes that the field of organizing will successfully engage the talents, political skills, and religious vision of Latino grassroots leaders, pastors, and, especially, organizers. Bringing more Latino organizers into the field and cultivating their talents represent continuing challenges, at which the networks have succeeded only partially and in specific geographic areas. To engage the Latino community fully, organizers must build on that progress.

Moreover, this optimism represents a challenge to talented young Latinos and those who work with them. As a professional career with wide-open growth opportunities and organic links into Hispanic communities, faith-based community organizing has a great deal to offer: professional wages, exciting work linked to their faith traditions, and real service to one's community. But it cannot offer the financial rewards of legal and corporate careers premised on uprooting oneself from low-income sectors of the Hispanic community.[25] Forming Hispanic youth with the wisdom to choose well is a challenge to all of us who have the privilege of working with them.

NOTES

My thanks to the Pew Charitable Trusts and the convenors and participants at the Hispanic Churches in American Public Life conference for valuable feedback on this chapter. I gratefully acknowledge funding from the Lilly Foundation through the Center for Ethics and Social Policy in Berkeley, California, which made this research possible. (Correspondence to rlwood@unm.edu.)

1. Though I understand the competing preferences within the community, I use "Hispanic" and "Latino" interchangeably here.

2. See Sanford Horwitt's *Let Them Call Me Rebel: Saul Alinsky—His Life and Legacy* (New York: Knopf, 1989).

3. For an excellent scholarly account of the COPS experience, see Mark Warren's *Dry Bones Rattling* (Princeton, NJ: Princeton University Press, 2001). For a popular, if somewhat hagiographic account, see *Cold Anger* by Mary Beth Rogers (Denton University of North Texas Press, 1990).

4. For a theoretical argument and case studies elaborating the importance of both contestation and compromise for effective participation in democratic institu-

tions, see Richard L. Wood, "Religious Culture and Political Action," *Sociological Theory* 17 (November 1999): 307–332.

5. These are listed in order, from largest to smallest. Full disclosure: my own research has been within PICO and the IAF. Although I have had costs of two brief research trips subsidized by each organization, I have received financial compensation from neither. Prominent smaller networks include InterValley Project in New England, RCNO in Los Angeles, and the Organize! Leadership and Training Center in Boston.

6. One reason for their relative anonymity is that these organizations carry different names in each local area: for example COPS in San Antonio, OCO in Oakland, BUILD in Baltimore, MICAH in Milwaukee, SFOP in San Francisco. Again, the content of these acronyms vary, but most either spell out a prophetic figure from scripture (such as Micah) or include the word interfaith," "organizing project," "community organization," "organizing," "people together," and so on. The prior anonymity of the field in academic circles has changed with three books recently published: Richard L. Wood, *Faith in Action* (Chicago: University of Chicago Press, 2002), Stephen Hart's *Cultural Dilemmas of Progressive Politics* (Chicago: University of Chicago Press, 2001), and Warren's *Dry Bones Rattling.*

7. These and the following figures are from a study sponsored by Interfaith Funders (Richard L. Wood and Mark R. Warren, "A Different Face of Faith-Based Politics: Social Capital and Community Organizing in the Public Arena," *International Journal of Sociology and Social Policy*, 22:11/12, [Fall 2002]: 6–54). This is the first study to gather data on the entire field of faith-based community organizing. All figures listed are approximations, projected as follows: The study managed to locate and interview the directors of 75 percent of the faith-based community organizations around the country that we could identify (network-affiliated or independent, with the criteria for inclusion being that they had to practice a form of organizing recognizable as faith-based community organizing and had to have at least one full-time staff member on the payroll at the time of the study). The numbers given were then calculated from data from the 100 responding organizations; weighted according to reflected network representation projected upward to the total universe of 133 organizations known to exist; and rounded off to reflect the preliminary and projected nature of the data.

8. On the PICO California Project, see Wood, *Faith in Action*; on the Texas IAF, see Warren, *Dry Bones Rattling.*

9. See Sidney Verba, Kay Lehman Schlozman, and Henry E. Brady, *Voice and Equality: Civic Voluntarism in American Politics* (Cambridge, MA: Harvard University Press, 1995).

10. See Wood and Warren, "A Different Face." Unfortunately for our purposes, the study collected data only on *institutions* participating as members of local organizing groups, not on *individual* participants. Interpreting what these data mean about individual-level involvement of Hispanics is problematic: on one hand, many of the Hispanic-majority churches may have sizeable non-Hispanic minorities; on the other hand, many of the other 80 percent of congregations may have sizeable Hispanic minorities not reflected in the survey.

11. This interpretation is based on (1) three years (1992–1995) of intensive ethnographic work inside the PICO network for my dissertation; (2) nine years of subsequent continuing contact with PICO; (3) three years (1997–2000) of contact with the IAF; (4) periodic interaction with organizers or clergy from these four networks and smaller regional networks linked to the InterValley Project, RCNO, and the Organize! Leadership and Training Center; and (5) longstanding contacts with scholars and fun-

ders connected with all these networks. Though this positions me, I believe, as the scholar with the best breadth of contact across the high barriers between networks, note that my primary ethnographic exposure has been within PICO and the Southwest region of the IAF-both of which may over-represent Latino involvement.

12. For this critique, see Gary Delgado's *Beyond the Politics of Place: New Directions in Community Organizing in the 1990s* (Oakland, CA: Applied Research Center, n.d., [c. 1993]).

13. Ibid.

14. No full list of Hispanic lead organizers exists, but a partial listing includes Elizabeth Valdez, Joseph Rubio, and Ramón Duran in Texas; Liz Calanche, Gina Martínez, Manuel Toledo, and Julia Lerma in California; Ana García-Ashley in Wisconsin; Sister Consuelo Tovar in St. Louis, Missouri, and Denise Collazo in Florida, and Petra Falcón in Arizona. A total of about seventy-five Hispanic professional organizers work in faith-based community organizing around the country.

15. About 35 percent of member religious congregations are Catholic; about 34 percent are liberal or moderate Protestant (in order of concentration: United Methodists, Lutherans, Episcopalians, Presbyterians, and United Church of Christ); about 16 percent are Baptist congregations, including many Missionary and other African American Baptists; the remaining 15 percent are other Christian, Jewish, Unitarian, and "other non-Christian" congregations.

16. See the Interfaith Funders study (Wood and Warren, 2002, Table II). In addition to this national money, local branches of CCHD often fund local faith-based organizing work.

17. The best scriptural and theological work connected with this effort is that of Robert C. Linthicum, especially *City of God, City of Satan: A Biblical Theology of the Church* (Grand Rapids, MI: Zondervan, 1991).

18. Faith-based community organizing has received about a third of *all* the funds distributed by the Catholic Campaign for Human Development in recent years. In fiscal year 1999 this came to more than $3 million.

19. Of course, this is too facile a summation of complex Hispanic political and economic interests. As a summary, it holds historically—and broadly—today, but it does not adequately reflect (a) the changing economic interests of Hispanics as they move up socioeconomically, (b) Hispanics' changing cultural values as they are more fully influenced by consumer culture, or (c) the diminished appeal of the GOP to some-Hispanics, as some party strands back anti-immigration legislation.

20. This political profile parallels that of African Americans in the mid-twentieth century, following the Great Migration from the South. As Douglas McAdam argues, the changed political opportunities occasioned by this profile was crucial in generating the civil rights movement. See McAdam, *Political Process and the Development of Black Insurgency, 1930–1970* (Chicago: University of Chicago Press, 1982).

21. Conferencia General del Episcopado Latioamericano. "Iglesia y Liberación Humana: Los documentos de Medellín." Barcelona: Editorial Nova Terra, 1969; National Conference of Catholic Bishops. "Economic Justice for All: Pastoral letter on Catholic social teaching and the U.S. economy" Washington, DC:NCCB, 1986.

22. Full details are available in Louis DeSipio, *Counting on the Latino Vote: Latinos as a New Electorate* (Charlottesville: University Press of Virginia, 1996); F. Chris Garcia, ed., *Latinos and the Political Ssystem* (Notre Dame, Ind.: University of Notre Dame Press, 1988); F. Chris Garcia, ed., *Pursuing Power: Latinos and the Political System* (Notre Dame, Ind.: University of Notre Dame Press, 1997); Harry Pachon and Louis DeSipio, "Latino Elected Officials in the 1990s," *Political Science and Politics* 25

(1992): 212–217; and Christine Marie Sierra, "Latino politics in the Eighties: Fact, Fiction, and Fantasy," presentation at Colorado College, Department of Political Science, Colorado Springs (1985).

23. See U.S. Census Bureau, *Voting and Registration in the Election of November 1992*, as analyzed in Jeff Manza and Clem Brooks, *Social Cleavages and Political Change: Voter Alignments and U.S. Party Coalitions* (New York: Oxford University Press, 1999), 305.

24. All the more so, given that "social connectedness" appears to be a primary factor determining voter participation (Ruy Teixeira, *The Disappearing American Voter* (Washington, DC: Brookings Institution, 1992); thus, anything that spurs social connectedness both within the Latino community and between it and other communities and institutions (that is, "bonding" and "bridging" social capital) holds promise to increase Latino electoral influence.

25. Of course, young African Americans and Anglos/whites, as well as other racial and ethnic groups, face the same set of choices—and the same challenge.

10

"Dangerous Times Call for Risky Responses": Latino Immigration and Sanctuary, 1981–2001

María Cristina García

During the 1980s, religious and civic groups engaged in one of the most important acts of resistance of the late twentieth century—sanctuary—a grass-roots movement that protested both U.S. foreign policy in Central America and U.S. immigration policy. Dozens of publications have analyzed this movement, from newspaper articles covering the trials of individual sanctuary "workers" to the more scholarly studies of its religious and political origins. Most of the early books on sanctuary, written by journalists or participants in the movement, recounted its history for a popular audience. These included Miriam Davidson's *Convictions of the Heart* (1988), Robert Tomsho's *The American Sanctuary Movement* (1987), Ann Crittenden's *Sanctuary: A Story of American Conscience and the Law in Collision* (1988), and Renny Golden and Michael McConnell's *Sanctuary: The New Underground Railroad* (1986). Gary MacEoin's *Sanctuary: A Resource Guide for Understanding and Participating in the Central American Refugees' Struggle* (1985) compiled a number of essays addressing the philosophical, theological, and legal foundations—and implications—of sanctuary. Within the last decade, a number of scholars have written important ethnographic studies of the movement, among them Susan Bibler Coutin's *The Culture of Protest: Religious Activism and the U.S. Sanctuary Movement* (1993), Hilary Cunningham's *God and Caesar at the Río Grande* (1995), and Robin Lorentzen's *Women in the Sanctuary Movement* (1991).

So why another essay on sanctuary?

Civic reaction to migratory policies on the U.S.–Mexico border today compels a reassessment of sanctuary. Since 2001, U.S. president George W. Bush and Mexican president Vicente Fox have engaged in discussions of migration issues, including border enforcement policies and the possibility of creating a new bracero program and granting amnesty to thousands of undocumented workers in the United States. Trade policies, unstable currencies, low wages, and high unemployment have driven Mexicans and Central Americans to the United States in ever growing numbers, where they provide cheap, unskilled labor for the service-sector economy. Hundreds of people die each year trying to cross over to *el norte,* some left stranded by their "coyotes" in railroad cars, in tunnels, and on the open desert. Unfortunately, these stories of abandonment and death are all too common on the U.S.–Mexico border, as are the stories of exploitation for those fortunate enough to survive the crossing. Only the most shocking cases receive more than a few paragraphs in our daily newspapers. But as in the 1980s, religious and civic groups along the border are serving as our public conscience, alerting Americans to the state of affairs and lobbying for fairer and more humane policies. Some argue that the sanctuary movement is dead, but just as the 1980s movement drew on an American civic tradition, the work of today's border activists forms part of that historical continuum. Sanctuary, whether in 1981 or 2001, is a response to inconsistent and inhumane policies that target a specific population—in this case, immigrants from Latin America. This essay, then, reassesses sanctuary as it has affected the U.S. Latino population.

Origins of Latino Sanctuary

During the 1980s, thousands of Central Americans were killed or displaced by the civil wars in their countries. Close to a million Salvadorans, Guatemalans, and Nicaraguans were believed to be in the United States by 1990. The overwhelming majority of Central Americans arrived illegally across the U.S.–Mexico border. They were a cross-section of their societies: urban and rural dwellers, factory and agricultural workers, students and professionals, young and old. They included union leaders, former political prisoners, army deserters, church catechists, and housewives. Some traveled alone; others came as part of family units.[1] Some had been singled out for persecution; others were trying to escape the general climate of violence. All were in need of safe haven.

Polls conducted during the 1980s revealed that for most Americans, the refugees did not rank high on their list of concerns or priorities. As late as 1987, during the Iran-Contra scandal, only 32 percent knew that Nicaragua was located in Central America. But for some Americans, the migration of Central Americans presented a moral dilemma. They believed that the United States had a responsibility to assist these displaced people, given the role the government and U.S. corporations had played in their displacement. A vocal segment of the U.S. population, reminiscent of the anti–Vietnam war protesters, kept Central America on the front page of U.S. newspapers. They challenged U.S. immigration policy as a means of protesting U.S. foreign policy in Central

Unidentified woman crying out to God on behalf of undocumented immigrants fleeing cross the U.S.–Mexico border (Courtesy of Jimmy Dorantes/Latin Focus)

America. Indeed, one cannot separate the protests against deportation from the larger cultural protest against U.S. involvement in the region.

According to Justice Department officials, the majority of Central Americans did not qualify for asylum in the United States under the terms of the recently passed 1980 Refugee Act. The 1980 act adopted the definition of refugee drafted by the 1967 United Nations Protocol in an attempt to regularize the highly politicized process by which people were officially recognized as refugees and asylees in this country.[2] A petitioner for asylum now had to prove "a well-founded fear of persecution for reasons of race, religion, nationality, membership of a particular social group, or political opinion."[3] The challenge, then, was to provide evidence of "clear probability" of persecution. In a letter to the *New York Times,* a spokesperson for the State Department's political asylum division clarified the government's position: "It is not enough for the applicant to state that he faces the same conditions that every other citizen faces. [Under the terms of the 1980 Refugee Act we ask] Why are you different from everyone else in your country? How have you been singled out, threatened, imprisoned, tortured, harassed?"[4] Thus, while in some countries, refugee status was extended simply by membership in a particular group or "class" of people, in the United States the burden of proof was placed on the individual applicant. And the evaluation of evidence continued to be politicized.

Officials in the Reagan administration argued that there were many opportunities for safe haven throughout the region and there was little need for

Central Americans to travel all the way to the United States. The fact that many chose to do so anyway suggested that they were economically rather than politically motivated and thus were not true refugees. But from a practical perspective, the Reagan and Bush administrations could not offer blanket asylum or safe haven to the Central Americans because to do so signified an admission that the governments that they propped up with millions of U.S. tax dollars were despotic regimes that violated human rights. Thus, refugee policy became a pawn of foreign policy interests.

Since the Reagan administration regarded Central American migration as an economic rather than a political migration, it is not surprising that few were admitted to the United States as refugees or were granted asylum. From June 1983 to September 1990, not more than 3 percent of Salvadoran and Guatemalan asylum applications were successful (2.6% for Salvadorans and 1.8% for Guatemalans). The Nicaraguans had a slightly higher acceptance rate, although not as high as generally assumed: 25.2 percent during the period 1983–1990. (Asylees from the USSR, by comparison, had an asylum rate of 76.7%, and Cubans a 17.2% approval rate.)[5]

The Reagan and Bush administrations also resisted the calls for a protected status that would allow Central Americans to remain temporarily in the United States until conditions in their homelands improved. Immigration legislation allowed for such a protected status: Eventual Voluntary Departure (EVD) is a discretionary status given to a group of people when the State Department determines that conditions in the sending country make it is dangerous for them to return. Since 1960, EVD had been granted to Afghans, Cambodians, Chileans, Cubans, Czechs, Dominicans, Ethiopians, Hungarians, Iranians, Lebanese, Poles, Romanians, Ugandans, and Vietnamese. But officials resisted the idea of EVD for Central Americans on the grounds that the violence in El Salvador, Nicaragua, and Guatemala was not sufficiently intense or widespread to warrant such an action. They also claimed that existing adjudication procedures were sufficient recourse for any "deserving aliens," and they disputed claims that the deportees faced certain death if returned to their homelands.[6] The sheer number of Salvadorans also made EVD impossible. It was one thing to grant EVD to 5,000 Poles when martial law was imposed in Poland in 1981; it was quite another to grant EVD to the 100,000-plus Salvadorans believed to be in the United States by 1983.[7] Officials also worried that EVD would lure even more people to the United States.[8]

The Justice Department instructed the Immigration and Naturalization Service (INS) to increase its surveillance of the U.S.–Mexico border and expedite the deportation of undocumented aliens. Of particular concern to the Justice Department were the petitions for asylum that they regarded as frivolous and that bureaucratically tied up the courts. The goal, then, was to discourage such "frivolous" claims and expedite deportation. Bail bonds were gradually raised from $200 to as much as $5,000 per person to prevent a detainee's release—and disappearance—into U.S. society.

Detention centers along the U.S.–Mexico border filled to capacity. Immigration attorneys and representatives from religious and human rights groups reported a systematic violation of civil liberties on the part of INS officials trying to expedite the deportation process. The list of abuses was considerable: living quarters were unsanitary, and medical attention was inadequate; correspondence was photocopied for government prosecutors; money and property were stolen; phone calls were tapped; refugees were denied access to translated forms and documents; and many were denied access to legal counsel. Central Americans were regularly tricked into signing deportation papers: one common tactic was to separate family members and tell one spouse that the other had already signed a request for "voluntary repatriation." Abuses at two detention centers, in particular at Port Isabel in South Texas (popularly know as *el corralón*) and El Centro in California, prompted lawsuits against the INS, but temporary injunctions were repeatedly violated.

As early as 1980, community groups that assisted immigrants noticed a steady increase in the number of Central Americans arriving at their offices and asking for help. Those fortunate enough to survive the crossing—the harsh terrain, the lack of food and drink, the beatings by Mexican police and bandits—told horrible tales of the wars in their homelands: aerial bombardments that destroyed their towns and villages; friends and relatives kidnapped by guerrilla groups or murdered by government security forces; threats of rape, mutilation, and death if they challenged the existing order in any way. Throughout the southwest, churches, soup kitchens, shelters, and legal aid offices that assisted Mexicans, Chileans, Cubans, and other immigrants stretched already tight resources to finance the bail bonds and legal expenses of the Central Americans and to supply them with basic needs such as food, clothing, and housing. By 1981, dozens of religious and civic groups from Texas to California were assisting the Central American refugees in some way. Among the more prominent of these groups were the Border Association for Refugees from Central America (BARCA), Proyecto Libertad, El Rescate, the Central American Refugee Center (CARECEN), the Río Grande Defense Committee, and the Immigrant and Refugee Rights Project. Shelters such as Casa Oscar Romero, in San Benito, Texas, housed hundreds of refugees each night.

It is out of this context that sanctuary arose. In Tucson, Arizona, during the summer of 1981, Jim Corbett, a committed Quaker, began his personal campaign to assist the Central Americans detained in INS prisons. When his property could no longer accommodate the dozens of refugees he bonded out of prison, he appealed to his friends in the Tucson community for help. Corbett envisioned a network of "safe houses" for the refugees, similar to the Underground Railroad of the antebellum period that hid escaped slaves. He traveled to Nogales and established contacts with volunteers on the Mexican side of the border to assist with his secret network. They agreed to find ways to transport Central Americans across the border to the United States, where they had a slightly better chance of securing asylum. Fluent in Spanish and a longtime resident of the borderlands, Corbett was familiar with the terrain and the various INS check points, and he volunteered to direct refugees across the safest routes to sanctuary sites. As the safe houses filled up, Corbett asked his friend Reverend John Fife of Southside Presbyterian Church if the church might serve as a sanctuary site. In November 1981, the church session voted in favor of serving as a safe house for the Central American refugees.

In a parallel development, several church congregations in the San Francisco Bay area were also discussing the idea of sanctuary and voted to serve as safe houses for Central American refugees. Many of those involved in the underground movement felt that they had to make their activities public, as a means of both raising consciousness about Central America and U.S. foreign and refugee policy and combating the INS contention that they were merely smugglers and lawbreakers hiding under the cloak of religion.[9] In January 1982, members of these churches voted to make a public declaration of sanctuary. Coordinating their actions on March 24, 1982 (the second anniversary of Archbishop Oscar Romero's assassination), Southside Presbyterian and five churches in Berkeley, California, publicly declared themselves to be sanctuaries for Central American refugees. In a letter to Attorney General William French Smith, Reverend Fife explained their actions:

> We take this action because we believe the current policy and practice of the U.S. government with regard to Central American refugees is illegal and immoral. We believe our government is in violation of the 1980 Refugee Act and international law by continuing to arrest, detain, and forcibly return refugees to terror, persecution, and murder in El Salvador and Guatemala.[10]

Over the next few years, more than 200 churches, temples, and synagogues across the country followed suit, representing a variety of denominations: Baptists, Episcopalians, Roman Catholics, Lutherans, Mennonites, Methodists, Presbyterians, Quakers, Unitarians, and conservative and Reform Jews. The support network also encompassed hundreds of churches, as well as religious and civic groups in the United States, Mexico, and Canada that assisted the sanctuary sites in their work, with either volunteers or financial and other material contributions. Thus, the movement was transnational in both composition and influence. More than twenty U.S. religious bodies endorsed the sanctuary movement, including Pax Christi, the American Lutheran Church and the Unitarian Universalist Service Committee.[11] A resolution passed by the National Council of Churches of Christ urged member communities to "give serious consideration to the sanctuary movement as an expression and embodiment of the Christian's duty to the suffering, and to afford affirmation and support to those persons and congregations who choose to pursue this difficult path."[12]

Beginning in 1982, the Chicago Religious Task Force (CRTF) on Central America served as coordinator and clearinghouse for this vast national network.[13] The CRTF, which eventually formed the National Sanctuary Alliance, distributed manuals (including *Sanctuary: A Justice Ministry* and *Organizer's Nuts and Bolts*) instructing churches on ways to assist the movement; in addition, newsletters and mailings kept supporters informed of the latest legal developments. The CRTF and its member groups organized activities that would guarantee media attention: They organized speaking tours for visiting activists and religious leaders from Central America who gave eyewitness accounts of what was happening in their countries. They trained refugees for public speaking so they could give press conferences. They organized ecumenical prayer services, candlelight vigils, and processions and caravans to honor the victims of war. They sponsored lectures, concerts, and festivals of Central American arts and crafts.

These activities no doubt played a critical part in focusing attention on U.S. policies, but it was the rank-and-file volunteers in individual communities—many of them housewives and retirees of varied backgrounds—who engaged in the riskiest activities: sheltering refugees or transporting them to safe houses or across the border to Canada. They worked anonymously and quietly, without the media fanfare and praise of sympathetic journalists—and often without the approval of the CRTF and other coordinating boards who wished to keep the movement closely supervised.

Those involved in the underground claimed to be following not only a Judeo-Christian tradition but also an American civic tradition. Examples of sanctuary could be found in the American revolutionary war, the antebellum and civil war periods, and, more recently, the Vietnam era, when dozens of churches hid conscientious objectors from arrest. Critics of the sanctuary movement, however, claimed that this movement seemed more concerned with challenging U.S. policy in Central America and with confronting the INS than with addressing the physical and emotional needs of the refugees. If the refugees were their primary consideration, they argued, they could do their work covertly, without the media hoopla and the open confrontation that risked the refugees' arrest by INS. The CRTF's "how to" manuals seemed to support the idea that this was a political movement using religion to justify its actions. But for those involved in precious sanctuary work, the religious and political content and motivations were inseparable. One could serve the refugees while making a political statement. The primary goal was to rouse an apathetic population that cared little about the world outside its national borders and that gave tacit support to immoral and illegal government actions.

Officials in the Reagan administration tried to discourage the growth of the sanctuary movement by dismissing this civic tradition and reminding activists that the principle of sanctuary was not recognized in common or statutory law. Whenever religious leaders wrote to inquire about the legality of sanctuary, a Justice Department official emphatically warned them that church workers and clergy were not exempt from prosecution. Violators faced fines of up to $2,000 and imprisonment for up to five years for harboring or smuggling and $10,000 fines and five years imprisonment for conspiracy to harbor.

During the 1980s, the work of these religious groups—and the influence they held over public opinion—were perceived as a serious threat to U.S. policy, and the administration tried to undermine their influence. Justice Department officials portrayed sanctuary workers and other peace activists as naïve and misguided at best, political extremists and terrorists at worst. The conservative Institute for Religion and Democracy, founded in Washington in 1981, branded liberation theology as a Marxist plot to undermine capitalism and the geopolitical order. It criticized sanctuary workers for using religion to manipulate the public to support their political agenda, and it pressured U.S. churches to sever ties to socially active church groups in Latin America and at home.[14] In Los Angeles and other cities, tax assessors warned churches that they would be stripped of their tax-exempt status if they provided shelter to Central Americans.[15] The FBI and other law enforcement groups began surveillance of sanctuary workers. In congressional testimony, the Center for Constitutional Rights reported a "growing number of . . . FBI visits, IRS audits, customs difficulties, mail tamperings, and break-ins, directed against . . . people involved in the sanctuary movement."[16]

But many sanctuary workers were willing to risk their freedom because they believed that they were answering a higher call. When Father Thomas Davis was arrested by the Border Patrol for transporting seven Nicaraguans and six Guatemalans from Laredo to Corpus Christi, Texas, he responded: "I felt we had a special obligation to these people. You have to do something as a Christian. We were caught between the laws of man and the laws of God. I chose the laws of God."[17] The chairperson of the Wellington Avenue Church in Chicago responded to the threats of fines and imprisonment: "Dangerous times call for risky responses. The consequences that may happen to Wellington are minimal in comparison to the pain that happens every day to the people of El Salvador and Guatemala."[18] Sister Darlene Nicgorski, convicted for her sanctuary work in Arizona, said: "And when all is said and done, I would rather be judged for having helped a refugee than for having defined what one is."[19]

The issue of sanctuary did divide religious congregations, however, as members debated the moral, theological, and legal implications of challenging the government. When clergy took a more liberal stance than their congregations were willing to accept, members defected, which brought the inevitable reprimand from superiors—and in some cases, expulsion—for neglecting their pastoral duties.[20] People of faith looking to the church for guidance were often frustrated since on the advice of their attorneys many churches chose not to speak out on the issue of sanctuary. As the largest Christian denomination in the border states, and in the country, Roman Catholics found sanctuary particularly confusing and divisive. Governing bodies such as the U.S. Catholic Conference and the National Council of Catholic Bishops chose to remain silent—a response some interpreted as tacit approval of the movement. Even Pope John Paul II gave mixed signals to Catholics. During a 1987 visit to the United States, he praised the "great courage and generosity" of those who protect illegal Central Americans from deportation; but when the press interpreted his statement as an endorsement of sanctuary, he clarified that he did not endorse lawbreaking.[21] Individual nuns and priests were more likely to take a public position on sanctuary, especially members of the Maryknoll, Franciscan, and Jesuit orders, often risking censure from bishops more concerned with protecting the church's uneasy ties with the state.

The Justice Department began its surveillance of the sanctuary movement in 1982, and a number of individuals were indicted soon thereafter. Their penalties varied, depending on the location of the trial and the sympathies of the judge and jury. In 1984, in Brownsville, Texas, Stacey Lynn Merkt, an employee at Casa Oscar Romero, was sentenced to 269 days in prison. She became the first sanctuary worker to be imprisoned for her activities, and soon after Amnesty International declared her a prisoner of conscience. Jack Elder, the director of Casa Oscar Romero, was convicted on six counts of conspiracy and transporting illegal aliens through south Texas. He served 150 days in a halfway house for parolees. In 1985, Elder's successor at Casa Oscar Romero, Lorry Thomas, was sentenced to two years in prison for transporting a Nicaraguan refugee. The arrests did not stop sanctuary activities, however, and like Merkt and Elder, many of those imprisoned were repeat "offenders."[22]

The biggest sting against the sanctuary movement occurred in Tucson, Arizona, in 1984–1985: a covert operation called "Operation Sojourner," which led to the indictment of sixteen sanctuary workers. The FBI infiltrated four men—two paid informants and two INS officers—into various sanctuary sites, targeting Southside Presbyterian Church in particular. The two paid informants, Jesus Cruz and Salomon Delgado, had been arrested for smuggling illegal immigrants for a Florida rancher.[23] Posing as concerned volunteers, they gained the trust of the sanctuary workers and attended their meetings, where they taped the conversations with concealed recorders. With the 100 tape recordings of meetings and conversations gathered over a ten-month period, the Justice Department charged sixteen people—including Corbett and Fife—with seventy-one counts of conspiracy and transporting/harboring illegal aliens.[24] (Charges against five were eventually dropped.) More than eighty other people—refugees and the church workers who transported them—were arrested as coconspirators.[25]

At the pretrial hearings, U.S. Prosecutor Donald Reno introduced a motion to block any evidence relating to the defendants' religious and humanitarian motives, U.S. foreign policy in Central America, and human rights abuses in the region, as well as any information on the asylum process—to strengthen the government's case that sanctuary workers were simply smugglers using religion as a cover-up for their criminal actions.[26] (Indeed, the prosecution argued that the defense should not even be allowed to refer to the Central Americans as "refugees.") The defense counsel, in turn, introduced a motion to dismiss all charges based on the defendants' constitutionally protected religious beliefs and the illegal infiltration of church activities that violated the separation between church and state.[27] The judge ruled in favor of the prosecution, and the trial began. After six months of evidence and testimonies, the jury found eight of the eleven guilty of various charges, including conspiracy. While deliberating on the sentences, Judge E. H. Carroll received hundreds of letters urging leniency, including one signed by forty-seven members of Congress.[28] All defendants were given suspended sentences of three to five years probation. (Three years later, a federal appeals court upheld their conviction.)[29]

The Justice Department claimed success. In an interview, INS Commissioner Alan Nelson remarked, "Above all, this case has demonstrated that no group, no matter how well-meaning or highly-motivated, can arbitrarily violate the laws of the United States. . . . Perhaps now that this verdict is behind us, those of the sanctuary movement can redirect their energies in a manner that is within the law."[30] Prosecutor Reno called the verdict "the death knell for the sanctuary movement."[31] However, if the Justice Department planned to intimidate sanctuary workers into silence, the plan backfired. The arrests and trial dominated television, radio, and the printed press. Radio networks such as Pacifica and National Public Radio covered the trial, as did international networks such as the BBC. Dozens of magazines, newspapers, and television stations covered the story. Even newspapers like the *Los Angeles Times*, which generally favored tougher immigration controls, criticized the government's infiltration of the movement. One editorial cartoon showed a Border Patrol agent arresting Jesus Christ and his apostles.

The public outcry against Operation Sojourner was so great that more than 200 new sanctuaries emerged during the trial of the eleven activists. By December 1987 the number of sanctuaries had reached 450, two states and twenty-eight cities, 430 distinct religious bodies in thirty-nine states and more than 70,000 active participants.[32] The Inter-American Symposium on Sanctuary, held in Tucson a week after the arrests, drew more than 1,500 people rather than the expected 200 or 300.[33] Two hundred representatives from Christian and Jewish congregations traveled to Washington to protest the arrests and to demand a congressional investigation of the Justice Department's surveillance and intimidation practices. In the years after the trial, no other sanctuary workers were arrested—partly because members became "savvier" about their activities, and partly because the Reagan and Bush administrations could not afford more negative publicity about its Central American policy.[34] More important, the number of deportations also slowed.

In the end, the sanctuary sites of the 1980s assisted only a small percentage of the hundreds of thousands of Central Americans who crossed over to the United States, in large part because word spread through the informal immigrant networks that media attention brought government surveillance.[35] But the public debates that resulted from sanctuary ultimately facilitated the legal changes that gave Central Americans certain protections in U.S. society. Legal cases such as *American Baptist Church et al. v. Richard Thornburgh, et al.* (1991) reinforced the rights of Central American detainees in immigration prisons; congressional legislation such as the Central American Studies and Temporary Relief Act (1989) and the Nicaraguan Adjustment and Central American Relief Act (1997) gave Central Americans the temporary protected status they needed and, finally, the opportunity to legalize their status as permanent residents. The sanctuary movement also served Americans, although in a very different fashion, by focusing attention on constitutional and philosophical issues important to a democratic society: the relationship between church and state and the dialectic between power and resistance, civil disobedience, and civil initiative. These issues would emerge once again in the late 1990s.

The New Sanctuary?

While some argue that the sanctuary movement is dead, newspaper articles of the past twenty years suggest that the movement inspired many of this current generation to continue this civic tradition: to commit itself to social justice projects and, when necessary, to engage in acts of civil disobedience. A host of new organizations dedicated to assisting victims of violence and war have emerged across the United States, and many cite the sanctuary workers as their inspiration. Civic and religious groups along the U.S.–Mexico border are currently engaged in activities reminiscent of the 1980s movement. Indeed, some of the activists are familiar names—former sanctuary workers who have transferred their attention to a new cause and a new group of people. They cite the same religious motivations for their work and are engaging in similar strategies to challenge what they consider to be an unfair, inconsistent, and inhumane immigration policy.

For several decades now, and especially since the implementation of NAFTA, the border has experienced uncontrolled growth resulting in infrastructure problems such as depleting water supplies, dangerous roads, and growing *colonias* that are out of reach of needed municipal services. The border population is now 10 million and is expected to double in the next twenty years. The population growth and resultant competition for jobs and resources have spurred many to risk it all and cross to the United States illegally in search of higher-paying jobs. The number of INS apprehensions and deportations grew steadily throughout the 1990s. Close to 200,000 immigrants were deported in the year 2000 alone.

To stem this illegal movement, in the early 1990s the Border Patrol launched "Operation Hold the Line" in El Paso and "Operation Gatekeeper" in California. These more than doubled the agents working in the field and expanded their use of high-tech equipment to track border crossings—equipment such as ground sensors and infrared cameras, as well as the more traditional steel fences and electric lighting. Similar strategies are now used at other major points of entry along the 2,000-mile border. Not surprisingly, the number of undocumented workers apprehended at these traditional points of entry has dropped, not because these people are discouraged from trying but, rather, because they are attempting to enter through other—more dangerous—areas where police surveillance is not as vigilant, such as the Arizona–Mexico desert. Newspapers have reported that ranchers in Douglas were detaining, and sometimes shooting, immigrants who crossed their property. Smugglers are redirecting their human cargo into these dangerous areas, often abandoning them there without food or water. In fiscal year 2000, close to 150 people died in the Arizona desert; and from January to August 2001, the Border Patrol rescued 13,000 people along the Arizona–Mexico border. More than 400 people died in 2001 trying to cross the border at various locations.[36]

Residents of towns on both sides of the border have long assisted the migrants, providing them with food, clothing, and shelter. Residents are known to drop off food and jugs of water at spots where migrants are known to camp. Some residents have deliberately broken immigration laws transporting the immigrants to whatever destination they requested. Mexico's migrant-protection agency, Grupo Beta, patrols the areas where migrants are known to pass on their way to the United States and halt the vehicles transporting the would-be migrants to give them "orientation sessions." In these sessions, the agents inform them of the many dangers that they will encounter in the desert, and if they are still unable to discourage them from crossing, they ask the migrants to take their free "survival kits" that consist of water, packets of electrolytes to prevent dehydration, and antibacterial and antisnake-bite lotions. In one four-week period during the summer of 2001, Grupo Beta "oriented" 15,600 migrants—more than 400 of them children. President Vicente Fox's administration has also created a new federal office, Mexicans Abroad, that trains volunteers in border towns to give similar orientation sessions and distribute similar "survival kits" as part of its campaign "Leave Safe, Return Safe."[37]

On the U.S side of the border, civic and religious groups are currently discussing strategies to deal with what they believe is an emergency situation. In a familiar scene, representatives from various organizations met at Southside Presbyterian Church to discuss their "border strategy" to protest migratory policy, a strategy that includes acts of civil disobedience such as dismantling portions of the border fence and lobbying at the national level for a new immigration policy. The group Humane Borders, consisting of eleven churches from the Tucson area, committed itself to creating several hundred water stations across the desert—each a quarter-mile apart—to provide sealed gallons of water for border crossers. The stations are marked by thirty-foot tall metal poles, with blue flags with the logo of the Big Dipper and North Star. The group is also handing out bumper stickers with the same logo as a symbol of their opposition to U.S. immigration policy, and to signify to migrants that the group is willing to give aid. In order to circumvent the law, Humane Borders will set guidelines so members know how to assist migrants without breaking the law through "aiding in the furtherance of an illegal alien." However, the decision of how far to go in aiding border crossers will be left to the individual volunteer. Not surprisingly, the Border Patrol is discouraging such stations for both humanitarian and legal considerations.[38]

As in the 1980s movement, the new activists are called to do this work because, as one sanctuary worker put it twenty years ago, "dangerous times call for risky responses." Religious and humanitarian concerns once again factor into their decision-making, and the media attention they are attracting has focused attention on U.S. policy. However, this time they may have even more difficulty convincing an apathetic American public of the nobility of their cause because these undocumented border crossers are in need of jobs, not safe haven. A thin line always separates political and economic motivations, of course, but U.S. policy—and the U.S. public—have always made a strict distinction between the two and have favored the political refugee as the "worthier" immigrant. Once again the goal is to make Americans cognizant of the role their foreign policy plays in producing migration—and the exploitation of these workers that will inevitably follow.

NOTES

1. Aurora Camacho de Schmidt, "U.S. Refugee Policy and Central America," *Christianity and Crisis* 49 (September 25, 1989): 283.

2. U.S. law makes a distinction between refugees and asylees. Refugees must apply for protection from outside the United States, usually from a third country; if they are already within the United Sates and petition—and are granted—asylum, they are known as asylees. Once in the United States, refugees and asylees have the same status under American law. One year after they are granted asylum or refugee status, they may apply for legal permanent resident status, at which point their cases are reviewed to determine whether country conditions have changed sufficiently to merit withdrawing asylum or refugee status. Letter from John D. Evans, Director of the Resource Information Center, U.S. Department of Justice to the Immigration and Refugee Board of Canada, December 15, 1994.

3. U.S. Comptroller General, Report to the Congress of the United States, "*Central American Refugees: Regional Conditions and Prospects and Potential Impact on the United States,*" Washington, D.C.: General Accounting Office (July 20, 1984), 41.

4. Laura Dietrich, "Political Asylum: Who Is Eligible and Who Is Not," *New York Times* (October 2, 1985): A-26.

5. "Asylum Cases Filed with INS District Directors Approved and Denied, by Selected Nationalities," *Refugee Reports* (December 21, 1990): 12.

6. "Judge Refuses Summary Judgment on EVD," *Refugee Reports* 10 (October 20, 1989): 9.

7. "Why Poles but Not Salvadorans?" (Editorial) *New York Times* (May 31, 1983): A-20.

8. Sid L. Mohn, "Central American Refugees: The Search for Appropriate Responses," World Refugee Survey (1983): 46.

9. Hilary Cunningham, *God and Caesar at the Río Grande: Sanctuary and the Politics of Religion* (Minneapolis: University of Minnesota Press, 1995), 30–31.

10. Gary MacEoin, "A Brief History of the Sanctuary Movement," in Gary MacEoin, ed., *Sanctuary: A Resource Guide for Understanding and Participating in the Central American Refugees' Struggle* (San Francisco: Harper & Row, 1985), 21.

11. For a list of endorsers (by 1985), see ibid., 26.

12. "Resolution on Refugee Protection and Sanctuary," *Migration News* 4 (1985): 49.

13. The CRTF is a coalition of religious and social action groups formed largely in response to the murders of the four American women in El Salvador in 1980. Cunningham, *God and Caesar*, 39.

14. David Kowalewski, "The Historical Structuring of a Dissident Movement: The Sanctuary Case," *Research in Social Movements, Conflicts, and Change* 12 (1990): 95.

15. Glenn F. Bunting and Paul Feldman, "Assessor Threatens Tax Status of Churches that Provide Asylum," *Los Angeles Times* (February 1988): 3.

16. "Break-ins at Sanctuary Churches and Organizations Opposed to Administration Policy in Central America." *Hearings before the Subcommittee on Civil and Constitutional Rights.* Committee on the Judiciary, House of Representatives. 100th Congress, First session, February 19 and 20, 1987.

17. Ron Hamm, "Sanctuary Movement Raises Hard Political Questions," *National Catholic Register* (February 12, 1984): 7.

18. Mohn, "Central American Refugees: The Search for Appropriate Responses," 46.

19. Dan Walter, "Courage in the Sanctuary; Nun Says She Must Aid Refugees," *Bergen Record* (April 1, 1986): A-19.

20. See, for example, Kathy Boccella, "Controversial Priest Ousted in Hempstead," *Newsday* (May 29, 1988): 2.

21. Don Schanche and J. Michael Kennedy, "Pope Lauds Sanctuary for Central Americans," *Los Angeles Times* (September 14, 1987): A-6.

22. Merkt was granted an early release from prison because of complications in her pregnancy. This allowed her to serve eighty-three days of her sentence under house arrest. "Sanctuary Activist Gets Early Prison Release," *Los Angeles Times* (April 18, 1987): 3. Sue Fahlgren, "Elder Gets 150 Days in Halfway House," *Corpus Christi Times* (March 28, 1985): A-1, A-4.

23. "Sanctuary Activists Convicted," *Bergen Record* (May 2, 1986): A-1.

24. Ronald Ostrow, "Clergy, Nuns Charged with Alien Smuggling," *New York Times* (January 15, 1985): A-1; Stephanie Overman, "Refugee Crisis Challenges U.S. Policy," *Florida Catholic* (January 25, 1985): 8; Gerard E. Sherry, "Symposium Focuses on Sanctuary for Refugees," *Our Sunday Visitor* (February 24, 1985): 4; Wayne King, "Use of Informers Questioned in Inquiry on Aliens," *New York Times* (March 2, 1985): 6.

25. Wayne King, "Church Members Will Press Sanctuary Movement," *New York Times* (January 23, 1985): A-24.

26. Wayne King, "Trial Opening in Arizona in Alien Sanctuary Case," *New York Times* (October 21, 1985): A-10; Mark Turner, "Sanctuary Evidence Suppression Sought," *Arizona Daily Star* (March 29, 1985): B-1.

27. Susan Bibler Coutin, *The Culture of Protest: Religious Activism and the U.S. Sanctuary Movement* (Boulder, CO: Westview Press, 1993), 134–136.

28. Ann Crittenden, *Sanctuary: A Story of American Conscience and the Law in Collision* (New York: Weidenfeld & Nicolson, 1988), 335.

29. "Sanctuary Co-founder Gets Probation," *Los Angeles Times* (July 2, 1986): 1; "Court Upholds Conviction of Arizona Sanctuary Workers," *Los Angeles Times* (March 30, 1989): A-1.

30. "Sanctuary Activists Convicted," *Bergen Record* (May 2, 1986): A-1.

31. "Despite Prosecutions, Sanctuary Movement Is Still Vital, Growing, Its Activists Insist," *Los Angeles Times* (July 11, 1987): 5.

32. These cities included Berkeley and Los Angeles, California; Cambridge, Massachusetts; Madison, Wisconsin; Ithaca and Rochester, N.Y.; New York City; St. Paul, Minnesota; and Chicago, Illinois. Victor Merina, "Cities vs. INS," *Los Angeles Times* (November 17, 1985): 1. According to Kowalewski, Catholics provided 17.4 percent of the sanctuaries, while Unitarians, Quakers and Jewish sites were somewhat overrepresented in terms of their proportions of U.S. believers. See Kowalewski, "Historical Structuring, 103; Miriam Davidson, *Convictions of the Heart, Jim Corbet and the Sanctuary Movement* (Tucson: University of Arizona Press, 1988), 85.

33. Sherry, "Symposium Focuses on Sanctuary for Refugees."

34. In July 1987, for example, the Border Patrol stopped Ken Kennon, Rabbi Joseph Weizenbaum, and a group of refugees near the border, but the Border Patrol let the two men go without even taking fingerprints. Davidson, *Convictions of the Heart*, 160.

35. Kendall J. Wills, "Churches Debate Role as Sanctuary," *New York Times* (June 16, 1985): 35; Hamm, "Sanctuary Movement Raises Questions."

36. Arthur H. Rothstein, "New Faith Group Hopes to Place Water in Desert Areas to Help Migrants," Associated Press release, December 26, 2000; Karen Brooks, "Hispanics Note Conflicting Laws," *Fort-Worth Star Telegram* (June 7, 2001): 9; James Pinkerton, "Deportation Case Flood Is Predicted," *Houston Chronicle* (June 27, 2001): A-17.

37. Susan Ferriss, "Mexico Group Aids Migrants Crossing Desert into U.S.," *Austin American Statesman* (August 19, 2001): A-21; Susan Ferriss, "Mexicans Pursue Survival Training for Migrants," Cox News Service (May 18, 2001).

38. Ken Ellingwood, "Humanitarians Test the Law in Aiding Border Crossers," *Los Angeles Times* (December 19, 2000): A-1.

PART II

Contemporary Struggles

11

Public Lives in American Hispanic Churches: Expanding the Paradigm

Daniel Ramírez

La Biblia es la bandera de la celeste tierra
Sus franjas, sus estrellas nos hablan de su amor
Ciudad de redimidos, refugio de mi Cristo
Comprólo con su sangre a precio de expiación

Yo soy un ciudadano de esa ciudad eterna
Por fe fuí redimido y hoy ciudadano soy
Es Cristo el gobernante de esa gloriosa tierra
Y al flotar su bandera anuncia redención

The Bible is the banner of the celestial land
Its stripes, its stars speak to us of His love
City of the redeemed, refuge where my Christ
Purchased with his blood, expiation's price

I am a citizen of that eternal city
By faith I've been redeemed and am now a citizen
Christ is the governor of that glorious land
Whose floating banner announces redemption

—Juan Concepción, *Ecos de vida*, n.d.; translation mine

In the fall of 1994, as anxiety gripped many in the California immigrant community, the lyrics to Puerto Rican composer Juan Concepción's hymn, "La Biblia es la Bandera" seemed, like the Negro slave spirituals on the eve of Emancipation, to acquire a double meaning. Folks around me—many of them undocumented immigrants—lustily belted out the chorus's declaration of celestial and, hence, terrestrial dignity, all the while keeping an eye cocked for light-green *migra* (Immigration and Naturalization Service; INS) vans and ears alert for news of Proposition 187. I was struck then by the metaphorical subversion, multivalent meaning, and mobility of the decades-old composition.[1]

Concepción's hearty *vals* (waltz), penned in the midst of the Boricua colonial and diasporic experience and performed widely within Chicano, Mexican, and Central American Pentecostal churches, never entered the canon of Mainline Latino Protestant hymnody.[2] Its exclusion mirrors others—among these, the dismissal of Pentecostal and Evangelical congregations as sites of political empowerment. However, in terms of ideology and in contrast to Mainline hymnody, the song strikes a dissonant note against a blind loyalty to the imagined nation-state and its symbols. Patriotism may represent not only the last refuge of scoundrels but also an idolatrous impediment to God's more universal design for humankind.

Such religio-cultural texts—*himnos, coritos, testimonios* (hymns, choruses, testimonials) also remind us of the tentative nature of the social scientific paradigm(s) we would employ in our analysis of the Hispanic church in American public life. The study must remain elastic in its definition of "public life" and its components (e.g., politics, education, business, social programs, advocacy, activism) in order to take in the breadth and depth of life-in-community, including that life lived in the public margins and in the margins between two publics. It must look beyond the traditional markers of public engagement (e.g., voter registration, campaigns, rallies) to appreciate the scope of engagement and solidarity at the micro- and macro-levels. Hispanic-American churches would be seen, then, as venues of American public life, as the communities' preferred sites of discourse, and as public squares of the communities' own creation. Here many find, debut, and hear affirmed their public voice. For a marginal proletariat on the move, U.S. Latino congregations serve not only as anterooms to the public square but also as critical sanctuaries where transnational identities are forged and where intergenerational and intraethnic ties are strengthened. The agency reinforced on one side of the border can then be leveraged to assert rights and prerogatives on the other side.

With this spatial reconfiguration in mind—of congregation as public square and of public square as transnational sphere—this essay seeks to explore Latino Protestant responses to two situations of duress: the experience of undocumented immigration and residency in California and the post–Proposition 187 expanding labor diaspora in the U.S. Southeast. The geographical shift will parallel a methodological one: from an analysis of cultural texts to ethnographic description. To be sure, this interdisciplinary move does not seek to diverge far from the social scientific approach; rather, it seeks to complement it by pointing to previously overlooked pathways that broader and more nuanced survey instruments can help to illuminate.

Latino Pentecostals protesting against drug trafficking (Courtesy of Rogelio and Armando Razo)

Contested Paradigms: Sociology's *Huelga Social* vs. Ethnography's *Agency*

It would be fruitful to recall the metanarrative set in place over three decades ago by students of Latin American Pentecostalism (and extrapolated northward to Latino Pentecostals in the United States)—namely, the one that spoke of social and economic deprivation, psychosocial stress, and stunted liberation. Take, for example, Swiss sociologist Lalive d'Epinay's description of Chilean Pentecostal Churches as urban, religious replicas of rural *hacienda* society, on "social strike" and uselessly disengaged, in apolitical enclaves, from meaningful societal and political participation.[3] Set against socialism's heady possibilities, Pentecostalism's opiate threatened to stymie proletarian projects of economic and political liberation throughout the hemisphere. Subsequent events in Chile, especially the cooptation of Protestant Church leadership by Augusto Pinochet in the wake of his 1973 overthrow of the leftist government of Salvador Allende, seemed to confirm d'Epinay's dire warning.

More than two decades later, d'Epinay's pessimism resurfaced in anthropologist Lesley Gill's study of Aymara female domestic workers in LaPaz, Bolivia. She found these women to be politically alienated and thus especially susceptible to the escapist and moralistic rhetoric heard in Pentecostal Churches.[4] For Gill, Pentecostalism had inserted itself into Bolivian working-class society at a strategic moment of economic and political frustration. Instead of heading to the union hall on Sunday afternoon to bone up on Marx, Aymara women could be found speaking in tongues, banging tambourines, and ejaculating antiphonal aleluyas to Bible-thumping *machista* harangues. Paradoxically for Gill, they also spent the hours that could have been dedicated to labor conscientization espying and snaring reformed (from *machismo*) men in the *templos* (temples) the women had occupied for much of the day. Opiate light, with some improved marital possibilities.

Further to the north, sociologist Abelino Martínez concluded that Nicaraguan Pentecostalism's otherworldly discourse ("salvation offer-and-demand") and conservative social practice, being eminently religious in nature, did not "stimulate the politicization of its members, but rather perpetuated their [political] indifference."[5] Still, given the violent context of Ronald Reagan's Contra war and the persistent recruitment by counterrevolutionaries and their U.S. sponsors, such a stance at least ensured scant comfort to the enemies of Sandinismo. Costa Rican sociologist Jaime Valverde was less forgiving of Pentecostal *sectas* (sects) in his country. For Valverde, Pentecostalism's sharp dichotomy between spirit (or spiritual life) and body (or politics) engendered a false consciousness among the proletariat. The resultant theological discourse coincided with the given social order and its imposed rules of the game, thereby maintaining both. Rather than joining the class struggle, adherents viewed the reigning economic and social crisis as the fulfillment of biblical prophecy; hence, they adopted submissive attitudes toward their economic oppression, therefore guaranteeing its continuance.[6]

The quarter-century (from d'Epinay to Gill) of frustrated attempts at and disenchantment with liberation projects prompted a reframing of the question. Several new anthropological studies sited themselves in different and specific locales. From these points of particularity, they challenged d'Epinay's universalizing description by offering, in line with their subdisciplinary ethnographic method, more in-depth analyses of conversion factors at the ground level of gender, symbolism, mobility, and indigenous identity. To name two salient ones: Elizabeth Brusco's *The Reformation of Machismo: Evangelical Conversion in Colombia*,[7] a description of Colombian women's promotion of Protestant (or Pentecostal) conversion as a "female collective action" and a "strategic woman's movement" aimed at the "reformation of machismo," and Carlos Garma's "Poder, conflicto y reelaboración simbólica: protestantismo en una comunidad totenaca" (Power, Conflict and Symbolic Re-elaboration: Protestantism in a Totenaca Community),[8] a study of the attempts of Totenaca Indians in southern Mexico to leverage competitive healing powers and outside (denominational) support against the local monopolies of traditional shamans and merchants and corrupt union elites.

Also, John Burdick's study of gender, race, and religion in Brazil found Black Pentecostals had actively sought out racial solidarity in the hemisphere, and he suggested that they have proven adept at refashioning received elements into uniquely Brazilian products—products that, unfortunately, were denied the imprimatur of *movimento negro* orthodoxy.[9] Burdick appreciated the complexity of religious discourse among the subaltern. On the one hand, the sublimation of ethnic identity to a universal one of Christian brotherhood seemed to militate against Black Power. On the other, the Pentecostal *culto* was replete with the rhythms, intonations, and corporeal movements and sensibilities of Africa. Most striking for Burdick was the implicit and explicit upending of the oppressive racial aesthetic hierarchy of Brazilian society, especially as that system militates against the self-esteem and worth of its lowest members: Black women. The countercultural redefinition of feminine beauty inoculated Pentecostal women against much of the media's daily psychological assaults and freed them to construct an alternative, oppositional identity to wield against a racist and sexist world not of their making.

The sum of these and other findings represented an ethnographic challenge to the d'Epinay thesis on societal alienation and invited continued open-ended inquiry into the process of religious conversion and praxis and societal engagement. Equally important, given their common methodology (in-depth interviews, participant-observer status, etc.), the studies evidenced a disposition to hear their subjects' side of the story and to accord them greater dimensions of self-agency and self-representation. It is a cue we would do well to follow.

Incomplete Paradigms: Latino Faith and Political Practice

The extrapolation to U.S. Latino Pentecostals of findings drawn from the many studies of Latin American Pentecostalism owes as much to the absence of similar studies in the United States as it does to the absence of religious variables in political and other social scientific studies of U.S. Latinos. Here again, Pentecostal faith and practice are among the most conspicuous absentees.

The problem lies partially with the additive approach, wherein religious variables are folded in to survey instruments designed to capture more traditional dimensions of Latino political and social behavior (e.g., party affiliation, voting record, religious affiliation). Thus, the groundbreaking 1992 Latino National Political Survey (LNPS) queried 2,817 Latino (Mexican American, Puerto Rican, and Cuban) respondents (and 456 non-Hispanic whites) on only five religious variables: religious preference (Catholic, Protestant, Jewish, No Preference, Something Else), denominational affiliation (several Protestant choices were offered), "born again" experience, religious guidance, and religious service attendance. The low number of religious variables (the survey posed almost 200 questions in all) naturally resulted in an equally low utility of the religious data, even when this was combined with the responses on volunteer activities and affiliations and "hot-button" political issues. The authors' conclusion that native-born Mexican Americans "are not particularly likely to indicate that religion significantly influences their daily lives" seems hardly surprising, especially given the 59 percent of respondents who confessed to zero or minimal ("a few times a year") service attendance.[10]

The same research cohort undertook a complementary survey, the Latino Political Ethnography Project (LPEP), to hone in on "grass-roots political participation in conventional electoral politics."[11] Using the election year of 1990 as a frame, researchers fanned out into five of the largest and oldest Latino *barrios* in the country: Boyle Heights in East Los Angeles, Pilsen in Chicago, Magnolia in Houston, El Barrio in East Harlem, and Calle Ocho in Miami. While many respondents and focus group participants in the three predominantly Mexican American communities underscored the importance of Catholic parishes as bases for voter registration and community organization drives (e.g., against prison and waste facility construction projects), the researchers again did not move beyond these traditional markers of public engagement. Only one of thirteen core questions posed to respondents invited mention of church engagement, and that only in a limited manner: "Do established neighborhood organizations (churches, clubs, union locals) participate in these [electoral] activities?" The two following questions asked about the organizers and attendees.[12]

More promising is the long-standing (since 1982) binational Mexican Migration Project (MMP) based at Princeton University and the Universidad de Guadalajara. For several years now, MMP researchers, employing both sociological and ethnographic methods, have honed in on the complex social processes (e.g., networks, identity formation) and the knitting of ties between "sending" communities in western Mexico and "receiving" communities in the United States.[13] The scholarly output has been considerable, especially in the area of migration as social process.[14] Still, explicit religious questions were not posed to respondents until 1999, when the MMP initial questionnaire was adjusted to query, "In your trips to the United States, have you belonged to a social/religious association?" Previously, researchers had asked, "In your last trip to the United States, did you belong to any social associations?"[15] While the open-ended questions about networks, contacts, and solidarity may yield data about the role of congregations, the project has yet to present substantive findings on the role of religious networks. Not that the variable is unimportant to the researchers. Principal investigators Jorge Durand and Douglas Massey's catalogue of migrant ex-voto *retablos* (small paintings on sheets of tin, which, in this case, attest to miraculous healings, interventions against border-crossing dangers, and salvation from calamities in the United States), collected from shrines throughout Mexico, augurs well for a long-overdue thematic shift in this valuable research enterprise.[16]

Finally, a host of recent localized studies of *cambio religioso* (religious change) and pluralism in Mexico, especially change ushered in through returned migrants (beginning in 1942 with the Bracero era and exploding with post-amnesty migratory flows), awaits comparative work in the United States that would allow scholars to overlay and mesh the religious cartographies of transnational religious life.[17]

Expanding Paradigms: Culture and Religion as Politics

A little-noticed (in this country, at least) 1993 essay by political scientist Jesús Martínez, "Los Tigres del Norte en Silicon Valley," offers fruitful new ways of looking at the political behavior of Mexican immigrants. According to Martínez, political scientists traditionally viewed this population as "simply cheap labor or *braceros*, not as citizens with rights and responsibilities in the republics to which they are bound through historical accident, social ties, or economic necessities."[18] Through his study of the discography and repertoire of the Tigres del Norte, arguably the most popular northern Mexican (*norteño*) musical group in both the United States and Mexico, Martínez argues that these troubadours of the immigrant experience (who have lived in the San Jose area since the late 1960s) have given public voice to millions of compatriots in their celebration of transgressive movement, "Que Vivan los Mojados" ("Long Live the Wetbacks"); of trickster tales, "Contrabando y Traición" ("Contraband and Betrayal"); of pined-for villages and lost loves, "Plaza Garibaldi"; of Mexican topography, "Bajo el Cielo de Morelia" ("Beneath Morelia's Sky"); and even of Chicano activism, "Cuando Gime la Raza" ("When the Race Shudders"). Martínez fleshed out his analysis with a thick ethnographic description of a concert and dance in the new, cavernous San Jose Convention Center. The Tigres' power of convocation summoned 7,000 attendees, many drawn from the janitorial work force of the Silicon Valley, and many probably later involved in successful labor organizing. Concert as public event, especially in the looming shadow of Proposition 187, Martínez's creative appraisal of the Tigres proved prescient. In 2000, the Grammy Award–winning group established the Tigres del Norte Foundation at the University of California at Los Angeles, endowing that university's Chicano Studies Research Center with generous resources for "the study, preservation, and dissemination of folk music in Spanish." The remarkable recovery of public voice began with the transfer into digital form of the Arhoolie Frontera collection, consisting of 15,000 phonograph discs mainly produced in the United States between 1910 and 1950.[19]

The study of borderlands religious musical culture may build on foundational analyses undertaken elsewhere in the Southwest. Américo Paredes' seminal folklore study of border *corridos* (Western ballad) and Manuel Peña's more explicitly ethnomusicological treatment of *tejano conjunto* (Texas folk group) music point to alternative ways of discussing subordinated communities and their public articulation of power, and internal contestations over identity through musical cultural practice.[20] To be sure, none of these musical practitioners have developed systematic critiques of societal inequities or programs for liberation. Neither have most religious practitioners. Students of both fields have been challenged to theorize creatively about the interplay between practice and theory. Accordingly, drawing from his study of popular Latino Catholic practice, theologian Roberto Goizueta has articulated a complex "liberating praxis" and "theology of accompaniment" that remain "rooted in and attend to the particular experience of U.S. Hispanics as aesthetic, ethical-political, rational—and preferred."[21]

While the strains and dance movements of *norteño* music were prompting Martínez to rethink traditional measurements of political behavior, several blocks over a team of researchers headed by anthropologists Renato Rosaldo and William Flores were busily querying area residents about their notions of "cultural citizenship." The researchers asked respondents about the sites in which they felt most welcome and observed "social practices, which, taken together, claim and establish a distinct social space for Latinos in this country."[22] The research charter was beguilingly simple: to study "the process of 'affirmation,' as the community itself defines its interests, its binding solidarities, its own space, and its membership—who is and who is not part of its 'citizenry.' " Centering on four sites (a high school in Eastside San Jose, a large outdoor flea market, a public park, and a community hospital) and a number of public celebrations (Cinco de Mayo, Día de San Juan), Rosaldo et al. described a "new politics of citizenship," one through which "people in subordinated communities struggle to achieve full enfranchisement and . . . search for well-being, dignity, and respect in their *ordinary everyday* lives" (emphasis mine). Multiplied thousands of times over, the aggregation of such a politics at the microlevel may result eventually in "a renegotiation of the basic social contract of America."[23]

Rethinking Public Voice

The studies just discussed help to cast a different light on the behavior of Latino faith communities in California, especially during periods of xenophobic scapegoating. They have informed my redaction of transgressive narratives, *testimonios ilegales* (my term)—that is, public and semipublic accounts of "illegal" border crossings by members of Latino Pentecostal congregations. I believe they exemplify many of the claims to citizenship and strategies underscored by Martínez, Rosaldo, and others. Also, when accompanied by the exchange of more material goods (housing, employment, "love offerings," advice, contacts, and other elements of the social processes outlined by Massey, Durand, et al.) or when set in the public frame of Pentecostal liturgy, these symbolic *testimonios* articulate a public voice for a community otherwise thought to be apolitical and voiceless. Take, for example, this case from the San Francisco Bay Area:

> Cuando ya habían pasado dos días sin escuchar nada de ellos, sabíamos que se habían perdido. Los hermanos se pusieron a orar para que Dios cuidara a mis dos hijitos.
>
> (When two days had gone by without hearing from them, we knew that they were lost. The brethren began to pray for God to watch over my two dear sons.)

As I helped her with her family's citizenship applications, *Hermana* (Sister) Socorro (not her real name) testified how God had watched over her adolescent sons' border crossing in the company of other undocumented immigrants several years ago. As the *migra* swooped down around them, the band of *pollitos* (illegal border crossers) scattered in small clusters and hid in the mountainous terrain to await their *coyote's* (smuggler's) instructions. Miraculously, a guardian angel appeared and ended up in the same group as the frightened and disoriented lads. He was a young *hermano* (brother) who had often stayed at their family's home in their native state of Michoacán. Two days later, their protector phoned the anxious and prayerful mother from a safe-house in Los Angeles. A member of the congregation's youth group was hastily dispatched in the church's vehicle southward with the requisite cash balance owed to the *coyote* to rescue the lost sheep. Hermana Socorro rose in the following Sunday evening service to testify joyfully about God's goodness and to thank the congregation for their prayers and support. One of the boys in the story now repairs jet engines in Dallas; the guardian angel of the story is now an Apostolic pastor in Michoacán.[24]

Hermana Socorro's narrative describes a conflicted border zone, one where a nation-state has funneled transgressive pilgrims into dangerous terrain in a cynical attempt to weed out women and children from the undocumented immigrant flow. Since the implementation of Operation Hold-the-Line in El Paso and Operation Gatekeeper in San Diego and Río Grande, more than 1,600 people have ended up as dehydrated, frozen, drowned, or brutalized cadavers—many of these anonymous.[25] Yet, in Socorro's testimony, the zone has been transformed into one of fraternal solidarity. Gospel parables of lost sheep and Good Samaritans come easily to mind for the many hermanos—including U.S.–born parishioners—celebrating news of their children's safe arrival. U.S. Border Patrol agents are consigned bit parts as relentless persecutors whose morality ranks slightly above that of Jericho Road thieves. The legalistic caution of the comfortably situated Pharisee is of no use in this grey zone of ethical engagement.

In instances where immigrants have already integrated themselves into congregational life, the web of solidarity can prove resilient against tearing. In an incident in California's central valley, a surprise Friday immigration raid on a carpentry shop netted an Apostolic congregation's youth auxiliary president and a companion. The congregation's consternation was owing to the timing of the events; the youth president was scheduled to preach in that evening's *culto juvenil* (youth service), and the companion was to have directed the service. The liturgical and sermon duties were hastily reassigned to the pastor's niece and son, respectively. Afterward, the women's Dorcas auxiliary president (the pastor's sister) hatched a plan to rescue the deported *hermanitos* (little brothers). A car was dispatched to the United States–Mexico border. Contact was made with the young men in Tijuana. Discreet phone signals were arranged. An *ofrenda de amor* (love offering) was even more discreetly raised. Prayers were lifted on their behalf. In short, an efficient, church-run *coyote* operation restored the lost sheep to the joyful congregation in time for the Sunday night evangelistic service.

The facility of contact with the deportees in Tijuana is not surprising. Researchers found at least twenty-two Apostolic congregations in that city in 1987; a decade later, a church historian placed the number at forty-two.[26] Again, the quiet mobilization of several elements within a multigenerational and multistatus congregation expands the political paradigm, or simply reminds us that politics remains the art of the possible. Although Latino Pentecostals may not have been invited to the immigration policy table, they certainly have not acquiesced abjectly to its decisions or settled for its crumbs.

In my research I have been hard-pressed to find instances, in the past decades of cyclical persecution, of any disclosure to immigration authorities by Latino clergy and laity of the presence of so many undocumented immigrants within such easily identifiable religious and cultural communities. And the examples of sheltering, employing, feeding, and transporting—all actions declared illegal by Congress in 1952[27]—are legendary. During one period of frequent immigration raids in Los Angeles, a senior pastor and former Apostolic Assembly President who had baptized hundreds of immigrants reassured anxious members of his flock with a paraphrase of Jacob's epiphanal declaration: "Esta no es oficina de inmigración; es casa de Dios y puerta del cielo!" (This is not an immigration office; it is the house of God and the gateway to heaven!).[28]

Several testimonios resemble holy "trickster" tales, like the one where a young woman in an Orange County Apostolic Church was rushing out the door, late for the rendezvous with the coyote who was delivering her mother, and paused to ask the pastor's wife for the loan of her large, black-leather-bound *Reina y Valera*, the age-old favorite Bible of Spanish-speaking Protestants the world over . . . and the agreed-upon signal for the clandestine exchange. Often befuddled Border Patrol agents serve as the trickster's hapless antagonists. For example, on the drive up Interstate Highway 5 from San Diego under overcast skies, a *coyote* noticed that his two middle-aged matronly *pollitas* had that unmistakable look of *aleluyas* (Holy Rollers). Their conservative attire; make-up-free faces, and tied-back and uncut hair betrayed their identity.

"Parece que son cristianas, verdad?" (Looks like you're Christians, right?)

"Sí, Señor," came the nervous reply.

"P'os pónganse a orar pa' que venga la lluvia. Cuando hay lluvia, se meten los agentes a la estación de San Onofre y dejan de revisar a los carros." (Well, start praying for rain. When there's rain, the agents at the San Onofre station go indoors and stop checking the cars.)

Drawing from deep reservoirs, Hermana Godínez and her companion clasped hands and prayed in the words of the old *corito*: "Manda la lluvia, Señor!" (Send down the rain, Lord!) As they sped past San Onofre and toward Los Angeles and church and kin, the only *mojados* (wetbacks) were the Border Patrol agents seeking refuge from the downpour.

Hermana Godínez and her companion knew to report to a certain hotel in Tijuana upon their arrival in that city. It served as the border node between their home congregation in Guatemala City and a sister congregation in Los Angeles. Prior pilgrims and fellow congregants, including Hermana Godínez' son, had already marked the way.

During the journey's final leg, one document probably assumed greater importance as the pair neared their destination—namely, a letter of recommendation from their home congregation. Unable to secure legal admission into the modern nation-state, many pilgrims resort to this ancient literary genre, in order to attest to good character and faithful Christian service. Letters from Mexican and Central American Apostolic Churches often insert a key phrase: "I beg you to receive my recomendee as is the custom among us ('Do not forget to practice hospitality, for thus, some have entertained angels unaware.' Heb. 13:2), that you extend him/her the right hand of fellowship, and that you help him/her with counsel and the orientation that may be necessary."

The public reading of a letter of recommendation in the receiving congregation's hearing transforms the otherwise ordinary document into an empowering credential of legitimacy. Thus, an immigrant whose labor and personal worth as a farmworker, gardener, domestic, or busboy is held in low esteem, and is meagerly compensated by an aloof, capitalist society during the day or through the graveyard shift, regains and is accorded a large measure of self-esteem and worth when gathered with his or her *hermanos en Cristo* (brothers in Christ) and when entrusted by them with the congregation's various offices and projects. For Latino congregations, the symbolic, when invested with deep theological significance and rearticulated thousands of times over in rituals of welcome (including thematic hymnody), impinges as much on the community's life as do the macroeconomic and macropolitical.

When necessary, the band of pilgrims provides anonymous protection from the heavy and capricious hand of officialdom. Such protection can buy valuable time and carve out breathing space for important personal reconstruction. For example, in 1994, a member of a San Francisco Bay Area congregation was struck and killed by a speeding car while he was bike riding to work. Hermano Efren, a fifty-two-year-old undocumented immigrant, whose thirty-year alcoholic habit had devastated his life, family, and body, had joined the congregation ten months earlier and discovered not only a new purpose in life but a new and large family as well. (Efren frequently requested and relished the performance of a *ranchero*-style hymn: "Una llaga podrida era mi vida/Y tirado en la basura Tu me econtraste." ("My life was a festering sore/And You found me discarded in the waste heap.") His sudden death took everyone by surprise. Calls to the Mexican consulate and the California Highway Patrol were of little avail; he was bereft of both U.S. and Mexican documents—a man without a country; legally absent in one jurisdiction and illegally present in another. An unsent letter found in his meager belongings yielded the address of an aged aunt in Guadalajara who had given him up for dead many years earlier. Anticipating her relay of power of attorney, the pastor and households in the congregation assumed legal and financial responsibility for recovery and burial of Efren's body. As the casket was lowered into the manicured Silicon Valley cemetery plot to the words of the melancholy, but hopeful hymn, "Mas Allá del Sol" ("Beyond the Sun"), the women of the congregation wept and embraced one another. After the ceremony, the hermanos recessed to the church's *comedor* (dining room) for the traditional postburial chicken *mole* dinner. Hermano Efren's sudden passing was deeply felt, and he—who in is earlier life could have starred in one of Pete Wilson's darkly alarmist pro-proposition 187 "They Keep Coming" commercials—would be sorely missed.

Given the far-off possibilities of formal political enfranchisement for many like Efren, our inquiry into Latino religious and civic life should press the point: Was the rescue, embrace, and empowerment of a marginal laborer by a marginal faith community any less relevant than that community's formal engagement at the various levels of civic life? To be sure, several members of Efren's congregation participated actively in grassroots community-wide efforts to combat the impending Proposition 187. Some served as liaisons to African American congregations—the task came easily, since they, unlike Catholic activists, spoke the same religious language in a cadence familiar to the Black Church. Others brought musical and public speaking skills—forged in church settings—to the anti-187 marches and rallies. If political scientists can compare notes with biographers of public leaders and families, surely we should balance our concern with voice and behavior in the public square with an attention to the interior lives of marginal communities and persons who inhabit parallel squares. The interior can affect the exterior. Often, like Mordecai and his royal niece Esther, the voiceless may deputize the enfranchised to speak on their behalf.

Hermano Efren's case offers another stark reminder in our age of economic globalization. It exemplifies poignantly the postmodern human condition: atomization, dislocation, and fragmentation. This situation obtains not only in the subordinated countries of the global economy but also in the lives of millions of American citizens. As the national public square disintegrates into a cacophonous multiplicity of digital venues, albeit venues controlled by fewer and fewer economic interests, the work of faith communities in the United States may focus more intently on what veteran liberation theologian Richard Shaull in his joint study (with Waldo Cesar) of Brazilian Pentecostals, has characterized as "the reconstruction of human life beginning at the most basic level."[29]

To conclude, when viewed against the twentieth century's backdrop of *capricious* nation-states and powerful elites,[30] the *constant* ethos and praxis of proletarian religious solidarity captured in the *testimonios ilegales* suggest an alternative view of politics, as well as a corrective to the long-standing paradigm of Latino Pentecostal Churches as disengaged sectarian enclaves. An expanded, interdisciplinary methodology should seek to capture these features.

Public Voice in the Diaspora

The 2000 U.S. Census counted 378,963 Latinos in North Carolina.[31] The figure represented a 394 percent increase from the Bureau's 1990 estimate. The newcomers have elicited widespread interest as the latest advance agents of an ever-expanding labor diaspora. The borderlands now encompass Charlotte, Clinton, Durham, Raleigh, and Siler City. The ethnographic part of this essay represents an initial, modest attempt to describe Latino faith and practice in this new region and to assay comparisons with sites of earlier settlement. Given disciplinary convention and the inevitable intimacy of Latino Christian hospitality, the ensuing description will echo the self-reflexivity of participant-observer experience.

Like other academics in the Research Triangle, I welcomed an opportunity to study some of the new (and old) stories unfolding around us. I went in search of the pilgrims, seeking to eavesdrop on their prayers, singing, and conversations, in order to glean a few insights into immigrant life, faith, and solidarity in *Carolina del Norte* and to pose a few questions. Although I had observed a December 1997 march for the Virgen de Guadalupe in downtown Durham—complete with indigenous Otomi dancers from Mexico State (contiguous to Mexico City)—I had missed by several months the touchstone event in Durham Latino Catholic history, the public exodus of angry Latinos from the largely African-American Holy Cross parish. The newcomers had taken umbrage at one-too-many perceived slights by the priest and had stormed out at the height of Sunday mass, pausing only to rescue Our Lady of Guadalupe from the altar for transport to a more hospitable site.[32] (The community soon found a welcome at the larger and wealthier Immaculate Conception Church in downtown Durham.)

I began my search at point zero, in Durham, a place where the hemispheric economic chickens have come home to roost somewhat uncomfortably. Within the span of a few weeks I visited three Mainline churches and one Pentecostal church, all of which had initiated "Hispanic ministries" in the past one to four years. At one Mainline church, I found an orphaned group of Mexican immigrants (three adults and five children) meeting in a fellowship hall on a Sunday afternoon after the main congregation's 11:00 a.m. service. The tiny flock milled about patiently, waiting to see if a shepherd, any shepherd, would show up. A married couple from the sponsoring congregation greeted arrivals. They had been assigned to play "hosts" for any newcomers but planned to leave before the service's conclusion. Finally, two young Guatemalan men arrived from Mt. Olive, an hour's drive away. They apologized for the delay (this was their second service of the day) and for the absence of their minister, and then proceeded to cobble together a service. Afterward, one of them informed me that he was departing that Tuesday for Chiapas, Mexico, to join his wife, who had purchased a house and store there with his North Carolina earnings. The investments would serve as a base for ministry among their Mayan cousins. From our conversation it was obvious that the sponsoring church was oblivious to the dark-skinned, indigenous Billy Graham in their midst. Yet, his was the very transnational identity that researchers of *cambio religioso* in Mexico and of migration social processes in both countries would find intriguing. Clearly, religious variables had weighed as much as, if not more than, economic ones in the intrepid, trinational evangelist's decision to pull up stakes. A modest *ofrenda de amor* and *Vaya con Dios* (Go with God) for the journey seemed the least that an ethnographer could offer.

A week later and a few blocks over, I attended the evening service of another Mainline ministry. The regional denominational jurisdiction had ordained the pastor, a Duke Divinity graduate, for Latino ministry in 1997. Here, the number was double that of the other church, with the same ratio of children to adults. The pastor, a light-skinned *caribeño* (Caribbean native) married to an Anglo woman, was assisted by another seminary couple, who were Anglo. The meeting was held in a room that could pass for a makeshift chapel. There were observable class differences between lay and clergy. The moderately literate Spanish-speaking congregants, all dark-skinned *mestizos* (mixed-race people), sat restlessly through a liturgy and homily that, although well-meant and trenchant with liberation themes, seemed not to resonate with their immediate realities and needs. After the service, as the women picked through a donated clothes closet, the weary pastor apologized to me for the low turnout. "Come back on the second Sunday of the month. We get a full house for our potluck dinner."

A third Mainline service, this one in neighboring Chapel Hill, presented a wholly different set of class and gender dynamics. The incorporation of lively Pentecostal *coritos* carried the service along quickly. The sermon was practical and down-to-earth. The class differences between a South American woman pastor (with an Anglo spouse) and the several Mexican and Colombian working-class families seemed to be mitigated by the common ground of female experience. But a glance around renewed my questions about marginalization. In relegating immigrants to fellowship halls and side chapels, many Mainline churches unwittingly replicate the alienating spatiality of the public square.

It took a February 2000 visit by Louisiana State Senator and Klansman David Duke to entice me to Siler City, a town about thirty minutes to the southwest of Chapel Hill and about thirty years behind the Research Triangle. I had read about that town's Love's Creek Hispanic Baptist Church, the church's Mexican pastor, and its brand new sanctuary in the region's left-leaning independent weekly. The juxtaposition of xenophobic race baiting and take-no-prisoners soul-saving in a Tar Heel town seemed too ironic to resist.

The congregation was comprised of determined folk who have claimed symbolic and physical turf on twelve acres of Tar Heel land. The very first interview with Reverend Israel and Ruth Tapia suggested to me that the divine power invoked on Sunday could last all the way to Saturday. The Tapias shared that they had decided to view the David Duke rally on behalf of their vulnerable parishioners. They were two of a handful of Black and Latino dissenters. After the Grand Wizard stepped down from the courthouse steps, and as he worked the crowd, Reverend Tapia called out after him, "David Duke! David Duke!" When the cool hatemonger turned to the voice, Tapia delivered a Gandhian message: "Jesus loves you!" Ruth Tapia added a coda to her husband's ministration: "Yeah, Jesus loves yuh, and He don't lahk whut you're doin'!" She is certain that the man's face fell in shame as he slipped away. For his part, Reverend Tapia, an immigrant Baptist preacher from Chihuahua, feels that his task is to create an environment that will inoculate the church's children against the David Dukes of the world.

Ruth Tapia was born and raised in the Texas Panhandle and met her husband during his ministerial studies. The summoning call to North Carolina had taken her by surprise, but her husband's response to it had not. She usually defers to his more public profile and thus shied away from journalists' inquiries at the David Duke rally. Such are the dimensions of silence—of inarticulate silence and of being silenced—in the public square in the country of one's birth. She was particularly pained at the attack by one rally speaker against Latinos' patriotism; she recalled a number of Chicano veterans back home, including cousins, who served in Vietnam. She expressed admiration for African Americans and their abolitionist and civil rights struggles. Soon after our interviews, she accepted an outreach job with the Chatham County WIC program. I encountered her months later staffing a table at the regional Fiesta del Pueblo in Chapel Hill. As she wields and hones skills first acquired in her church community in Texas and North Carolina (the anteroom to the public square), Ruth Tapia may soon step up to Sojourner Truth's platform to claim her prerogatives of citizenship. In the meantime, her guerrilla-like interjections into and against the David Duke discourse represents merely the beginning of a long series of speech acts, acts in concert with the identity that her husband is intent on creating, interpellations that the New South will be forced to heed.[33]

Another event, the new temple dedication service, reinforced the import of this issue. In an earlier interview, the Tapias had confessed to a patient acquiescence toward Pentecostal music, a decision born out of an earlier disappointment in their Siler City pastorate and the defection of musicians to the Iglesia de Dios (Church of God). On this day, the "sensurround" approach to music seemed to discomfit the forty visitors from area's Southern Baptist Churches. Ever-polite Southerners, they endured the cacophony. But what for Mainline outsiders may have sounded like liturgical babble was for an insider (weaned on Black and Brown gospel music), sweet harmony, and for an ethnographer (attuned to unspoken meanings at play in the production of sounds and rhythms), an invitingly rich cultural text.

The music provided a frame for power contestation in the dedication service. The first congregational song was a bilingual rendition of the Swedish import, "How Great Thou Art," a standard whose debut by Billy Graham's lead soloist, George Beverly Shea, has left the incorrect impression that it is an original American composition. The congregation alternated between English and Spanish versions, ending up with a couple of simultaneously bilingual choruses at the end. Initially, the musicians and the English-speaking visitors seemed out of synch with each other, but the subsequent Spanish section smoothed the jagged dissonance. Thereafter, things flowed smoothly. Without realizing it, the visitors—several were movers and shakers in this town and probably Jesse Helms supporters—adapted to the *bolero* rhythm that the musicians insisted on applying to the song, being true to their liturgical memory. Thus, a religious musical text ostensibly exported southward from the United States decades ago, resurfaced in repackaged form in the stubborn hands of Salvadoran troubadours in the heart of the Bible Belt. In their construction and maintenance of a religio-cultural identity, folks at Love's Creek Hispanic Baptist Church have not offered a *tabula rasa* for inscription by more powerful agents. Rather, they have been busily constructing a self, a self in negotiation with the wider world. Our study of that process should proceed with an understanding of these ethnopoetics.

Conclusion

By taking seriously Latino believers' cultural artifacts and thickly describing the course of their life-in-community, we will arrive at a fuller, more complex understanding of the stakes as they see them at the intersection of faith and civic life. While the quantitative assessment of civic engagement will certainly yield valuable and overdue indices of behavior and attitudes, we would be remiss as students of this phenomenon if we did not also inquire about questions that arise, that have always arisen, within the hearts and minds of pilgrims still sorting out their way to Zion. Our efforts to better understand the attempt by a subaltern ethnoreligious community to carve out its own space, to execute its cultural practice, and to self-represent, may require some paradigm shifts. These are shifts we should welcome.

NOTES

I thank Eliseo Ramírez and Israel and Ruth Tapia and gratefully acknowledge my debt to other exemplars of the praxis outlined in this essay: the late Rosalva Arias de Martínez, Tomás Oceguera, Elías Castillo, and Salvador Arias.

1. Concepción's second verse reinscribes supranational meanings on familiar patriotic elements: "Sesenta y seis estrellas/Que hay en la bandera/Representan los libros/Que en ella encontrarás/Sus franjas que son doce/Sus tribus representan/Y el asta en que ella flota/El Cordero Pascual" (The sixty and six stars/Upon the banner/Represent the books/In which you will find/Its stripes which are twelve/representing its tribes/And the pole from which it waves/the Paschal Lamb). The third verse heralds a moment of universal reunion beyond terrestial boundaries: "De todo pueblo y raza/De toda tribu y lengua/Se formará una tribu/En la celeste Sión/Y allí todos reunidos/Bajo de esa bandera/Cantaremos las glorias/De paz y redención" (From every people and race/From every tribe and tongue/A tribe shall be formed/In the celestial Zion/And gathered together there/Under that banner/We will sing the glories/Of peace and redemption). Juan Concepción, ed., *Ecos de vida: selección especial de himnos y canciones espirituales por compositores hispanos* (Brooklyn, NY: Editorial Ebenezer, n.d.; translations mine).

2. In terms of mobility, Latino Apostolic missionary and migrant streams carried the song southward; it appears in the hymnals of Mexican American, Mexican, and Nicaraguan Apostolic churches: *Himnos de Consolación* (Los Angeles: Apostolic Assembly of the Faith in Christ Jesus, 1980), 6th ed.; *Himnario de Suprema Alabanza a Jesús* (Guadalajara: Iglesia Apostólica de la Fe en Cristo Jesús, 1996), 6th ed.; *Himnario de Suprema Alabanza, Aumentada* (Managua: Iglesia Apostólica de la Fe en Cristo Jesús, n.d.), 2nd ed. Note the hymn's re-working of patently norteamericano symbols (stars and stripes) in the latter two countries. Also, the difficulty in tracing precisely the dissemination of most Pentecostal hymns and choruses suggests that these ride in the luggage and in the hearts of a very mobile religious proletariat that often does

not bother to check in with civil and ecclesiastical authorities. Their dissemination, performance, and multiple meaning remind us of the permeability and elasticity of borders, both geographic and disciplinary.

3. Lalive d'Epinay, *Haven of the Masses: A Study of the Pentecostal Movement in Chile* (London: Lutterworth, 1969).

4. Lesley Gill, *Precarious Dependencies: Gender, Class and Domestic Service in Bolivia* (New York: Columbia University Press, 1994).

5. Abelino Martínez, *Las sectas en Nicaragua: oferta y demanda de salvación* (San José, Costa Rica: Editorial Departamento Ecuménico de Investigaciones, 1989), 112.

6. Jaime Valverde, *Las sectas en Costa Rica: pentecostalismo y conflicto social* (San José, Costa Rica: Editorial Departamento Ecuménico de Investigaciones, 1990), 80–81.

7. Elizabeth Brusco, *The Reformation of Machismo: Evangelical Conversion in Colombia* (Austin: University of Texas Press, 1995).

8. Carlos Garma, "Poder, conflicto y reelaboración simbólica: protestantismo en una comunidad totenaca" (Licenciado Thesis, Escuela Nacional de Antropología e Historia, México, D. F., 1983).

9. John Burdick, *Blessed Anastacia: Women, Race and Popular Christianity in Brazil* (New York: Routledge, 1998).

10. Rodolfo de la Garza, Louis DeSipio, F. Chris García, John A. García, and Angelo Falcón, *Latino Voices: Mexican, Puerto Rican, and Cuban Perspectives on American Politics* (Boulder, CO: Westview Press, 1992), 14, 58.

11. Rodolfo de la Garza and Louis DeSipio, "Overview: The Link between Individuals and Electoral Institutions in Five Latino Neighborhoods," in *Barrio Ballots: Latino Politics in the 1990 Elections*, ed. Rodolfo de la Garza, Martha Menchaca, and Louis DeSipio (Boulder, CO: Westview Press, 1993), 1.

12. Ibid., 21.

13. Douglas S. Massey, Rafael Alarcón, Jorge Durand, and Humberto González, *Return to Aztlán: The Social Process of International Migration from Western Mexico* (Berkeley: University of California Press, 1987).

14. Jorge Durand, *Más allá de la línea: patrones migratorios entre México y Estados Unidos* (Mexico, D.F.: Consejo Nacional para la Cultura y las Artes, 1994); Douglas S. Massey and E. Parrado, "Migradollars: The Remittances and Savings of Mexican Migrants to the United States," *Population Research and Policy Review* 13 (1994): 3–30; Douglas S. Massey and Audrey Singer, "The Social Process of Undocumented Border Crossing among Mexican Migrants," *International Migration Review* 32 (Fall 1998): 561–592. For a valuable thick ethnography of transnational (Los Angeles and San José de la Laja, Jalisco) identity at the nuclear family level, see (MMP researcher) Victor M. Espinosa, *El dilemma del retorno: migración, género y pertenencia en un contexto transnacional* (Zamora,: Colegio de Michoacán, 1998).

15. Web site: http://mmp.opr.princeton.edu/home-en.aspx

16. Jorge Durand and Douglas S. Massey, *Miracles on the Border: Retablos of Mexican Migrants to the United States* (Tucson: University of Arizona Press, 1995).

17. The Subsecretariat for Religious Affairs, the agency in Mexico's Interior Ministry charged with implementing the 1992 constitutional revisions on religious freedom, sponsored a peer-reviewed journal in which most of the country's religion scholars (e.g., Roberto Blancarte, Carlos Garma Navarro, Renée de la Torre, Patricia Fortuny Loret de Mola, José Luis Molina, and Rodolfo Casillas) published on themes of religious change and pluralism: *Religiones y Sociedad* (Mexico, D.F.: Secretaría de Gobernación). The several Centro de Investigación y Estudios Superiores en Antropol-

ogía Social (CIESAS) regional research units, together with the several regional Colegios (de Michoacán, de Jalisco, de la Frontera Norte, and de México), the Universidad de Guadalajara, and the Universidad Autónoma de México-Iztapalapa, have proved particulary fecund sites for research in this field. See Luis R. Morán Quiroz, *Alternativa religiosa en Guadalajara: una aproximación al estudio de las iglesias evangélicas* (Guadalajara: Universidad de Guadalajara, 1990); Eliseo López Cortés, *Ultimo cielo en la cruz: cambio sociocultural y estructuras de poder en Los Altos de Jalisco* (Zapopan: El Colegio de Jalisco, 1999); Patricia Fortuny Loret de Mola, coord., *Creyentes y creencias en Guadalajara* (Mexico, D.F: Instituto Nacional de Antropología e Historia, 1999); Lourdes Celina Vázquez, *Identidad, cultura y religion en el sur de Jalisco* (Zapopan: El Colegio de Jalisco, 1993); Miguel J. Hernández Madrid, "Los movimientos religiosos poscristianos en perspectiva global y regional," *Relaciones: estudios de historia y sociedad* 72 (otoño 1997): 157–178; Aída Hernández Castillo, "Identidades colectivas en los márgenes de la nación: etnicidad y cambio religioso entre los mames de Chiapas," *Nueva Antropología* 45 (abril 1994): 83–106; and Alberto Hernández H., "El desarrollo de las alternatives religiosas en la Frontera Norte," El Colegio de la Frontera Norte (unpublished paper), 1999.

18. Jesús Martínez, "Los Tigres del Norte en Silicon Valley," *Nexos* 16 (Noviembre 1993).

19. http://www.sscnet.ucla.edu/csrc/tigres1.html.

20. Américo Paredes, *With a Pistol in His Hand* (Austin: University of Texas Press, 1958); Paredes, *Folklore and Culture on the Texas–Mexican Border* (Austin: Center for Mexican-American Studies, 1993); Manuel Peña, *The Texas–Mexican Conjunto: History of a Working-Class Music* (Austin: University of Texas Press, 1985). For a parallel ethnomusicological study in an altogether different setting of subordination—namely, apartheid—see Veit Erlmann, *Nightsong: Performance, Power, and Practice in South Africa* (Chicago: University of Chicago Press, 1996). For a literary analysis of border *corridos*, see María Herrera-Sobek, *Northward Bound: The Mexican Immigrant Experience in Ballad and Song* (Bloomington: Indiana University Press, 1993).

21. Roberto Goizueta, *Caminemos con Jesus: Towards a Hispanic/Latino Theology of Accompaniment* (Maryknoll, NY: Orbis Books, 1998).

22. William V. Flores and Rina Benmayor, "Constructing Cultural Citizenship," in *Latino Cultural Citizenship: Claiming Identity, Space and Rights*, ed. William V. Flores and Rina Benmayor (Boston: Beacon Press, 1997), 1.

23. Renato Rosaldo and William V. Flores, "Identity, Conflict, and Evolving Communities: Cultural Citizenship in San Jose, California," in Flores and Benmayor, ibid., 57–96.

24. The accounts were first compiled for a column syndicated by Pacific News Service in the wake of Proposition 187: Daniel Ramírez, "Proposition 187 and the Latino Church," Pacific News Service, San Francisco, February 13, 1995. The informants and congregations remain anonymous for attribution.

25. The most comprehensive binational study conservatively placed the number of fatalities at 1,600 for the years 1993–1997. See Karl Eschbach, Jacqueline Hagan, Nestor Rodríguez, Rubén Hernández-León, and Stanley Bailey, "Death at the Border," *International Migration Review* 33 (Summer 1999): 430–454.

26. Alberto Hernández Hernández, "Sociedades religiosas protestantes en la frontera norte: estudio sociográfico en tres localidades urbanas," *Frontera Norte* 8 (enero-junio 1996): 107–132. Samuel López Torres, *Historia de la Iglesia Apostólica de la fé en Cristo Jesús en Tijuana: 1927–1997* (Tijuana: Samuel López Torres, 1999), 138.

27. U.S. Congress, 8 USC §1324, 1952.

28. Interview with Benjamin Cantú, Los Angeles (September 20, 1994).

29. Richard Shaull and Waldo Cesar, *Pentecostalism and the Future of the Christian Churches: Promises, Limitations, Challenges* (Grand Rapids, MI: Eerdmans, 2000), 116.

30. The flux in immigration policy (e.g., the massive repatriation of 1 million Mexicans *and* Mexican Americans during the 1930s; the seductive bracero guest-worker program of 1942–1964; the punitive Operation Wetback of the 1950s; the Immigration Reform Acts of 1964, 1976, 1978, 1986, and 1998; the scapegoating ballot initiatives and criminalizing border enforcement measures of the 1990s) continues to bedevil—or energize—American politicians. In spite of amply documented abuses in the bracero program, President George W. Bush voiced preference for the broad expansion of guestworker programs over a general amnesty for undocumented immigrants. "Fox y Bush acuerdan impulsar nueva política migratoria," *La Jornada,* (February 17, 2001). On repatriation, see Francisco E. Balderrama and Raymond Rodríguez, *Decade of Betrayal: Mexican Repatriation in the 1930s* (Albuquerque: University of New Mexico Press, 1995). On the bracero program and Operation Wetback, see Ernesto Galarza, *Farm Workers and Agri-Business in California, 1947–1960* (Notre Dame, IN: University of Notre Dame Press, 1977); and Julian Samora, *Los Mojados: The Wetback Story* (Notre Dame, IN: University of Notre Dame Press, 1971).

31. http://www.census.gov/population/estimates/state/rank/hisp.txt.

32. "Durham Churches Reach Out to Hispanic Faithful," Durham, NC *Herald-Sun* (October 26, 1997): A14.

33. "The interpellation is an originary speech act, with which the pauper erupts into the real community of communication and producers (in the name of the ideal), and makes them accountable, demands a universal right, as a human being-part of the community; and, in addition, expects to transform it by means of a liberation praxis (which is also frequently a struggle), into a future, possibly more just society." Enrique Dussel, *The Underside of Modernity: Apel, Ricoeur, Rorty, Taylor, and the Philosophy of Liberation,* translated by Eduardo Mendieta (Atlantic Highlands, NJ: Humanities Press International, 1996), 36.

12

"The Ladies Are Warriors": Latina Pentecostalism and Faith-Based Activism in New York City

Elizabeth D. Ríos

In this essay I examine the narratives of Puerto Rican Pentecostal women in ministry in New York City. They have led ministries that have sought to live and teach a holistic gospel.[1] They have been able to usher in some level of urban social transformation in their communities. These "Progressive Pentecostals" have simultaneously taken a traditional *vertical focus* on being more like Jesus and a *horizontal focus* that is demonstrated through Jesus' ministry calling (Luke 4: 18–19).

Many black American Pentecostals, including Pastor James Forbes of New York City's Riverside Church, call their ministry style "progressive Pentecostalism."[2] This style blends a passion for transformative social action with an urgency to win souls to the Kingdom. I apply this concept to Puerto Rican Pentecostal women.[3]

Latina Pentecostal activists have not allowed gender biases, fear, or other obstacles to hinder them from serving others. These activists have made major strides over the past few decades. Latina Pentecostals base their activism on Joel 2:28. They see it as a call to service where only God's approval is needed. This call sets them free to do Christian work, globally and locally—in the church and outside of it.

While it may be true that some Pentecostals fall into the stereotype that they are "so heavenly-minded that they are no earthly good," others have been actively engaged in social justice. In New York, evangelical men and women established faith-based nonprofit agencies or holistically-minded churches that have and continue to address some of the social ills in their communities.

Latina Pentecostals' desires to impact society are rooted in their belief that God is concerned with the person as a whole. To them, it is not an option to sit idly and do nothing as people suffer. It was the call of God over their lives that moved them beyond the four walls of the church to depart altogether from traditional church ministry to do what some may have deemed "ungodly" work—addressing drug addiction, the HIV/AIDS crisis, the mental health issues, children with disabilities, and teen pregnancy.

Manoel de Mello, a Brazilian Pentecostal pastor whose followers number in the millions, reflects the Progressive Pentecostal mindset when he asked his listeners, "What good does it do to convert a million people if at the same time the devil unconverts ten million through hunger, disease and military dictatorship?" He went on to state, "these sort of things one can't overcome by holding wonderful religious services but by organizing one's forces and joining with others who have similar interests. We must join now with other Protestants and even with Roman Catholics to help each other."[4]

Contrary to stereotypes, the Latino Pentecostal movement has a social vision, although they never articulated their work in those terms. As such, they have been active serving their community. However, while the Puerto Rican Pentecostal community was familiar with addressing the end result of a problem, they were not used to challenging the systemic "structural sins." Therefore, if trying to help someone in the church led to critiquing the systems, the minister was considered to be *fuera de orden* (out of order) and plunging into unchartered and restricted territory.

As Gastón Espinosa and Daniel Ramírez show elsewhere, the Latino Pentecostal movement has a tradition of social service by providing housing, food, and medical services for migrants and immigrants. Pentecostal ministries served as ad hoc social workers, taxi drivers, counselors, and relief service providers. They have assisted ex-convicts in securing jobs and helped welfare mothers purchase groceries. They felt that it was not their place as Christians to challenge the system at large because they were suspicious of legislatures. This is why Pentecostal ministries served jobless moms and starving households, instead of advocating for better policies that would have enabled these families to get the skills necessary to find permanent jobs.

The first generation of Latino Pentecostal leaders had a social vision of transforming the community primarily through *"Jesus y la palabra"* (Jesus and the Word) and not through advocacy, policy analysis, or engaging politicians in forums. This is the key difference between second- and third-generation Latino Puerto Rican Pentecostals. The younger emerging Latino Pentecostal population believe that just because a better world is expected, they should not accept all injustice with patience while waiting for the Lord's second coming. Rather, their hope is that they can do something about structural evil. Unlike the first generation who did not see that as an option because of their social, economic, or educational status, this emerging group is dealing with systemic and structural "sins" in addition to personal sin. They are more open to partnerships with secular institutions and non-Christians than the first generation was. For this reason, I call them "Progressive Pentecostals."

Rev. Aimee García Cortese in the 1970s (Courtesy of the Flower Pentecostal Heritage Center)

As people who see themselves as servants of God, Progressive Pentecostals advocate for liberation against personal and structural sin.[5] Some Latina faith-based activists have functioned like Progressive Pentecostals because they are able to translate their faith into social action. Although Progressive Pentecostalism begins in the worship experience, it finds its ultimate expression in community service.[6] It is these Latinas that I seek to expose. I seek to demonstrate the dynamic effect of Puerto Rican Latina Pentecostals in New York City, as well as to explore their faith as they moved across denominational and socially constructed barriers to create holistic and organic models of leadership since the 1940s. The organizations these women have created, along with their models of ministry and their continued involvement in New York City civic life, has served as a source of encouragement to numerous emerging Latinas today. If the "whole" church is to take the "whole" gospel to the "whole" world, it must have a holistic spirituality. However, the Pentecostal mindset historically has been defined as one that ministers only to the individualistic and personal element, which makes it inner-directed and vertical. The missing element of social transformation (which includes social action, social service, and social witness) is outer-directed and horizontal.

Nueva York: The Mosaic That Is

The granting of U.S. citizenship to Puerto Ricans in 1917 and the increased economic influence of America produced what we have come to know as the "great Puerto Rican migration." By the early 1930s, New York City's Latino population was predominately Puerto Rican.[7] Then came the end of World War II, which began a new migration of Puerto Ricans to New York. The increase of Puerto Ricans from the "Enchanted Island" to New York was large. The Latino demographic profile began to change when in the late 1960s U.S. immigration laws and a host of other issues in Latin America began to prepare the way for a new migration of Cubans, Dominicans, Colombians, and other Latinos.

Today, the ethnic mosaic in New York City is very different. The 2000 census summary statistics from the New York Department of City Planning reported that among those of a single race, white non-Hispanics remained the largest group, accounting for 35 percent (2.80 million) of the city's population. Hispanics were the largest single minority group, numbering a 27 percent share (2.16 million) of the population.[8] Black or African Americans accounted for 24.5 percent, and Asian or Pacific Islanders for 9.8 percent. The numerical and percentage growth of the Hispanic community showed an increase of 377,043, or 21.1 percent; of that figure, the Bronx accounted for the highest percentage (49.5), which is attributed to the Puerto Rican community, followed by Dominicans in Manhattan at 20.6. However, this shows a steady decline from census statistics in 1960, which found that 80 percent of all Latinos in New York City were of Puerto Rican ancestry. This number continued to drop from 68 percent in 1970 to 61 percent in 1980 and to 50.3 percent in 1990. Some attribute the decrease to return migration to Puerto Rico, urban flight to the suburbs, and a change to warmer climates, particularly Florida. The Puerto Rican population decline in the city has been a focus of press attention, as people try to predict the future of the city's growing and ethnically diverse population.[9]

There are now Latino communities in all New York City boroughs, and 27 percent of New Yorkers are identified in the census as Latinos. As mentioned previously, the Bronx accounts for the largest number of Latinos (644,705), followed by Manhattan (417,816), Queens (556,605), Brooklyn (487,878), and Staten Island (53,550).[10]

Las Raices: We've Come a Long Way

The Pentecostal movement began in April of 1906 at the Azusa Street Revival. It was led by William J. Seymour (1870–1922), an African American Holiness evangelist from Louisiana. The Latino Pentecostal movement traces its roots back to this revival. The movement split in 1913 into two theological camps—Trinitarian and Oneness. In 1915, H. C. Ball, Rodolfo Orozco, and Alice Luce founded the Latin District Council of the Assemblies of God, and in 1916, Francisco Llorente and Antonio Casteñeda founded the Oneness Apostolic Assembly of Faith in Christ Jesus. As Gastón Espinosa notes, almost every indigenous Latino Pentecostal denomination prior to 1940 in the United States traces its genealogy back to one of these two denominations.[11] The power to radically turn one's life around with the help of the Holy Spirit was one of the defining claims of this new movement. Pentecostalism quickly drew those left at the margins of a society. It was no surprise then that Latinos—feeling increasing subjugation from the California Anglo population—became part of the movement. At the onset of this faction, reactions to Pentecostalism were almost unanimously negative. Many of the respected church leaders and theologians dismissed it by not even considering it worthy of criticism. Due to this lack of attention from the religious leaders, those who practiced Pentecostalism were seen as disturbed, mentally challenged, emotionally unstable, psychologically deprived, and pathological. By the 1990s, the movement began to be taken more seriously because of its global scope. David Barrett startled many in 1980 when his statistics suggested that classical Pentecostalism was the largest unit in the Protestant family.[12] By this time, Latino evangelists had already introduced Pentecostalism all over New York, Puerto Rico, and Latin American communities.

One of these early evangelists was Francisco Olazábal (1886–1937). He was considered by many to be one of the most effective Latino preachers in the early days of the Pentecostal movement. Espinosa points out that his invitation to New York City came by way of Rev. Francisco Paz, a Mexican American Assemblies of God minister who had invited Olazábal to Spanish Harlem. After numerous campaigns, he began to cross racial boundaries to influence black Americans, Italian Americans, and Anglo-Americans. Olazábal organized the Latin American Council of Christian Churches (CLADIC)[13] in 1923 and reportedly helped organize 130 churches that attracted 50,000 followers from across the United States and Mexico. On many occasions, Olazábal traveled with a young woman and eventually became a key player in the ministerial development of that emerging unknown Latina in New York City. The unknown woman was Leoncia Rosado Rousseau, or "Mama Leo," as she has come to be known today. In the 1930s she began her ministerial career that eventually birthed some of New York City's greatest contemporary Pentecostal leaders.

Rev. Paz, the Assemblies of God minister who had also been greatly persuaded by Olazábal's ministry, impacted a New York City Puerto Rican Pentecostal giant: Rev. Ricardo Tañon.[14] Another key figure in the Latino Pentecostal movement in New York City was Juan León Lugo. Originally having migrated to Hawaii from Puerto Rico, Lugo converted to Pentecostalism in 1913 and went on to study under evangelists affiliated with the Assemblies of God denomination. Lugo moved to New York in 1931 to personally supervise what is now coined a "church plant" in Greenpoint, Brooklyn. A man of vision and seeing the tremendous increase in Puerto Ricans in Manhattan, Lugo went on to establish a new "church plant" on East 104th Street in Manhattan.[15] In general, most Puerto Rican Pentecostals did what they could do in the early years as they were watching from the wings as they, like black Americans, were the victims of the dominant power structure that enshrined Jim Crowism.

Due in part to the work of these men of God, many people were moved not only to spread the gospel but also to become beacons of light in the midst of the many challenges of life that the Puerto Rican community faced in that era. It was then that Latino Pentecostals began to make great contributions to urban ministry in the United States. Though unknown to the wider church, women and men in New York like "Mama Leo" and Rev. Ricardo Tañon, both of whom were significantly influenced by Francisco Olazábal, revolutionized methods to minister to drug addicts, alcoholics, and youth. Rev. Tañon, a former student of Olazábal, was known to be a charismatic preacher. Tañon organized the John 3:16 youth program in Olazábal's church, which later developed into "Iglesia Cristiana Juan 3:16" in the South Bronx, and he went on to establish many churches in the Northeast, Puerto Rico, and Dominican Republic. For Latino Pentecostals in New York, he was a spiritual and moral voice, not only for them but also for other churches and civic organizations.[16] The new wave of articles from white Evangelical's speaking of a "new focus on social ministry" by Pentecostals is not news to the Latino community as they have had their own "Convoys of Hope"[17] for decades.

Tañon has gone on to shape the work of Eldin Villafañe, another Puerto Rican Pentecostal from New York City. Eldin Villafañe's book, *The Liberating Spirit: Towards an Hispanic American Pentecostal Social Ethic*, has encouraged many Latino Pentecostals to establish separate nonprofit corporations. He reminds us that Latino Pentecostal leaders have created soup kitchens, after-school programs, and support groups—all of which fulfill important needs in the Hispanic community. He sees these ministries, whether big or small, as prophetic signs to all those who, for various reasons, have chosen flight instead of fight.[18]

Latinas in Ministry: The Ladies Are Warriors

Today, while still not nearly enough, there are Latina preachers, pastors, seminarians, college professors, theologians, chaplains, faith-based nonprofit CEOs, and powerfully creative lay leaders in the church. The Latinas who have remained active in ministry in New York City all attribute their longevity to faith, prayer, patience, and, more than anything else, their undying belief that as Pentecostals their work is a mandate of God. These women warriors have shown the world how God manifests His power through earthly vessels *regardless* of gender.

These Latina women were "warriors" because God gave them their directives, and they did not let anything stand in their way of fulfilling their divine mandates. They used the tools of faith, prayer, and patience even while not receiving the full support of others in the community of faith. As Progressive

Pentecostals, these Latinas have demonstrated that the church's mission includes engaging in power encounters with the sinful structures of society. They have sought as their life's work to respond to both the vertical and horizontal elements of life, which then becomes holistic in nature and thus breaks the "chains of injustice" and introduces a "chain of change" to transform their urban communities. They are defined as warriors because, as far as they are concerned, they are *doing* what many others are still *discussing*.

Theology of Presence: Holistic Faith-Based Ministry Models in the City

While some are better known than others, all have developed a holistic methodology to solving specific problems in their communities. They have gone forward to develop an approach that is different from most traditional Christian work. "As Pentecostals, many of us get passionate and involved in one area of need and think to ourselves that if we solve a particular problem in a person all other things will work themselves out," Rev. Ana Villafañe stated. Founder of Way Out Ministries in the Bronx, the 67-year-old activist went on to claim, "we have found that even though a person may make a personal commitment to Jesus Christ, the rest of the problems in his or her life may not be solved instantaneously."[19] What is evident in Latina Pentecostal faith-based activism is that the old individualistic salvation model proved to be too limited. Pentecostals often found themselves blaming *el Diablo* (the devil) for everything, when, in reality, the problems were social and structural. "Solving the housing problem does not solve the emotional struggles a person has to deal with of being homeless."[20] The models in this essay are organized by decade. These organizations use a methodology that deals with the spiritual, social, economic, political, cultural, emotional, physical, moral, justice issues, and educational or family life of each individual that walks through its doors. Rooted in their faith, these programs have altered the civic and social issues of their day.

Damascus Christian Churches: Rev. Leoncia Rosado Rousseau, Angel to the Outcasts

Born on April 11, 1912, Rev. Leoncia Rosado Rousseau or "Mama Leo," as she is affectionately called by many, came to New York City by boat on September 22, 1935. Although when I met her, she was ninety years old and suffering from the beginning stages of a progressive, neurodegenerative disease, Mama Leo could still recall her dramatic beginnings in ministry. From the seedy corridors of some of New York City's worst barrios, her ministry to "the outcasts" of society—the drug addicts, gang members, prostitutes, and alcoholics—has birthed some of today's greatest preachers, pastors, and evangelists, like Nicky Cruz, who went on to establish a worldwide evangelistic ministry; Jim Jimenez, who pastors the Rock Church in Virginia Beach, Virginia; and Bishop Jerry Kaufman, now deceased, who was a Jewish drug addict and went on to become a well-known figure in New York City after leaving John 3:16 to establish Love Gospel Assembly in the Bronx, to name just a few.

"It was in the mountains," she says "of Toa Alta, Puerto Rico, when God spoke to me and told me I had to go to New York City."[21] After having a huge argument with her mother about this "voice," she arrived in New York, where she met Rev. Francisco Olazábal, who she credits for opening many doors of ministry for her. "I would go to services with him where he would be the invited speaker and out of nowhere he would say, 'I feel from the Lord to have Leoncia speak,' " she recalls. "You could see the disapproval of all the male ministers on the pulpit" but "I walked through every door God opened," she said.

A great opportunity for city government sponsorship of her program came when Nelson A. Rockefeller was governor. "She actually said no to $12 million dollars!" said Sonia Gamboa, Mama Leo's personal assistant for the last eleven years and a frequent participant of the Center for Emerging Female Leadership. "The *New York Times* actually wrote about her for this situation. Rockefeller offered her $12 million in state assistance to help fund the program she developed for drug addicts and prostitutes of the street but there was a catch, she had to take out the name of Christ in her programming." Sonia believes that the exact statement Mama Leo told them was "you can keep your $12 million, I will keep my Christ."

When asked about the discouragements and struggles she faced as a Latina in ministry, she said, "I was rejected by many." Sonia, her assistant, explained: "Cops didn't like [Mama Leo] because she was working with these really bad people who already had records in the police department. Ministers didn't like her because she was a women 'doing a man's work.' It would have been easier to deal with" said Sonia, "if Mama Leo had other Latina sisters to talk to, but at that time not many of them were doing what she was doing. She was isolated." Another struggle she faced was money for operating costs. It was difficult to meet some basic needs for her program participants, although she says, "God always provided."

Today, while the drug and alcohol rehabilitation program no longer exists, she says it does live on through the legacies of the people she touched. However, Damascus Christian Church still operates successfully and has a Latina woman heading its operations as bishop. Mama Leo still attends the church she started in the 1970s, "Iglesia Cristiana de Jamaica," which currently has a membership roster of about 150 people. Mama Leo went to the toughest neighborhoods, talked and ministered to some of our society's less desirables, because she knew without a shadow of a doubt that God had called her. Perhaps that is what is missing in some of our emerging Latinas, a sense of divine purpose. Leo summed up her life with the quip, "if my life inspires other Latinas to get to know God then that is a good thing."

Way Out Ministries: Rev. Ana Villafañe, Friend of the Addicted

Born on April 6, 1934, in Brooklyn Heights, New York, and growing up in the early to mid-1960s, a Puerto Rican young woman named Ana Villafañe was about to embark on a life-changing journey in her life. It was during the 1960s while in her thirties that she first got involved in dealing with the heroin epidemic that devastated the New York City Puerto Rican community. As a graduate of Mama Leo's alcoholic rehab program, she felt an earnest desire to make a difference in people's lives. However, before the establishment of Way Out Ministries, she was involved with the Community Progress Corporation (CPC), which was a program funded by the City of New York. CPC ran a rehabilitation station for many in the city, in addition to other programs that they operated for housing and medical treatment. This was a time when "the Bronx looked like an atomic bomb had hit it"[22] and "there were no programs really dealing with drug addicts that were faith-based other than Teen Challenge and Mama Leo's Christian Youth Crusade, which was part of the Damascus Christian Church. Although new secular programs like Day Top, Phoenix House, and Inwood House were being established," CPC had locations in the Stuyvesant area of Brooklyn, in Queens, and in Hunts Point of the Bronx. After about ten years and a series of events at CPC, she left to become a senior counselor with the Methadone Maintenance Treatment Program. It was at this time that she and her husband, Eddie Villafañe, began Way Out Ministries. Members of the Catholic, Lutheran, Baptist, and Reformed Churches were most helpful to Rev. Villafañe at the beginning of Way Out; for three years, she received monetary support from these churches. The City of New York became aware of her program and gave her $1 million for three years from tax levy monies. Today, however, Way Out exists entirely on private individual donations. For the last twenty-seven years the organization has been operating purely on the faith of its founder. "Very few churches, you won't believe it, support us," says Rev. Ana Villafañe. Although this program mostly services a Latino population, little support actually comes from Latino Pentecostal churches. "I do have a few Pentecostal churches, but not as much as I know I can be supported by. The Hispanic Pentecostal *Concilios* should be doing more to help, but they are not."

The operating costs and funding issues that she has encountered have been very discouraging, but she still maintains a positive attitude. She said, "you have no idea what I have gone through, but I am here because God has me here and because I am unrelenting." She went on to say, "I know what God has started he will finish." Interestingly, the majority of her employees are women, and only two of them (her part-time bookkeeper and her secretary) actually receive a stipend for their work. All others are volunteers who she personally had to educate in the area of volunteerism.

However, while Rev. Villafañe holds on to her unrelenting faith, the future of Way Out is literally in the hands of its community, and she is hoping they come through for her. Currently, she is undertaking a $2 million fundraising campaign to build a new residence in the East 148th Street area where her program now resides. This is the first time in their history that she has embarked on such a challenge to raise support. "It not because of pride, but because I was happy with the way things were." Unfortunately, she has had a tough time, as people have not fulfilled their pledges of support from her radio campaigns and fundraising dinners.

Way Out has as its goal to minister to substance and alcohol abusers, individuals with AIDS, the homeless, the needy and afflicted individuals in order to help them break out of their destructive lifestyles and prepare them to accept responsibilities. Throughout the past thirty-three years, many people have been drug free and law-abiding citizens. Some have even chosen to help others by becoming directors of residences, shelters, soup kitchens, and pantry programs.

Crossroad Tabernacle: Aimee García Cortese and Joseph Henry Cortese, Latina Pioneer and Hip Hop Evangelist

Aimee García Cortese, now seventy-three years old, is pastor emeritus and founder of the Crossroads Tabernacle in the Bronx, New York. Her thirty-four-year-old son, Pastor Joseph Henry Cortese, took over at Crossroads in January 2002 from his mother, who founded the church in 1983. Pastor García Cortese has been written about in Pentecostal literature and has even appeared in various articles on women in ministry.[23] While the church is still part of the Assemblies of God (AG) denomination, its mission and ministry are unique and quite unlike any other AG church in New York City. When asked how she feels she is affecting her community through her church, she stated, "Our impact is the obedience to proclaim the gospel to all people."[24] The doctrine of Crossroads is based on "Bible truth as found in the scriptures and I make no apology for its truth because in it I find the mind of God."

The legacy of Pastor García Cortese and the church she founded continues as the Reverend Joseph Henry Cortese, or "Pastor Joe," as he is called, has transitioned into the role of senior pastor. Pastor Joe is known in the city as the "Hip-Hop Evangelist" because of his use of drama and music to reach the teen culture. He was born in the East Bronx in 1967 and is the youngest of four children. Currently, he is supervising the church's $3 million renovation, slated for completion in 2002. The project is transforming a 1939 movie house into one of the largest and most sophisticated theaters and recording studios in the Bronx borough.

The building, at 1320 Castle Hill Avenue, has been transformed into the Boden Center for the Performing Arts, which features concerts and plays, as well as teaching dance, music, and drama to neighborhood kids. The church has already completed the Studio on the Hill, a state-of-the-art audio and video recording studio. "Although our paradigms and our models are drawn from scriptures—the bare necessities of ministry as Jesus called it—Crossroads has taken those bare functions and translated them in such a way that they work here in Castle Hill in 2001." Pastor Joe goes on to say, "ministry for us is becoming more and more radical, even though it's still very historic."[25]

"We're really pulling away from fundamental tradition and moving into real living, breathing spirituality," said Rev. Joe García, "and that translates at the bottom into some very non-religious things in terms of outreach, such as providing services for the community that are not based on church membership or doctrinal lines."[26] He plans to make the church a beacon for the Gospel and hip-hop artists and teens throughout the Bronx. He also hopes to provide education and job training. He even hints at the possibility of opening a laundromat and restaurant to serve the community.

In thinking about the philosophy of ministry found at Crossroads, Rev. García says, "Jesus' ministry met all human needs. First and foremost, knowing. He knew who he was, and where he came from." From Pastor Aimee's perspective, a community needs to understand its identity. "He cared about hunger in his community," she goes on to say; "therefore it is fitting for churches to feed the hungry—spiritually and physically."[27]

Coming from what she calls a legalistic "raja-tabla" Pentecostal background,[28] Pastor Aimee has gone through many metamorphic stages due to her treatment within the Pentecostal community. She mentions how she was asked to leave "Spanish Assemblies of God" many times, only to return. Reflecting on her struggles, she says that she came to the following conclusion: "I know who I am—actually God knows who I am." In her times of ministerial mêlées, she says, "I cried out to God—I'm yours, Lord. Do what you please with me; place me at your service, and I will follow and not turn back." Although her church is meeting the needs of their community as Jesus modeled in His day, Pastor Aimee would not necessarily use the term "holistic" because as she says, she is "still dealing or, better yet, struggling, with the concept." Yet, with over fifty years in ministry, Pastor Aimee García states, "if being holistic and impacting our community means reaching out, meeting needs, touching the sick, helping them receive medical assistance, seeking betterment for our children by advocating for better schools and health plans, then we are very much holistic!"[29]

Bruised Reed Ministry and Rev. Rosa Caraballo, Healing Caregiver

Born in San Juan, Puerto Rico, on January 21, 1954, Rosa grew up Baptist and was introduced to the Pentecostal movement when she met and began to date Pentecostal preacher Hermes Caraballo. During her formative years in ministerial training, she worked at New Life for Girls, with Cookie Rodríguez, a former prostitute and drug addict in New York City who became a Christian and turned her life around.

After having married Hermes Caraballo, an Assemblies of God minister at that time pastoring Glad Tiding Church in the Bronx, she was thrust into the reality of HIV/AIDs when someone in her congregation in 1985 was diagnosed with the disease. That sparked the beginning of Bruised Reed Ministry. In 1986, due to this death, she began to develop formal relationships with Montefiore Medical Center, Bronx Lebanon, and North Central Bronx through her hospital visitation ministry at Glad Tidings. "I never planned on this, I was just walking through the doors that God opened for me."[30]

As a bilingual faith-based, nonprofit organization, its mission is to deliver and help others render holistic compassionate services to persons afflicted, affected, or abandoned because of HIV/AIDs. In 1993, they incorporated and moved into donated office space. In 1996, an opportunity to expand arose when Rev. Raymond Rivera provided office space in his building at virtually no cost. Some of the challenges Rev. Caraballo has faced are similar to what Rev. Ana Villafañe mentioned previously; she lamented that "there is very little financial support for our organization. It's discouraging to see that very few Latino churches see people with HIV/AIDs as a mission field to be won for the Lord." She goes on to say that "men of God and vision like Rev. Ray Rivera, Rev. Marcos Rivera of Primitive Christian Church, Rev. Lou Carlo, Pastor of Wounded Healer and Professor at Alliance, Rev. David Anglada [a former AG youth leader who is now assistant to the bishop for Hispanic/Latino Ministries in the Metropolitan New York Synod of the Lutheran Church], Rev. Franklin Simpson, the pastor of Resurrection Lutheran Church in the Bronx, have all been supportive to me personally or to my ministry through financial donations." However, she stated that most of her support has come from the non-Christian AIDS community.

Rev. Rosa Caraballo indicated that while it is wonderful that more Pentecostals want to get involved in faith-based efforts to deal with societal conditions, she fears that some may be doing it now due to the new Charitable Choice law which "makes it easier to take the risk from some one else's funding than your own church's budget." Currently, Rev. Caraballo has a dual role of serving as executive director of Bruised Reed and chaplain for the HIV Palliative Care Services Division of Montefiore Medical Center, a partnership that fits nicely with her vision to one day open up Villas de Esperanza, a home that will provide respite for caregivers of HIV/AIDs-afflicted families.

Latino Pastoral Action Center (LPAC)

At the core of the Latino Pastoral Action Center's establishment (in 1992) was a 1970s organization known as Acción Civica Evangelica de las Iglesias Hispanas de Nueva York. This organization was cofounded by the now deceased, Rev. Dr. José Caraballo, an Assemblies of God minister and the dean of Hispanic studies at New York Theological Seminary. This was the first major and widely recognized attempt to organize Latino Pentecostals in hopes of religion changing social and political issues. The organization was able to have representatives from every major Pentecostal council in New York City. "Some of

New York's best and brightest youth ended up working for us and going on to become scholars and voices in the city for a different generation," said Rev. Rivera reflecting on Acción Civicas history.[31] "The organization ultimately ended in closure due to lack of funding sparked by an investigation from the mayor's office due to an innocent minister's demand of all youth employees to tithe from their summer paychecks."

However, the theology of a holistic gospel that would facilitate social transformation always stayed in the mind of Rev. Dr. Raymond Rivera, and thus when an opportunity became available, he established the Latino Pastoral Action Center (LPAC) in 1992. LPAC was instituted as a faith-based, nonprofit organization to holistically educate, equip, and empower people to serve effectively in church and society. Rev. Luís Lugo and Rev. Danny Cortes of the Pew Charitable Trusts were instrumental in the genesis of this organization. "Danny promised me start-up funding if I could find a fiscal conduit." At that time, the New York City Mission Society (NYCMS), the oldest church-based organization and social service agency in the city, had a Puerto Rican layperson, Emilio Bermiss, for the first time in its history serving as executive director.[32] "Emilio Bermiss did not hesitate to give us an opportunity and that was a miracle as I never met him before that moment."[33] After approval, LPAC officially became a division of NYCMS, but it was autonomous from the start as "we came to them, they did not invite us." LPAC started out providing technical assistance to other grassroot Latino organizations. It now operates an urban ministry complex that serves the entire generational cycle, while being a model for holistic ministry to urban leaders throughout the United States.

It is LPAC's aim to assist the many grass-roots level organizations that exist and continue to come into existence in their development, organizing, advocacy, and networking activities. "The lack of sustainability is the major downfall of many organizations; it is even harder for Latino/a-led agencies," Rev. Rivera stated. It is because of his experience that he tirelessly works to help other Latino organizations in New York City get funded and provides the necessary technical assistance to educate them on the advantages and disadvantages of starting faith-based ministries in the city. He does all this while still struggling to financially secure his own organization.

LPAC has been able to advocate, organize, and create a network that follows a holistic ministry paradigm as a complementary alternative to existing traditional models of service. Experienced and emerging leaders of the city and leaders across the country have felt LPAC's impact. Its visibility has increased due to Rev. Rivera's four-principle philosophy of "transformation, liberation, community, and healing,"[34] which has been a requested seminar topic around the country. Rev. Rivera has been a great advocate for women in ministry and has helped Bruised Reed, Angels Unaware, Mission of Mercy, and the Center for Emerging Female Leadership and many others with monetary donations, space, funding sources, or general encouragement and support.

Latinas in Ministry and the Center for Emerging Female Leadership (CEFL)

The Center for Emerging Female Leadership was founded after a reorganization of the Latinas in Ministry program that was started by Dr. María Peréz y González. In the beginning, Latinas in Ministry served only a predominately Spanish-speaking, first-generation community. It began when the New York Mission Society won a grant from the Lilly Endowment to do a study on Latinas in Ministry following a Black Women in Ministry model already present at the organization. It was a groundbreaking study.[35] No doubt, that study was initiated by Emilio Bermiss, the first Puerto Rican lay minister serving as executive director. The first study, which began in 1992 and was completed in 1993, raised some issues about leadership development within the Latino community for women. Representatives on their advisory board were respected Latinas in Ministry such as Rev. Frances Rivera (Baptist pastor), Rev. Olga Torres Simpson (Pentecostal minister's wife and now founder of a faith-based organization), Isabel Ramos Wing (a Christian social worker), Marilyn Calo Rivera (a Christian Board of Education principal), Rev. Rosa Caraballo (Pentecostal pastor's wife and founder of a faith-based ministry).

Soon after, a retreat was held in 1994, which attracted eighty-six women to address some of the issues raised in the study and to pay tribute to Latina pioneers, such as Pastor Aimee Cortese and Mama Leo. Funding from the Lilly Endowment was exhausted. Dr. Peréz y González and others were not able to commit to the time necessary to build the program and also maintain their already active lives as ministers, professors, chaplains, and wives.

Latinas in Ministry is now a program under the Center for Emerging Female Leadership umbrella. While the leadership, focus, and target group were Latinas, it is open to everyone. Eventually it began to attract many black American women as well. Most of the Latinas involved with the program, however, are second- and third-generation Latinas. Initial attempts to work with Latinas who were first generation did not work due to the issue of language. As was discovered from the Latinas in Ministry study, one of the concerns of many Latinas was culture/language.[36] The changes that have occurred caused some of the earlier advisors and members of Latinas in Ministry to feel estranged as they felt they lost ownership of the program. It is the Latinas in Ministry's desire to develop a way to bridge the generations, but they have yet to find a clearcut solution. The greatest challenge has always been getting enough support from volunteers to operate programs since this is done out of passion not payment.

CEFL has held eight conferences that have attracted people from Florida, California, Texas, and Massachusetts. Its last conference, which was held in March of 2002, attracted 630 women (and some men). The conference is said to be one of the only gatherings in the city that brings together many women from different denominations. It is unique in that it blends Latina Spanish Pentecostal traditions with black American Pentecostalism in its worship services and preaching delivery. Topics chosen for the conferences deal with many of the realities of women, such as domestic violence, sexual abuse, and economic stabilization, in addition to topics that help attendees grow in their faith and spirituality. Other CEFL programs include women's retreats, Women in God's Service retreats (WINGs—only open to women in ministry or theologians), and intermittent seminars. Having gone through a tremendous transition, as it was a program of the Latino Pastoral Action Center, CEFL is now in the process of getting its own 501(c)3. It has its own board of directors and a national board of advisors. It hopes to become a national organization. It plans to hold a bi-annual Latinas in Ministry convocation. It also hopes to resurrect one of the key features of the Latinas in Ministry program of the past—fellowship groups in each borough. At present, the Center for Emerging Female Leadership is also exploring the interest of the Lilly Endowment to do a second Latinas in Ministry study. Dr. María Peréz y González has indicated interest in serving as principal investigator. Dr. Elizabeth Conde-Frazier and Dr. Milagros Peña have also accepted seats on the national advisory board of the organization.

Regardless of the differences of opinion on how the program should be run, it has been very successful. In December 1997, *Latina Magazine* did a brief article on the program, which yielded many inquiries from all over the United States about when we will get programs going in their state. The future of CEFL looks bright, as interest for the continued development of female leaders, especially the Latina women who have less resources available than their black American counterparts, is needed. Funding will be needed to operate a full-fledged organization with its own executive director and staff. This way, CEFL can move forward to meet the needs of all women, including the needs of Latinas.

Mission of Mercy (MoM): Iris Sánchez, Emerging Leader

Iris Sánchez, who is more than fifty years old, began her work with the hungry and homeless of Sunset Park, Brooklyn. With the support of her Pentecostal pastor, Apostle Luciano Padilla Jr., and his church, Bayridge Christian Center, she sought to make a difference in the lives of other women. Herself a victim of domestic violence, she organized women around that issue and substance abuse and general health care of women. Starting out as a ministry of the church and having received tax exemption status from the federal government with the help of the Latino Pastoral Action Center, Mission of Mercy (MoM) has been able to contract with the Human Resources Administration of New York City to operate a Welfare to Work demonstration project, which is a multimillion-dollar project. In addition, she was given the responsibility to oversee other Brooklyn agencies that also participate in the program as service providers. As a newcomer to the faith-based nonprofit world, it is truly in a unique position to be in and quite challenging. MoM's programs include but are not limited to providing food and clothing to clients; establishing new connections within the community by providing resources, training, and education in order to facilitate individuals to earn their GED; and advocating and educating the church and community about key issues that affect their section of Brooklyn. Due to her domestic violence background, she hopes to open a safe haven for battered and abused women over 18. But ultimately, as she says, "we are diffusing the idea that it is impossible to make a difference."[37]

Revisiting the Latina in Ministry Study

On June 24, 2002, two Latina in Ministry Focus Groups were held at Alliance Theological Seminary. The topic of discussion was the first study of Latinas in Ministry. The groups totaled twenty and were a mixture of first- and second-generation Latinas, with varied backgrounds of ministry experiences. All, however, had more than ten years of experience in ministry. The issues that were raised in the first report—such as empowering women and culture and language—were felt to still be issues today. Maribel Acosta, a well-spoken, educated, second-generation Latina who attends a first-generation church, talked about the struggle of language: "Sometimes I feel that first-generation Latinas don't understand our educational and social needs." She went on to say, "I don't want to give up my cultura." Many in the group agreed with that statement. Evidently, the perception seems to be that if you give up your Spanish language, you give up your "cultura." Furthermore, many felt that although empowering women is seen much more from the pulpits, it still needs to get more individualized attention.[38]

Another concern they had which was also brought out in the initial study is educational support. Unlike many of the Anglo denominations that provide mentoring, financial support, and resources for education, they felt the Latino Pentecostal church was still behind in that area. According to Rachel Miranda (a Latina in ministry who wears many hats in her church and their outreach ministry to the community), "saying you empower me is one thing, show me the money that proves to me you are willing to invest in my education."[39] All these women felt that investing in their education is an investment in your church or faith-based ministry, as they would fittingly give back from what they have learned.

The last predominant issue that came up with all the leaders who were interviewed for this essay, as well as the participants of the focus group, was the lack of support networks. This was also listed in the initial study. According to Rev. Villafañe, "I went through a very public separation with my husband which was very devastating to me personally. Not one pastor came to me to console me or encourage me, to say 'sister Ana we are with you.' It would have been great to at least get one of my sisters in the faith to say that." She also mentioned, "I do get lonely. I have no mentorship. The only time I get a woman to call me is when they want me to go to an event they are hosting. I would like a support group with peers."[40] Carmen Acosta, an Assemblies of God licensed minister shared, "although I didn't have a real mentor, I watched my pastor's daughter because she had an education. It was mentorship by osmosis, so to speak." Rev. Caraballo went on to say, "women supporting women is also about showing emerging leaders how to do ministry and avoid the mistakes we made. I learned street ministry from Cookie Rodríguez. I saw compassion in action from a Mennonite woman who befriended me. These women helped me grow into my call. That is what is lacking now. Latinas rarely mentor other Latinas."[41]

A New Paradigm for Ministry

The Latinas highlighted here as Progressive Pentecostals are getting involved in the daily socioeconomic issues confronting their cities, and there are many others like them that have not been mentioned. Progressive Pentecostalism will no doubt create urban social transformation, as demonstrated by the stories of these Latina activists. In post-9/11 New York, the church, its ministers, and lay people, are poised to be key instruments to do what it has wanted to do all along—evangelize the masses. But this time the paradigm seeks to challenge systemic conditions and structures, in addition to providing direct services. It is a paradigm that is willing to look at the "sinful" social structures in society. The context we presently find ourselves in has challenged ministers, lay people, church planters, and senior pastors to work toward a prophetic imagination where God and His gospel touch every area of life. Politics and civic participation are no longer seen as taboo as they once were. Anthony Stevens-Arroyo states that although advocating on behalf of issues that impact the Latino community may still not be popular in organized religion, churches are doing it anyway. He believes it could be attributed to the fact that religion actually helps believers survive the harsh realities of urban dwelling.[42] The Latino community in New York and across the globe needs a prophetic voice, as Walter Wink argues in *Naming the Powers: The Language of Power in the New Testament*. It is a voice that will "name, unmask, and engage the powers" of destruction that are currently determining the existence of the Latino communities here in New York and elsewhere. African Americans have captured the prophetic imagination and have developed the confrontational voice and presence needed that has been able to rally their people to unity and shake the corridors of power that are responsible for the inequality, pain, abuse, and death of their communities. Latinas can learn from the many New York City African American pastors who have led their churches or developed nonprofit organizations that are holistic in nature and prophetic in deed.[43]

Concluding Reflections

Urban social transformation in New York City has taken place at various levels because Progressive Pentecostal Latina women (and men) have taken their place in ministry and are redefining for themselves and for those who watch them, what it means to be a Pentecostal. They have worked to add the missing social element in our contemporary definition of Pentecostalism. All social structures and institutions "have moral values entrenched in them. They can be good or evil."[44] These Latinas have been able to improve the city through the work of nontraditional church ministry and faith-based nonprofit organizations that challenge the structures. They have used the resources available to them, regardless of the obstacles before them, whether it was gender bias, racial discrimination, lack of support, or denominational baggage.

While Latinas have come a long way, we still need to address issues that will not go away until we call them out of the darkness and into the light. Latinas need to begin support networks, provide intentional mentoring opportunities for emerging Latina young women, learn to fellowship instead of hiding the scars of ministry for no one to see, involve themselves with ministries for women like CEFL and other organizations that are working to support women who have decided to follow God to the barrios of our cities across the United States. In addition, Latino Pentecostal churches must learn to become more involved financially with ministries that are being effective and efficient in "engaging the powers" and that are working to continue to transform our urban neighborhoods. It is no longer enough to support Latinas by mouth either via the pulpit or the occasional "el señor te esta usando" (The Lord is using you). It is time, especially in light of what has happened to our post 9/11 world, to help ministries like the ones highlighted here with the money, support, and resources they need to continue to impact society and challenge the structural sins of our institutions of power. There is no reason for them to continue to struggle alone. The call to Progressive Pentecostalism that impacts society and transforms neighborhoods is for everyone who claims to have the power of God. Latina faith-based activists, *You are proclaimers of the word, rebuilders of our cities, and restorers of our hope. You are God's oaks of righteousness; He will display His splendor through you! [Read Isaiah 61:1–4.] ¡Siempre P'alante Latinas de fe!*

NOTES

I thank Rev. Dr. Lou Carlo, director of the Urban Studies Program and assistant professor at Alliance Theological Seminary, New York City; Rev. Edna Quiros, ordained minister of the Spanish Eastern District of the Assemblies of God; and Rev. Dr. Raymond Rivera, president and founder of the Latino Pastoral Action Center for their support with the critical feedback, focus group coordination, research, and writing of this essay.

1. The word "wholistic" is commonly used in the context of alternative medicine or the New Age movement. I intentionally use the spelling "holistic" to differentiate myself from the alternative medicine movement and its use of the word, not from the understanding that it entails a total system view, taking into account mental, spiritual, physical, and psychological aspects.

2. James Forbes, *The Holy Spirit and Preaching* (Nashville, TN: Abingdon Press, 1989), 15.

3. This includes organizations such as Christian Community Benevolent Associ-

ation, Youth Ministries for Peace and Justice, Angels Unaware, and Vision Urbana, along with newer emerging groups such as the Northeast Clergy Group and its program, the Ground Zero Clergy Taskforce, and Young Progressive Ministers.

4. Cited in Walter J. Hollenweger, "The Critical Tradition of Pentecostalism," *Journal of Pentecostal Theology* 1 (1992): 7–17. See also "Charismatic and Pentecostal Movements: A Challenge to the Churches," in *The Holy Spirit*, ed. Dow Kirkpartrick (Nashville, TN: Tidings, 1974), 209–233.

5. This is based on the Four Principles of the Latino Pastoral Action Center as developed by Rev. Dr. Raymond Rivera. http://Livedtheology.org/pdfs/Rivera.pdf.

6. Carl S. Dudley, Jackson W. Carroll, and James P. Wind, *Carriers of Faith* (Louisville, KY: Westminster–John Knox Press, 1983), 65–94

7. Gabriel Haslip-Viera, "The Evolution of the Latino Community in New York City: Early Nineteenth Century to the Present," in *Latinos in New York: Communities in Transition*, ed. Gabriel Haslip-Viera and Sherrie L. Baver (Notre Dame, IN: University of Notre Dame Press, 1996), 7, 3–30.

8. Population Division, New York City Department of City Planning. U.S. Census Bureau, 2000 Census Summary. Available: http://www.nyc.gov/html/dcp/pdf/pub/soc001. [July 3, 2002].

9. For example, Janny Scott, "Master of the Mosaic That Is New York City; Expert Keeps Tabs on Changing Population," *New York Times* (September 1, 2001); Susan Sachs, "Hispanic New York Shifted in 1990's, Puerto Ricans Lost Their Plurality," *New York Times* (May 22, 2001); Mireya Navarro, "Puerto Rican Presence Wanes in New York," *New York Times*, (February 28, 2000).

10. Race categories are from the 2000 Census and are not strictly comparable with categories of previous years, which would make the count seem slightly off. Population Division, New York City Department of Planning, U.S. Census Bureau, *2000 Census* 94–171. Available: http://www.nyc.gov/html/dcp/pdf/pub/soc001.pdf[July 3, 2002].

11. Gastón Espinosa, "*El Azteca:* Francisco Olazábal and Latino Pentecostal Charisma, Power, and Faith Healing in the Borderlands," *Journal of the American Academy of Religion* 67 (September 1999): 597–616.

12. David Barrett, ed., *World Christian Encyclopedia: A Comparative Survey of Churches and Religions in the Modern World* (New York: Oxford University Press, 1980).

13. Espinosa, "*El Azteca*," 604.

14. Eldin Villafañe, "A Spiritual Father and Spiritual Leader: Rev. Ricardo Tañon—An Apostle in the Bronx," *The Catalyst: Magazine of the Latino Pastoral Action Center* 1 (July–September 1998): 16.

15. Luis A. Carlo, "Let Us Overturn the Tables: Toward a New York Puerto Rican Pedagogy of Liberation" (Ph.D. diss., Teachers College/Columbia University, New York, 2002), 148–151. This chapter is a general overview of Hispanic Evangelicalism and its influences. See chapter six of Espinosa's dissertation on the origins of the Latino Pentecostal movement in New York City: Gastón Espinosa, "Borderland Religion: Los Angeles and the Origins of the Latino Pentecostal Movement in the U.S., Mexico, and Puerto Rico, 1900–1945" (Ph.D. diss., University of California, Santa Barbara, 1999), 217–245.

16. Eldin Villafañe, *The Liberating Spirit: Towards an Hispanic American Pentecostal Social Ethic* (Grand Rapids, MI: Eerdmans, 1993), 97–98.

17. Rose Marie Berger and Susannah Hunter, "Between the Lines: Raising the Roof," *Sojourners Magazine* (September–October 2001). Available: http://www.sojo

.net/magazine/index.cfm/action/sojourners/issue/soj0109/article/010942i.html[July 7, 2002]. This article speaks about the new acceptance Pentecostals are receiving since it has become public knowledge that they are focusing on social ministry through "Convoys of Hope," which bring health clinics, food, clothing, and other such items to over 25,000 people every weekend.

18. Villafañe, *Liberating Spirit*. 9.

19. Telephone interview with Rev. Ana Villafañe, conducted by Elizabeth Rios in the Bronx, New York City (July 8, 2002).

20. Personal interview with the Rev. Dr. Raymond Rivera, conducted by Elizabeth Rios in the Bronx, New York City (July 5, 2002).

21. The following quotations are from a telephone interview with Leonicia Rosado, as told to Sonia Gamboa, personal assistant, conducted by Elizabeth Rios in the Bronx, New York City (July 8, 2002). Due to "Mama Leo's" frail condition, she spoke through her personal assistant who translated into English her answers to my questions.

22. The following quotations are from a telephone Interview with Rev. Ana Villafañe, conducted by Elizabeth Rios in the Bronx, New York City (July 8, 2002).

23. For a discussion on women and ministry and early social action, see Gastón Espinosa, " 'Your Daughters Shall Prophesy': A History of Women in Ministry in the Latino Pentecostal Movement in the United States, in *Women and Twentieth-Century Protestantism*, ed. Margaret Lamberts Bendroth and Virginia Lieson Brereton (Urbana: University of Illinois Press, 2002), 25–48.

24. The following quotations are from an e-mail interview with Pastor Aimee Cortese, conducted by Elizabeth Rios in the Bronx, New York City (July 9, 2002).

25. Emily Fancher, *Bronx Times*, January 10, 2002.

26. Ibid.

27. E-mail interview with Cortese.

28. "Raja tabla" is a figure of speech in Latino Pentecostal circles which means "to preach so hard that it splits wood." It has legalistic underpinnings.

29. E-mail interview with Cortese.

30. The following quotations are from a telephone interview with Rev. Rosa Caraballo, conducted by Elizabeth Rios in the Bronx, New York City (July 8, 2002).

31. The following quotations are from a personal interview with the Rev. Dr. Raymond Rivera, conducted by Elizabeth Rios in the Bronx, New York City (July 5, 2002).

32. The New York City Mission Society was a nondenominational Mainline Protestant organization that was instrumental in the early history of New York Latino Protestantism. See Espinosa, "Borderland Religion," 221–222.

33. This and following quotation from personal interview with Rivera.

34. The four-principle philosophy is available by contacting LPAC. Rev. Rivera is currently working on a book entitled "Ministry in a Situation of Captivity."

35. See "Latinas Altar Place in Church," *New York Daily News* (October 1994).

36. Ibid, p. 7.

37. Telephone interview with Ms. Iris Sánchez, conducted by Elizabeth Rios in the Bronx, New York City (July 7, 2002).

38. Latina in Ministry Focus Group, conducted by Elizabeth Rios at Alliance Theological Seminary, Manhattan, New York City (June 24, 2002).

39. Ibid.

40. Telephone Interview with Villafañe.

41. Latina in Ministry Focus Group.

42. Anthony M. Stevens-Arroyo, *Latino Barrio Religion*, Available: http://home.adelphi.edu/catissue/articles/arroyo96.htm [July 3, 2002].

43. See Testimony of the Honorable Floyd H. Flake to the Senate Committee, March 14, 2001. Retrieved online at http://www.senate.gov/finance/031401fftest.pdf [July 4, 2002]. See also *New York Post* article "Drowning Kids in Failure," March 20, 1999. Retrieved online at http://www.manhattan-institute.org/html/_nypost-drowning.htm [July 4, 2002]. See also biographical data on the Rev. Calvin O. Butts, retrieved online at http://www.upenn.edu/chaplain/pucfsn/buttsbio.html [July 4, 2002].

44. Francis X. Meehan, *A Contemporary Social Spirituality* (Maryknoll, NY: Orbis Books, 1982), 9.

13

Chains of Liberation: Poverty and Social Action in the Universal Church of the Kingdom of God

Jill DeTemple

Every Friday night, liberation is enacted in Boston. People emerge from subway stations at Park Street and Downtown Crossing and make their way through Boston's central shopping and park district to a small storefront church nestled in the midst of shoe stores and the Massachusetts Commission for Education. Among the shops and offices, the beginning half of the church's anthem hangs boldly on a faded red awning over the front door: "*Pare de Sufrir!*" (Stop Suffering!).[1] The second stanza of the anthem is reserved for those who enter into the sanctuary, the large gold letters that dominate the back wall reading: "Jesus Christ is the Lord!"

As the service begins, an electronic organ plays and the congregation rises, clapping and singing an invocation of the Holy Spirit that is at the same time an expulsion of demons, which they identify as the specific cause of drug abuse, alcoholism, prostitution, and mental illness. Inside the small church in Boston there is no place to be silent, no passive observation. Everybody sings, expelling evil spirits by stomping and flinging them away from their bodies as the Holy Spirit comes down in conceptual tongues of fire, and everybody is liberated as workers make their way around the congregation, laying their hands on each head in the crowd. All are given a space to speak, and everyone is touched. Individual suffering is expressed, and met, by communal voices, by communal hands. The silent and often isolated world of the immigrant in a major metropolitan area is, for the moment, dissolved.

Liberation is effected by the casting out of demons and their oppressive effects and by the collective roar of the congregation *clamando a Dios* (shouting out to God) for the end of suffering. It is a liberation and a transformation that is immediate, communally enacted, and uniquely rooted in the history and practices of the church and the people it serves. It is liberation as enacted by the Iglesia Universal del Reino de Dios (Universal Church of the Kingdom of God, henceforth IURD), a small but rapidly expanding Pentecostal congregation that challenges societal oppression, and many models of resistance to that oppression, by engaging the experience of poverty at its locus in the individual.

Writing about the IURD, or indeed any religious group that emphasizes the enthusiastic and unmediated experience of the Divine, is something akin to photographing the sunset or the particular way moonlight shines on a mountain peak. At best, it is a two-dimensional representation of certain colors or moods; a tool that allows one to imagine the depths and subtleties of what it seeks to capture. At worst, it is a flat and lifeless souvenir that can call into question the actuality of the experience itself. The problem here is compounded by the additional emphasis on action in the public domain. In examining the IURD as a Hispanic church engaging in American public life, I am trying to describe not only some of the infinite colors of the Holy Spirit but also the particularly slippery alchemy of making the Spirit concrete.

To be more specific, social action that works for social justice does not simply emerge in a time and space of need. Antonio Gramsci contends that leaders are required to articulate and enact strategies for overcoming oppression, and that these leaders are most effective when they are rooted in the subaltern strata they seek to raise up.[2] Many authors in this volume, for example Moffett, León, Busto, Barton, and Ríos, describe a process of conscientization and action that exemplifies this framework of change, and César Chávez and Reies Tijerina, among others, have been effective as organic intellectuals fighting for a transformation in the power structures of hegemony that Gramsci so aptly describes. These men are prime exemplars of a particular process that turns articulation into action: capable leaders that read the signs of the times and then act as a kind of catalyst, the necessary element that creates a reaction which, in turn, leads to an organized political movement engaging oppression openly and on a grand scale. This is social action writ large, the stuff of strategies and national campaigns.

But is this the only model for the historical and social processes that lead to activity in the public realm? Does it address the needs and actions of those so removed from public enfranchisement that they have not achieved the subaltern's collective identity, and thus the concomitant recognition of their potential for power? This essay will argue that, for many on the margins of society, acting to change the system via the organized and group-oriented methods *of* the system is neither a logical nor a tangible initial path. Rather, a more radical reordering of power structures is required—one that removes, at least temporarily, the specter of the system altogether.

It is this alternative kind of process that the Universal Church of the Kingdom of God in the United States employs. While it is an immigrant church dedicated to "meeting and assisting the needs of all those [in need],"[3] the means

Universal Church of the Kingdom of God (Courtesy of Eric Kramer)

it uses to accomplish this goal are focused less on the overarching strategies that challenge systemic oppression with systematic and organized opposition, and more on tactics designed to address particular experiences of poverty and injustice. The demons of the system—daily injustices, poverty, isolation, and disenfranchisement—are unseated from their daunting position in an overwhelming and almost untouchable whole, and they are made personal via the theology and practice of the church. These demons become maladies that, once they have been named by their victims, can be exorcised away. To return to the metaphor used above, the power of the catalyst is taken from the articulations of a leader and given over to the expressions and actions of individuals—though, and this must be noted, these are individuals defined by and within the community of the church. A different sort of catalyst is utilized. A distinct kind of movement toward social action is in play.

Brazil

The roots of this action can be found in the history of the church itself. Born in Brazil at a time of burgeoning Pentecostal growth, the Iglesia Universal was founded in 1977 by Edir Macedo, a former Río de Janeiro state lottery official who continues to serve as the leader of the organization, having adopted the title of "bishop." From humble beginnings in a converted funeral parlor in downtown Río, Bishop Macedo saw the church through more than twenty-eight years of remarkable expansion. Beginning with an initial foreign mission to Argentina in 1980, the organization has placed churches in more than seventy countries and currently claims upward of eight million members worldwide.[4] Perhaps even more notably, it has become the largest media rival to the predominant *TV Globo* in Brazil, having purchased the São Paulo–based Record Television Network for $45 million in 1991. Currently, the church's holdings in Brazil include the television station and a related radio network, a large and active press, a bank, and an up-and-coming national soccer team.[5]

Indeed, the IURD acquisition of the Record Television Network marked the church's entry into the public arena as Carlos Magno de Miranda, a former bishop and outspoken critic of the organization, accused the IURD of financing the purchase with Colombian drug money.[6] In 1995, the church continued to make headlines as it protested the broadcast of a soap opera on TV Globo. The *telenovela*, "Decadence," featured a charismatic evangelical becoming a millionaire through his preaching and continual pleas for money, a characterization that upset many evangelicals and especially the Universal Church as it charged that the lead character was cast to physically resemble Edir Macedo.[7] Shortly after this incident, IURD churches were attacked by angry protesters across the country when Sergio Von Helder, an IURD pastor who hosted a daily program on Record Television, kicked a statue of Our Lady of Aparecida, the patron virgin of Brazil, while on the air. This event, which Von Helder intended as a demonstration of the IURD's staunch disapproval of idolatry, was so shocking to the largely Catholic populace of Latin America that stations all over the continent continued to play footage weeks after the event itself had passed.

Clearly, then, the church has gained a place in the popular consciousness of Brazilians, but what about the public domain of politics or civic action? Is the IURD using its tremendous resources to effect change outside its organizational boundaries?

No clear answer to these questions can be attempted without first exploring how the IURD defines these boundaries and its place as a religious organization chartered under the specific commandment to Stop Suffering(!). IURD theology roots suffering in the presence of malevolent spirits that roam the earth as the result of the Fall. In a chapter of his book *Nos Passos de Jesus* (In the Steps of Jesus), entitled, "The Origin of Chaos," Macedo writes:

> Just as the earth was created perfect, so, too, was man created perfect so that Adam did not have only one eye, much less suffer from any kind of sickness, no! He was created in the image and likeness of the Highest, and was perfect in every way. But, just as Satan penetrated the earth and made it without form and empty, he also subtly penetrated the life of Adam and Eve and wrapped them up in such a manner that they stopped listening to the Word of God in

> order to pay attention to Satan. And so began the great tragedy of humanity, its chaos and emptiness, because, in no longer submitting to God, they became subordinate to Satan.[8]

Just as Satan achieved a reintroduction of chaos into the physical world when he was cast down from Heaven, so, too, did he inhabit the lives of men and women, robbing them of the fullness of the indwelling of God and casting them into the current state of fallen grace, a state marked by moral, emotional and material shortcomings. Suffering, in other words, is the embodied result of a poverty that can be traced directly to evil forces at play in the world.

While these forces cause suffering in individuals, they are also manifested in societal structures. Macedo continues:

> Impotent, outwardly religious, scientific, cultured, elegant, the world is dominated by satanic principles; under its false external appearance is a boiling cauldron of national and international ambitions, commercial rivalries, and tears hidden under a smile. Satan and his hierarchy of evil spiritual beings are the invisible agents and the true power and intelligence of dictators, kings, presidents, and governors who are the visible leaders.[9]

The oppression of individuals by governments and the effects of globalization and unchecked commercial interests are thus explained as the action of evil on earth, a maleficent force that has penetrated all the way from the singular individual in Adam to global systems in international ambitions and government actions.

The response to this prevalent demonic state, according to church theology, lies in the example of Jesus, who in the gospel tales cast out demons and ended the suffering of all who asked. The key to the cessation of suffering is thus a two-step process of faith and action. First, one must believe that the power of God through Jesus is greater than the power of Satan and his demons that roam the earth. Second, one must take the necessary steps to invoke that higher power, calling out to God and seeking baptism in the Holy Spirit for physical, emotional, and financial healing.

All of this appears to favor individual action over organized social movement. Indeed, it has long been a criticism of evangelical churches in Latin America, and especially of Pentecostals, that they have not been socially engaged.[10] Yet a closer examination of IURD rhetoric and practice, as well as academic literature utilizing the experiences of church members, reveals a real emphasis on social issues, especially on the experiential aspects of poverty.

Writing about the IURD, Andrew Chesnut links poverty and Pentecostal practice, arguing that Pentecostalism's invitation to personally experience divine power via baptism in the Holy Spirit can only be understood in terms of the sense of profound powerlessness experienced by the disprivileged.[11] The IURD and other Pentecostal churches, he contends, directly address this powerlessness by placing the impetuous to change in the hands of the faithful. Richard Shaull and Waldo Cesar's more recent exploration of Pentecostalism in Brazil furthers this study, concluding that the emphasis on personal action in the church often translates to an improved sense of autonomy, as well as motivation for action outside of church walls.[12] This transformation of the experience of poverty will be discussed more fully below and in the context of the church as it expands in the United States. What draws our attention in Brazil is the broadening of action beyond the individual to the formation of groups working to combat the results, and the roots, of poverty at the societal level.

Within the IURD, perhaps the best example of this kind of action is the 1994 formation of a charitable group intended to address the mounting agricultural crisis in Brazil's draught-stricken northeastern region. Under the guidance of Bishop Marcelo Crivella, the Associação Beneficente Cristã (Christian Charity Association) organized and financed a comprehensive irrigation system and extensive community-building project that erected the town of Nova Canaã (New Canaan) from the dust of the dry *Sertão*. Crivella raised money for the project by releasing a compact disc of his music in conjunction with Sony Records, and the Christian Charity Association has grown within the church to include literacy, disaster relief, drug addiction, and homelessness assistance programs.[13] Thus, the IURD has become active, not only on Brazilian airwaves and in its newspapers but also on the streets and in the dirt of the Brazilian countryside.

The IURD is also beginning to insert itself into politics. The church has actively supported candidates in recent local and national elections, both on its own and as a part of a greater consortium of evangelicals in Brazil, and its popular newspaper, the *Folha Universal*, frequently addresses social issues such as abortion, the minimum wage, and the role of the government in health care.[14] In all of these issues, IURD bishops, who are the designated communicators of IURD theology and social teachings, emphasize personal responsibility and action as the basis of hope, which, in turn, is the path to knowledge of God and a better society. Thus editorials favor the minimum wage and expanded access to health care, while at the same time warning against the establishment of a comprehensive welfare state, which church thinkers believe would rob the poor of their greatest asset—hope in a fulfilled future.[15]

Thus the IURD in Brazil, while continuing to emphasize the individual and embodied experiences of poverty, has also begun to address the conditions of poverty and systemic oppression through political and civic action that requires the commitment and vision of the group as a whole. The power of individual salvation, defined by the church as the direct experience of the Holy Spirit in the exorcism of demons, has been transformed into a power of social consciousness and the very real actions of development and social change. The church is no longer in the headlines only for scandal but has come into Brazil's public life as a representative of a faith-based organization working within its theology to affect the world.

The United States

The Universal Church of the Kingdom of God in the United States is not yet fielding official political candidates and, for the most part, has refrained from large-scale social action movements such as those currently under way in Brazil. One reason for this more conservative stance is the relatively small size and diverse geographic locations of church chapters within the United States. Having begun its North American ministry with the establishment of the New York congregation in 1987, the IURD has since expanded from coast to coast, and congregations meet in converted theaters and storefront churches in twelve states across the country. At this time, most of the congregations are almost exclusively comprised of Latin American and West African *immigrants*, and the majority of the services are in Spanish or Portuguese.[16]

Still, the church is growing rapidly in its North American setting and, as a result, is beginning to engage more directly in the public sphere. What follows is an exploration of the process this engagement is taking, a glimpse at a model of social action that focuses as much on the colors of poverty as the systems and historical operations that produce it.

Como Vencer en este País: La Decisión es Suya

Walking through the front doors at the IURD church in downtown Boston, newcomers are handed a small pamphlet with an American flag and the words *Como Vencer en este País* (How to Win/Overcome in This Country) on the cover. Inside, a checklist of suffering includes problems with family, drug and alcohol abuse, mental illness, difficulty in obtaining medical care, and probable demonization by witchcraft or spells. The solution to any and all of these problems, the pamphlet declares, begins with an action on the part of the reader: *La Decisión es Suya* (The Decision Is Yours). The reader who agrees that his or her life is in need of a radical change and wants to stop suffering is instructed to say in a loud voice, "I want to stop suffering. I'm going to the Universal Church!"[17]

Indeed, it is this emphasis on individual action and motion that makes up the core of IURD theology and liturgy and also the church's subsequent involvement in public life. While Friday services are dedicated to liberation from evil spirits, the same which Macedo links in his theological writings to Satan and the introduction of evil and chaos to the world, *cadenas* (chains) of services presented, on average, three times daily, focus on specific forms of suffering so that members of the church may choose to attend the *culto* that best addresses their particular need. The *Cadena de Empresarios* presented every Monday centers around financial issues, while the *Cadena de Salud* on Tuesday (which is the second most popular of the daily programs after the Friday *Cadena de Liberación*), focuses on physical health and mental well-being. Wednesday and Thursday are dedicated to family issues, and Sunday is reserved for the

"Grand Encounter with God," where church members are encouraged to "thank God for all of the victories [they] have received."[18]

Thus, the element of individual choice is emphasized in the act of joining the church, in "going to the Iglesia Universal," and in the very structure of the liturgy that the church offers. Unlike traditional church services where pastors and priests decide the order of the day and congregants never know if their specific concerns will be addressed, the IURD offers tailored and predictable help. While the world outside of the church may be unsteady and difficult to forecast for the new immigrants the IURD serves, the space inside the church provides a constant atmosphere where participants are, in some sense, in control. In the words of one pastor, "Your family may fail you, the state may fail you, even I may fail you, but God never will."[19]

Thus the beginnings of the long road to civic empowerment are located by the practice and rhetoric of the church in local relationships that emphasize individual choices and expectations. In choosing which cadena to attend, IURD members are able to exercise a degree of control in a public arena. As indicated by the words of the pastor, they are also engaged in an active and critical recognition of their relationship with the world around them as it is expressed in family, state, church, and God. While IURD participants acknowledge that mortal relationships may fail, what stands out is the explicit sense of expectation in one's surroundings, an articulation of one's basic rights as a member of a family or religious organization, as a citizen, and as a child of God, as someone with the rights and capabilities to challenge that which unfairly oppresses.

This theme of individual choice, power, rights, and ability is predominant in every church service but is perhaps most clearly expressed in the following excerpt from a November 1998 sermon. Reading a passage from Joshua in which God stops the sun in the sky so that the Israelites might gain victory (Joshua 10:12–14), the preacher told the congregation the following:

> Faith! Faith is what stopped the sun in the sky. We all know that there are twenty-four hours in a day, three-hundred and sixty-five days in a year, but that day, in that year, there were three-hundred and sixty-six! Imagine what even the smallest bit of faith on your part could do! *There is no such thing as destiny*. . . . You have the power, through God, by accepting God into your hearts, to change your life and to defeat evil. God doesn't ask for money, He only asks for your love; for your open hearts.[20]

To understand the revolutionary nature of this message is to understand that, especially in Latin American contexts, suffering is tied inextricably to destiny, both of which are linked to, and lived out as, the condition of poverty.[21] To be poor is to be largely in the hands of others, either for work or welfare, and is regularly a condition of destiny via class structure. Certainly this continues to be true in the United States where many recent Hispanic immigrants find themselves relegated to low-wage or dangerous jobs and are commonly excluded from all but emergency medical care.[22]

Moreover, poverty is often experienced as isolation. To be poor in Los Angeles, São Paulo, or Beijing is often to be cut off: from friends or family who have moved to cities in order to find work, from the land, from medical services, from the basic technology that much of the world takes for granted, and from the political, commercial, and civic powers that influence and inform the daily environment. It is often, paradoxically, to be utterly dependent on, and voiceless in, a system entirely outside of one's own control, be it Immigration and Naturalization or the whims of the official who may or may not grant an appointment after several hours of waiting. All of this makes the experience of being poor an "already and not yet" reality bordered by the visible proximity of something other: of not being poor, of having access, of bringing forth a voice in the public domain that challenges the political, civic, and commercial interests that, wittingly or not, support the conditions of material and social oppression and want.

So the reality of poverty in urban life is a reality that eventually comes to rest at the heart of every individual; it is a reality couched in the us-not-them terms of destiny. It is a reality that is, at some level, purely personal, even as it is explained, and in some senses, experienced, within the larger context of class or caste. To be poor is to know that one is bound to be on the losing side, tied to other sufferers by status and situation, not by choice or effort.

Suffering as a result of poverty, then, as a result of being in the class of the disenfranchised, becomes the direct result of destiny. In stating that there is no such thing as destiny, the pastor at the IURD was actively challenging this prevalent cultural theme, in effect, turning it on its very head. If there is no such thing as destiny, then suffering can no longer be considered inevitable; poverty can no longer be accepted as a condition rooted in the body and minds of those who live in its grip. Most important, it is something that the individual, without waiting for an entire group to join in the action, can do something about: in the home, on the streets, or in the houses of government. In other words, to stop suffering within the context of the IURD is to take individual action; to make a motion; to recognize and challenge the failed relationships of families, churches, and states. In the parlance of the church in Boston, it is to make a first move toward the civic domain, to start down the long road of public action that allows one to "overcome in this country."

Pare de Sufrir! Existe una Solución!

The first step in the process of overcoming, once IURD adherents have recognized the potential for individual action, is naming the obstacle to their success. On Friday nights, workers and pastors ask patrons to name their tormentors so that they might be specifically cast out, and testimony about the subsequent experience of healing and power plays a central role in most services. Indeed, it is in these many public acts of naming obstacles and tormentors that the articulation of oppression and injustice is accomplished. Experiences of illness and hardship are called up for examination and removal, as are the demons of frustration and shame. Returning to Gramsci's model of the subaltern move to power, we see in the IURD an alternate paradigm. Instead of relying on a single organic intellectual for the formulation of a conscious need for change, every individual is required to take the job upon him- or herself.

Once the problem has been named, however, a second and important process occurs within the space of the church, still rooted at the individual level. This process is a transformation of experience that re-forms many of the aspects of poverty and powerlessness in the world outside the church into an actualization of potential inside church walls. Where the life of an immigrant in the United States is often one of silence or fighting against the barriers of a strange language, inside the church, language is a source of prestige and power as congregants are invited to the symbolically central location of the altar to give their testimony. Indeed, language can be altogether superseded as shouting out to God is often accomplished through *glossolalia*. The move toward collective power is rooted not simply in mortal articulation but in the language of God himself.

In a similar manner, the way in which the IURD conducts its frequent requests for tithes and offerings offers the chance to transform the financial aspects of poverty. Where $10 is inadequate for a date to the movies around town, it can, in a sense, "buy" the IURD participant who walks from his or her chair down the center aisle of the church to place money on an open Bible a certain amount of prestige, and again, power, in having seen an opportunity, made a decision, and then acted upon it, all in front of an approving and supportive audience of peers. What is in the public world outside of the church a symbol of powerlessness or want becomes, in the course of a two-hour service, a sign of God's favor—a sure mark of (and way toward) "victory."

Indeed, it is this transformation of experience, and the subsequent feeling of empowerment, that members cite when asked about the public role of the church. Pastors frequently remind their congregations that "faith doesn't stop at the door," and testimonies commonly recount how a realization of power, almost invariably described as "the power of God," gave a woman the strength to tell an abusive husband to get help or get out; gave a younger woman the gumption to stand up and demand a living a wage from her employer; gave an older man the sense of charity to help a beggar on the street.[23] The chancellor for the IURD in the United States also points to this central motif when asked about the public role of the church. In a pamphlet distributed by the church, he linked the transformation of lives via faith and the word of God with church-sponsored blood drives in California, prison outreach programs in several metropolitan areas, and a nationwide effort to send clothing to the victims of Hurricane Mitch.[24]

More than these small and individual experiences of empowerment, often described by IURD members and literature as "victories," however, the transformation enacted within the church is one from the singular helplessness of the dispossessed to the relatively mighty position perhaps best characterized as membership on a winning team. The IURD in Brazil quite consciously holds rallies in packed soccer stadiums, and a bishop working in England published literature with the title "Keeping the Faith and Running to Win."[25] Through the process of naming the demons of their oppression, of making the decision to Stop Suffering(!) and then acting upon it, IURD members are able to overcome the isolating experiences of poverty and actively engage the relationships of family, church, and state with the support and encouragement of a dynamic and motivated community. In the space of the church framed in the rubric of individual choice and movement, IURD participants create the road to communal action, the framework for mobilization and engagement at the civic and political levels.

The Alchemy of Action

Following this model of individual action which leads to community formation, the civic engagement of the church takes place at two distinct levels: one focused on individual crisis and the necessary realization of potential that seeks to discredit poverty as destiny, and the other a more traditionally conceived, group-oriented charitable wing that further reinforces the status of a "winning side" by seeking out and aiding those the church deems less fortunate. One IURD pastor explained that the church in the United States consciously focuses on the "dispossessed," which he identified as the drug-addicted and mentally ill. "Even in the first world," he commented in response to my questions about IURD social action in the United States, "so many people live in the shadow of God. They think they are alone. We give them a chance to fight. The government here teaches people to read, feeds the poor, takes care of some physical illnesses. But we do what they can't. We cure people, and then show them that they can be men of God." In his estimate, the IURD in Boston alone helps as many as ten serious drug addicts monthly, many of whom, he was sure to point out, had failed in other attempts at rehabilitation. "They come to us empty," he said, "then God fills them and there is no more room for drugs. This is our service to them, to society."[26]

In other words, the IURD in the United States seeks initial public engagement on the small scale, at the level of individual crisis with an eye toward individual transformation. The dispossessing demons of drug abuse, mental illness, and violence are recognized but are squarely removed from a remote conceptualization of society and are placed, instead, at a personal level where they can, at the will of the individual, be exorcised away. These sorts of demons, pastors and church administrators assured me, are almost always better handled at this level of personal transformation. But it is the hope of the church, once a larger core of people have experienced and begun to live this transformation, and once Americans "overcome their pride" and realize that immigrant churches have something to offer, to begin larger social action projects along the lines of those currently conducted in Brazil.

Until that time, however, the public work of the IURD is that of an alternate and inside model of the move to power, public work that progresses from individual transformation to collective capability, from the helplessness and isolation of poverty to the assurance and hope of a motivated and mobilized community. It is work that moves along the lengthy and often slow road leading to the hard-won recognition of potential. In chains of liberation that cast off the shackles of destiny, it is work that addresses the isolated condition of poverty in a way that larger, more formal and group-oriented outreach programs simply cannot. It reminds us that communities and groups that strive toward social justice do not simply arise magically from a vacuum of need and cannot be created solely by the alchemy of political planning. Perhaps most of all, it is work that reminds us that civic engagement meant to benefit the poor on the large scale may miss altogether the lived reality of the condition it targets, incorrectly assuming that the demons of systemic injustices and poverty are experienced, and can only be addressed, by a collective mass or movement.

NOTES

1. This and all other translations from Spanish and Portuguese are my own.

2. Antonio Gramsci, *Selections from the Prison Notebooks* (New York: International Publishers, 1999). See especially section I part 1, "The Intellectuals."

3. Regina Cerveira, chancellor, Universal Church of the Kingdom of God, United States, personal correspondence (November 17, 2000).

4. Universal Church of the Kingdom of God, *Universal Web Site*. Available: http://www.igrejauniversal.org.br [July 5, 2000].

5. Gary Richman, "When the Topic Is the Universal Church of the Kingdom of God," Río de Janeiro: AP Worldstream (November 28, 1995).

6. Rev. José Bittencourt Filho, *Alternativos dos desperados: como se pode ler o pentecostalismo autônomo* (Río de Janeiro: Centro Ecumênico de Documentaçao e Informação, 1991), 107.

7. "Brazilian Church Assails T.V." *Globo* (UPI Wire Story Río de Janeiro) (September 21, 1995).

8. Edir Macedo, *Nos passos de Jesus* (Río de Janeiro: Editora Grafica Universal, 1986), 21.

9. Ibid.

10. See Harvey Cox, *Fire from Heaven* (Reading, MA: Addison-Wesley, 1995). See also Richard Shaull and Waldo Cesar, *Pentecostalism and the Future of the Christian Churches* (Grand Rapids, MI: Eerdmans, 2000).

11. R. Andrew Chesnut, *Born Again in Brazil* (New Brunswick, NJ: Rutgers University Press, 1997), 66.

12. Shaull and Cesar, *Pentecostalism*, 50–51.

13. Universal Church of the Kingdom of God, *Nova Canãa* (Video recording). Brazil: Universal Church of the Kingdom of God, 2000.

14. Universal Church of the Kingdom of God, *Folha universal*. Available: http://www.uol.com.br/folhauniversal [November 12, 2000].

15. Ibid. [November 16, 2000].

16. Cerveira, personal correspondence. No official membership figures are available from the church, though congregations seem to range in size from fewer than 100 (Brockton, Mass.) to more than 1,000 (New York) people.

17. Universal Church of the Kingdom of God, "*Comer Vencer en este País*," Pamphlet Boston, 1998.

18. Ibid.

19. Sermon delivered at the Universal Church of the Kingdom of God, Boston (November 12, 1998).

20. Ibid.

21. For a further discussion of poverty and the Universal Church of the Kingdom of God, see R. Andrew Chesnut, *Born Again in Brazil.*

22. According to Census Bureau figures from 1993, nearly 25 percent of all Hispanics in the labor force over the age of sixteen worked in technical, sales, and administrative support positions. There are no records of migrant farmworkers and "under the table" wage earners. Some 40 percent of all Hispanics were poor in 1993, the most recent statistics from the Census Bureau, meaning that they lived at the poverty level as established by the Census Bureau for at least two months of the year. Additionally, 10 percent were chronically poor, meaning that for a two-year period they were poor each of the twenty-four months. In the same year, Hispanics were the largest group to enter a condition of poverty, at a rate of 8.6 percent compared to 3 percent overall. Source: United States Census Bureau, United States Census Bureau Web Site. Available: http://www.census.gov [May 5, 1999].

23. Universal Church of the Kingdom of God, Boston, MA. (testimonials by IURD participants), April 5, 1999.

24. Universal Church of the Kingdom of God, *Pare de Sufrir!* Pamphlet. Los Angeles, CA, November 12, 2000.

25. Bishop Renate Cardoso, "Keeping the Faith and Running to Win," Universal Church of the Kingdom of God, Universal Web Site. Available: http://www.igrejauniversal.org [November 18, 1998].

26. Telephone interview with the pastoral staff, Universal Church of the Kingdom of God, Boston (July 21, 2000).

14

"The Lord Requires Justice": Lessons on Leadership from the African American Church for Mexican American Catholics

Alberto López Pulido and Santos C. Vega

The evolving relationships between race or ethnicity and religion in the history of the United States have underscored the establishment and consistent development of political and civic leadership within the African American Church. From its inception, through civil rights to contemporary politics, the African American Church is both the pillar and the foundation for political leadership in the African American community. The church has persisted as a place of freedom where African Americans have openly expressed their thoughts and emotions about their continual oppression.[1] Yet the relationship between religion and politics established within the African American Church has not been replicated by other communities of color in the United States, specifically, Mexican American Roman Catholics.

Whereas religiously inspired political leaders such as César Chávez can be identified in Mexican American history, these examples represent more of the exception rather than the rule within institutional Roman Catholicism. For the most part, Latino Roman Catholic political leaders have been absent from within the formal structures of Roman Catholicism and the larger community. As Dolores Huerta, vice president of the United Farm Workers reminds us, "talking about religion is still a political issue, especially when you talk about the history of the Chicano." Referring to her experiences in working with Latino churches in New York, Huerta states that priests would get up and talk about how many angels you could put on the head of a pin but could never talk about anything political. "The sermons were not relevant to the politics affecting the people's lives."[2] Consider that a 1982 survey of 995 Latinos exploring their relationship with the Catholic Church discovered that the second most common source of bad experiences identified was "little or no help with social problems."[3] These findings are compounded by the historical reality that the important contributions of popular religious practices that typify Mexican American Roman Catholic experiences have been silenced or gone unrecognized by the American Catholic hierarchy.[4]

In contrast, African Americans have developed political leaders and social movements through their religious structures and traditions. As John Hope Franklin and Alfred A. Moss point out, "the establishment of separate houses of worship gave African Americans an extraordinary opportunity to develop leadership."[5] Over the years, the African American Church has continued "as a base for building a sense of ethnic identity and a community of interest among its members."[6]

In an attempt to understand the relationship between religion and political leadership for Mexican American Roman Catholics, the purpose of this essay is to compare and contrast a Mexican American Roman Catholic Church with an African American Baptist Church to demonstrate strategies for political and civic engagement implemented by the African American Church. We use these experiences as examples and teachings that Mexican American Roman Catholics can learn in order to foster and increase civic and political involvement in their communities. A structural, historical, and theological analysis of both religious institutions is presented. We conclude by underscoring the important role and function of the national parish in the history of the American Catholic Church, the *Cursillo* and National *Encuentro* movements, and recommend these institutional strategies as viable avenues for political and civic engagement for Mexican American Roman Catholics in the United States.

Context and Objectives

This essay is based on research in two churches located in Phoenix, Arizona. We examined the Mexican American Roman Catholic parish of Immaculate Heart Church (IHC) and the African American congregation of First Institutional Baptist Church (FIBC), with an eye toward interpreting and analyzing political and civic leadership for Mexican American Roman Catholics from everyday concrete experiences.[7] These churches were chosen because of similar composition and location. Both churches are located within a few blocks of each other in the inner city of Phoenix, with congregations of 2,000–3,000 members led by stable and long-term leadership. Reverend Dr. Warren H. Stewart Sr. has served FIBC for the past twenty-eight years. Up until 1998, Father Tony Sotelo had served as the parish priest of IHC for the past fourteen years. In 1999, Father Sotelo chose to leave the role of parish priest and is now full-time in prison ministry.

A Latino and an Anglo-American Catholic priest carry a cross in a pilgrimage in California to protest the shoddy treatment of Latino laborers (Courtesy of Jimmy Dorantes/Latin Focus Photos)

We recognize that IHC represents a working-class immigrant church in comparison with the middle-class composition of FIBC. Nevertheless, we believe that the issues of religion, ethnicity, and class mobility must be placed within the historical development and evolution of each congregation. Whereas there is historical evidence of an emerging middle-class community from within IHC, they no longer represent the majority of the institution. In contrast, one could argue that the solid middle-class composition of FIBC is directly related to the leadership skills fostered by the church.[8] Nonetheless, these issues represent important topics for future research that go beyond the scope of this essay. Of greater significance is the fact that both churches are actively involved in political movements and civic engagement. We examined the questions of religion and political and civic leadership within both a contemporary and historical context, with research methods that included interviews of the leadership, attending religious services, and a review of pertinent historical church documents.

Unsettled feelings continue to plague each generation of Mexican American Roman Catholics with regard to their role in the American Catholic Church. Does this religious community that comprises close to half (44%) of the Roman Catholic population in Phoenix feel secure in expressing its cultural and linguistic traditions? Are these beliefs and practices understood and embraced by the institutional church, or merely tolerated? Most important, how do these issues of personal and religious identity influence the active participation of Mexican American Roman Catholics in politics and civil rights issues?[9] These questions will guide us in discerning and understanding the dynamics of political leadership and social change for Mexican American Roman Catholics in Phoenix, Arizona.

The Story of the Immaculate Heart Church

The history of Roman Catholicism in the American southwest is best characterized as a ubiquitous religious tradition that is impossible to contain within the institutionalized boundaries of American Roman Catholicism as it traversed northern to southern geographical regions in the Americas. Catholicism flourished with little direction or support from the centers of colonial power in Mexico. As a result, Mexican American popular religious expression has functioned to establish and provide community and create collective action as people coalesce around religious symbols that bear little institutional imprint. This is the history that encapsulates the origins of Immaculate Heart Church.

In the late nineteenth century, Mexican Americans coalesced as Roman Catholics in the home of Jesús Otero, a mission to Immaculate Conception Church in nearby Florence, Arizona. After a series of transformations, the church acquired the name of St. Mary's and, in 1903, the overwhelmingly Mexican American congregation constructed a "basement church." During the next ten years, foreign clergy and laity arrived in the region, bringing with them different traditions and languages and the power to implement these new experiences and expressions into the recently established American Catholic Church. By 1913, construction on an "upper church" above the initial basement church began. Since the basement church had been constructed and supported by Mexican Americans, church leaders saw no reason in modifying such arrangements even though a fully adorned church in the Mission Revival style had been built on top of the original house of worship. As a result, this hierarchical edifice relegated all non-English Catholic expressions and language to the basement of the church. It appears that from the perspective of the hierarchy, Mexican American Roman Catholic identity became synonymous with "basement" Catholics.

In 1915, following a baptismal mass where the Mexican children and their families had been directed to the church basement to partake in the ceremony, the community organized itself and coalesced into the "Mexican Catholic Society" and presented a petition signed by 1,500 Spanish-speaking residents requesting a separate parish.[10] Mexican Catholics demanded equal rights with other members of the congregation because "their forefathers were the first founders of the mission in Phoenix" and they had "contributed their full share toward the creation of the church and toward its maintenance."[11]

It was from this conflict that IHC was established.[12] From its inception, IHC represented a firm spiritual and sacramental foundation for Mexican American Roman Catholics. It became a focal point for their spiritual life as they participated in a range of church-sponsored organizations and activities. The most important of these activities began in the 1960s through their involvement with the Cursillo movement.[13] IHC became the first permanent center for Cursillos in Phoenix, Arizona.

The process through which political and civic leadership is created and fostered at IHC is through the education of the membership regarding issues that affect their daily lives and inevitably enter the political arena. It is a perspective that envisions and embraces a common good for the larger community, obligating one to engage in political action in order to change or resolve community issues.[14] The most salient of these issues for IHC is immigration.

The immigrant experience has shaped the evolving character and identity of IHC. Today, it is a church shared by the successful children of immigrants, the working poor, and undocumented Mexican nationals. Over the past ten years, the church has overwhelming transformed into an immigrant church with 90 percent of its membership comprised of Mexican immigrants. In response, the church presently offers ten Sunday services, nine of which are in Spanish.

Consequently, through the leadership of Father Tony Sotelo, IHC became directly involved with Valley Interfaith Project (VIP), a nonprofit organization whose main objective is to carry out community-organizing efforts in Arizona.[15] As a result, the politics of IHC, with assistance from VIP, placed an emphasis on immigration issues. Beginning in 1996, an immigration leadership project was formed, and a citizenship campaign was established. The project trained 165 church members to conduct citizenship workshops. Out of all that attended the workshop, 1,125 submitted citizenship applications, and between 600 and 700 church members became U.S. citizens. The 165 leaders trained at IHC went on to train an additional 20 leaders at nearby churches within the diocese. The results of this work are not known. The training of the initial 165 leaders was conducted by the United Neighborhood Organization out of Chicago, Illinois.[16]

From Father Sotelo's perspective, education is at the core of leadership formation for Mexican American Roman Catholics. It is his belief that "the church should foster political awareness and participation through education. The mission of the church is to educate the poor and get them out to vote." Issues such as labor organizing, workers rights, civil rights, and the education of children need to be placed alongside religious instruction for baptisms and confirmations.[17] The belief is that issues that directly impact the congregation of IHC need to also be part of the educational process.

The Story of First Institutional Baptist Church

During the nineteenth century, the independent Black Church movement emerged in response to the evils of slavery and racism in America. Within this movement was the community of Black Baptists who were struggling to carve out a religious niche in the midst of the southern plantations that defined their lives as slaves.[18] This space would become the only sphere of black experience that was free of white power.[19]

In Arizona, Baptists arrived through the work of James C. Bristow in 1875 near Camp Verde. By 1905, Reverend John B. Bell began preaching to African Americans in the Phoenix area. His work led to the creation of the Second Colored Baptist Church. This community went through several transformations, and with the construction of a new edifice, were renamed the First Colored Baptist Church. In 1951, another new church was built and renamed the First Institutional Baptist Church.[20]

The story of resistance and protest in the formation of the African American Church is at the core of FIBC. The leadership is consciously aware of the fact that "the African American Church arose out of political protest." It is this history that drives the agenda of this church. Similar to IHC, politics is about a common good. It represents a personal belief or action with a goal toward benefiting the majority of the larger community. For Pastor Stewart, politics are holistic and inseparable from ideology, religion, and ethics in one's everyday life.[21]

To tell the story of protest and resistance for the African American Church reinforces the collective memory and the story of struggle for liberation in African American history. These teachings become models for the membership to follow and emulate and are reinforced by biblical scripture. As one church member underscores, everything a church does must be scripturally based. Such a foundation calls people into social action issues, which, in turn, bring them into the political arena.[22] The church uses biblical prophets as a pattern for speaking up against injustices and the status quo. As Pastor Stewart states, beginning back in the eighteenth century, the African American Church has consistently used biblical prophets such as Isaiah, Jeremiah, Elijah, Hosea, and Micah as models for leadership that arose and spoke against injustices and the status quo and called for a balancing of equality and equal rights.

African American leadership definitely looks to the Bible for direction and guidance to foster political leadership. A key text for FIBC is drawn from Micah 6:8, where "the Lord requires us to do justice and to walk humbly with your God." Another function of scripture is to educate one about the need to emancipate the downtrodden and oppressed, as presented in Luke 4:18–19: "The Spirit of the Lord is upon me, because he anointed Me to preach the gospel to the poor. He has sent me to proclaim release to the captives, and recovery of sight to the blind, to set free those who are downtrodden, to proclaim the favorable year of the Lord."[23] Finally, the interpretation of the sacred (God) is one that is actively involved in the liberation of humankind. "Resurrection occurs every time we set someone free from some kind of death. We feel it is our business to set people free from racism, sexism, substance abuse, etc.," states the pastor of FIBC.[24] From the leadership's perspective, the most critical issues for FIBC are youth, racism, computer literacy, and education.

Comparisons and Findings

For both IHC and FIBC, stable and long-term leaders have provided leadership opportunities. Such stability has allowed for the planning of programs and confidence in the membership to become involved in their respective churches. Both pastors have ministered to as many as three generations of families during their tenure. At IHC, the citizenship campaign described above represents a good example. In addition, Father Sotelo had begun working on a "mutual aid society" for immigrants in the parish before his departure. Under Pastor Stewart's leadership, FIBC has more than seventy ministries, with a majority focusing on issues of social justice.[25] Aside from these similarities, we discover major differences regarding historical responses, theological interpretations, and church structures for both institutions.

It is interesting to note that IHC shares a history with the African American church. Both experienced segregation and exclusion as a result of their differences. Yet, whereas Mexican Americans *requested* their own parish within the same structure, African Americans *forced* their own agenda and established their own *autonomy*. Such liberation gave African Americans full control of those sacred expressions deemed unacceptable by the powers that be, including interpretations of religion and politics for their community. This history represents the legacy of FIBC.

In contrast, Mexican Americans from IHC chose a semiautonomous relationship within the hierarchical structures of American Catholicism that influenced, and at times restricted, their interpretations and actions regarding religion and politics for their community. During the "heady days" of the Chicano movement, there was discussion by activist priests to establish a separate church, but according to Moises Sandoval, this was never an option for Mexican American Catholics. There have never been bishops, clergy, or religious leaders to lead such an institution. The only recourse has been to be an appendage within the existing institution and, in that way, create for Hispanics a home within the larger church.[26] As a result, such an arrangement has limited the independence of the IHC congregation and its decision-making process.

Furthermore, as stated earlier, the historical transformation of this parish regarding its membership is worth noting. As a church that has transformed into a predominately immigrant church, the agendas and perspectives regarding the needs of Mexican and Mexican American Roman Catholics have changed. The proximity of IHC to the U.S.–Mexico border, the high percentage of Latino and Mexican immigrants, and the impact of the Spanish language and culture demands an advocacy type of leadership from the Catholic Church hierarchy. Priests and laity must be called to a community advocacy leadership in the twenty-first century. Human rights issues and political activism will motivate the need for advocacy by single-issue groups, and the political response by government units at all levels will bring to the forefront the social needs of immigrants. These social needs grow out of globalization enterprises like the North American Free Trade Agreement (NAFTA), the industrialization of Mexico, the more than 2,000 *maquiladoras* (border factories) operating along the U.S.–Mexico border.[27] These economic and political policies have magnetized the immigration stream to the United States, searching for better jobs, higher wages, and improved home life. The immigrants bring with them diverse Catholic churches where immigrants seek spiritual space, sacramental services, and social support. IHC must deal with this variety of religious needs coupled with the variety of social needs.[28] The church leadership will have to aid the particular concerns of immigrants and assist them in creating their own community organizations. One example is the ongoing effort to organize a nonprofit union or community organization comprised of immigrant families.[29] Most important, the newness of immigrants and their concerns have yet to be fully realized and actualized as part of a larger political agenda as active Roman Catholics in the United States.

It is clear from this essay that the collective actions and interpretations from the African American Church are grounded and justified through sacred scripture. Scripture serves to orient the community regarding political and civic leadership. It is very common for Pastor Stewart to interweave a religious interpretation of social issues and their political implications in his sermons. For example, at a service, within the context of "giving thanks to God," he made mention of an Urban League report that stated the quality of life for African Americans had improved. Furthermore, the sermon entitled, "My Harvest Is Appointed" focused on transforming the community. It was an affirming message on how one should expect God to work in their lives.[30]

In comparison, none of the leadership at IHC drew from scripture to interpret or explain social issues within the Mexican and Mexican American community. The homily at a recent mass focused on "faith," "hope," and "God's divine plan." It was a somber message expressed through reverence and was silent regarding political and civic leadership for the Mexican American congregation. During the time for prayer petitions, there was a request to pray for immigrants by the pastor.[31]

There is much that can be said regarding the structure of both churches and their relationship to political and civic leadership. The autonomy of the African American Church enables it to take positions on political issues directly from the pulpit. Consider, for example, that FIBC is a lifetime member of the National Association for the Advancement of Colored People (NAACP). Every year, the church picks a life member, and the head of the NAACP comes to church to present the award from the pulpit and encourage the church body to become members of this political organization. No comparable activity was discovered at IHC. In addition, it is critical to point out that we discovered the existence of five African American pastors who serve on the board of directors for the NAACP. In contrast, there exist zero clergy on the board of the National Council of La Raza (NCLR), a comparable civil rights organization for Latinos. Despite the fact that the NCLR is absent of clergy participation, Raul Yszaguirre, former president of NCLR, claims that the vision for "Hispanic empowerment" is through the building of institutions that live for and are committed to the betterment of Hispanics, such as the Roman Catholic Church.

Described by one writer as a deeply religious man, "Yszaguirre's faith in the church includes a hope to change it, to restore it to the forefront in the struggle for liberation and progress for Hispanics in America."[32]

Our research revealed only one recent example of political and civic leadership at IHC. As discussed earlier, political and civic leadership was facilitated by Valley Interfaith Project. It was successful because it received the full support of the local pastor. In contrast, FIBC underscores the issue of political and civic leadership throughout seventy church-based ministries, as noted earlier. It is interesting that VIP had established a partnership with FIBC, which, from the pastor's perspective, was unsuccessful at his church because VIP represents a "single-issue" organization. According to Pastor Stewart:

> That is why it is hard to rally our people to really get involved in Valley Interfaith because our people are just involved in the total livelihood of the community. We have the assistant to the mayor here, the city manager here, firemen here, we have politicians here, principals here, and superintendents here. They are involved. So we didn't need Valley Interfaith to be that one organization to get us politically involved.[33]

Recommendations

Having examined an African American Church in relation to a Mexican American Church, we offer the following recommendations for the enhancement of civic and political leadership for Mexican Americans as members of the Roman Catholic Church. It is essential for Mexican American Roman Catholics to establish an autonomous identity for purposes of creating and maintaining community. The challenge will be to create a common story and legacy from among its various constituencies, including the larger and ethnically different Roman Catholic hierarchy. This will require leadership with vision and insight into the range of stories that comprise the Mexican American experience. It will require Mexican American Roman Catholics to uncover, acknowledge, and celebrate their history and tell their own story. Historically speaking, within the structure of the American Catholic Church, the function and purpose of the national parish, the cursillo movement, and the national encuentro movement offer us excellent examples of where this has occurred.

National parishes have played a critical role in the historical development and evolution of ethnic Roman Catholics in the United States. For example, they became the "focus of life" for Irish immigrants in New York. They functioned as a weapon to confront discrimination and "served as a center of social life and organization [preserving] their religious, cultural, and national identity."[34] Joseph Fitzpatrick's research on Puerto Ricans in New York uncovered that the national parish has historically served three major functions: (1) to maintain effective contact between immigrants and the church that maintains a strong religious faith and practice, (2) to provide the basis for a strong community life, and (3) to give newcomers a sense of cultural and ethnic identity. The physical building of the parish, and their identity as parishioners, gave them a sense of belonging and represented the symbols by which they were known to the larger community.[35] For a variety of reasons, the Catholic Church began phasing out national parishes by the 1920s. In 1916, there were more than 4,700 foreign-language parishes that dwindled down to a little over 1,500 by 1948.[36]

Consider that, despite the fact that national parishes solidified such an effective structure to maintain cultural and community solidarity, in 1939 Francis J. Spellman moved to create what came to be called "the integrated parish" representing a territorial parish with at least one priest who could speak the language of whatever ethnic group was present in its territory. Services were offered in the ethnic group's language, in addition to its regular English service. Policy of the integrated parish has many factors. The most important factor, which led to the creation and support of the integrated parish, was with an objective of integrating Puerto Ricans into the American Church. Spellman, along with other leaders of the Catholic Church, observed national parishes as negative church structures that served to reinforce ethnic identity and retard cultural assimilation into the mainstream. He also saw them akin to the segregated churches that had been imposed on black Americans and a denial of the opportunities that came with integration into the greater American community.[37] Such a perspective directly contradicts the historical realities of African Americans in relation to their religious traditions and formations. As FIBC underscores, the Black church survived and moved forward the political agenda of African Americans because of its independent and autonomous structure. American Catholic history has revealed that national parishes serve to reinforce Mexican American ethnic identity and foster leadership from within the institutional church. We believe that such institutional structure can serve in positive ways to develop political and civic leadership within Mexican American communities.

In addition, we believe that Mexican American Roman Catholics need to take a closer look at the history of the Cursillo movement in the American Catholic Church. It is the first movement within the church to stress the leadership potential of the Mexican American community. The significance of the Cursillo movement regarding Mexican American leadership is the use of the Spanish language, the Mexican cultural milieu, and the group dynamics that come with shared experiences. A critical case study can be found in the work of Antonio Soto and his discussion of an extremely successful Chicano Deacon Program in California Parishes. According to Soto, the Cursillo movement was the first movement to stress the leadership of Chicanos and to dramatically change their role within the church. As something that began on the Island of Mallorca in January of 1949, it is characterized as an intense three-day workshop in leadership formation and Christian living. It consists of in-depth discussions, led by a team of laymen and a priest, of the fundamentals of the Christian message and its relation to the modern world. The Cursillo eventually spread from Mallorca, with the first one in the United States taking place in

May of 1957 in Waco, Texas, led by two Spanish airmen Bernardo Vadell and Agustín Palomino, who teamed up with a local priest by the name of Father Gabriel Fernández.[38]

Important lay leaders such as César Chávez, Willie Velasquez, and Ernie Cortez are known to have actively participated in Cursillo. As one Cursillista wrote more than thirty years ago about the Cursillo experience, "I rediscovered my own people, or perhaps they redeemed me. Only Spanish was spoken. I was cast in a spiritual setting which was a perfect background for reviving my Chicano soul." It has been described as a movement of self-assertion for Mexican-American Roman Catholics that has no equal. According to Soto, "it was a means of redemption for the Spanish-speaking people who were suddenly released from traditional understandings of religion and presented with a new vision of the church in which they could say 'We are the church.' "[39] Therefore, we recommend a comprehensive study of the Cursillo movement in the American Catholic Church and its implications for Mexican American identity and political leadership.

Finally, we believe it is important that Mexican Americans Catholics revisit the national Encuentro process that is responsible for bringing forward issues of Latino Catholic leadership at both local and national levels.[40] The national Encuentro process brought the issue of Latino Catholics to the forefront of the American Catholic Church. The first national Encuentro for Spanish-speaking Catholics was held in June of 1972, at Trinity College in Washington D.C., with a focus toward changing the Catholic Church's policy of assimilation to one of cultural pluralism. This gave birth to a division for the Spanish speaking that became a special Office of the Secretariat within the American Catholic Church. In addition, the Bishop's Committee for Hispanics was established, more Hispanic bishops were named, and a special edition of diocesan newspapers in Spanish was incorporated. Among other things, Basic Christian Communities were considered a low priority; the establishment of nonterritorial parishes for Spanish-speaking and the training of all candidates for the priesthood in spoken Spanish and Hispanic culture were rejected by the hierarchy.

Five years later, a second Encuentro, also held in Washington D.C., was heavily shaped and molded by input from the laity. Nearly 100,000 Hispanic Catholics were surveyed regarding their views and needs from the church. A common thread in all the documents of the second Encuentro was the encouragement and recognition of lay ministers by the church. One of the most significant resolutions from this gathering was to form Basic Christian Communities. The belief was that "future leaders are born and fostered" in Basic Christian Communities. In 1983, a pastoral letter was approved by the American Catholic bishops, which described Hispanics as a blessing from God and authorized the third Encuentro. A major outcome of this event was to unify Hispanics in the United States around the broad outlines of a national pastoral plan for Hispanic ministry. The plan was approved by the bishops in 1987, but with no funds allocated for implementation, some Hispanic leaders compared it to a beautiful new car without wheels.

The Encuentro process appeared on the scene more than thirty years ago and addressed key issues. Yet, from our perspective, many of these issues remain unresolved. For example, what became of the pastoral plans? Which Encuentro strategies were successful, which failed, and why? How were the issues of political autonomy for Mexican American Roman Catholics addressed through the Encuentro process? We believe these are critical issues for the future of Latino political and civic leadership.

Examples from the histories of national parishes and the Cursillo and Encuentro movements provide us with profound dimensions for creating and fostering leadership for the larger Latino community in the United States. Research has revealed that leadership issues are important for Latino Catholics, in particular, at a local level. According to one study, Latino adults are seeking religious formation and training for ministry where they have the opportunities to exercise their ministry in parishes and are given a degree of responsibility when working with others. This is in direct response to the perception that training for leadership roles within the church has had a tendency to separate the laity from their community in accomplishing their work.[41]

This perspective is reinforced by Soto's research of Our Lady of Guadalupe Church in Santa Clara County in California. His work underscores that, given the opportunity and proper cultural environment, Mexican Americans can excel in providing leadership for their own people. As a result, church-sponsored leadership for the Cursillo movement, the Catholic Council for the Spanish Speaking, and the Chicano Deacon Program emerged from this parish. Amazingly, of the ten permanent deacons in the San Francisco archdiocese listed in its directory for 1977, nine came from the Guadalupe parish. As early as 1964, Guadalupe parish was one of the first to have a parish council elected by the people.[42]

A parallel example in the contemporary context can be found at San Fernando Cathedral in San Antonio, Texas. In the words of the current pastor, David García, San Fernando "has helped integrate, affirm, support, develop, challenge, and ground many generations of south Texas. They come to celebrate who they are, where they come from, and where they can go together in this faith community that has wielded such a remarkable influence over so many people in its 267 years of existence."[43]

The Catholic Church hierarchy, parish priests, and laity should be encouraged to provide leadership in community organization-building efforts by Mexican Americans and Latinos through parish leadership development in both spiritual Encuentros and Cursillo opportunities. Diocesan-wide issues and problems bordering on discrimination and inequality should not be allowed to fester as in the past. Because of these issues, the IHC was brought into existence. These conditions are grounded in historical, political, and social experiences of the Mexican American people and can serve to motivate political and social leadership training and organization building.[44] In view of the diminishing numbers of Roman Catholic priests, the role of the laity will be paramount for the future of the church regardless of ethnic background. To fulfill this challenge, the Roman Catholic laity will need to develop a strong sense of ownership of the church in concert with the hierarchical leadership. As the largest sector of the church, we believe Latino Roman Catholics must play a central role in the re-imaging and transformation of this religious institution.[45]

Leadership issues for Mexican American Roman Catholics are critical for the future of American society. To suffer the consequences of social and political injustices to family, life, and soul becomes essential if there is not another generation of Mexican American Roman Catholics who are concerned about being denied access to such issues in the future. As our African American brethren have taught us, leadership based on advocacy within institutional religious structures is the promise for the Mexican American and larger Latino Roman Catholic community in the twenty-first century.

NOTES

1. Aldon D. Morris, *The Origins of the Civil Rights Movement* (New York: Free Press, 1984), 4.

2. Andrés Guerrero, *Chicano Theology* (Maryknoll, NY: Orbis Books, 1987), 83.

3. This represents a total of 11.8 percent of the 30.3 percent respondents who reported negative experiences. Office of Pastoral Research, *Hispanics in New York: Religious, Cultural, and Social Experience,* Volume 1 (New York: Archdiocese of New York, 1982).

4. Alberto L. Pulido, "Mexican-American Catholicism in the Southwest: The Transformation of a Popular Religion," in *En Aquel Entonces: Readings in Mexican-American History,* ed. Manuel G. Gonzáles and Cynthia M. Gonzáles (Bloomington: Indiana University Press, 2000), 87–95.

5. John Hope Franklin and Alfred A. Moss, *From Slavery to Freedom* (New York: Knopf, 1994), 103. See also Benjamin E. Mays and J. W. Nicholson, *The Negro's Church* (New York: Institute for Social Research, 1933), 3.

6. Hart M. Nelsen and Anne Kusener Nelsen, *Black Church in the Sixties* (Lexington: University of Kentucky Press, 1975), 11–13.

7. Michael Buroway, *Ethnography Unbound: Power Resistance in the Modern Metropolis* (Berkeley: University of California Press, 1991).

8. C. Eric Lincoln and Lawrence H. Mamiya, *The Black Church in the African-American Experience* (Durham, NC: Duke University Press, 1990), 343.

9. Good examples would be language and immigration issues. These are key issues that daily affect the lives of Mexican Americans, both inside and outside the institutional Roman Catholic Church.

10. Julie A. Corley, "Conflict and Community: St. Mary's Parish, Phoenix, Arizona" (M.A. thesis, Arizona State University, 1992).

11. "Segregation of Congregations at St. Mary's: Appeal to the Bishops," *Phoenix Gazette,* June 26, 1915.

12. John Alba, "Heritage: Longstanding Leadership of Hispanics in Tucson Contrast Sharply with Their Development in Phoenix," *Metro Phoenix* (1988): 58. The most famous story surrounding the demands put forward by the Mexican basement Catholics asking for their own church is told by Mr. Adam Díaz, telephone interview with authors Phoenix, Arizona (February 6, 1996).

13. Examples include a Catholic *Apostolado* comprised of the male members and women such as the *Guadalupanas* as early as 1935. Catholic youth organizations were

formed in the 1940s; and by World War II, Mexican American men were active in the Knights of Columbus and the St. Vincent De Paul Society. Roman Catholic Diocese of Tucson/Phoenix, Immaculate Heart of Mary File, Phoenix, Box 20.

14. Father Tony Sotelo, personal interview with authors, Phoenix, Arizona (July 20, 2000).

15. Monetary support for VIP comes from participatory donations made by Catholic and Protestant churches and synagogues in the area.

16. Francisco Navarette, personal interview with authors Phoenix, Arizona (August 3, 2000).

17. Personal interview, with Sotelo, July 20, 2000, Phoenix, Arizona. One of the biggest challenges for parish priests today, according to Father Sotelo, is to keep up with the multiple issues occurring in the church. In reflecting on his own experiences as a parish priest, he states that there was so many things on his agenda that he had to make sure to respond to all the different ministries of his parish, and VIP only represented one of them.

18. Lincoln and Mamiya, *Black Church*, 20. This movement has its roots in Philadelphia, Pennsylvania. It was led by Richard Allen, who established the first African Methodist Episcopal (AME) Church.

19. In addition, "the eschatological recognition that freedom and equality are at the essence of humanity and thus segregation and slavery are diametrically opposed to Christianity." James H. Cone, *Black Theology and Black Power* (New York: Seabury, 1969).

20. Personal interview with Annette Willis Smith, Phoenix, Arizona (August 3, 2000). See also Keith Jerome Crudup, "African-Americans in Arizona: A Twentieth Century History" (Ph.D. diss., Arizona State University, 1998). The earliest sign of African American religious expression in Phoenix was in 1889 with the establishment of Tanner Chapel AME church led by Reverend H. H. Hawkins. Matthew C. Whitaker, "In Search of Black Phoenicians: African-American Culture and Community in Phoenix, Arizona, 1869–1940" (M.A. thesis, Arizona State University, 1997), 35.

21. Personal interview, with Rev. Dr. Warren H. Stewart Phoenix, Arizona, July 22, 2000. The views of Pastor Stewart are supported by the work of the black theologian, J. Deotis Roberts, who states Black political theology is about the salvation of "blacks-in-community" in this life. See *A Black Political Theology* (Philadelphia: Westminster, 1974), 204.

22. Telephone interview with Michael Kelly, Phoenix, Arizona (July 27, 2000). Michael Kelly is the assistant to the mayor of the city of Phoenix. He runs several men's ministries as a member of FIBC.

23. *The New American Standard Bible.*

24. Personal interview, Reverend Dr. Warren H. Stewart, Phoenix, Arizona (July 22, 2000).

25. Personal interview, Annette Willis Smith, Phoenix, Arizona (August 3, 2000).

26. Moises Sandoval, *On The Move: A History of the Hispanic Church in the United States* (Maryknoll, NY: Orbis Books, 1990).

27. Olga Odgers Ortiz, "Cartografia de la Fe: cambios en la estructura territorial del catolicismo en las comunidades mexicanas del condado de San Diego," presentation at the Association for Borderland Studies and Western Social Science Association Joint Annual Conference, San Diego, CA (April 26–29, 2000).

28. Historically, Mexican Americans organized community groups for aid in their struggles against the devastating effects of the violation of their social and politi-

cal rights in the public arena. The majority of these community organizations inspired by "Mutualistas" of the 1800s have grown apart from the immigrant political issues at the local level. Most Mexican and Latino immigrants of today will have to organize their own community organizations; see Rodolfo Acuña, *Occupied America: The Chicano's Struggle Toward Liberation* (San Francisco: Canfield Press, 1972).

29. Francisco Navarette, personal phone interview with authors, Phoenix, Arizona, August 3, 2000.

30. We would describe this service as proactive and affirming. First Institutional Baptist Church service (July 30, 2000), 7:30 a.m.

31. Immaculate Heart Church service, September 6, 2000, 7:30 a.m.

32. Isidro Lucas, *The Browning of America: The Hispanic Revolution in the American Church* (Chicago: Fides/Claretian Press, 1981), 69–70.

33. Interview with Stewart. Valley Interfaith Project organizer Petra Falcon made an interesting observation as to FIBC's involvement with VIP. Ms. Falcon believes that the African American church is more effective and successful in working on its own. It is her belief that they may fear being swallowed up by a coalition due to their smaller numbers, which could explain their lack of involvement with VIP in Phoenix. Petra Falcon, telephone interview with the authors, Tucson, Arizona (August 2, 2000).

34. Office of Pastoral Research, *Hispanics in New York: Religious, Cultural, and Social Experiences*, Volume 2 (New York: Archdiocese of New York, 1982), 291.

35. Joseph P. Fitzpatrick, *Puerto Rican Americans: The Meaning of Migration to the Mainland* (Englewood, NJ: Prentice Hall, 1971), 123–124.

36. Moises Sandoval, *On the Move*, 63.

37. Jay P. Dolan and Jaime R. Vidal, eds., *Puerto Rican and Cuban Catholics in the U.S., 1900–1965* (Notre Dame, IN: University of Notre Dame, 1994), 73–74.

38. Antonio R. Soto, "The Chicano and the Church in Northern California, 1848–1978: A Study of an Ethnic Minority within the Roman Catholic Church" (Ph.D. diss., University of California, Berkeley, 1978), 199–200.

39. Ibid., 206–207.

40. This discussion on the National Encuentro movement draws heavily on the work of Sandoval, *On the Move*, 80–81.

41. Office of Pastoral Research, *Hispanics in New York* Volume 2.

42. Soto, "Chicano and the Church," 215.

43. Virgilio P. Elizondo and Timothy M. Matovina, *San Fernando Cathedral: Soul of the City* (Maryknoll, NY: Orbis Books, 1998), 119.

44. Santos C. Vega, "Pedagogy of Mexican-American Catholic Religious Practice as Based on Indicators of the Hispanic Ministry Encuentro Process, Historical Religious Experience, and in Relationship with the Treaty of Guadalupe Hidalgo, 1848." 1848/1898@TranshistoricThresholds Conference, file: D:\1848cd\papr.vega.html, a CDD-ROM. Arizona State University: Gary D. Keller and Cordelia Candelaria (Tempe: Bilingual Press/Editorial Bilingue, 2000).

45. Sandoval, *On the Move*, 135–136.

15

Pray for Elián: Religion and Politics in Miami

Miguel A. De La Torre

On Thanksgiving Day, while the United States feasted on the traditional turkey dinner, a small boy of five years of age was found off the coast of Fort Lauderdale clinging to an inner tube. Within a few days, Elián Gonzalez's name became nationally known. This child emerged at the center of a custody battle between the Exilic and Resident Cuban communities. Surrounding Elián's Miami home, both young and old, Catholics and Protestants, rich and poor, gathered to pray. Signs written in blue asked the nation to "Pray for Elián." Exilic Cubans held hands and surrounded the house to recite the rosary. These same worshipers were preparing to unclasp their praying hands and lock arms instead to prevent the U.S. government from taking this child. Some worshipers even claimed to have seen the Virgin Mary hovering over the house, while others referred to Elián as the miracle child or Miami's Jesus. Across the street from Elián's house in Miami lives a *santera,* a practitioner of the African-based Cuban religion known as Santería. For her, Elián is a child of Ochún, the quasi-deity of the sea. Followers of Santería believe that Ochún spared Elián's life to bear witness that she is still the mother of all Cubans.

While the world focused on the unfolding saga of a child named Elián, a subtext also developed. The Elián story illustrates how religion, politics, and power merge within the Miami Exilic community. The chapter's purpose is not to determine what the fate of Elián should have been. Rather, this chapter will explore how the power of the Exilic Cuban community in Miami formed their religious response to the Elián story and how that response masks a political agenda designed to maintain and increase the power base of that community. In other words, in this chapter I attempt to understand how a community of less than a half million Exilic Cubans amassed the power to contest the strongest government in the world, literally confounding the U.S. endeavor to return Elián to Cuba.[1]

Unfolding Saga

According to the official reports, a seventeen-foot aluminum boat left Cardenas, Cuba, for the United States on November 21, 1999, at 4:30 a.m. On board were fourteen individuals, one of them a boy named Elián, traveling with his mother and her boyfriend. Hours before the boy was rescued, the boat capsized off the Florida Keys. Except for Elián and two adults, all the others drowned, including his mother, Elizabeth Brotons.[2]

Meanwhile, two Broward fishermen, cousins, were on an early morning fishing expedition when they spotted an inner tube bobbing in the ocean shortly after 9 a.m., Thanksgiving morning. Upon seeing a hand move from within the tube, one of the fishermen jumped into the ocean and pulled Elián out of the water. Exhausted by the ordeal, Elián was taken to the hospital for medical treatment and was released the following day. At that time, the Immigration and Nationalization Service (INS) gave temporary custody of the boy to a distant relative living in Miami, Lazaro González, the child's great-uncle. This ensured the child's care while the agency determined the boy's immigration status. Nevertheless, on the following day, November 27, the boy's father, Juan Miguel González, from his home in Cardenas, Cuba, demanded the return of his son. At that moment, the boy became the epicenter of a political tug-of-war between the Exilic and Resident Cuban communities.

Four days after Elián was pulled from the water, November 29, he literally became the poster child for the Exilic community. It was believed that Fidel Castro might attend the World Trade Organization meeting that was going to be held in early December in Seattle, Washington. So posters and flyers were rapidly produced with a picture of Elián on a stretcher under the caption, "Another Child Victim of Fidel Castro." The political worth of Elián as a symbol against the Castro regime was obvious. Yet, Elián's true value to the community became apparent only with his transformation into a religious symbol. The metamorphosis of Elián into a sacred symbol was not the Machiavellian formulation of a few with political power; rather, it was a joint effort of the Exilic Cuban community, who attempted to comprehend the will of a Deity who had seemed silent during the past forty years of their Babylonian captivity in Miami.

How could Elián become a deific symbol? Because sacred language is rooted in symbols and myths, anything profane (a river, stone, star, animal, or human being) can be transformed into something sacred, a marker pointing to something greater than itself.[3] Specifically religious people (such as prophets or apostles) and religious objects (such as totems) are not the only or even the supreme representations of the Divine reality. Anything or anyone can reveal aspects of the Divine. Elián as symbol not only reflects the sacred, he comes into being in a sacred manner.[4]

Prayer vigil for Elián González in front of his uncle's home in Little Havana, Florida. Reinaldo Martinez holds a poster of Elián on Thursday night, November 2, 2000 (Courtesy of the *Miami Herald*)

His few hours in the ocean became two and a half days, raising the question, how can a child survive that long, alone, in the sea? The answer: a miracle from God. As the battle over Elián's immigration status became fierce, his symbolic worth increased, while the Exilic community began to speak of him in religious terms. An unconfirmed report, circulated widely within the community, recounted the tale of dolphins circling Elián's inner tube, protecting him from sharks. Dolphins, in the early Christian Church, symbolized salvation. Not only is Elián saved, he now comes to save. "He's a miracle," says María Rodríguez, age fifty-five, while attending the annual Three Kings Day Parade (January 9); "the fact that he made it for two days, with dolphins circling around him—that proves he's a miracle." At his great-uncle's modest home, religious candles line the sidewalk as the Exilic community begins to compare Elián to Jesus.[5]

The church was less subtle in its comparison of Elián to Christ. During a prayer vigil held on March 29, the clergy assured the crowd that God was on the side of the Exilic Cubans. "In Cuba, some people have made Elián a symbol of the new Che [Guevara], so it is not so unusual that some people in Miami are seeing him as the new Christ," said the Reverend Gustavo Miyares of Immaculate Conception Church, one of the prayer vigil organizers. María Ester Fernández, another of multiple prayer organizers in front of Elián's house, best summed up the convictions of the Exilic community when she said, "We continue praying that Elián stays, because God wants it. . . . Just as Christ died for us and on the third day was resurrected, so will the Cuban people be resurrected."[6]

Within a short time, the community began to point out that, like Jesus, Elián arrived just weeks before Christmas, at the end of the millennium, on the last official day thanksgiving is offered to God. Even the year 2000, the sixth millennium since the supposed creation of the earth, conferred upon Elián, like Jesus, the symbol of hope. Besides being likened to Christ, the community also believed Elián to be protected and watched by the Virgin Mary. As many as forty people attested to seeing the image of the Virgin on the glass door of TotalBank, located in Little Havana: she appeared to protest Elián's return to Cuba. The bank's location on 27th Avenue quickly became a pilgrimage stop for the multitudes who came with flowers, some rubbing their babies against the window pane for good luck.[7] One woman reported seeing a vision of the Virgin with child surrounded by two giant dolphins.[8] These stories are reminiscent of the Cuban tale of drowning fishermen being saved by *la Caridad del Cobre* (the Virgin of Charity), Cuba's patron saint. Even la Virgen de Guadalupe, believed to have appeared to a Mexican indigenous peasant more than 400 years ago, made an appearance as a spot on a mirror in the bedroom where the boy slept.[9]

The community created religious rituals that bound the sacred with the secular. On Mother's Day, May 14, 2000, dozens of women and children *vestido de luto* (dressed in mourning black), gathered by the sea wall behind the Shrine of Our Lady of Charity to honor Elián's mother. A prayer service was held, culminating with the tossing of roses into a makeshift raft. Ana Rodriguez, thirty-five, a mother of three who participated in the event said, "It's for her and all the mothers that have died for freedom. Not only Cuban mothers."[10] Elevated to the realm of martyrdom, the community continued to honor her memory by naming a street after her (87th Court in Hialeah Gardens) and erecting a shrine to her at the Bay of Pigs memorial on 13th Avenue in Little Havana.

As the sacred and political shared the same space, the boundaries between the two became blurred in the minds of the supporters who gathered before Elián's house to pray. Jorge Mas Santos, the chairperson of the Cuban American National Foundation (CANF), the most powerful Exilic Cuban political lobbying organization in the United States, helped complete this fusion when he said, "Praying in a religious ceremony is the best way to show our support."[11] In spite of the fact that the official Catholic Church hierarchy of Miami took a position of neutrality, citing "moral uncertainty," local priests became major players in the unfolding saga.[12] Reverend Francisco Santana, of the Shrine of Our Lady of Charity, literally brought the church into Elián's Miami home. Six nights a week, he celebrated a private mass for Elián's family, and while not specifically praying for Elián to stay—so as not to contradict the church's hierarchy—he led prayers that God would touch his father, Juan Miguel, so that he could love as a father over any prevailing political pressure.[13] Ergo, that Elián would stay.

As Miami's Jesus, the miracle child, Elián is credited with forging new ties between Catholic priests and Mainline and Evangelical Protestant pastors, historic rivals in both Miami and La Habana. Father Santana surrounded by fellow Catholic priests and Protestant ministers made ecumenical history when they officially turned the protest for justice in front of Elián's house into a daily prayer vigil. Santana proclaimed, "We are transforming, as of this moment, the cries demanding justice in front of Elián's house into a permanent prayer vigil, so that God can complete the miracle that He himself begun."[14] Elián, as a sacred symbol, brought healing to centuries of religious rivalry, a task beyond the ability of mere mortals. Six Catholic priests and six Mainline Protestant pastors (the twelve disciples of Christ) took turns leading the nightly prayer vigil. On Fridays, they led joint prayer services. Presbyterian pastor Manuel Salabarria said it best, "We have a common ground, a common interest, and a common purpose." To maintain this alliance, the Reverend Santana put aside the devotion to Mary so as not to "offend" the Protestants.[15] During one of these massive prayer vigils, a cross composed of 10,000 Exilic Cubans marched downed Calle Ocho (8th Street), as both Catholic priests and Protestant ministers joined forces in proclaiming the miracle child.[16]

But Elián as symbol is not limited to Catholics and Protestants. Practitioners of Santería also saw in the boy religious symbolism. Although it is impossible to document the exact number of worshipers, scholars estimate that about 5 million in the United States are identified with the religion of Santería.[17] One of the side stories that emerged during the Elián saga centered on a note Lazaro González, the boy's great-uncle, wrote for Elián's grandmothers. He entrusted the note to Sister Jeanne O'Laughlin, host to the boy's grandmothers in late January during their trip to the United States. Sister O'Laughlin forgot to pass the note on, finding it in her pocket days later. The note was a warning to the grandmothers that Castro wanted the child so that he could make a ritual sacrifice of Elián. This concern is based on the most-repeated rumor on the streets of Little Havana, that Castro was forewarned of a child saved by dolphins in the sea who will overthrow his regime. Castro had to acquire the boy to prevent the fulfillment of prophecy. Elián (Jesus) was being sought by Castro (Herod), who wanted to kill the messiah who threatened his rule. Even Auxiliary Bishop Agustín Roman was quick to make the comparison between Castro and Herod after reading the Scriptures about Herod wanting Jesus killed to preserve his reign.[18] According to resident and Exilic practitioners of Santería, Castro participates in this Afro-Cuban religion, even traveling to Africa to be initiated into its mysteries. But somehow Castro has offended Elegguá, the first and most powerful *orisha*, according to the annual oracles. Elegguá is believed to be depicted as a child, and some see Elián as being the child that Elegguá has destined to overthrow Castro. Hence, Castro's obsession in having Elián returned.[19]

References to Judaism are also used to show the significance of Elián as the miracle child. Roberto Sánchez, sixty-five, an Exilic Cuban Jew, waved Israel's Star of David flag in front of Elián's Miami home. He said, "Elián is the Moses of the year 2000. This is a sacred child, so the flag of the Holy Land is appropriate here, because this street is holy land."[20] Like Moses, Elián is drawn from the waters, escaping the Pharaoh Castro. And like Moses, the hopes are that Elián will lead his people to the promised land of Cuba. One Exilic Cuban magazine pictured Elián on its back cover over the caption: "A Cuban Moses." Jewish Exilic Cubans have even quoted the Talmud to justify the struggle of keeping Elián in the States: "To save a human is to save the entire world."[21] Rabbi Solomon Schiff, vice president of the Rabbinical Association of Greater Miami compares the Elián saga to the ship, St. Louis, which in 1937, while carrying 937 Jewish refugees from Germany, was turned away from Cuba and the United States. Elián reminds him of the immense value of human life. So also is the Koran, the sacred book of Islam, quoted. Reference is made to a passage that refers to a messenger who will be a child coming from the sea named Elián. Rabbi Schiff points out that Christians, Jews, and Muslims (I would add Santero/as) have identified with Elián for different reasons, but under one similar idea: "Every human being is like an only book which deserves respect, dignity, and a quality of life."[22]

History is simply repeating itself, according to Santiago Aranegui, professor of antiquity and history at Florida International University. Every new age occurs when a "chosen" person sets out on a grand, earth-changing mission. These epochs are usually announced by the appearance of a child, as was the case with Moses and Jesus. For Adventist pastor Charles Vento, an Exilic Cuban, Elián, like the prophets of old, has the divine power to change the destiny of nations and liberate oppressed people.[23] Mirta Rondon, sixty-one, who led a chant in front of Elián's Miami home, believed Elián to be a messiah. "I have a feeling that he will be the one. He will be the one who brings change to the history of Cuba."[24] In the streets of Miami, protestors routinely shouted, "Elián is king of the Cubans."[25] Exilic Cuban superstars like Gloria Estefan, Willy Chirino, Arturo Sandoval, and Andy Garcia made pilgrimages to Elián's house. Even the Fox Family Channel produced the first Elián movie, which aired in September 2000.

Why all the fuss over Elián? Exilic Cubans read their story in the story of Elián. Frank Calzón, executive director of the Center for a Free Cuba (CFC), located in Washington D.C., puts into words what the community felt: "Each one of us sees himself in that small child, in the suffering of his tragedy."[26] Elián represents the ultimate sacrifice of a parent seeking liberty for their child. One reason why Cubans gathered at Elián's house is to somehow prevent what they themselves experienced. The story of Margarita Aguiar, fifty-six, a Miami-Dade Community College counselor who took off work to stand before Elián's house, is typical of those who came and prayed. She recalled her brother being shot when Castro's soldiers took over her parochial school and invaded her church in February 1961. She stated that her father placed her on a plane, exchanging being with her for her freedom, the same choice she wants for Elián: "He was a father who loved me enough to say, 'I'll never see her again, but she will live in freedom.' "[27] Part of the Exilic Cuban collective memory is the Pedro Pan (Peter Pan) flights, a massive Catholic operation that removed over 14,000 Cuban children from Cuba during the early 1960s. Regardless of the importance of the family unit, Exilic Cubans have historically subordinated the parent–child relationship for the sake of "saving" the child from communism. Ernesto Betancourt, founding director of Radio Martí, the station responsible for broadcasting U.S. propaganda into Cuba, explains: "We [Exilic Cubans] see that the repression of a regime still pursues the child; the world only sees that he still has a father."[28]

During the last days of the custody standoff, when it appeared as if the battle for Elián was lost, the community continued to expect God to perform a miracle. When a flock of birds in "V" formation flew over Elián's Miami home on April 13, at 2:40 a.m., it was immediately taken as a sign of hope from God. Notwithstanding, in the pre-dawn hours of April 22, 2000, federal agents raided the home Elián was staying in and, through force, reunited him with his father who was waiting in Washington, D.C. His forceful removal by Janet Reno and the Justice Department occurred on Holy Saturday. Again, Catholic and Protestant ministers joined forces to speak as one, believing that unless they came together, the Exilic community would be lost. They denounced the Clinton administration's sacrilege of violating Holy Week and called the community to prayer and peaceful demonstration. However, the religious symbolism of Holy Saturday's extraction was not lost on the Exilic community. Pastor Humberto Cruz illustrated the connection by stating, "They say in the Scriptures that a shadow fell on Jerusalem when Jesus was crucified. A shadow has once again fallen, this time on our city" [of Miami].[29]

On Easter morning, the day after the raid, pulpits throughout South Florida prayed for Elián, his Miami family, and the community at large. At St. Juan Bosco, the church Elián's Miami relatives usually attend, an eleven-year-old Milena Libertad (whose last name means "liberty"), herself a rafter who came to Miami in the previous year, belted a song she composed about Elián: "If you love me, hear me, dad. I don't want to go back to Cuba." She brought the church to tears. Concepción Pelaez, seventy-six, summed up the importance of worship when she said, "I cry for the child. The mass did me good because as we cry, we release our pain."[30] Later that evening, during the evening mass at Our Lady of Charity shrine, Elián's little cousin, Lazarito Martell, prophesied to the delight of the 300 attendants that Elián was going to stay in the United States. The congregation, carrying prints of Jesus Christ on the cross with his blood dripping down over the island of Cuba, heard Reverend Santana proclaim, "Elián is staying and Fidel is leaving." When Elián's Miami family stood before the congregation, the parishioners waved miniature Cuban flags as they burst into the Cuban national anthem.[31] These services epitomize the merging of the Exilic Cuban political agenda with religious fervor. But when and how did this fusion occur? To answer that question, we now turn to the historical antecedents of the Exilic Cuban political religiosity.

Antecedents to the Saga

The reaction of Catholic priests and Protestant ministers to the Elián saga can never be understood apart from the historical fight of the Cuban churches against "godless communism." The Cuban Catholic Church, prior to the Cuban revolution of 1959, was highly influenced by the denunciation of communism presented in the papal encyclical *Divini Redemptoris*, which understood Catholicism and Marxism as mutually exclusive. This 1937 pontifical document was written as a reaction to the excesses of the Spanish Civil War and the religious persecutions that occurred in Mexico and Russia. The Cuban priesthood was predominately from Spain. Of the 3,000 Catholic priests in Cuba on the eve of the Revolution in 1959, approximately 2,500 were from Spain, trained during the Franco dictatorship and highly influenced by the bitter Spanish Civil War victory over communism—a victory clothed in heavy religious overtones. These priests transplanted the atmosphere of a religious crusade against communism from Spain to Cuba. No room existed for dialogue; instead, Cubans were forced to choose between "Roma o Moscú."

The Cuban Revolution occurred prior to the radicalization of the churches in Latin America due to the Second Vatican Council (1962–1965), which dealt with the challenges of the modern world, and the 1968 conference of Latin American bishops in Medellín, Colombia, which articulated the basic tenets of liberation theology. These gatherings emphasized the responsibility of Christians toward the poor and afflicted. Not benefiting from these theological developments, the pre-Revolution churches of Cuba concentrated their efforts in running schools, which were staffed by foreigners, located in the cities, and (due to their high tuition) exclusive of both people of color and low-income families. In an effort to increase their political power, these churches attempted to establish and maintain links with the different political regimes that ruled Cuba, regardless of their corruption and disregard for socioeconomic justice.

Paradoxically, during the Cuban Revolution, before Castro proclaimed his Marxist-Leninist orientation on December 1, 1961, both Catholic and Protestant chaplains actively served in the columns of the Castro brothers and Juan Almeida. Many Protestant leaders cooperated with the guerrilla forces in that nationalistic attempt to eliminate Batista. Two early martyrs of the revolution were Frank and Josué Pais, Baptists who were killed by Batista's soldiers for leading an uprising in Santiago; also Esteban Hernández, a Presbyterian, was tortured and killed by Batista's police. The boat that brought the rebels to Cuba, *Granma*, was purchased with the help of a $10,000 donation from a staff member with the National Council of Evangelical Churches. Additionally, homes of Protestant leaders served as underground headquarters for the Revolution.

Catholic leaders also partook in the insurrection. For example, Father Sardiñas served as chaplain to the rebel army and was promoted to the rank of *comandante*, Father Madrigal was treasurer of the July 26 movement, and Father Chabebe relayed coded messages to the rebel forces via his religious radio program. Although the church hierarchy remained silent during the insurgence, a significantly large percentage of Catholics, like the martyred Catholic student leader Echevarría, participated in the uprising, fighting the forces of Batista as Cubans who happened to be Catholics.[32] If Christ's mission was to bring about a just social order, then as followers of Christ, they felt commissioned to this task. They saw the revolution as the vehicle by which to put their faith into action, specifically through solidarity with those who were marginalized and oppressed in Cuba.

Many churches were at first pleased with the government's initial move to end gambling, prostitution, and political corruption. After helping to eliminate Batista, they returned to their church ministries. However, the early optimism of church and state cooperation gave way to disillusion as the new regime took a more leftist tilt. A closer relationship with the Soviet Union, the promoters of "godless communism," along with land and education reform (which curtailed church autonomy), led to the eventual break a few years after Batista's overthrow. Catholics, as well as Protestants, became engaged in counterrevolutionary activities, openly supporting and praising the United States, which was intent on annihilating the Revolution and reestablishing its former authority on the island.

The churches took the position that Cuba needed to be "saved" from atheism. By Christmas 1960, Archbishop Pérez Serantes, a social reformer, critic of the Batista regime, and an early supporter of Castro, wrote a pastoral letter that presented Cubans with an ultimatum, titled "With Christ or Against Christ." He clearly laid out the existing dichotomy in eschatological tones: "The battle is to wrestle between Christ and the Anti-Christ. Choose, then, each to who they prefer to have as Jefe."[33] By 1961, the government nationalized all church schools and declared most foreign clergy persona non grata, in response to three Spanish priests and one Methodist minister who participated as chaplains in the April Bay of Pigs invasion. One of the priests, Father Ismael de Lugo, read a communiqué to the Cuban population:

> The liberating forces have disembarked on Cuba's beaches. We come in the name of God. . . . The assault brigade is made up of thousands of Cubans who are all Christians and Catholics. Our struggle is that of those who believe in God against the atheists. . . . Have faith, since the victory is ours, because God is with us and the Virgin of Charity cannot abandon her children. . . . Long live Christ the King! Long live our glorious Patron Saint![34]

As retribution for the Christians who opposed Cuba's new Marxist orientation, both Catholics and Protestants faced expulsion, were denied running schools as a form of income, and had their private media nationalized. Also, church members were routinely watched by the government, while several bishops, priests, and ministers found themselves placed under house arrest. Christians were refused entry into the Communist Party, a sure path toward economic advancement, and denied high-level positions in the government and university. Many, mostly the middle class, chose flight, rather than fight, as an alternative, creating a brain-drain on the island and further weakening the churches' power base. Monsignor Pérez Serantes, a critic of Castro's Marxist leaning, best summed up the church's predicament: "All that is happening to us is providential. . . . We believed more in our schools than in Jesus Christ."[35]

Those Christians who chose Miami as their response to Castro's crackdown on the churches brought the religiously cloaked sentiments about communism which originated in Franco's victory in Spain. The dialogue that developed between the left and the church after Vatican II and the rise of liberation theology came too late for Cuba. The Exilic Cuban mind was set. To be an Exilic Cuban Christian meant to participate in the crusade against communism and Castro. To recognize any achievements accomplished in Cuba, or to have an opinion that might in any way be construed as somehow benefiting or complimenting present-day Cuba, is to betray one's fidelity to God and instead proclaim an allegiance with Satan. For example, during the Elián saga, several demonstrators, armed with "Pray for Elián" placards and posters of Attorney General Janet Reno (a Miamian) with diabolical horns sprouting from her head, took their protest to her Miami home.[36] One poster read, "Elián is Christ. Reno is Lucifer. Castro is Satan."[37] Immediately after the federal raid of Elián's Miami home, Mayor Joe Carolle denounced the seizure in religious tones. "What they did was a crime. These are atheists. They don't believe in God."[38]

In one of the protest marches following the raid, Cubans dressed in black and laid flowers, a silver cross, and the Cuban flag beneath a photo of Elián's mother, which was erected at the Bay of Pigs monument. Many cooled themselves from the 80-degree temperatures with circular paper fans which read, "I vote Republican." Within this atmosphere, religion, politics, and power are fused and confused. From Miami, an Exilic Cuban worldview is constructed where *La lucha* becomes a sacred space representing the cosmic struggle between the "children of light" (Exilic Cubans) and the "children of darkness" (resident Cubans), complete with a Christ (Martí), an anti-Christ (Castro), a priesthood (CANF), a promised land (Cuba), a Babylon (the United States), and martyrs (those who gloriously suffer in the holy war against Castro). Add to this cosmology a Messiah child—Elián.

Understanding Exilic Cubans

The non-Cuban Hispanics in the United States look at the Elián saga and shake their heads in bewilderment. They, like the rest of the nation, have difficulty understanding the passions that permeate Miami. Part of this misunderstanding is based on the social location of Exilic Cubans, which is radically different from any other Latino/a group in this nation. Miami Cubans are whiter, as well as more economically, politically, and educationally established,[39] mostly due to the economic enclave they carved out for themselves.[40] These pronounced differences between Exilic Cubans and other U.S. Hispanics have created misinterpretations and, at times, mistrust.

To understand the Exilic Cuban mindset, the reader must realize that for

Miami Cubans, the universe is conceived and perceived in its relationship to one person, Fidel Castro. Castro is an all-consuming fire central to the construction of every opinion, action, and resolution that may originate in Miami. Castro, as the incarnation of Satan, informs the daily experience of the Exilic community. La lucha, the very struggle of life, is geared against the figure of Castro. Jaime Suchlicki, director of the Institute of Cuba and Cuban-American Studies (ICCAS) at the University of Miami, reminds us that the fight is not so much about Elián as it is about Fidel.[41] This sentiment is expressed by Isaura Felipe, eighty-six, at the Buena Vista Social Club, a Little Havana center for the elderly. While clutching the gold crucifix around her neck, she exclaimed, "[If Elián is returned] I will cry, because that would be giving Fidel Castro pleasure, and he will be making fun of us."[42] Sonia Ruiz, thirty-six, while keeping an all-night vigil, echoed the feelings: "Why are they going to give [Elián] to that Communist dad? Our government has betrayed us again. Why are they letting Castro win?"[43] The Elián saga has more to do with Castro than it does with Elián.

Studies conducted by sociologists Alejandro Portes and Rubén Rumbaut suggest that Cuban émigrés differ from other Latino/a groups because their immigration was rooted in the changing political situation in the homeland.[44] Thus, the Exilic Cuban interest in politics focuses on the United States' foreign policies toward Cuba. Other U.S. Latina/o groups pursue a political agenda with a variety of issues that encompass bilingual education, immigration, affirmative action, improving social services in *los barrios*, and police brutality—just to mention a few. Exilic Cubans, in contrast, are politically focused on the elimination of Castro. As one local bumper sticker put it: "No Castro—No Problem."[45]

It will be a mistake to think that the repatriation of Elián signals the demise of the Exilic Cuban resolve to view the world through an anti-Castro lens. On the contrary, the Miami community's determination of maintaining fever-pitched hostility toward anything that might appear pro-Castro is only stiffened as right-wing hard-liners are accused of not standing firmer in its defense of Elián. The Elián saga is but the latest example of how the community formulates its actions, even religious actions, based on the supposed impact it will have on Castro. Nothing else matters.

NOTES

1. For more on Elián, see my book, *La Lucha for Cuba: Religion and Politics in the Streets of Miami* (Berkeley: University of California Press, 2003). Specifically, according to the 1990 U.S. Bureau of the Census, of the roughly 22 million Latino/as residing in the United States, about 1 million (or 4.8%) are of Cuban origins. Over half this number lives in Dade County. They compose 29 percent of the total Dade County population of 1.9 million, or about 562,000 Cubans, making Dade the county with the highest concentration of Cubans. Seven out of every ten residents in Hialeah (a city in northwest Dade) are Cuban-born, followed by Miami with six out of every ten residents. This makes Hialeah and Miami the top two cities in the nation with the

highest foreign-born ratio. The only city in the world with a larger number of Cubans is La Habana, Cuba.

Exilic Reverend Ramos (a Protestant) and auxiliary Bishop Román (a Catholic) estimate Exilic Cubans have a higher level of religious participation than when they lived on the island. For example, about 15 to 20 percent attend Catholic services, compared with 5 to 8 percent prior to Castro's revolution (Marcos Antonio Ramos and Agustín A. Román, "The Cubans, Religion and South Florida," in *Cuban Exiles in Florida: Their Presence and Contribution*, ed., Antonio Jorge, Jaime Suchlicki, and Adolfo Leyva de Varona (Coral Gables: University of Miami Press, 1991), 121). While the majority of Cubans may claim to be Catholic, it is important to realize that most profess the old Cuban idiom, "*Soy católico a mi manera*" (I am Catholic in my own way). Many practice their Catholicism while engaging in other religious tradition, like Santería, without finding any internal contradiction.

2. Alfonso Chardy, "Family Ties Spurred Rafters on Elián Trip," *Miami Herald* (June 23, 2000).

3. Mircea Eliade, *Patterns in Comparative Religion*, translated by Rosemary Sheed (New York: Meridian Books, 1963), 11.

4. Mircea Eliade, *The Sacred and the Profane: The Nature of Religion*, translated by Willard R. Trask (New York: Harcourt, Brace & World, 1957), 20–65.

5. Eunice Ponce and Elaine de Valle, "Mania over Elián Rising," *Miami Herald* (January 10, 2000).

6. Alejandra Matus, "El fevor religioso aumenta entre los manifestantes frente a la casa de Elián," *El Nuevo Herald* (April 22, 2000).

7. Joaquim Utset, "Devotos de la Virgen dicen ver una señal contra el regreso del niño," *El Nuevo Herald* (March 26, 2000).

8. Matus, "El fevor religioso."

9. Meg Laughlin, "Prayer Vigil Lifts Elián Fervor to New High," *Miami Herald* (March 31, 2000).

10. "Ceremony Set to Honor Elián's Mom," *Miami Herald* (May 14, 2000).

11. Amy Driscoll and Sandra Marquez-Garcia, "Thousand Join Glowing Prayer Vigil," *Miami Herald* (March 30, 2000).

12. D. Aileen Dodd, "Catholic Leaders Low-Profile," *Miami Herald* (April 15, 2000).

13. D. Aileen Dodd, "Elián a Bridge Linking Rival Faiths," *Miami Herald* (April 10, 2000).

14. Rui Ferreira, "Vigilia permanente en casa de Elián," *El Nuevo Herald* (April 5, 2000).

15. Dodd, "Elián a Bridge."

16. Joaquin Utset, "Miles de personas participan en virilia en Miami," *El Nuevo Herald* (April 11, 2000).

17. Migene Gonzalez-Wippler, *Santería: The Religion* (New York: Harmony Books, 1989), 9.

18. Laughlin, "Prayer Vigil."

19. Maria Travierso and Charles Cotayo, "Elián, un niño 'milagroso' hecho símbolo," *El Nuevo Herald* (March 6, 2000).

20. Paul Brinkley-Rogers, "Protestors from Abroad Flock to Home," *Miami Herald* (April 19, 2000).

21. Daniel Shoer Roth, "Los cubanos se ven reflejados en el niño balsero," *El Nuevo Herald* (January 7, 2000).

22. Travierso and Cotayo, "Elián, un niño 'milagroso.' "

23. Ibid.

24. Ponce and de Valle, "Mania over Elián."

25. Joaquin Utset and R. Ferreira, "De la protesta cívica al júbilo popular," *El Nuevo Herald* (January 9, 2000).

26. Roth, "Los cubanos."

27. Karen Branch, "Adult Exiles Recall Cuban Childhoods," *Miami Herald* (April 15, 2000).

28. Roth, "Los cubanos."

29. Daniel A. Grech, "Pastors Join Criticism, But Appeal for Calm," *Miami Herald* (April 23, 2000).

30. Andrea Robinson, "A Community Looks to Heal," *Miami Herald* (April 24, 2000).

31. "Little Cousin's Dream Strengthens Exiles' Faith Boy Will Stay in U.S.," *Miami Herald* (April 24, 2000).

32. John Kirk, *Between God and the Party: Religion and Politics in Revolutionary Cuba* (Tampa: University Presses of Florida, 1988), 48–49.

33. Manuel Maza, "The Cuban Catholic Church: True Struggles and False Dilemmas" (M.A. thesis, Georgetown University, Washington D.C., 1982), 91.

34. Kirk, *Between God and the Party*, 96.

35. Aldo J. Büntig, "The Church in Cuba: Toward a New Frontier," in *Religion in Cuba Today*, ed. Alice Hageman and Philip E. Weaton (New York: Association Press, 1971), 111.

36. Karen Branch, "Crowds Target Reno's Home," *Miami Herald* (April 6, 2000).

37. Laughlin, "Prayer Vigil."

38. Carolyn Salazar and Manny Garcia, "Federal Agents Seize Elián in Predawn Raid," *Miami Herald* (April 22, 2000).

39. The socioeconomic location of Exilic Cubans is radically different from that of other Latino/a groups. Most of the Cubans who came to this country during the early 1960s were economically middle and upper class. The vast majority of the first wave (1959–1962) composed an elite of former notables who were mostly white (94%), middle-aged (about thirty-eight years old), educated (about fourteen years of schooling), urban (principally La Habana) and literate in English. The second wave (1962–1973) was predominately white, educated, middle class, and willing to work below minimum wages. While all strata of Cuban society were represented in these first two waves, it was obvious that the vast majority consisted of those from the upper echelons and the middle class who had most benefited from the pre-Castro regime. They represented the top echelons of the country's governmental and business community, facilitating their reestablishment in a foreign land. See Miguel A. De La Torre, "Miami and the Babylonian Captivity," in *Sacred Text, Secular Times: The Hebrew Bible in the Modern World*, ed. Leonard Jay Greenspoon and Bryan F. Le Beau (Bronx, NY: Fordham University Press, 2000), 269.

40. The flight of capital from Latin America to the economic and political security of the United States provided an economic space for Exilic Cubans to manage said funds leading to the creation and growth of banks. Once secured in banking positions, they provided "character loans" to their compatriots to encourage business. It mattered little if the borrower had any standing within Euro-American banks, little collateral, or spoke English. Loans (usually from $10,000 to $35,000) were provided based on the reputation of the borrower in Cuba. This policy was discontinued in 1973 because the new refugees, who were not from the more elite first wave, were

unknown to the lenders. This practice contributed to the development of an economic enclave. See Alejandro Portes and Alex Stepick, *City on the Edge: The Transformation of Miami* (Berkeley: University of California Press, 1993), 132–135.

41. Paul Brinkley-Rogers, Curtis Morgan, Elaine Dreviewle, and Audra D. S. Burch, "Case Provokes Harsh Feelings, Hope," *Miami Herald* (April 5, 2000).

42. Paul Brinkley-Rogers, "Exiles Tearful over Boy's Future," *Miami Herald* (April 8, 2000).

43. Paul Brinkley-Rogers, Curtis Morgan, and Eunice Ponce, "For Most in Miami, Ruling Draws Restrained Reaction," *Miami Herald* (June 2, 2000).

44. Alejandro Portes and Rubén G. Rumbaut, *Immigrant America: A Portrait* (Berkeley: University of California Press, 1996), 133.

45. Guillermo J. Grenier and Hugh Gladwin. FIU 1997 CUBA POLL, Institute of Public Opinion Research (IPOR) of Florida International University and the *Miami Herald*. Available: http://www.fiu.edu/orgs/ipor/cubapoll/index.html, #28 [Accessed May 2, 1998].

16

Intifada: Church–State Conflict in Vieques, Puerto Rico

Lester McGrath-Andino

This essay explores the role played by the Ecumenical Coalition of Churches for Vieques (ECCV) in the formation and struggles of a broad-based civil disobedience campaign being carried out since 1999 by the people of Vieques and Puerto Rico against the U.S. Navy.[1] As a result of the ECCV's leadership, the campaign was conducted in a peaceful manner and contributed to the defeat of the pro-statehood administration in the November 7, 2000, local elections. This movement may significantly contribute to the creation of an ecumenical social agenda for the Puerto Rican people as they enter the twenty-first century. Thus, a group of religious leaders of eight Christian denominations has had a direct influence on the political and social development of Puerto Rico, even though in this religious context social commitment and activism are not seen as the responsibility or the everyday task of the church.

In his classic work on the social sources of power, Michael Mann points out that a society is constituted by multiple overlapping and intersecting sociospatial networks of power. He indicates that the best way to understand a society is through the study of the four social networks of power: ideology, economics, politics, and the military-industrial complex.[2]

Mann's model is important to understand the close relations that exist in Puerto Rican society between the various networks of both local and U.S. power. The importance of this model to understand Puerto Rican society is clear and based on two points. First, and contrary to other societies and contexts where some of the power networks may appear to be hidden, Mann's model fits well with Puerto Rico's colonial reality. The modern history of Puerto

Rico is a perfect example of the interaction between the power grids mentioned by Mann.

Second, during Puerto Rico's five centuries of colonial history, religion has been used as a source of ideological production to sustain the imperial power of Spain and the United States. While the usual and more obvious colonial power sources (economics, military, and politics) have always been present and visible, the importance of religious ideological control lies concealed, apparently hibernating while the Puerto Rican Church builds temples and institutions, completely oblivious to the capacities and inner activity of the hidden ideological power. In the meantime, its "objective, neutral, nonpolitical" discourse carries a constant message of prudence, patience, and submission to the authorities.

The reasons for this invisibility are varied. On one side, most people define ideology negatively, in terms opposed to their own perceptions and religious beliefs. Very few define their political or social vision as an ideology. They prefer to use the term against their adversaries, as if their own arguments were ingenious, objective, truthful, and neutral, while those tainted by "ideology" are false, subjective, and utopic. For others, the term "ideology" is defined politically and disconnected from their daily religious activity, which tends to be steered toward peace, order, and a virtuous lifestyle. Finally, for the rest it is difficult to establish a connection between everyday theological discourse and the social and mental formation of the brethren, assuming that this occurs only when you are openly debating specific themes, as if the process of ideological formation and formulation could not happen implicitly.

I should point out that for most conservative Latin American Protestants, politics is a very dangerous field, not to be entered for fear of your salvation, not to be preached about at church, and always looked upon with suspicion. The political field is seen as highly contaminated with hidden worldly agendas and conflicts. Many Protestants claim that it is not a place for "God-fearing" Christians. Pastors and religious leaders who minister and preach a committed, politically influenced social agenda are looked upon with suspicion, persecuted, fired, or shunned. Of course, in Puerto Rico as in most places, there exists a double standard at the moment of exercising pressure on these leaders. Due to our colonial relations with the United States, pastors who sympathize with the two annexationist political parties in Puerto Rico—the New Progressive Party and the Popular Democratic Party—are a majority, and their political actions are tolerated or swept under the rug. Their social commitments are seen as part of their ministry and never associated in any way with their political loyalties. In contrast, pastors who favor independence for Puerto Rico, notwithstanding their centrist or social-democratic credentials, are considered "radicals" whose every social commitment and action falls under suspicion because of their obvious hidden agendas and "ideology."

Mann's study helps us understand the hidden ideological presuppositions of religious discourse. He points out that religion, as a source of ideological power, serves three functions: it provides meaning to our observations and sense perceptions; establishes adequate norms of conduct; and creates ritual

Rev. Luís Rosario, general minister of the United Church of Christ, along with an unnamed mother and son, prepares to be arrested at one of the fourteen nonviolent civil disobedience camps outside of the Vieques U.S. military base (Courtesy of Farrique Pesquera)

or aesthetic practices such as song, dance, and visual art forms. These sources create considerable power when wielded by conservative groups, who may have the backing not only of reason and logic but also of God, tradition, and the Bible. As all but the most fervent materialist recognize, where meaning, norms, and aesthetic and ritual practices are monopolized by a distinctive group, it may possess considerable extensive and intensive power to manipulate and control people.[3]

These functions are constantly active in religion. Religion is the site where meaning and society are taught from a particular perspective (while ignoring others). Religion preaches an ethical discourse to believers about how they should live in submission to the God-ordained powers of law and order (while avoiding a questioning of the status quo or the root sources of evil, injustice, and oppression). It is also a place where carnal passions and instincts are tamed, while an ideological message is planted through the use of art, oratory, symbols, and Sunday rituals. It is for these reasons that Mann concludes that religious movements provide the most obvious examples of ideological power acting in modern society.[4]

Puerto Rican Religious, Political, and Military Context

Puerto Rico has been a colony of two empires for the last five centuries. Until 1898, the island was a colony of Spain, and its population was 99 percent

Roman Catholic. Since 1898 Puerto Rico has been a colony of the United States as a result of the Spanish-American War. The new rulers encouraged the entry of Protestant missionaries from a dozen denominations, who collaborated with the empire in its civilizing mission of transforming the Spanish colony into a future "showcase" American territory. The relation between the Roman Catholic hierarchy and Protestant missionaries was initially conflictive, tense, and occasionally violent. On the one side, the Puerto Rican Catholic Church was formed and nurtured by the religious ideological monopoly, which Spain had enforced over its colonies during four centuries, while the Protestant missionaries came imbued by the Manifest Destiny worldview of America as a beacon of law, order, and civilization. On the other side, for the missionaries, Protestantism was seen as the purest form of Christianity, while Spanish Catholicism was perceived as imposing, conservative, traditionalist, and exclusive.[5] Both groups used their publications to condemn the actions and motivations of each other. The arrival of Pentecostalism to Puerto Rico in 1916 only served to increase religious fragmentation and the simmering tensions already described. Contrary to what may have been expected, Pentecostals did not join Protestants in an anti-Catholic front, for their fundamentalism and puritan morality served to keep both Catholics and Protestants at bay.

Throughout the twentieth century, the distance between the Catholics, Protestants, and Pentecostals has closed somewhat, to the extent that a respectful cordiality is kept among the three, while each continues to work in isolation. Due to the "stronghold" mentality fostered by each group, it has been very difficult to promote genuine dialogue and mutual respect among these three branches of Christendom. As a result, the ecumenical movement in Puerto Rico has developed slowly, hesitantly, on a very small scale, and only during the second half of the twentieth century.

In terms of Puerto Rico's present political life, the three main political parties respond to variant conceptions on how Puerto Ricans should solve their colonial dilemma. The ruling political organization from 1992 to 2000 was the New Progressive Party (PNP), a pro-American group that favors federated statehood for the island. It has shared power since 1968 with the Popular Democratic Party (PPD), an organization that wants to maintain its current territorial relation with the United States but seeks to enhance its present constitutional powers vis-à-vis the American Empire. The third political formula is represented by the Puerto Rican Independence Party (PIP), a progressive, social-democratic party that wants separation from the United States, along with a number of smaller, usually more radical, groups.

Finally, in terms of the military presence in the island, the United States controls the Caribbean through its military bases in Puerto Rico. Teddy Roosevelt's "splendid little war" of 1898 had as its purpose the conquest of the United States' future Caribbean *mare nostrum* to protect the Panama Canal and its hemispheric interests in Latin America. Today, Puerto Rico still responds to the geopolitical interests of the United States of America and its Armed Forces. Puerto Rico is surrounded by military bases, two of which are Roosevelt

Roads Naval Base in Ceiba and Camp García on the small island of Vieques, four miles across from the Puerto Rican mainland.

Struggle for Vieques

The island of Vieques measures twenty miles long by three miles wide. With a population of 10,000 inhabitants, during World War II, 26,000 of its 33,000 acres were expropriated by the U.S. government, which has tried to buy the rest of the island ever since. So desperate has the Navy been to take over the Vieques, that during the Kennedy administration a plan was proposed to move both the Viequenses and their cemeteries to St. Croix.[6]

At present, the Viequenses live in a narrow corridor right in the middle of the island. For neighbors they have 120 magazine and bomb depots in the western part of Vieques, comprising some 8,000 acres, and a live bombing range in the eastern part, which is used year-round by North American, Latin American, and NATO naval forces.[7] The range comprises some 18,000 acres and has been used in the past as a launching pad for military interventions in Cuba, the Dominican Republic, Panama, Granada, and Haiti.[8] Here, military weapons are tested in sea-to-land and air-to-land bombing runs. Both napalm- and uranium-tipped ammunitions were originally tested in Puerto Rico (and both actions initially denied by the Pentagon) before being used in Vietnam and Iraq.[9] The area is also used for multinational military exercises. In addition, the facilities were rented out to various nations through the Internet until the present crisis forced the U.S. military to withdraw their ads.[10] Since the United States is not a signatory country of the Tlatelolco Treaty, which calls on Latin American countries to avoid the presence, use, and proliferation of nuclear weapons, Puerto Ricans have always feared the presence of nuclear weapons at both Roosevelt Roads and Vieques. In fact, a nuclear accident did occur in these waters in 1966. This is confirmed by documents recently released under the Freedom of Information (FOI) Act.[11]

The recent struggle to free Vieques from the U.S. military presence started on April 19, 1999, with the death of David Sanes, a Puerto Rican civilian employee at the U.S. Naval base. His job was to direct the bombing runs from his observation post near the bombing range. He was killed after a jet accidentally dropped two 500-pound bombs near the observation post he was manning.[12] The governor of Puerto Rico, Honorable Pedro Rosselló, immediately asked the Navy and the president of the United States to stop all bombing practices on the island.[13] He also formed a commission to study the controversy and recommend a course of action.[14] The Comisión de Vieques issued its first report in June of 1999. It contained four recommendations: (1) the immediate end of all bombing, (2) the cleaning of all contaminated lands, (3) the total withdrawal of the Navy from Vieques, and (4) the return of all expropriated lands to the islanders.[15]

Although the governor initially accepted these recommendations and strongly lobbied in the U.S. Congress for a satisfactory solution to the crisis, he eventually acquiesced to the Clinton White House's pressure to back off.[16] While this was happening, Puerto Rican civil society mobilized and organized to prevent a renewal of the bombing.[17] Various groups initiated a civil disobedience campaign, which eventually evolved on three different fronts. On the first front, students, politicians, teachers, union organizers, and religious activists organized fourteen disobedience camps that were created to stop the bombing.[18] They met with success and were able to stop bombing raids for thirteen months. The second front was the Coordinadora Todo Puerto Rico con Vieques (CTPRV). This umbrella organization was a coalition of professional associations, cooperative groups, labor unions, university students, religious organizations, and leaders from the three major political parties. The third front, and the main theme of this paper, was the formation of an island-wide coalition of Christian Churches, which united the Baptist, Disciples of Christ, Episcopalian, Lutheran, Methodist, Presbyterian, Roman Catholic, and United Evangelical Churches.

Ecumenical Coalition of Churches for Vieques

The Ecumenical Coalition of Churches for Vieques (ECCV) was formed early in 2000 as a result of the failure of the Puerto Rican government to continue supporting and participating in the consensus formed in 1999.[19] After nine months of activities in favor of the Navy's exit, the governor capitulated on January 30, 2000, by accepting the presidential directives imposed by the Clinton White House.[20] The directives called for three more years of bombing practice with inert or dummy bombs, a maximum of ninety days of bombing per year, a $40 million grant to enhance the Vieques economic infrastructure, and a referendum to be celebrated in Vieques nine months before or after May 1, 2001.[21] This referendum would be administered by the Navy and would present only two options to the Viequenses. The first option was to leave the island after three more years of inert bombing, with the return of all expropriated land to the government of Puerto Rico. The second option was to maintain the continued presence of the military, a renewal of the use of live ammunition by the Navy, and a gift of $50 million in additional funds to the people of Vieques.

Most Puerto Ricans refused to accept the presidential directives for various reasons.[22] First, the monetary grants were interpreted by the Viequenses as a bribe. Second, the religious groups maintained that the civil rights and health concerns of the people should not be negotiable. In the words of Roman Catholic Bishop Alvaro Corrada del Río, "no bomb can be sufficiently inert to make it morally acceptable to the Puerto Rican people."[23] Finally, most questioned the objectivity and prudence of having the Navy run a referendum over a matter in which they were an interested party. After all, the Secretary of the Navy, Richard Danzig, had publicly acknowledged that they had hired a public relations firm to convince the Viequenses about the merits of the Navy's case and that they would do everything in their power to win the referendum.[24]

Meanwhile, the Puerto Rican consensus against the Navy was slowly disintegrating. The members of the two government commissions complained that their work and recommendations had been completely ignored by the governor.[25] The ruling party (PNP) left the consensus table, while the PPD straddled the fence for political reasons, leaving leftists alone with labor, students, and religious activists. The PNP administration immediately went on the offensive, attacking its critics by calling them separatists and radicals with a political anti-American agenda.[26]

While all of this was happening, the Christian Churches planned a mass rally to let Clinton know the island's feeling about Vieques. It is important to point out that the leaders of this church coalition were San Juan Archbishop Roberto González and Pentecostal leader Wilfredo Estrada, General Secretary of the Bible Society of Puerto Rico, both members of the two Vieques Commission. Late in 1999, Reverend Estrada was approached by one of his fellow commissioners with a suggestion to hold a mass demonstration to try to sway the president's decision in favor of Vieques. He also added that since Puerto Ricans had limited trust in their political parties, it was crucial that the march should be organized by the churches, which did enjoy their confidence. Reverend Estrada called a meeting of various pastors, and since the civil consensus was still active around this issue got a number of religious and political figures of all political parties to accept the idea of organizing a civic march on February 20, 2000.[27]

By January, the denominations organizing the civic march had decided to form the Ecumenical Coalition of Churches of Vieques.[28] As the day of the Marcha por la Paz de Vieques approached, the governor accepted the presidential directives on January 30, immediately pulled his party out of both the consensus table and the civic march, and asked the PNP militants not to go to what was now, in his eyes, an antigovernment and anti-American event.[29]

The Vieques march was a success. Both the national and international media estimated that approximately 150,000 persons marched in Puerto Rico's largest mass event ever.[30] For the governor, the success of the march was perceived as an insult to his aspirations of having the people accept the presidential directives and as a political attack on his administration.[31] Immediately, the PNP administration started attacking the motivations of the churches, which comprised the Ecumenical Coalition.[32] Meanwhile, the churches had organized two camps at the eastern bombing range in Vieques. These were the Evangelical Council camp (October 1999), manned by the laity and clergy of five Protestant denominations,[33] and the Roman Catholic camp (January 2000), manned by the laity and clergy of the Caguas diocese.[34] In addition, since the annexationist parties had abandoned the consensus by January 30, it is obvious that the sectors manning the disobedience camps would tend to be the political and social fringe: students, labor, environmentalists, peace advocates, and those who favor independence for Puerto Rico. Using this fact, the state accused the churches of being a front for radical and separatist groups pushing their own political aspirations.[35]

Eventually, the Ecumenical Coalition's call for a civil disobedience campaign would be answered by the government, who called on the faithful to practice religious disobedience against the church authorities.[36] The state's argument was that the churches had no political mandate to preach against social and civil matters, while they (the PNP) had won the election, and had a mandate of one million votes in their favor. Letters were even sent to the Vatican complaining about the "political activism" of San Juan Archbishop Roberto González and Caguas Bishop Alvaro Corrada del Río.[37]

It is under this atmosphere that the Ecumenical Coalition met Governor Pedro Rosselló face to face on April 19, 2000, the first anniversary of David Sanes's death. Since January, the Coalition had been trying unsuccessfully to meet with President Bill Clinton at the White House.[38] Since his answer was that he "did not want to say no to a group of bishops," the consolation prize was to meet White House aide Jeffrey Farrow, Governor Rosselló, and his Secretary of State at the governor's mansion, La Fortaleza.[39] The Coalition went to the meeting with the following points for discussion: to continue the "no more bombing" policy until the proposed referendum, to promote an early date for this consultation (August of 2000), and to include an additional option in favor of an immediate and permanent end to all bombing practices and the eventual withdrawal of all military personnel from Vieques. It became quite clear in that meeting that the White House was unwilling to change any of the presidential directives and the governor favored the U.S. government's position. It was also discovered that the governor had been playing the Pentecostal card against the Ecumenical Coalition, with what would eventually be negative results for the administration.[40]

The Pentecostals in Puerto Rico comprise the majority of all Protestants, with almost 1 million followers. Their largest denominations united some years ago to form the "Pentecostal Fraternity" (FRAPE). Due to their conservative nature, Puerto Rican Pentecostals tend to favor the status quo, very rarely enter the political arena, and prefer to keep away from public social issues and controversies. They proudly refer to themselves as "apolitical" and have never liked the social activism of the mainline Protestant denominations associated with the Evangelical Council of Puerto Rico and, more recently the Ecumenical Coalition. Finally, local Pentecostals tend to demonize Catholicism and have problems with ecumenism in general. It is under these assumptions that Governor Rosselló tried to play what he perceived were "his Pentecostals" against the Ecumenical Coalition's so-called radicals.

Unknown to the Coalition, the governor had arranged a meeting with the Pentecostal leaders right after his encounter with the Ecumenical Coalition, expecting a solid backing from them in front of the assembled press corps.[41] Unfortunately, the Pentecostals, led by Reverend Ángel Marcial, told the governor publicly that his assumptions had been wrong the whole time. The Pentecostals affirmed that they had personally (although not publicly) backed the goals and purpose of the February march, that most of their leaders had been present at the march, and that they favored the Ecumenical Coalition's positions of *ni un tiro más* and the withdrawal of the Navy from the island.[42] They did not commit themselves to join the Coalition because of their concerns with any civil disobedience campaign run by Catholics and because of their so-called political neutrality.

The night of the meeting with the governor, and to commemorate the anniversary of David Sanes's death, twenty of Puerto Rico's cultural, social, religious, and political leaders took over El Morro castle, a Spanish fortification which is also a U.S. National Park Service monument, for twelve hours in an act of civil disobedience.[43] The purpose of this action was to show the United States the unity of Puerto Ricans around the Vieques struggle.

Situation after the Evictions

By the end of 2000 the Vieques conflict seemed to be at a standstill. Events had run their expected course since the evictions of early May. On May 4, 2000, the federal authorities removed the protesters who had lived for thirteen months at the disobedience camps in Vieques. Pastors, priests, and nuns were arrested and transported to Roosevelt Roads Naval Base in full view of the nation, thanks to the heavy media coverage. That evening the Ecumenical Coalition led a candlelight vigil in the Old City, where major speeches were given by various religious leaders, among them Reverend Wilfredo Estrada, Methodist Bishop Juan Vera, and Roman Catholic Bishop Alvaro Corrada del Río. For the next few days most university centers erupted in protests, while the Federal Court and Fort Buchanan Army base in San Juan were surrounded by hundreds of marchers demonstrating against the arrests.[44]

Since January the U.S. Congress had also been active, slowly diluting the main elements of the presidential directives, as Republican legislators introduced change after change in various pieces of legislation. The western area of Vieques was not returned to the government of Puerto Rico by December 31, as stated in the directives. Nothing was said about the environmental cleanup of the area. Meanwhile, the $40 million economic development grant was being used by the Navy to buy votes for the newly announced November of 2001 referendum, as their public relations firm worked and maneuvered among the newly elected officials.[45]

The elections of November 7, 2000, completely changed the insular and national panorama, as the Popular Democratic Party defeated the Rosselló administration and the Republican Party defeated the aspirations of Vice-President Al Gore. Most local political observers believed that the issue of Vieques was vital in the local defeat. Others pointed out that it was the televised statement by PNP gubernatorial candidate, Dr. Carlos Pesquera, that "the issue of Vieques had been solved [by the presidential directives]," was a turning point in the campaign.[46] Victorious, Governor-elect Sila Calderón had expressed early in her campaign her commitment for a prompt solution to the Vieques problem once she was elected. Her strategy seemed to be based on legal challenges to the Navy's violations of health and environmental laws. After her inauguration, the Puerto Rican Independence Party, the Ecumenical Coalition, and the leaders of the struggle asked President Bill Clinton for a presidential decree before the end of his term ordering the Navy to leave Vieques.[47]

The Republican victory in the United States was a blessing in disguise for the cause of Vieques. Paradoxically, purging Washington of Jeffrey Farrow of the Clinton administration, and his advisors, permitted the opening of new venues of dialogue and negotiations with the Republican administration. Soon after the presidential election, the Navy restarted bombing Vieques with inert bombs, while hundreds of protesters entered the bombing range during their maneuvers. A few practices were prevented, others were delayed, and plans were made to paralyze future maneuvers. Over a thousand persons had entered the range in approximately forty different operations, through both land and sea, in preparation for the next naval maneuvers planned for January and May of 2001.[48]

The Ecumenical Coalition has been trying to find its way since May 4, 2000, in the new and uncharted waters of civil disobedience. The coalition was aware that most Puerto Ricans were waiting for its direction, but insisted on not having others dictate its policies and future actions, while maintaining a policy of patience and dialogue. An example of this is their low profile during the months before the 2000 presidential elections.

Quo vadis, Vieques?

On May 1, 2003, after sixty years of military control, land expropriations, and bombing practices, the Republican administration of George W. Bush ordered the U.S. Navy to cease operations on the island of Vieques. This event was the culmination of four years of political pressure on two administrations in both Puerto Rico and the United States, which were forced to push the issue of Vieques forward as a decades-long civil and human rights problem for the world's most influential democracy. During most of this time, thousands of persons—including bishops, priests, nuns, and ministers of various denominations—participated as "human shields" to block the Navy from carrying out military maneuvers, first through civil disobedience camps and later by the authorized entrance of small groups of activists into the bombing ranges to disrupt the bombing practices. Eventually over 1,600 Puerto Ricans, and over 300 North Americans and Puerto Ricans in the United States, would be arrested and tried in Federal Court under trespassing charges. Some of the personalities arrested were U.S. Representative Luís Gutiérrez (D-Ill.), Rev. Al Sharpton, Robert Kennedy Jr., actor Edward James Olmos, ex-boxing champion José "Chegui" Torres, Jacqueline Jackson (wife of Rev. Jesse Jackson), Adolfo Carrión Jr. (D-N.Y.), and many others.

Throughout the four years of this process, the Navy consistently denied the impact of the disobedience campaign, but in recent exit documents the Navy leaves little doubt about the effectiveness of the protest movement and the civil disobedience actions designed to upset military activity in Vieques. A memorandum sent by the Chief of Naval Operations to the Secretary of the Navy on January 10, 2003, states that

> [the] physical security at Vieques is becoming ever more difficult and costly to maintain, given the civil unrest which accompanies the Navy's presence on the extremely aggressive and costly multi-agency security actions. The level of protests, attempted incursions, and isolated successful incursions generally remain high when Battle Group training occurs on the island.[49]

It is interesting to mention the strong activism shown by the Puerto Rican Diaspora in the United States, especially in New York. The three ethnic Puerto Ricans in the House of Representatives—Rep. Nydia Velázquez (D-N.Y.), Rep. José Serrano (D-N.Y.), and Rep. Luís Gutiérrez (D-Ill.)—lobbied long and hard through the Hispanic Caucus of the U. S. Congress against the Navy's interests to sweep this matter under the political rug, and kept the issue of Vieques at the forefront of Washington politics.

Various other factors contributed to the Navy's withdrawal. The American and international press gave wide publicity to the perceived violations of the human and civil rights of the Viequenses. The State Department and the White House received constant diplomatic pressure from various nations and world organizations to leave the island. Another important factor was the constant support of the Puerto Ricans who time and time again expressed their desire for the Navy's withdrawal, as shown in the various polls taken by the Catholic Church in Vieques and by private concerns in Puerto Rico. This support leveled at around 70 percent of the population in Puerto Rico and around 89 percent of the population in Vieques.[50] Finally, for most observers, the church's presence through the activities of the Ecumenical Coalition was vital in keeping all groups working and moving in the same direction. Even as the people of Vieques celebrated the end of the Navy training, various civil and religious groups had been preparing for the next phases of the struggle for environmental cleanup, return of the lands to the people of Vieques, and a sustainable, community-controlled development.[51]

On May 1, 2003, administrative jurisdiction of 18,000 acres of the Navy's Camp Garcia on the eastern end of Vieques was transferred to the Fish and Wildlife Service of the Department of the Interior, to be classified as Wilderness Refuge Areas. The Department will administer these lands during the process of decontamination, which is expected to take a number of years, if similar cases in Panama and the Philippines are any example. For the local community groups, however, the only legitimate administrator of these lands should be the people of Vieques. This has been reiterated many times to various federal and Puerto Rico government agency representatives. The Viequenses have underlined their commitment to use civil disobedience again, if necessary, to push for environmental cleanup and the transfer of lands to the Puerto Rican government. However, the majority of Navy-held lands are not contaminated and could be designated for public use almost immediately. The Puerto Ricans will continue to struggle for the return of lands that belong, by natural right, to the present and future generations of Viequenses.[52]

In this historical process, the role of the Ecumenical Coalition was highly visible and important as a catalyst for the mobilization of thousands of persons who would have never demonstrated or participated in a civil disobedience campaign of this magnitude. The struggle of Vieques has empowered the church to create new possibilities for social outreach, which breaks with previous stereotypes about faith-based activism (or the lack of) in Puerto Rico. Until recent times, many conservative Christians believed in a dualist, cold war worldview that promoted a submissive, apolitical, socially passive and ideologically "tame" Christianity, which frustrated its followers' aspirations for an active church preaching a revitalized vision of an empowered Kingdom of God. Vieques awakened denominations, leaders, and lay people to consider new possibilities for communal change and to develop new strategies for the type of social change envisioned in the gospel's message.

It is my view that the Ecumenical Coalition is in a very important stage, due to the expectations that many people have about the future of this organization and its potential to deal with other important issues of our nation's future, such as the final status of Puerto Rico. For the last two decades, the three main political parties have agreed that Puerto Rico is a colony of the United States and have annually gone to sessions of the United Nations Decolonization Committee to press for actual changes in this relation. The U.S. government has blocked all attempts to discuss this issue in the U.N. General Assembly. In Puerto Rico, the issue of the island's final status has been the object of intense discussions since 1898, and many feel that this matter is too important to leave in the hands of the political parties. The people of Puerto Rico have seen their trust in politicians eroded badly during the last few administrations due to corruption, hidden agendas, and a lack of new ideas for the achievement of the final status of the island, while the Christian denominations enjoy a very high degree of trust among the general population. It may well happen, after the victory of civil society in Vieques, that the Puerto Rican people may place such an important issue in the hands of the Ecumenical Council or a similar group. Maybe it is unfair to put so much pressure on the back of what is essentially a small group of denominational leaders, acting many times without the full support of their denominations. But still, the Ecumenical Coalition is the only forum where Protestant and Catholic leaders exchange views and ideas, work for the common good, and envision a new Puerto Rico.

If there is a surprise in the whole Vieques process, it may well be the actual withdrawal of the Navy after all. There were quite a few moments when it appeared that the struggle would lose its momentum, when there were problems getting volunteers to enter the bases as *desobedientes* due to the excessive jail sentences given by the Federal Court, and even when the religious' theological rhetoric ran ahead of what some of the leaders were willing to do in terms of disobedience. For the first time in recent Puerto Rican history, the

Cold War rhetoric of the conservative, annexationist sectors did not sway the decisions of the religious leaders, as they stood united and firm against the public relations machinery of the Navy, the political pressures of the pro-Navy minority in both Vieques and Puerto Rico, and the subtle pressures of church members who preferred a nonconfrontational, passive, and anemic gospel.

What legacy has the Vieques struggle had on faith-based political and civic activism in Puerto Rico? As a result of the Vieques struggle, faith-based groups have mobilized to push, with the use of new strategies, their particular social agendas. Denominations are awakening to their social responsibility, as well as to their power to change society. The interesting point is that their issues may fall on either side of the liberal-conservative spectrum.

One example of this has been the formation of a coalition of conservative Catholic, Protestant, and Pentecostal groups who joined to stop the government's attempt to eliminate from the newly proposed penal code Section 103 of the previous code which condemned sodomy.[53] For a long time these groups paralyzed the Puerto Rican legislature's approval of the new penal code by threatening legislators who voted for elimination of Section 103 with an electoral boycott during the next elections. At the last moment, the U.S. Supreme Court came to their rescue with a ruling banning all sodomy laws from the nation and its territories. Before Vieques these groups would have never used pressure to achieve their goals.

Another attempt to change society was that of a group politically "neutral," pro-American Evangelicals who accused the Ecumenical Coalition of being anti-American and of using radical and political tactics to achieve their victory in Vieques, against what they consider was their correct reading of the gospel. To attack these so-called liberals, the Evangelicals fell into a contradiction, for they decided to create a political party, precisely what they were accusing the liberals of doing all along. In addition, since local Christians are supposed to maintain the facade of neutrality, the only way they could subtly indicate their pro-American inclination, without being too open in terms of the status discussions already mentioned, was through their group's name, for the initials of Evangélicos Unidos en Acción, EUA, are also those of the United States of America, the Estados Unidos de América, in Spanish.[54]

Finally, Vieques has served to awaken the social aspirations of many individual Christians, who would have depended in the past for their denominational bodies to respond, in a very passive way, to issues of society. There seems to be more liberty now for individual Christians to support, or oppose, social and political issues in the press and other forums and to come out publicly for these issues.

The liberation of Vieques may be a sui generis case in terms of church–state relations when the nation concerned is the United States. Groups in Okinawa, Japan, and Lancelin, Australia, are presently studying the Vieques process in terms of their own problems with nearby U.S military bases, but it is difficult to ascertain to what extent the strategies and methods used in Vieques can be repeated. It would seem that the victory of the Viequenses over the world's greatest military power and nation may have depended more on the vast coalition of groups, and on the unity and sacrifice of thousands of people, than on any particular strategy or method. God knows how many things were tried, with varied success.

In July 2003, a new round of legal battles started in the U.S. Federal Court in San Juan with the arrest of a dozen activists who participated on May 1, 2003, in the destruction of the concrete entrance to Camp García, a symbol of the sixty years of military control over two-thirds of Vieques territory.[55] The same actions that enthralled the American public in 1989, as the Germans destroyed their Iron Curtain and, more recently, toppled dozens of statues of Saddam Hussein in Iraq, are considered seditious and an act of treason under the Homeland Security Act and are used as an excuse to once again imprison the Viequenses.

As of this writing, the activists who led the civil disobedience campaign have turned their attention to the decontamination and development of the former military base. They have received little help from the U.S. Government. Both Democratic and Republican administrations are notorious for dragging their feet when the subject is the cleaning up of military-held lands, as Panama has so sadly taught Puerto Rico. Puerto Rican issues have always had a backseat to other more important domestic or foreign interests. President Bush's decision to close the Roosevelt Roads Naval Base near Ceiba, on the Puerto Rican mainland, has been interpreted by many as an act of revenge on the civil and local government because of their support for the Vieques campaign. The Southern Army Command was moved from Roosevelt to Florida, a move that both pacifists and political groups in Puerto Rico welcomed with great joy, but that has had a mixed impact on the local economy. The Ecumenical Coalition is in a serious effort to define its future goals. Although the first of its four goals (returning the military-held lands to Puerto Ricans) has been met, it is still struggling to realize the other three goals (demilitarizing the island, decontaminating the lands, and developing the island's economy). Unfortunately, most of the eastern lands around the former Vieques base have been handed over to the Department of the Interior. People fear that this may be a trick to take the land back in the future during a period of national crisis or emergency, since this land was taken away from one federal dependency and given to another "for protection." The Department of Interior has hired public relations personnel to pacify the local population and activists, a goal that has met with moderate success.

Vieques land prices have increased by 50% during the last 18 months. However, many viequenses are having a hard time buying land on their own island. People with cash show up on people's porches trying to buy land and many succeed. A few shady land deals have occurred, and the local government has been working on their own development plans, ignoring an environmentally friendly development plan created by a group of university professors and social scientists associated with the Ecumenical Coalition. Viequenses hope for some ecologically sound development, but there is no consensus on the matter. Today Vieques is experiencing a tourist boom and some additional hotels have been constructed. However, it is too early to measure employment and increases in the standard of living, but if the nearby island of Culebra is the pattern, unemployment will be reduced by half, and income could increase by as much as 20–30% during the next decade.

After all is said and done, the fact is that the people of Vieques and Puerto Rico—led by their religious leaders with the support of a wide coalition of students, labor unions, civic groups, professional associations, and political parties—were able to pressure the government of the United States into returning what was essentially the "crown jewel" of military bases in the Caribbean to its rightful owners, the Viequenses. A new day has begun for Vieques, free of bombing runs and practices, free of a military presence, and free to experience peace and justice for the first time after sixty years of an undeclared war against their people's well-being.

NOTES

1. This essay was originally written in December 2000. The last section ("Quo vadis, Vieques") updates the essay to July 2003.

2. Michael Mann, *The Sources of Social Power*, Vol. 1 (Cambridge: Cambridge University Press, 1986), 1.

3. Ibid, 23.

4. Ibid, 302.

5. Samuel Silva Gotay, *Protestantismo y política en Puerto Rico: 1898–1930* (San Juan: Editorial de la Universidad de Puerto Rico, 1997), 59–65.

6. The islanders immediately baptized it the "Dracula Plan." The plan was soon dropped by the Navy. This was the last of the various attempts by the U.S. Military to move the viequenses out of their island.

7. *El Mundo*, May 25, 1999, p. 3. *El Mundo* will hereafter be cited as *EM*.

8. "Vieques vital para la defensa nacional," *EM*, April 25, 1999.

9. "Marian reconoce haber usado balas de uranio," *EM*, May 28, 1999; *El Nuevo Día*, July 19, 1999, p. 4. *El Nuevo Día* will hereafter be cited as *END*.

10. *END*, May 3, 1999, p. 12.

11. "A negociar para limpiar el uranio," *Primera Hora* (daily newspaper), January 8, 2000; "EPA Agrees to Waste Clean-Up," *San Juan Star* (daily newspaper), January 11, 2000. *Primera Hora* and *San Juan Star* will hereafter be cited, respectively, as *PH* and *SJS*.

12. "Vieques Bomb Error Leaves 1 Dead, 4 Hurt," *SJS*, April 20, 1999.

13. "Condena total por tragedia Vieques: voces unánimes," *END*, April 21, 1999.

14. *END*, May 12, 1999, p. 8.

15. *END*, July 1, 1999, p. 4.

16. "Rosselló accede a la nueva política y rechaza ser un traidor," *END*, February 1, 2000.

17. "Obispo Álvaro Corrada se une a la desobediencia civil," *EM*, January 31, 2000.

18. "Toman ímpetu los campamentos en zona restringida," *EM*, November 7, 1999.

19. "Religiosos convocan marcha multitudinaria pro-Vieques," *EM*, February 23, 2000.

20. "Acuerdo final con Casa Blanca sobre Vieques," *END*, February 1, 2000.

21. At the end of 2000, the Navy informed the government of Puerto Rico that

the referendum would be celebrated on November 3, 2001. Events ran ahead of this poll, and it was never celebrated.

22. "Business As Usual in Vieques Civil Disobedience Camps," *SJS*, February 6, 2000.

23. "Obispo Álvaro Corrada se une a la desobediencia civil," *EM*, January 31, 2000.

24. "Secretario Richard Danzig sin garantias traspaso tierras," *END*, August 27, 2000.

25. *END*, December 16, 1999.

26. *END*, February 14, 2000, p. 5.

27. *END*, February 22, 2000.

28. "La marcha mas grande en nuestra historia," *Claridad*, February 25, 2000. *Claridad* will hereafter be cited as *CLA*. This is a political weekly.

29. *END*, February 20, 2000.

30. "Mar humano . . . por Vieques," *END*, February 27, 2000.

31. *END*, February 27, 2000.

32. " 'Guerrilla' sin armas de desobediencia en Vieques," *PH*, March 18, 2000.

33. *SJS*, September 25, 1999, p. 7.

34. *EM*, January 31, 2000.

35. *END*, February 14, 2000, p. 5.

36. *El Vocero*, April 14, 2000. *El Vocero* will hereafter be cited *VOC*.

37. Late in 2000, the Vatican announced that Caguas bishop Álvaro Corrada del Río was being named Bishop of Tyler, Texas, effective January 6, 2001. Most political observers saw this "promotion" as the result of intense Puerto Rican and North American administrations' pressure on Rome to rid themselves of this fiery thorn. See *END*, December 10, 2000.

38. *VOC*, April 14, 2000.

39. "Decepcionados religiosos luego de reunion Jeff Farrow," *VOC*, April 19, 2000.

40. Ibid.

41. Ibid.

42. *END*, April 29, 1999, p. 163. The phrase means "Not even one more shot" and was first used by historian Ivonne Acosta.

43. "Grupos pro-Vieques se apoderan de El Morro," *SJS*, April 19, 2000. I participated in this action.

44. "Desalojos con guantes de seda," *SJS*, April 5, 2000.

45. "Navy tags $3.5 million for pre-vote campaign," *SJS*, September 8, 2001.

46. *VOC*, August 7, 2000, p. 2.

47. *VOC*, November 11, 2000, p. 8.

48. "Navy resume training amid renewed protests," *SJS*, August 3, 2001.

49. *END*, February 2, 2003, p. 8.

50. *END*, November 8, 2002, p. 6.

51. *END*, May 18, 2003, p. 6.

52. "Vieques Awakens," *New York Post*, June 10, 2003, p. 8.

53. *END*, June 20, 2003, p. 10.

54. *SJS*, June 1, 2002, p. 18.

55. "Continuan los arrestos en Vieques," *END*, June 28, 2003, p. 2.

17

Latino Clergy and Churches in Faith-Based Political and Social Action in the United States

Gastón Espinosa

Conventional wisdom holds that except on rare occasions, Latino religious leaders, churches, and religious organizations have not been proactive in political and social action[1] and in some cases have tacitly approved of the oppressive conditions under which Latinos have had to live and work.[2] However, this essay and this book challenge that wisdom. There has been a de facto tradition of Latino political and social action over the past 150 years, especially in the Southwestern United States. Juan Gómez Quiñones, F. Arturo Rosales, Carlos Muñoz Jr., and Mary S. Pardo briefly note the important role that faith-based political and social beliefs had in fighting for social justice during the 1960s and 1970s.[3]

In the early 1990s, Sidney Verba, Kay Lehman Schlozman, and Henry E. Brady argued in *Voice and Equality: Civic Voluntarism in American Politics* that Latino churches and faith-based organizations provided critical leadership and capacity-building skills that could later be transferred into the political and social arena. Despite this fact, Latinos lagged behind Anglo-Americans and blacks on almost every measure of political mobilization and participation.[4] The notable exceptions were in campaign work and board membership (i.e., nonmonetary forms of participation), where Latino citizens matched Anglo-American participation and, in one case, they even surpassed their black counterparts (Table 17.1).[5]

However, when broken down by religious affiliation, they found that Latino Protestants were more likely to engage in political activities than Latino Catholics were. In fact, Latino Protestants were just

TABLE 17.1. Political Activities by Race (% active), 1995

Political event	Whites	Blacks	Latinos
Voting	73	65	41
Campaign work	8	12	7
Campaign contributions	25	22	11
Contacting public officials	37	24	14
Protesting	5	9	4
Board membership	4	2	4
Political organization affiliation	52	38	24

Source: Verba et al., *Voice and Equality.*

as likely to be politically active as their white and black counterparts. Verba et al. hypothesize that this is because Latino Protestants devote twice as much time to religious and to nonreligious activities (both inside and outside of the church) as Catholics. For this reason, they contend that Latino Protestants are more likely than Catholics to engage in skill-endowing activities that can be later transferred into the political arena.[6] They also found that churches and religious organizations (often unwittingly) provided critical capacity and leadership skills and opportunities (e.g., leading a Bible study or catechism class or leading a board, fund-raising, youth, or women's committee meeting) that can also be transferred into the political arena.[7] Perhaps the best example of this kind of church-based leadership and capacity building is found in the black community. Frederick Harris and R. Drew Smith found that churches have often served as key sites for political and social mobilization and for developing leadership and capacity building skills that are directly transferable into the "secular" political and civic arena.[8] This kind of important research has continued into the mid-to-late 1990s. Rodolfo de la Garza, Louis DeSipio, Jongho Lee, Chris García, and Peggy Levitt have all briefly referred to the role that clergy and churches play in political and social action.[9]

Despite the growing revisionist historiography, scholars know very little about faith-based political and social action among the national Latino population and among political, civic, and religious leaders today. This is no longer true. My analyses of the Hispanic Churches in American Public Life (HCAPL) national survey data indicate that Latino clergy, churches, and religious organizations are much more actively engaged in political and social action than hitherto realized. In fact, Latinos in general and civic leaders in particular believe not only that clergy and churches are active in addressing educational, social, and political issues but also that they should become *more* involved. I also found that there is a positive correlation between immigrant status, income, education, and religious activity and the degree of political and social engagement.[10]

I further confirmed the finding by Verba et al. that Latino Protestants are more proactive than Catholics in most forms of political and social action. This

President George W. Bush meets with Latino clergy and religious leaders to discuss his faith-based initiatives program at the White House on May 22, 2001. Latino Protestant and Catholic clergy and lay leaders include Pedro Windsor, Lisa Treviño-Cummins, Jesse Miranda, Armando Contreras, Luís Cortés, Daniel De León, Jim Ortíz, Raymond Rivera, and Rudy Carrasco (White House Photo by Eric Draper)

study breaks new ground by further comparing Catholics to Protestants, then Catholics, in turn, to Pentecostals, non-Pentecostal Evangelicals, Mainline Protestants, and Alternative Christians (e.g., Jehovah's Witness, Mormon and Christian Science).[11] I also examine the role of religious leaders and churches in educational, political, and social issues. This is followed by a brief discussion of what Latino Catholic and Protestant churches are doing to address social issues in local congregations and parishes and the growing interest in presidential politics.

The findings in this chapter are based on the Hispanic Churches in American Public Life (HCAPL) national surveys and community profile interviews and recent scholarship on Latino Catholic and Protestant faith-based political and social action. The HCAPL project was a three-year (1999–2003) nonsectarian study funded by a $1.3 million grant from The Pew Charitable Trusts. It is the largest study in U.S. history on Latino religions and politics and was directed by Virgilio Elizondo of the University of Notre Dame and Jesse Miranda of Vanguard University and managed by Gastón Espinosa of Claremont McKenna College. We commissioned and collaborated with Harry Pachon, Rodolfo de la Garza, and Jongho Lee of the Tomás Rivera Policy Institute (TRPI) to conduct three national surveys and produce eight community profiles. The findings in this chapter draw on research from all five phases of the HCAPL project: (1) a national random sample telephone survey of 2,060 Latinos; (2) a mail-out survey of 434 Latino civic (229) and religious leaders (205); (3) community profiles of 266 religious clergy and laity in forty-five congregations representing twenty-five denominations and religious traditions in eight cities and urban locations in Los Angeles, San Antonio, rural southern Colorado, Chicago, rural Iowa, Miami, New York City, and San Juan, Puerto Rico; (4) seventeen commissioned scholarly studies on the history of Latino religions and faith-based political, civic, and social action; and (5) three years of primary and secondary research on the topic.[12]

Latino Churches and Political Action

The data from the HCAPL national survey (N = 2,060) confirms the finding by Verba et al. that Latinos nationwide are not as active as whites and blacks on most measures of political action. It found that 26 percent of Latinos nationwide said that their churches or religious organizations gave people a ride to the polls on Election Day; 24 percent said that they advocated on behalf of a specific ballot issue, proposition, or referendum; 20 percent handed out campaign materials; 18 percent organized or participated in protests or rallies; and 16 percent asked people to support a certain political candidate. The only exception was voter registration, in which 39 percent of all Latinos said their churches and religious organizations were actively involved. When I analyzed only US-born nonimmigrant Latinos, the voter registration rate rose to 47 percent and the other six measures increased by one to four percentage points. Given high immigration rates and low levels of literacy and education, Latinos were more active than I originally hypothesized.

When I analyzed the findings by Protestant and Catholic religious affiliation, Latino Protestants were more likely than Catholics to indicate that their churches and religious organizations engaged in political action such as voter registration (39% vs. 37%), giving people a ride to the polls (31% vs. 24%), handing out campaign materials (23% vs. 19%), asking people to support certain political candidates (20% vs. 14%), and organizing and participating in protests or rallies (19% vs. 18%). In contrast, Catholics were only slightly more likely (24%) than their Protestant counterparts (23%) to indicate that their churches asked them to advocate on behalf of a specific ballot issue, proposition, or referendum (Table 17.2).

An analysis of church-sponsored political action by religious family groupings confirmed several widely held stereotypes and discovered several trends (Table 17.3). First, and consistent with previously held stereotypes, Latino Mainline Protestants were likely or more likely than their Catholic, Evangelical, Pentecostal, or Alternative Christian counterparts to indicate that their churches engaged in political action. Second, and counter to sectarian and apolitical stereotypes, Alternative Christian traditions were the second most likely self-described Christian religious family group to indicate that their

TABLE 17.2. Political Mobilization (%) by Catholic and Protestant Affiliation in the HCAPL National Survey, October 2000

During the last five years, which of the following activities has your church or religious organization been involved with?

Answer	Latino Catholic	Latino Protestant
Helped in voter registration	37	39
Given people a ride to the polls on Election Day	24	31
Handed out campaign materials	19	23
Advocated on behalf of a specific ballot issue, proposition, or referendum	24	23
Asked people to support certain political candidates	14	20
Organized or participated in protests or rallies	18	19

churches and religious organizations helped in four out of six measures of political action. Third, and counter to Catholic social teaching, liberation theology, and farmworker union-support stereotypes, Catholics scored their churches as low or lower than the other four religious family groups on three out of six measures of political mobilization. Fourth, and counter to various sectarian, anomie, and apolitical stereotypes, Latino Pentecostals scored their churches as high or higher than did their Catholic counterparts on all six measures of political mobilization.[13] In fact, Pentecostals were the only religious grouping that reported as high or higher scores on all six measures of political action than their Catholic counterparts.

TABLE 17.3. Latino Political Mobilization (%) by Religious Family Grouping in the HCAPL National Survey, October 2000

During the last five years, which of the following activities has your church or religious organization been involved with?

Answer	Catholic	Mainline Protestant	Evangelical* Protestant	Pentecostal Protestant	Alternative Christian
Helped in voter registration	37	50	32	41	44
Given people a ride to the polls on Election Day	24	36	28	31	31
Handed out campaign materials	19	32	20	23	25
Advocated on behalf of a specific ballot issue, proposition, or referendum	24	21	24	24	19
Asked people to support certain political candidates	14	25	21	15	25
Organized or participated in protests or rallies	18	18	21	18	13

*Non-Pentecostal or Charismatic Evangelical Protestants include all Southern Baptists, Adventists, Christian Reformed, and similar groups.

Factors Shaping Latino Political Action

Why are Hispanic Catholics generally less likely than Protestants to say that their churches and religious organizations are engaged in political action? There are at least four factors that help explain why: (1) immigration, (2) income, (3) education, and (4) religious participation. First is the fact that U.S. Latino Catholics are more likely to be immigrant (54%) than their Protestant counterparts (33%). The HCAPL national survey found that immigrants are significantly less likely than their nonimmigrant counterparts to become involved in political or social action. When two index variables containing six measures of political action and seven measures of social action from the HCAPL national survey were analyzed by immigration status, there was a strong negative relationship between political (−0.141) and social (−0.132) action.[14] This may indicate that Latino immigrants are less likely than their nonimmigrant counterparts to attend churches that engage in political and social action.

There are a number of reasons why one's immigrant status may negatively affect a church's decision to become politically and socially active:

a. Immigrants are less likely to have had courses on U.S. civics and politics and thus less likely than nonimmigrants to know how to engage in political and, to a lesser extent, social activities.
b. Almost one-third (32%) of all Latino Catholics are non-citizens and therefore cannot vote in elections.
c. A large number of immigrants may be reluctant to engage in political and social dissent because they come from countries where these kinds of activities were repressed. One Evangelical Baptist woman from war-torn El Salvador said in an HCAPL community profile interview, "I can't say that I've gotten involved in political issues. In social issues, yes. In my country there were so many things going on. There, politics is violence. When you come to this country you are afraid to get involved in political issues because you are not used to it. When I came here I saw a protest in front of my house, a protest by teachers, and I got scared, because in my country there would be police and even deaths."
d. Immigrants (especially those from Central America, the Caribbean, and South America) who arrived after 1980 are less likely to be aware of and draw on the de facto tradition of Latino and especially Mexican American faith-based political and civic activism of the 1960s and 1970s.[15]
e. Immigrants may have genuine philosophical objections (especially given their experiences in their home countries) to mixing religion and politics. David Vargas, for example, is a Catholic parishioner from Los Angeles who said in his community profile interview, "No, [I don't support congregations getting involved in politics]. There should be a political organization for the laity. But clergy shouldn't

intervene directly in politics because it's not their role. It's not [their] role to be political. [They] should be involved in such a way that it promotes and encourages the laity to become interested in politics, to fight for their rights, [so] that their petitions are respected. . . . In all these things clergy should make people aware." María González, a member of a Latino Mormon Church in Chicago, said that she agreed with the separation of church and state because "in my country there was a time when they were not separated, and it was bad because there was not religious freedom, there was only one religion [Roman Catholic]. If they are separated, then we all have religious freedom, we can believe in and pray to whomever we want." Carlos Segundo, a Pentecostal leader from Argentina now living in Miami concurred when he said, "Separation of church and state? I agree with the separation. I come from a country where they are not separated, so I saw the other side of the coin. There, a Christian Evangelical is a second-class citizen. Until the 1960s, when an Evangelical died, there was no place to bury him. The cemeteries were Catholic."

f. Immigrant-serving churches may have less money to engage in political and social activities. Rev. Julia Hernández, an associate pastor of an American Baptist Church in New York City, said that churches do not do more "because they do not have big budgets to develop community programs."
g. Some immigrants may fear that their political and social activities may contribute to either their deportation or lack of visa renewal for them or a family member.

Second, there is a direct positive correlation between high income and political and social action. The HCAPL national survey found that Latinos who lived below the poverty line ($24,999) were much less likely to say that their churches engaged in political and social action than Latinos that had higher incomes and thus were middle class ($25,000–$64,999) or upper middle class ($65,000+). Although the difference between the two groups is not statistically significant for political action (1.39 lower class vs. 1.55 middle and upper middle class), the difference was statistically significant (2.46 vs. 2.79, or 95% level) for social action. Why Latinos living in poverty were less likely to attend churches that engaged in political and social action is uncertain, though one may hypothesize that Latino churches located in economically disadvantaged and underdeveloped neighborhoods do not have adequate staffing to prepare and lead Hispanics in political and social activities.

Hence, although often significantly larger than their Protestant counterparts in numerical size, raw income, material resources, and denominational support, Catholic churches may be handicapped precisely by their large size as one or two priests and a handful of lay leaders may have to minister to a thousand or more families. This is in contrast to the average Protestant church, which, although it may likewise have only one or two clergy, may also have only 130 parishioners. Disparity in ratio of clergy (and lay leaders) to parishioners may be further exacerbated by other potential obstacles like lack of Latino clergy, fluency in Spanish, and understanding of Latin American history, popular traditions, and culture.

This last point may speak to the Catholic situation since there is a shortage of both Spanish-speaking and Latino priests. For although there are over 47,000 priests in the United States, only 6 percent are Latinos and two-thirds of these were born outside of the country. This is in sharp contrast to Latino Protestant immigrant churches which are pastored almost exclusively by Latin American and second- or third-generation U.S. Latinos themselves. It would seem reasonable to hypothesize that Latin American and U.S. Latino clergy may be more likely to engage in political and social action than their Anglo-American Hispanic-serving counterparts because they have more personally invested in the outcome. While clearly a large number of dedicated Anglo-American priests and lay leaders have given up everything to serve their Latino Catholic parishioners, on average it may be that they simply are not as committed to political and social engagement or at the very least have made it less of a priority.

Third, there appears to be a positive relationship between the level of education and the likelihood that Latino churches and religious organizations engaged in political and social action. The HCAPL national survey found that Latino Protestants are more likely than Catholics to have graduated from high school (27% vs. 23%) or have some college (28% vs. 21%). Furthermore, Catholics (19%) are more likely than Protestants (13%) to say that they have only an elementary school level education. Thus perhaps some Latino Protestants are more likely to say that they attend churches that engage in political and social activities because they are more likely to have attended or graduated from high school or have attended some college, which has given them the confidence to engage in such activities. The lower levels of parishioner education may also hinder or retard an otherwise politically and socially active priest or lay leader from equipping larger numbers of lay people for activism.

Fourth and finally, there appears to be a positive relationship between participation in religious activities and political and social action. The HCAPL national survey found that Latinos who read their Bibles, lead a Bible study, and attend church are more likely to say that their churches engage in political or social action than are those who never read their Bibles, never lead a Bible study, and never attend church. For example, Latinos who read their Bible once a month or more are more likely to attend churches that engage in political or civic activism than are those who report that they never read their Bible. After indexing political and social action, those who read the Bible everyday were more likely to attend churches that engage in political action than those who read their Bible once a month or less, a few times a month, or a few times a week. Likewise, those who read their Bible everyday were also more likely to engage in social action than those who never read their Bible. Similarly, Latinos who attend church once a month or more are twice as likely to engage in political or social activism than are those who never attend or attend once a year or more. When a mean index for political and social action by church attendance was created, it revealed that those who attend church almost every week were more likely to say that their churches engaged in political action (1.60) than those who never attended church (1.29). Likewise, those who attended church almost every week were more likely to say that their churches engaged in social action (2.80) than those who never attended. However, those who attended once a week or more had lower scores (1.41 and 2.61) on both indexes. Thus, we cannot assume that higher levels of religious intensity are always correlated with higher levels of political or social action. Furthermore, when I created an index of political and social action that included leading a Bible study as such an action, I found that Latinos who had led a Bible study are more likely (1.51 vs. 1.39) to say that their churches engage in political action but are only slightly more likely to say that their churches engage in social action (2.57 vs. 2.56) than those who never had.

When analyzed by Protestant versus Catholic, Latino Protestants were significantly more likely to say that they read the Bible once a week or more (67%) than Catholics (25%). Similarly, Latino Protestants (69%) were significantly more likely to say that they attend church every week or more than once a week than Catholics (48%). Latino Protestants (42%) were also twice as likely to say that they had led a Bible study than Catholics (21%). However, these findings are biased in favor of Protestants, who are more likely to engage in these kinds of practices than Catholics, who might be just as spiritual and religiously active but in other ways, such as praying to saints, observing popular traditions, and participating in home altar devotions.

Nevertheless, there does appear to be a relationship between how much guidance religion provides in a person's life and the likelihood that their church is engaging in political and social action. Those individuals who said that religion provided some or a great deal of guidance in their day-to-day living were more likely to say that they attended churches that engaged in political (1.50) action than those who said that it provided no guidance at all (1.31). When Latino Catholics and Protestants are analyzed by the level of guidance that religion provides by their church's level of political and social action, Latino Protestants (67%) were significantly more likely than Catholics (48%) to say that religion provides a great deal of guidance for their day-to-day living. Unlike the other three questions regarding religious participation, this particular question is not biased in favor of Protestants. All of these factors, but especially religious guidance and leading a Bible study (a leadership skill that could later be transferred to political and social arenas and a skill that is common among Catholic Charismatics—who make up 22% of all Latino Catholics), may help explain why Protestants were more likely to report that their churches engaged in political and social action.[16]

In short, socioeconomic factors like immigration, income, education, and religious participation are positively related to Latinos who attended churches that engage in political and social action. Although being Protestant is not significantly tied to all six measures of political activism equally, it is nonetheless correlated to political activism in general. In addition, being Protestant is significantly related to social action. In fact, Catholics have the lowest mean index of all five religious family groupings for both political and social action. However, this should not be pushed too far, as Latino Pentecostals (49.2%) and Alternative Christians (56%) have as high or slightly higher poverty rates than Catholics (49%) have. Latino Catholics are also more likely to have graduated from college (14%) or graduate school (4%) than either Pentecostals (10% and 2%) or Alternative Christians (9% and 0%). But Mainline Protestants (1.80 and 2.84 for political and social action, respectively) and Alternative Christians (1.55 and 2.83) have a higher mean of both political and social activism than do Catholics (1.34 and 2.45), Pentecostals (1.53 and 2.66), and Evangelicals (1.46 and 2.76). In conclusion, Latino Protestants are more likely than Latino Catholics to be engaged in social activities because Catholics are more likely to be immigrants, live in poverty, have lower levels of elementary education, and have lower levels of religious participation.

Latino Civic Leaders' Perception of Church Involvement in Political Mobilization

Latino civic and political leaders gave their Catholic and Protestant churches and religious organizations mixed reviews concerning their attempts at political mobilization. In fact, they gave them lower scores than did the general Latino population on four out of the six measures of political mobilization (Table 17.4). Further, although 40 percent of civic leaders surveyed said their churches or religious organizations advocated on behalf of a specific ballot issue, 38 percent helped in voter registration, and 25 percent said their churches or religious organizations organized or participated in protests or rallies, only 14 percent of civic leaders said their churches and religious organizations asked parishioners to support a certain political candidate, 11 percent handed out campaign materials, and 5 percent gave parishioners a ride to the polls on Election Day.

TABLE 17.4. Political Mobilization (%) by Latino General Population, Civic Leaders, Clergy, and Black Clergy in the HCAPL National Surveys (2000) and Leadership Surveys (2001)

During the last five years, which of the following activities has your church or religious organization been involved with?

Answer	Latino National	Latino Civic	Latino Clergy	Black Clergy
Helped in voter registration	39	38	60	84
Given people a ride to the polls on Election Day	26	5	11	64
Handed out campaign materials	20	11	19	31
Advocated on behalf of a specific ballot issue, proposition, or referendum	24	40	43	28
Asked people to support certain political candidates	16	14	14	
Organized or participated in protests or rallies	18	25	26	17
None of the above		38	20	

Latino religious leaders took a more positive view of their work than their civic counterparts. Like civic leaders, religious leaders tended to view their churches and religious organizations as more likely to help in voter registration, advocate on behalf of a specific ballot issues or proposition, or organize a protest or rally than to hand out campaign materials, ask people to support certain political candidates, or give people rides to the polls on Election Day. When comparing the findings to their black counterparts in R. Drew Smith's study on the public influences of African American churches, black clergy were found to be significantly more likely than Latino clergy to say that they and their churches participated in voter registration (84% vs. 60%), gave people a ride to the polls on Election Day (64% vs. 11%), and handed out campaign literature (31% vs. 19%). However, Latino clergy were more likely than black clergy to report that they advocated on behalf of a specific ballot issue, proposition, or referendum (43% vs. 28%) and that they organized or participated in protests or rallies (26% vs. 17%).[17]

Latino Churches and Social Action

Much of the confidence that the Latino population in general and civic leaders in particular afford clergy, churches, and religious organizations may be due to the fact that they are perceived as providing badly needed social services and programs free of charge to the Latino community, thus taking pressure off local city and state governments. This seems to defy the stereotype in many university Latino studies programs that clergy, churches, and religious organizations are doing little to alleviate the suffering of the poor and, instead, preach a kind of naïve "pie-in-the-sky after you die" message of political and social complacency. Despite this stereotype, a high percentage of the Latino population reported that their churches were starting day cares, food coops, or child-care centers (44%); reaching out to gangs in an effort to reduce community violence (39%); helping newly arrived immigrants establish themselves (35%); helping members of their community secure jobs, better wages, or better working conditions (34%); starting drug and alcohol rehabilitation programs (32%); and starting English or citizenship classes (31%). This is consistent with the anecdotal observations of colleagues in this volume.

As is true with Latino political mobilization, there were differences when Latino Catholics are compared to Protestants. Latino Protestant churches are more likely to provide social services than their Catholic counterparts in five out of seven measures of social action, such as reaching out to gangs (44% vs. 36%); helping community members secure jobs, better wages, or better working conditions (36% vs. 33%); helping immigrants establish themselves (39% vs. 35%); starting day-care centers, food coops, or child-care centers (48% vs. 43%); starting ESL and citizenship classes (33% vs. 30%); and starting after-school programs (43% vs. 35%). This may be due to the fact that Latino Catholics have lower rates of church attendance, thus fewer opportunities for exposure to such social service activities. A slightly higher percentage of Latino

Catholics (33%) reported that their churches and religious organizations had started a drug or alcohol rehabilitation home than their Latino Protestant counterparts (32%). Likewise, when I cross analyzed church-sponsored social activities by religious family groupings in five out of seven measures (Table 17.5), Latino Catholics consistently gave their churches lower marks than did their Mainline Protestant, Evangelical, Pentecostal, or Alternative Christian counterparts on such issues as reaching out to gangs in an effort to reduce community violence, helping members secure jobs, starting ESL or citizenship classes, and starting day-care centers, food coops, and after-school youth programs for teenagers. Furthermore, Alternative Christian traditions reported a higher rate of social action on three out of seven measures than their Mainline Protestant, Pentecostal, Evangelical, and Catholic counterparts. Mainline Protestants ranked highest on three out of six measures and either ranked second or tied for second highest on six out of seven measures of social action.[18] Evangelicals and Pentecostals ranked highest or tied for highest on two (helping newly arrived immigrants and starting youth programs) and one (starting youth programs) measure, respectively.

While statistical evidence is lacking, one of the reasons churches were not more active may be due to lack of money. Although only anecdotal, Rev. Julia Hernández's comment that churches do not do more "because they do not

TABLE 17.5. Latino Social Services (%) Provided by Religious Family Grouping in the HCAPL National Survey

During the last five years, which of the following activities has your church or religious organization been involved with?

Answer	Catholic	Mainline Protestant	Evangelical* Protestant	Pentecostal Protestant	Alternative Christian
Reached out to gangs in an effort to reduce community violence	36	46	44	43	52
Helped members of your community secure jobs, better wages, or better working conditions	33	37	36	34	40
Helped newly arrived immigrants establish themselves	35	42	38	37	30
Started drug or alcoholic rehab program	33	35	28	34	38
Started English or citizenship classes	30	38	34	30	31
Started day care centers, food coops, or child-care centers	43	52	50	45	49
Started after-school youth programs for teenagers	35	35	46	43	42

*Non-Pentecostal or Charismatic Evangelicals include Southern Baptists, Adventists, Christian Reformed, and similar traditions.

have big budgets to develop community programs" is important. Despite this fact, her church, like many others, still managed to offer some nonmonetary-driven social services to the community, like counseling for victims of domestic violence and ESL classes for immigrants. Still other churches, like one Latino Reform Church in America, stated that they sponsored food pantry programs, Kids with a Promise tutoring classes, Boys and Girls Scout troops, Alcoholics Anonymous groups, computer training classes for older people to enhance their professional skills, ESL classes, fund-raising for base community organizations, and social worker advocacy for youth and the elderly. Similarly, several Pentecostal churches reported offering social programs, contacting politicians, and contacting the police to let them know about the needs and problems facing their community. Juana García, vice president of her Pentecostal church's women's organization, said that, although she does not get too involved with politics, she does fight for educational and social issues. Likewise, Jorge Sena of Chicago said that his Pentecostal church gave away 1,000 pairs of children shoes, provided food for the poor, sponsored a food pantry, and created after-school programs for youth. Other denominations appear to be doing the same. Father José Valle from Chicago said that their primary social focus is aimed at gangs, youth, and immigrants; providing ESL classes; addressing economic issues; and fighting for the rights of labor. He found that reaching youth in gangs was challenging because "the ones that are not killed, wound up in jail."

It is interesting to note that this commitment to social justice goes beyond a group's denominational community. A number of Latinos from different Christian denominations said their congregations had been actively involved in providing relief (especially food and clothing) and support (e.g., collecting funds) for victims of the 9/11 terrorist attacks in New York City, the Vieques Struggle in Puerto Rico, Hurricane Mitch in Honduras, Hurricane Andrew in Florida, the terrible earthquake that devastated El Salvador, and Afghan refugees. One Seventh-day Adventist pastor from Miami said, "We have a department that is dedicated to meeting the needs of our community, people that have financial woes, or social issues. . . . We have a disaster relief department that takes clothes and food; for example, we were very involved when Hurricane Andrew hit. . . . The relief department works at an international level . . . [in] the floods and earthquakes in Central America . . . and right now our institution is helping in New York." Similarly, a Pentecostal leader from Miami stated regarding social programming, "The Church participates in all events, like 9/11—our members donated blood, and our children gave money to Afghanistan. We help Central American countries." Networking in order to maximize social capacity is a prominent theme in Latino faith-based activism.

In this respect, Latino Protestants and Catholics have a common de facto social justice commitment that is community-based and yet national and international in vision and scope. The fact that 35 percent of all Latinos were born outside of the United States or come from countries where poverty and right-wing dictators often functioned like terrorists may help contribute to this sense of collective identity with people in other parts of the world.

How do civic and religious leaders view the church's role in providing social services? Civic leaders tend to be less optimistic than religious leaders about the church's effort to engage in social action. When compared to their religious counterparts, civic leaders were less likely than clergy to report that their churches or religious organizations reached out to gangs in an effort to reduce community violence (civic leaders 33% vs. religious leaders 35%); help members of their community secure jobs, better wages, or better working conditions (32% vs. 55%); help newly arrived immigrants establish themselves (33% vs. 55%); start a drug or alcoholic rehabilitation program (16% vs. 23%); start English or citizenship classes (36% vs. 47%); and start day-care centers, food coops, or child-care centers (35% vs. 36%). There were, however, two social measures in which civic leaders gave religious leaders slightly higher marks than the latter gave themselves: starting after-school programs for teens (36% vs. 35%) and organizing disaster relief (39% vs. 37%; Table 17.6).

In addition to church-sponsored social work, many social services are being provided by a growing number of faith-based organizations (FBOs).[19] Richard Wood has pointed out that the vast majority of the 133 faith-based organizations and 3,300 participating congregations in the United States are associated with a religious tradition. All combined, these FBOs reach an estimated 1.5 million people in just their own congregations. Twenty percent of the 3,300 congregations (660) are Hispanic and 16 percent of the 550 professional faith-based organizers are Latinos, 50 percent of whom are women. Thus Latinos are represented in faith-based organizing at a slightly higher rate than

TABLE 17.6. Social Services (%) Provided by Latino Churches by National Population, Civic Leaders, and Clergy in the HCAPL National Survey

During the last five years, which of the following activities has your church or religious organization been involved with?

Answer	National	Civic	Clergy
Reached out to gangs in an effort to reduce community violence	39	33	35
Helped members of your community secure jobs, better wages, or better working conditions	34	32	55
Helped newly arrived immigrants establish themselves	35	33	55
Started drug or alcoholic rehab program	32	16	23
Started English or citizenship classes	31	36	47
Started day care centers, food coops, or child-care centers	44	35	36
Started after-school youth programs for teenagers	37	36	35
Served as a site for labor organizing		4	10
Helped your members get affordable housing		27	43
Organized international assistance		30	36
Organized disaster relief		39	37
None of the above		16	10

their percentage (13.7%) of the U.S. population in 2004. This may be due to the rich heritage of Catholic social teaching, liberation theology, and largely Mainline Protestant faith-based organizing and social justice activism during the Mexican American and black civil rights movements of the 1960s and 1970s. However, there are also a growing number of Pentecostal and Evangelical FBOs springing up across the United States.[20]

Latino Attitudes on Clergy Involvement in Educational, Political, and Social Issues

Although Latino churches and faith-based organizations are very active in voter registration but not in most other traditional forms of political mobilization and participation, they still enjoy the overwhelming support of Latino civic leaders. When asked about how important Latino churches and religious organizations are in shaping current national discussions, 88 percent of Latino civic leaders and 82 percent of religious leaders surveyed indicated "very important" or "somewhat important." Fully one-third (35%) of all Latino civic leaders surveyed said clergy input in national discussions was "very important." Civic leaders also gave religious leaders remarkably high marks for shaping community affairs (75%), as well as addressing educational, social, and political issues (73%). This overwhelmingly positive support may be based on the recognition of the critical role that Catholic and Protestant churches have in the daily lives (baptism, marriage, last rites, Eucharist, programs, etc.) of ordinary Latinos. Although difficult to determine, it may also be due to the influence of Catholic social teaching, liberation theology, popular Catholicism, Our Lady of Guadalupe, faith-based Catholic charities, faith-based organizations like Communities Organized for Public Service (COPS), United Neighborhood Organizations (UNO), El Paso Interreligious Sponsoring Organization (EPISO), Alianza de Ministerios Evangélicos Nacionales (AMEN), and the fundamental recognition that Latino culture and values are largely tied to Christian morality and a Judeo-Christian worldview. Because 93 percent of all U.S. Latinos self-identify as Christian and thus share this worldview, it may be risky for an elected political official to criticize conservative Catholic or Evangelical Protestant Christian organizations.[21]

Notwithstanding general support for clergy, churches, and religious organizations, civic leaders were less enthusiastic about the idea of Latino churches and religious organizations becoming more involved in educational, social, and political issues. Despite this fact, 62 percent of the general Latino population, 74 percent of civic leaders, and 82 percent of religious leaders surveyed indicated that religious leaders should become more involved. However, this general support for greater Latino church and clergy participation in political, social, and educational issues dropped off significantly when survey respondents were asked whether they believed that religious leaders should try to influence public affairs. Only 50 percent of Latinos nationwide and 61 percent of civic leaders believe that religious leaders should try to influence public affairs. This contrasts with 92 percent of religious leaders. Notwithstanding, more than half (54%) of all Latino civic leaders surveyed indicated that they had seen an increase in the frequency of contacts by Latino religious leaders or organizations.

Despite the different levels of support for Latino church and clergy involvement in educational, political, and social issues, Latinos actively involved in church generally believe that their churches are taking positive steps to address social issues. For example, the HCAPL national survey found that 65 percent of the general Latino population believes that religious leaders and churches are talking about the pressing social and political issues of the day. As the work of other authors in this volume indicates, Latino religious leaders' involvement in the struggles over the Sanctuary movement, Proposition 187 in California, Elián González in Miami, and Vieques in Puerto Rico clearly indicate the commitment of some clergy, churches, and religious organizations to faith-based social and political action. Latino civic leaders recognize this: 63 percent believe that clergy or church parishioners have an important role in shaping issues in their political jurisdiction. Furthermore, 78 percent indicate that churches and religious organizations were at least somewhat important in shaping community affairs. This may explain why 62 percent of the national Latino population and 71 percent of civic leaders surveyed wanted their churches or religious organizations to become more involved in educational, social, and political issues. A Chicago Pentecostal reflected, "I think that from a social perspective we need to be more involved [in politics]. Politically, I think every Christian organization should have a voice and vote in what is going on politically. If we don't speak up, then people will speak for us. If we don't vote, then they will vote for us. Then it will be our fault." Perhaps reflecting the influence of Catholic social teaching or liberation theology, María Sánchez said, "We are called through Jesus to do that because he was our main example of helping the poor and fighting any injustice that we saw in our society. And so through government, which is the dominant power in our country, we are called to be involved. This church is not separate from society; it's within society. We have to work with society and try to change it for the better."[22]

Regardless of the widespread support Latino churches, clergy, and religious organizations enjoy, religious leaders have yet to capitalize on the confidence. For example, only 22 percent of all Latinos said that their churches or religious organizations had asked them to engage in social activities. Furthermore, only 19 percent of political and civic leaders said religious leaders routinely contacted them regarding specific political, civic, or social issues. This is probably due to the widespread perception among religious leaders that political and civic leaders are uninterested in clergy and church participation in public life. This appears to be confirmed by the finding that only 33 percent of all Latino civic leaders sought clergy support and input for their political campaigns and civic programs. In fact, it may also be the case that some highly assimilated, middle-class, and secular-oriented second- and third-generation Latino political and civic leaders simply do not know how to reach out to local Spanish-speaking congregations. A contribution of this book could be that since Latino religious leaders, churches, and religious organizations are highly valued, they could confidently network better with politicians and social service providers.

Roman Catholic Social Services Provided by Churches and Dioceses

The high level of confidence that civic leaders have in Latino Catholic and Protestant clergy and churches appears to be well founded. This is evident in the recent study of Diocesan Hispanic/Latino Ministry directed by Bryan T. Froehle and Mary L. Gautier at the Center for Applied Research in the Apostolate (CARA) at Georgetown University.[23] They found that a significant percentage of dioceses provide direct services as part of their social ministry to the Latino community. When asked, "What is the most important resource that your [Diocesan Hispanic Ministry Office] provides to the Hispanic/Latino community?" one leader from the Grand Island diocese wrote, "Pastoral formation program, awareness on social justice, multicultural ministry, sense of belonging and ownership, migrant ministry program, collaboration among parishes." Still another from Youngstown, Ohio, said, "Bilingual resources, prison ministry, care of migrant workers."[24] The Hispanic Ministry Offices appear to be meeting important needs. Three-fourths of the 106 Catholic dioceses (out of 176 nationwide) that responded to the Froehle and Gautier survey indicated that their Hispanic ministry offices collaborated with local Latino service agencies, the diocesan Office of Religious Education, and Catholic Charities. They also found that seven in ten respondents from western states provide naturalization assistance (vs. 27% from the Northeast, 36% from the Midwest, and 42% from the South) and more than six in ten from the West provide legal advocacy, although only half from the Northeast and South do the same. Further, more than two-thirds of those working in parish churches serving more than 9,000 Hispanics said they provided legal advice. However, the report did not state what percentage of smaller Hispanic-serving ministry offices provided support, although it would probably be considerably less and this could, in part, help explain their lack of participation in the survey.[25]

Despite this possibility, a significant percentage of Catholic diocesan ministry offices reported that they provide free legal advice (47%), naturalization assistance (42%), financial assistance (39%), food or clothing (37%), and health services (20%) to the Latino community. At the parish level, they found that a number of churches offer financial assistance to immigrants (78%), legal advocacy (66%), food or clothing (65%), social gatherings and events (64%), and health services (59%). Diocesan churches, however, are not trying to provide these social services alone. Approximately 81 percent of diocesan Latino ministry offices collaborate with local Latino faith-based organizations and secular social service agencies. They also collaborate with Catholic Charities (77%), Immigrant/Migrant/Refugee Services (72%), and Health Care Ministries (31%).

The critical role that the Catholic Church plays in providing social services to Latinos through collaboration and networking was evident in the finding that the most important resources that the diocesan office provides for Latino ministries is "services and advocacy." More than half (53%) of all diocesan offices said that this was the single most important ministry their office provided the Latino community, followed by "collaboration" with outside social service agencies (47%) and "leadership formation" (33%). Because a significant percentage of Latino Catholics are immigrants, it is not surprising that "advocacy" on behalf of those not able to advocate for themselves is the single most important social service the church provides its parishioners. When asked what advice Hispanic ministry officers would give to a diocese seeking to expand their Hispanic programs, leaders from Oklahoma City said, "One must get to know the needs and cultural customs of each community [and visit] parishioners, hospitals, prisons, [and] jails." They also encouraged them to visit the poor and form their own local Pastoral Parish Plan.[26]

The findings in the Froehle and Gautier study challenge the widely held stereotype that the Catholic Church is not providing social services and programs for Latinos. In fact, the Catholic Church provides millions of dollars worth of social services to the Latino community free of charge. The growing number of Catholic Hispanic ministry offices has directly shaped these services and increased support.[27]

Latino Protestant Social Services Provided by Churches

Although the long and rich tradition of Latino Catholic social teaching and faith-based activism make the findings about Catholic social work somewhat predictable, scholars in this book, such as Paul Barton, Daniel Ramírez, Elizabeth Ríos, Jill DeTemple, and Lester McGrath-Andino note a similar level of social service action among Latino Protestants. Today there are 8 million Latino Protestants in the United States. Of this number, 88 percent (7 million) self-identify with an Evangelical denomination or as "born-again" Christian. There are now more Latino Protestants than Jews or Muslims or Episcopalians in the United States. Their large numbers raise important questions about the kinds and types of social services they provide the Latino community.[28]

Scholars like Amy Sherman at the Hudson Institute are addressing this gap in the literature.[29] In cooperation with the Alianza de Ministerios Evangélicos Nacionales (AMEN), Sherman surveyed 452 Latino Evangelical, Pentecostal, and Mainline Protestant pastors and congregational leaders across the United States. Although the average Latino congregation surveyed had only 130 regular adult attendees, she found that a surprisingly high 72 percent of these congregations offered social service programs. In fact, Latino Protestant congregations offered a total of forty-nine different social service programs and regularly worked with schools, nonprofits, police departments, and local city governments. She found that the average congregation provided six social services to the community. The twelve most common types of social services provided by churches she surveyed were pastoral counseling (55% of all churches), food assistance (51%), family counseling (44%), clothing assistance (40%), referrals to other helping agencies (34%), emergency financial assistance (28%), aid to immigrants (20%), ESL classes (19%), aid to prisoners and their families (16%), tutoring programs (15%), and substance abuse, rehabilitation, and counseling (12%). Over 55 percent of churches said that they partnered with other churches, social service nonprofits, schools, the police, courts/probation/parole officers, and local government. Furthermore, 38 percent indicated that they partnered with secular social service providers. This led Sherman to the conclusion that Latino congregations are "at least as likely, and perhaps slightly more likely" than non-Hispanic churches to cooperate with non-church-based organizations in providing social programs for the Latino community.

Despite the surprisingly high percentage of congregations that were providing social services to the Latino community, 28 percent of those surveyed were not providing any social programs. The most common reason why Latino churches were not sponsoring social service programs, and consistent with the findings and testimonies cited earlier, were lack of "know-how" (55%) and their small size and lack of money (46%). Interestingly enough, and somewhat counterintuitive given the fact that 88 percent of all Latino Protestants are Evangelical or "born-again," only 8 percent said they were philosophically opposed to offering social programs. In short, despite their conservative theology and moral positions on abortion and homosexuality, 92 percent of Latino Protestant religious leaders surveyed by Sherman indicated that they already sponsored or were open to sponsoring social service programs for the community.[30] This indicates that the antisocial gospel specter of Anglo Fundamentalism may be largely absent in Latino Evangelical and Pentecostal churches and religious organizations.

Perhaps most surprising, and echoing the findings pointed out earlier in this essay, was that Latino Protestant churches are also just as likely to engage in social service programming as their black counterparts, a community with a long and rich tradition of social activism. For example, when Sherman compared her findings to Andrew Billingsley's study of black churches in the United States, she found that 72 percent of Latino churches indicated that they had one or more community-serving programs, compared with 69 percent of black churches in the Northeast, 66 percent of black churches in the North Central region, 66 percent of black churches in the Midwest, and 75 percent of black churches in Denver. Furthermore, 323 Latino Protestant churches offered more than 1,943 programs, and 80 percent offered more than three programs.[31]

The important news is that the 28 percent of those churches surveyed that do not presently sponsor social service ministries said they planned to do so in the near future. However, when compared to Anglo-American congregations in the Hartford Seminary's Institute for Religion Research Faith Communities Today survey (FCT churches), Latino churches tended to fall short in providing food assistance (51% Latino vs. 85% FCT churches), clothing assistance (40% Latino vs. 60% FCT churches), emergency financial assistance (28% Latino vs.

88% FCT churches), aid to immigrants (20% Latino vs. 14% FCT churches), and substance abuse, rehabilitation, and counseling (12% Latino vs. 32% FCT churches).[32] However, as we have just seen, this may have more to do with lack of money, resources, and time, than with desire. Despite this fact, there are a growing number of Protestant faith-based organizations sprouting up across the United States that are providing proactive faith-based social service ministries.[33]

Latino Clergy and the Presidency

One of the results of the growing number of Latino churches and faith-based social programs in the United States is greater interest in politics and the American presidency. Although Latino clergy are becoming increasingly visible in presidential politics in Washington, D.C., this is not a new development. In fact, one of the first major connections between a Latino faith-based social leader and a national political leader took place when Democratic presidential candidate Robert Kennedy took communion along with César Chávez to break Chávez's twenty-five-day fast for nonviolent protest in Delano, California. Since then, other Latinos such as Archbishop Patricio Flores of San Antonio have met with every American president since Richard Nixon. Furthermore, Father Virgilio Elizondo has met Lyndon B. Johnson, Jimmy Carter, Ronald Reagan, George Bush, Bill Clinton, and George W. Bush. Similarly, Rev. Jesse Miranda of the Assemblies of God has met Ronald Reagan, George Bush, Bill Clinton, and George W. Bush.

Furthermore, Latino clergy leaders like Seventh-day Adventist evangelist José Vincente Rojas served for President Bill Clinton in the late 1990s. On May 22, 2001, President George W. Bush invited 150 Latino Catholic and Protestant religious leaders to tour the White House. In a press conference, he lauded the important role that Latino clergy play in undergirding American life and stated that it was important for political leaders to work together with Latino clergy for social change. President Bush and John DiIulio later met with Armando Contreras, Rev. Jesse Miranda, Rev. Daniel de León, Rev. Pedro Windsor, Rev. Raymond Rivera, Rev. Luis Cortés, Lisa Cummins-Treviño, and Rudy Carrasco to discuss President Bush's faith-based initiatives. Miranda was given a one-on-one five-minute audience with the president at the White House to discuss trends in American religions and politics. Since then, Bush called a meeting of fifteen Latino bishops to meet at the White House; however, the event was cancelled due to the terrorist bombing of September 11th—the day they had planned to meet. In addition to these meetings, Bush has also made high-profile appointments, like *Pedro Pan* exilic Cuban refugee Mel Martínez to the Department of Housing and Human Development (HUD). Lisa Treviño-Cummins worked in the White House Office of Faith-Based Initiatives. In addition, Luis Cortés and Jesse Miranda organized the first National Hispanic Presidential Prayer Breakfast in Washington, D.C., on May 5, 2002. President Bush, Senator Joseph Lieberman, television show host Chris Matthews, and many others spoke to 750 Latino clergy and religious leaders from forty-nine states (all except Alaska). Bush continues to speak at this annual event.[34]

President Bush met with Latino religious leaders because he was hoping to garner their support for his faith-based initiatives and also to seek their support for his 2004 presidential race. The HCAPL national survey found that Bush has good reason to reach out to Latinos. Although the vast majority of Latinos supported Bill Clinton in 1996 (82% vs. 14% for Dole) and Al Gore in 2000 (Latino Catholics voted 76% for Gore vs. 24% for Bush, and Protestants voted 67% for Gore vs. 33% for Bush), nationwide Bush took 35 percent of the Latino vote (doubling Dole's Latino vote). More important, just weeks prior to the 2000 election, 37 percent of all Latinos self-identified as politically independent and 17 percent still had not decided who they planned to vote for, Gore or Bush. Bush and his Republican strategists realized that they stood a much greater chance of making political inroads among Latinos than among African Americans, who gave Gore over 90 percent of their vote. Bush's primary strategy has been to seek their support for his administration's position on controversial church–state and social issues, which Latinos tend to support. He was aware of the fact that the HCAPL and Pew Forum national surveys found that 70 percent of Latinos support prayer in schools, 61 percent support school vouchers, 81 percent support charitable choice, and 66 percent do not support homosexual sex relations. Given the fact that the South is becoming increasingly Republican and that Latinos constitute a growing swing vote in critical electoral vote–rich states like Florida, New Mexico, Arizona, Nevada, and Colorado, this Southwestern political strategy has in fact paid off. Exit polls from the 2004 presidential election indicate that Bush took 44 percent of the national Latino vote (versus Kerry's 53%) and 56 percent of Latinos in Florida, 44 percent in New Mexico, 39 percent in Nevada, 32 percent in California, and 30 percent in Colorado. By comparison, Bush took 58 percent of the national white vote but only 11 percent of the black vote. Religion may have been a decisive factor as nationwide 52 percent of Catholics, 59 percent of all Protestants, and 79 percent of Evangelicals voted for Bush, and those that attended church more than weekly gave Bush 64 percent of their vote. Furthermore, Bush saw a slight increase (+7%) in the Latino Catholic vote (from 24% in 2000 to 31% in 2004) and a major increase (+31%) in the Latino Protestant vote (33% in 2000 to 63% in 2004). Nationwide, moral values (22%) was the number one concern in shaping their decision to select a candidate, followed by the economy (20%), terrorism (19%), the Iraq war (15%), and healthcare (8%). This played well for Bush as he received 80 percent of the moral values vote versus Kerry's 18 percent.[35]

Bush's outreach to Latino clergy and religious leaders has met with mixed reviews by Latino Catholics and Protestants. Although this is largely due to the fact that they historically vote Democratic, it is also due to perceived inconsistencies in the Bush administration's views on immigration, big business, welfare and Aid For Dependent Children and other economic justice and civil rights issues. Some are highly skeptical of Bush's motives, and still others worry about losing their prophetic voice in society if they seek and secure government funding. The fact that Bush may be able to attract morally conservative Latinos to his cause is one reason for his proposal to grant work permits to Latin American immigrants, a proposal that has met with mixed reviews. Regardless of Bush's motives, it is clear that Latino clergy are being sought out by political leaders to support their public policies and electoral races. Although Latino clergy have made the long journey from second-class citizenship in the 1850s to the Bush White House in 2001, they still have a long way to go.

Interpreting the Significance of Latino Faith-Based Action

This chapter has but scratched the surface of the important role of Latino clergy, churches, and religious organizations in political and social action. Taken as whole, what can we conclude? First, these findings refine and modify the perceptions of previous scholarship. Although scholars correctly note that at some periods of time the hierarchy of the Catholic Church was not proactive in social action at the national level, he may have underestimated the role of individual Latino and Anglo priests, organizations, popular religiosity, and local parishes. This study found that Latino clergy, churches, and religious organizations are much more politically and socially active today than hitherto believed. In fact, they appear to be becoming more and more politically and socially active with each passing decade. Because the vast majority of Latinos are Roman Catholic, Pentecostal, or Evangelical and as neither Latino Pentecostalism nor Evangelicalism has had a reputation for political or social action, I expected to see much lower levels of participation and support. Instead, almost four out of ten (39%) Latinos nationwide indicated that their churches helped in voter registration, and one in four (26%) said that their churches had given people a ride to the polls on Election Day and advocated on behalf of a specific ballot issue, proposition, or referendum.

Second, these findings confirm and go beyond some of those in Verba et al.'s *Voice and Equality*. Latino Protestants are as active or more politically active than their Catholic counterparts on all six measures of political action in the HCAPL national survey. However, in addition to attending church more often, I argue that other socio-religious factors such as immigrant status, income, education, and religious participation help explain why Latino Protestant churches are more active than their Catholic counterparts.

Third, the Latino population in general and civic leaders in particular gave churches and clergy high marks for addressing educational, social, and political issues. However, they still lag behind Anglo-Americans and blacks in some respects, especially in political action.

Fourth, and perhaps not surprisingly in light of this finding, 62 percent of Latinos nationwide and 74 percent of civic leaders surveyed want religious leaders to become more involved in educational, social, and political issues. Given the lack of regular contact between Latino civic and religious leaders, it was surprising to find that Latino civic leaders gave churches and religious leaders consistently higher levels of support for their participation in educational, social, and political issues than the general population did. However, this affirmation drops off when asked whether they think religious leaders should try to influence public affairs.

Fifth, Latino churches and clergy are much more likely to get involved in social rather than political issues. Many factors may contribute to this finding, but the influx of millions of refugees fleeing military dictatorships in Central and South America in the 1980s and 1990s may have something to do with this, along with the fact that many Latin American immigrants and U.S. Latinos simply do not have the leisure time, money, or information about how to become more involved in political and social action.

Sixth, the fact that such a high percentage of Latinos are immigrants helps to explain why they are less likely than their African American counterparts to become involved in political mobilization. However, Latinos are actually as likely—or, in some cases, slightly more likely—to become involved in providing social services for their community than their African American counterparts.

Seventh, Latino Protestants not only tend to be more proactive in political and social issues because they are more involved in their churches, as Verba et al. point out, but also because they are less likely than Catholics to be immigrants, live in poverty, and have low levels of education and are more likely to attend church, read their Bibles, lead a Bible study, and say that religion provides "some" or a "great deal" of meaning for their day-to-day living.

Eighth, and perhaps somewhat predictably given the long tradition of Anglo-American Mainline Protestant political and social activism, Latino Mainline Protestant churches and religious organizations were more politically and socially active than Catholics, Evangelicals, or Pentecostals.[36]

Ninth, generally speaking, Latino Christians who have higher (although not necessarily the highest) levels of church attendance, Bible reading, and leading Bible studies were more likely than those who never attended church, never read the Bible, and never led a Bible study to say that their churches engaged in political or social action. Thus, there does appear to be a correlation between religious participation and political and social action.

Tenth, Alternative Christian groups (e.g., Jehovah's Witnesses, Mormons, and Christian Scientists) were the second most likely religious family grouping to indicate that they were involved in political mobilization and in providing social services—more so than their Catholic, Evangelical, and Pentecostal counterparts. By including Alternative Christian traditions, this study moves beyond the traditional paradigm of interpreting Latino Christianity in the United States.

Eleventh, Latino religious leaders are being sought out by American presidents and political leaders to support their domestic social policies as never before. No longer will organizations like the National Council for La Raza, the League of United Latin American Citizens, and the National Alliance of Latino Elected Officials (NALEO) be the only organizations purporting to speak on behalf of the Latino community. A growing number of clergy, churches, and faith-based organizations may also join their lobbying in Washington, D.C., in the years ahead.

All of these findings point to the general conclusion that Latino clergy, churches, and religious organizations are engaged in political and social action and have the widespread support of both the Latino population in general and civic leaders in particular. That evidence, as well as similar findings discussed in the other chapters in this volume, indicate that this trend in Latino faith-based political and social action is likely to continue well into the twenty-first century.

NOTES

I thank The Pew Charitable Trusts for funding the Hispanic Churches in American Public Life (HCAPL) research project, which has generated the survey data for this study. I also thank Jesse Miranda of Vanguard University and Virgilio Elizondo of the University of Notre Dame and lead data analysts So Young Kim of Florida Atlantic University and Han-Sun of Northwestern University for their assistance in analyzing the data for this publication. I also thank Edwin I. Hernández, Kenneth Davis, Milagros Peña, and Ulrike Guthrie for their critical feedback on early drafts of this essay. Unless otherwise noted, all of the quotes in this chapter were taken from the HCAPL community profile interviews. The names have been changed to protect the anonymity of the interviewees.

1. I use the terms "civic action" and "political action" interchangeably. I include under the category of "civic leaders" all public leaders in elected offices. This includes civic, city, state, government, and political leaders. By "religious leaders," I mean all ordained and nonordained persons in churches or religious organizations that provide leadership to their constituencies or organizations in either a paid or voluntary capacity. The findings in this chapter are based on the HCAPL national survey ($n = 2{,}060$) in the Fall of 2000. The national survey and civic and religious leaders surveys were conducted by the Tomás Rivera Policy Institute (www.trpi.org). More than 5,000 surveys were mailed out to civic and religious leaders in 2001. A total of 434 Latinos responded. The religious leaders surveyed were both Catholic and Protestant and included clergy and nonordained lay leaders. For more about the HCAPL study, see Gastón Espinosa, Virgilio Elizondo, and Jesse Miranda, *Hispanic Churches in American Public Life: Summary of Findings*, 2nd ed. (Notre Dame, IN: Institute for Latino Studies at the University of Notre Dame, 2003). This document will hereafter be cited as Espinosa et al., *Hispanic Churches.*

2. Rodolfo Acuña wrote: "The Catholic Church refused to promote social action and limited itself to meeting the minimal spiritual needs of the people. . . . [It] was a missionary group that, by its silence, tacitly supported the oppressive conditions under which Chicanos had to live and work." Protestants were not much better as they were "not interested in championing rights or promoting brotherhood." Acuña notes some positive contributions of the Christian church. Rodolfo Acuña, *Occupied America: A History of Chicanos* (Harper & Row, 1973), 148–149. Also see, Moises Sandoval, ed., *Fronteras: A History of the Latin American Church in the USA since 1513* (San Antonio, TX: Mexican-American Cultural Center Press, 1983), 398–399; José Angel Gutiérrez, *The Making of a Chicano Militant: Lessons from Crystal* (Madison: University of Wisconsin Press, 1998), 21, 24–25, 256, 280–281.

3. Juan Gómez-Quiñones, *Chicano Politics: Reality & Promise 1940–1990* (Albuquerque: University of New Mexico Press, 1990), 177–182; F. Arturo Rosales, *Chicano! The History of the Mexican American Civil Rights Movement* (Houston: Arte Público Press, 1997), 265; Carlos Muñoz Jr., *Youth, Identity and Power: The Chicano Movement* (New York: Verso Books, 1992), 50, 55; and Mary S. Pardo, *Mexican American Women Activists: Identity and Resistance in Two Los Angeles Communities* (Philadelphia: Temple University Press, 1998), 31–38, 171–181.

4. Sidney Verba, Key Lehman Schlozman, and Henry E. Brady, *Voice and Equality: Civic Voluntarism in American Politics* (Cambridge, MA: Harvard University Press, 1995); Rodolfo de la Garza, *Ethnic Ironies: Latino Politics in the 1992 Elections* (Boulder, CO: Westview Press, 1996); Rodolfo de la Garza, Louis DeSipio, F. Chris García, John A. García, and Angelo Falcón, *Latino Voices: Mexican, Puerto Rican, and Cuban Perspectives on American Politics* (Boulder, CO: Westview Press, 1992); Peggy Levitt, "Two Nations under God? Latino Religious Life in the United States," in Marcelo M. Suárez-Orozco and Mariela M. Páez, eds., *Latinos Remaking America* (Berkeley: University of California Press, 2002), 150–164.

5. Verba et al., *Voice and Equality*, 233.

6. Ibid., 230–231, 245–247, 320–332.

7. Ibid., 230–235, 245, 320–333.

8. Fredrick C. Harris, *Something Within: Religion in African-American Political Activism* (New York: Oxford University Press, 1999); R. Drew Smith, ed., *New Day Begun: African-American Churches and Civic Culture in Post–Civil Rights America* (Durham, NC: Duke University Press, 2003).

9. Verba et al., *Voice and Equality*; de la Garza, *Ethnic Ironies*; de la Garza et al. *Latino Voices*; Levitt, "Two Nations?" 150–164.

10. The HCAPL national survey has two batteries of questions about church participation in political and social action. The first is question number thirty-two. It reads as follows: During the last five years, which of the following activities has your church or religious organization been involved in? Helped in voter registration; given people a ride to polls on Election Day; handed out campaign materials; advocated on behalf of a specific ballot issue, proposition, or referendum; asked people to support certain political candidates; organized and/or participated in protests or rallies; don't know/refused to answer. The second is question number thirty-three. It reads as follows: During the last five years, which of the following activities has your church or religious organization been involved in? Reached out to gangs in an effort to reduce community violence; helped members of your community secure jobs, better wages, or better working conditions; helped newly arrived immigrants establish themselves; started drug or alcoholic rehabilitation programs; started English or citizenship classes; started day-cares, food coops, or child-care centers; started after-school youth programs for teenagers; don't know/refused to answer.

11. I use self-definition and self-identification as "Christian" as the basis for this classification system. Jehovah's Witnesses and Mormons self-identify as Christian.

12. Espinosa et al., *Hispanic Churches*, 13.

13. "Anomie" refers to the "moral meaninglessness" that uprooted immigrants, migrants, and people experience in the process of social dislocation. Some have suggested that Pentecostal growth in Latin America is due to the social dislocation created by the changes in Latin American society which has created "refugees from modernity" and "deprived searchers for some new form of psychological compensation." Harvey Cox and Emilio Willems challenge this interpretation of Pentecostalism; see Harvey Cox, *Fire from Heaven: The Rise of Pentecostal Spirituality and the Reshaping of*

Religion in the Twenty-first Century (Reading, MA: Addison-Wesley, 1995), 171–177; Emilio Willems, *Followers of the New Faith* (Nashville: University of Tennessee Press, 1967).

14. The political and social indexes were created by indexing all of the possible responses from questions 32 and 33 from the HCAPL national survey on political and social action. These questions are cited in full in note 10.

15. Espinosa et al., *Hispanic Churches*; Gómez-Quiñones, *Chicano Politics*, 88–92; Gutiérrez, *Making of a Chicano Militant*, 40–41, 331; Rosales, *Chicano*! 265; Muñoz, *Youth, Identity and Power*, 50, 55.

16. The HCAPL national survey found that 22 percent (5.4 million) of all Latino Catholics self-identified as "born-again" Christian and as a Pentecostal, Charismatic, or spirit-filled Christian. Espinosa et al., *Hispanic Churches*, 16.

17. The questions in the HCAPL national survey regarding voter registration, giving people a ride to the polls, handing out campaign materials, advocating on behalf of a specific issue, and participating in protests or rallies were taken directly from R. Drew Smith's national survey of black clergy and thus can be used for comparisons. Smith, *New Day Begun*, 9–10, 58–83.

18. These three measures were (1) reaching out to gangs in an effort to reduce community violence (52% for Alternative Christian vs. 46% for Mainline Protestants—the next highest scoring group); (2) helping members of your congregation secure jobs, better wages, or better working conditions (40% for Alternative Christian vs. 37% for Mainline Protestants—the next highest scoring group); and (3) starting drug or alcohol rehabilitation homes (38% for Alternative Christian vs. 35% for Mainline Protestants—the next highest scoring group).

19. For example, large faith-based organizations like Pueblo Nueva, Jim Ortiz's My Fathers House, and City Impact in southern California; Project Quest in San Antonio; Resurrection House in Chicago; Luís Cortés' Nueva Esperanza in Philadelphia; Ray Rivera's the Latino Pastoral Action Center in the Bronx; and Nehemiah House in New York City are sponsoring a growing number of social programs.

20. Richard L. Wood, *Faith in Action: Religion, Race, and Democratic Organizing in America* (Chicago: University of Chicago Press, 2002).

21. The HCAPL national survey found that 93 percent of all Latinos self-identified with a Christian tradition, indicated that they were a born-again Christian, or specified that they attended a denomination affiliated with the Christian tradition. Another 6 percent indicated that they had no particular religious preference/other, 1 percent was affiliated with a world religion or non-Christian tradition, and 0.37 percent indicated that they were atheist or agnostic. Espinosa et al., *Hispanic Churches*, 14.

22. For more on women and faith-based activism see Pardo, *Mexican American Women Activists*.

23. Bryan T. Froehle and Mary L. Gautier, *Ministry in a Church of Increasing Diversity: A Profile of Diocesan Hispanic/Latino Ministry* (Washington, DC: Georgetown University, Center for Applied Research in the Apostolate, 2002), pp. 1–33. Unless otherwise noted, this section on Latino Catholicism is based on the findings in this report. See also Bryan T. Froehle and Mary L. Gautier, *Catholicism USA: A Portrait of the Catholic Church in the United States* (Maryknoll, NY: Orbis Books, 2000), and Kenneth G. Davis, Eduardo C. Fernández, and Veronica Méndez, *United States Hispanic Catholics: Trends and Works 1990–2000* (Scranton, PA: University of Scranton Press, 2002).

24. Froehle and Gautier, *Ministry in a Church of Increasing Diversity*, 49, 52.

25. Ibid., 1–3, 5, 11.

26. Ibid., 9, 14, 25, 32–33, 56.

27. Ibid., 9, 14, 25, 32.

28. Espinosa et al., *Hispanic Churches*, 14–16. For a more refined analysis of Latino religious affiliation, see Gastón Espinosa, "Changements démographigues et religieux chez les hispaniques des Etats-Unis" (Demographic Shifts in Latino Religions in the United States), *Social Compass* 51(3) (September 2004): 303–320; Espinoza, "The Pentecostalization of Latin American and U.S. Latino Christianity," *Pneuma* 26:2 (Fall 2004).

29. Amy L. Sherman, "The Community Serving Activities of Hispanic Protestant Congregations: A Report to The Center for the Study of Latino Religions," Notre Dame University (Washington, DC: Hudson Institute Faith in Communities Initiative, 2003), pp. 1–29. Unless otherwise noted, this section on Latino Protestantism is based on the findings in this report.

30. Espinosa et al., *Hispanic Churches*, 14, 28, note 21.

31. See Sherman, "Community Serving Activities," 10–12 and Andrew Billingsley, *Mighty Like a River: The Black Church and Social Reform* (New York: Oxford University Press, 2002). The twenty-three service options listed in Sherman's survey were food assistance, clothing assistance, emergency financial assistance, referrals to other helping agencies, homeless services, tutoring, teen mentoring, Head Start, day care or child care, GED, ELS, substance abuse counseling or rehab, pastoral counseling, aid to immigrants, job training, health programs, citizenship classes, legal assistance, life skills, parenting classes, teen pregnancy prevention programs, family counseling, and aid to prisoners. Sherman, "Community Serving Activities," 10–12.

32. Sherman, "Community Serving Activities," 11.

33. These fifteen faith-based ministries are (1) the Association of Church-Based Community Ministries sponsored by the Latino Pastoral Action Center (LPAC) in New York City, led by Ray Rivera; (2) the Hispanic Clergy of Philadelphia and Vicinity, led by Luis Cortes; (3) the Latino Leadership Foundation in Chicago, led by Noel Castellanos, (4) the Mid-Atlantic Compassion Network in Washington, led by Rafael Guevara; (5) World Vision's Metro Seattle and Tacoma Hispanic Initiative, led by Tito Hinojo; (6) the Alianza de Ministerios Evangélicos Nacionales in Costa Mesa, California, led by Jesse Miranda; (7) World Vision's La Alianza in Los Angeles, led by Martin García; (8) Let's Partner Network/Eleazer Partnerships in Riverside, California, led by Lee de León; (9) Obras de Amor: The Kingdom Coalition in Santa Ana, California, led by Eric Adams; (10) Unidos por Jesucristo in Los Angeles, led by Miguel Batz; (11) the Hispanic Christian Church Association of Central Florida, led by Edgardo Luís López; (12) the Coalition for Hispanic Ministries in Orlando, Florida, led by David Byrne; (13) the Intercultural Leadership Network in San Antonio, led by Albert Reyes; (14) the Coalition of Latin American Ministers in Chicago, led by Daniel Matos-Real; and (15) the Informal Hispanic Evangelical Network in Chicago, led by Daniel Alvarez. Sherman, "Community Serving Activities," 15–22.

34. Espinosa et al., *Hispanic Churches*, José Vincete Rojas, *José: God Found Me in Los Angeles* (Hagerstown, MD: Review and Herald Publishing Association, 1999), 97, 138–147. See photo at the beginning of this chapter for evidence of President Bush's meeting with Latino clergy and lay leaders. Other observations in this and the following paragraph are based on anonymous conversations with Latino clergy and lay leaders. For evidence of the 2004 presidential election findings see, Roger Simon, "Second Act," *U.S. News & World Report, Special Election Edition*, November 15, 2004, pp. 16–30, especially 24; Dan Gilgoff, "The Morals and Values Crowd," *U.S. News &*

World Report, November 15, 2004, p. 42; Ricardo Alonso-Zaldivar, "Bush Snags Much More of the Latino Vote, Exit Polls Show," *Los Angeles Times*, November 4, 2004, A30; John C. Green, Corwin E. Smidt, James L. Guth, and Lyman A. Kellstedt, "The American Religions Landscape and the 2004 Presidential Vote: Increased Polarization," Available at: http://pewforum.org/religion-politics.

35. Espinosa et al., *Hispanic Churches.*

36. Ibid., Robert Wuthnow and John H. Evans, eds., *The Quiet Hand of God: Faith-Based Activism and the Public Role of Mainline Protestantism* (Berkeley: University of California Press, 2002).

Conclusion: Assessing and Interpreting 150 Years of Latino Faith-Based Civic Activism

Gastón Espinosa, Virgilio Elizondo, and Jesse Miranda

The essays in this volume challenge the long-standing perception that religion has had little positive influence on political, civic, and social action in the Latino community over the past 150 years. As we have seen, religious ideology, institutions, leaders, and symbols have shaped the motivations and trajectory of key Latino activists, organizations, and movements. This book both confirms and modifies Rodolfo Acuña's criticism that Catholic and Protestant churches refused to promote social action or champion the rights of Latinos, and thereby tacitly supported their oppressive conditions. We have seen that although most faith-based civic action carried out between 1900 and 1970 was conducted by Catholic and Protestant clergy, ex-clergy, or religious lay leaders, it was often (although not always) conducted without the formal blessing and support of their superiors and denominations—and sometimes in spite of them. However, Latino clergy and popular religious expressions have played an important role in Latino civic activism. After 1970 we begin to see various denominations and governing boards increasingly lend their considerable institutional financial and moral support on behalf of Latino struggles for social justice. This support varied according to time, place, situation, and circumstances. Today, most major Latino-serving denominations and clergy support various kinds of faith-based political, civic, and social action.

If we look at the seventeen essays as a whole, several themes stand out. First, we see that individual Catholic and Protestant clergy, religious, and churches have fought on behalf of the Latino community over the past 150 years. Padre Antonio José Martínez, José Felipe Ortiz, Juan Romero, Virgilio Elizondo, Gregoria Ortega, Gloria Gallardo, Rosa Marta Zaraté, Leo Nieto, Tomás Atencio, Jorge Lara Braud, Lydia Hernández, Aimee García Cortese, Leoncia Rosado Rousseau, Ana Villafañe, Ray Rivera, Wilfredo Estrada, and countless others have marched, prayed, fasted, and picketed on behalf of their *barrios* and *colonias*. Although they have not always been successful, they have served on the front lines of many past and present struggles.

Second, we found that many of the most important Mexican American civil rights movement leaders were profoundly shaped by their spirituality and popular religious traditions. César Chávez used his popular Catholic symbols and practices such as Our Lady of Guadalupe, pilgrimages, and fasts to fight for social justice on behalf of migrant farmworkers and the United Farm Workers Union. Reies López Tijerina based his land grant struggle on a Pentecostal-influenced magical-literalist reading of the Bible and the Spanish Catholic *Laws of the Indies*. Countless other Chicano/a activists also drew on religious symbols and their political spirituality to fight on behalf of the Latino community. In many ways, the early Mexican American civil rights movement was profoundly shaped by and was in certain respects a product of religious language, symbols, rhetoric, and notions of social justice.

Third, the struggle for political, civic, and social justice sometimes brought otherwise warring Catholics and Protestants together on the picket lines, in disobedience camps, in pilgrimages, and in prayer vigils in Delano, Miami, San Juan, and countless urban centers and border towns throughout the United States and Puerto Rico. In most cases where Latino activists have been successful, they have respectfully set aside sectarian and theological differences and joined forces, shared power, and worked together on behalf of the Latino community.

Fourth, Latino Catholics and Protestants have often pointed to activists outside of their own denominations and in some cases religion (e.g., Mahatma Gandhi) to challenge, threaten, or inspire their denominational leaders to become more involved in their struggles. César Chávez openly praised Gandhi's nonviolent activism. He also publicly praised the Protestant-led California Migrant Ministry before Catholic leaders for being the first to stand on the picket lines with him. Presbyterian Jorge Lara-Braud praised Catholics like Chávez and ex-Pentecostals like Tijerina for their work on behalf of the Latino community before the Presbyterian General Assembly. Latino activists have thus sometimes used the tactics of fear, shame, and competition to motivate their denominational leaders to act.

Fifth, Hispanic women have often provided the critical grassroots support for political action in the Latino community. Women like Leoncia Rosado Rousseau, Gloria Gallardo, Ana Villafañe, Rosa Marta Zaraté, and countless others have often been the first to rally the people to the cause of social justice and faith-based social ministry, and they have provided much of the often-unheralded behind-the-scenes labor. Despite these important contributions (or perhaps because of them), we still know surprisingly little about their work and that of thousands of other women. More work needs to be done to uncover, explore, and spotlight the critical role of Latinas in political, civic, and social action.

Sixth, many of the Latino/a clergy, religious, and laity (e.g., Juan Romero, Jorge Lara-Braud, Virgilio Elizondo, Elias Galván, Lydia Hernández) who initially risked speaking out on behalf of the Latino community were later named or recognized as leaders within their respective denominations. This was especially true for Protestant ministers and Catholic priests but less true for Catholic women like Rosa Marta Zaraté, and independent leaders like Reies López Tijerina. Today many of these former activists now shape their denomination's policies on a wide range of social justice issues dealing not just with Latinos but the entire denomination. They have thus been able to mainstream their once marginalized and "radical" views.

Seventh, the Chicano, civil rights, feminist, and liberation theology movements helped birth many grassroots religious organizations, associations, and faith-based groups that, albeit in different ways, have provided the critical long-term capacity to carry on political, civic, and social action in the Latino community over the past thirty years. Countless faith-based organizations like PADRES, Las Hermanas, MACC, the Latino Pastoral Action Center, the Latin American Methodist Action Group (MARCHA), COPS, UNO, EPISO, AMEN, Nueva Esperanza, and others have continued the struggle at the local level. This points to the importance of institutionalizing one's powerbase and building the organizational capacity to continue the struggle in the future.

Eighth, Latino activists have not had the money, time, or connections to exercise the kind of behind-the-scenes "quiet influence" of Anglo-American Mainline Protestants.[1] Like their black counterparts, Latinos have had to fight, claw, and picket their way into the national limelight in order to spotlight injustice. Unlike wealthy and well-connected Anglo-American Mainline Protestant denominations and leaders, Latino Catholic and Pentecostal traditions and leaders have not traditionally had the connections or resources needed to push their political agendas at the state house or in Washington D.C. This is slowly beginning to change.

Ninth, despite this fact, Latino clergy, churches, and religious organizations have been active in addressing the educational, social, and political needs of their communities. In fact, they have garnered more widespread support than has hitherto been realized and are presently actively involved in promoting political and social action. The relatively low levels of political and social action (at least compared to their Anglo and black counterparts) is largely due to their immigrant status, poverty, low levels of education, and varying degrees of religious participation, the latter of which can help develop skills that can later be transferred into the political and social arenas.

Tenth, Latino civic activism does not always take the form and method most often found in Anglo-American Protestant traditions. Latino activism has been profoundly shaped and limited by education, economics, capacity, social capital, and denominational support. For this reason, Latino engagement has often taken on a more behind-the-scenes or an occassionally more radical form. Many churches and clergy live among the poor. Often they *are* the poor. In light of this reality, there is a need to create new conceptual models for Latino political, civic, and social action. These new models of faith-based action and social engagement need to be judged by the context, standards, resources, and capacity within the Latino community itself and not by some outside standard that has little or no direct bearing on the realities of millions of Latinos living in economically marginalized and underserved *barrios* and *colonias.*

Eleventh, Latino clergy and faith-based organizations are being courted by American presidents and political leaders to support their domestic policies and political party platforms. A small but growing number of Latino clergy and lay leaders are beginning to gain access to the White House or key Washington insiders. However, what is beyond dispute is that sometime in the past 150 years Latino clergy and religious organizations have leaped over the back seat of politics, where they had been since 1848. Whether Latino faith leaders will be able to transform this access into real political clout that positively affects the Latino community remains to be seen.

Although this volume addresses a variety of ways that religion has affected Latino political, civic, and social action over the past 150 years, it has only scratched the surface of a new field of inquiry. What remains to be done? We need more research on the influence of religion on political, civic, and social action during the colonial Spanish and Mexican periods in Mexico, the Latin Caribbean, and the Southwest. Much more research needs to focus on the Spanish missions, church–state conflicts, and secularization's effect on Indians and mestizos between 1790 and 1848. Still more work is needed to look at how Latinos used their popular religious traditions to fight for social justice after the United States–Mexico War of 1848 and the Treaty of Guadalupe Hidalgo. In a similar vein, scholars need to explore more carefully the important ways that Latino Pentecostal, Evangelical, and Mainline Protestants fought for political, civil, and social justice in the late nineteenth and/or early twentieth centuries. New research needs to focus on how Alternative Christian and non-Christian religious traditions like Mormonism, Jehovah's Witness, Santería, Spiritism, Judaism, Islam, and Buddhism have enabled and empowered Latinos to engage in activism. Across all denominations and time periods, there is a need for more scholarship on the role that women have had in these struggles. Scholars also need to examine the impact of religion on the origins of ostensibly secular civil rights organizations like LULAC, the G.I. Forum, and the National Council for La Raza, and more needs to be written on the impact of religion in the Chicano movement and among Cubans, Puerto Ricans, and Central Americans living in the United States and on Latinos in New York, the Midwest, and Florida. Research also needs to be conducted on the relationship between Latino clergy and lay leaders and the American presidency. Finally, work needs to be conducted among "new" Latin American Catholic and Protestant/Pentecostal immigrants arriving in the United States who are not acquainted with the Latino faith-based activism during the civil rights and Chicano movements. In short, the field of Latino religions and political activism is wide open. We invite scholars to use this volume as a starting point for their own investigation into this increasingly vital and relevant field.

Although we hope this book moves the scholarly discussion on Latino political, civic, and social action forward, what kind of practical historical lessons and recommendations can be made to chart a new course for the future? First, Latinos need to realize that they represent a growing and potentially powerful segment of American society. Latinos are now the largest minority group in the United States and will continue to be so in the foreseeable future. They have something beautiful to give to American society, and they must not be shy about sharing it with their fellow Americans. They also have to realize that numbers alone will not translate into political, civic, and social power until Latinos register and actually mobilize their votes in city, state, and national elections. Voter registration drives, rides to the polls, and discussions about how the American political system works is crucial to transforming raw numbers of immigrants and U.S.-born Latinos into political power. The Latino community's goal should not be based entirely on self-interest. It must avoid numerical and cultural triumphalism and, instead, see the Latino community as one piece of the colorful fabric that makes up the American mosaic. Latino contributions in religion, history, music, art, architecture, cuisine, intellectual traditions, and values are not any more or any less important than those of any other racial or ethnic group.

Second, Latinos need to place greater emphasis on education, leadership training, and leadership development. Right now, Latino Catholic and Protestant communities are underserved and underrepresented in all segments of higher education and theological education, as well as in Washington, D.C. It is critical that Latino religious leaders work with academics and intellectuals in creating new programs and plans for future political, civic, and social engagement. Latino clergy need to be careful not to pretend to have expertise in something they are not qualified to address. The anti-intellectualism within the Latino religious community, but especially among some Evangelicals and Pentecostals, needs to be addressed in their congregations and denominations. The best way to address this issue is for clergy to model this role by partnering with scholars at Christian or secular colleges and universities, seminaries, Bible institutes, and pastoral institutes. This kind of strategic partnering may produce rich dividends. Likewise, it is critical that Latino academics and intellectuals writing on this topic maintain strong ties with the religious community and faith-based endeavors and yet not pretend to take the place of or speak for religious clergy. In short, there needs to be mutual respect and proactive collaboration. In light of this recommendation, socially engaged political organizaitons, caucuses, parties, colleges, universities, seminaries, Bible institutes, pastoral centers, and churches need to develop training programs that build capacity for greater educational, political, civic, and social engagement.

Third, Latino religious leaders and organizations need to work harder at networking and building bridges with secular Latino civil rights and political organizations such as the National Council for La Raza, National Alliance of Latino Elected Officials (NALEO), and the League of United Latin American Citizens (LULAC). In turn, these organizations need to do the same and to recognize the central role of religion and faith in the Latino community. When their needs and views are not respected or represented, Latino religious leaders need to exercise leadership by creating new civil rights organizations that will capture the rich diversity of opinions on a whole range of church–state (e.g., prayer in school), educational (e.g., vouchers), social (e.g., charitable choice), and political issues (e.g., immigration, Elián González, Miguel Estrada). In light of this reality, Latino religious and lay leaders need to create programs that build capacity for greater educational, political, civic, and social engagement. In those instances where these institutions and organizations do not exist, new ones may need to be created or sponsored by churches or nonsectarian religious coalitions. A creative curriculum also needs to be developed that addresses the unique needs of the Latino community.

Fourth, present Latino political, civic, and social action groups need to address the full range of needs, not only for first-generation Spanish-speaking immigrants, who make up 35 percent of all Latinos, but also for the other 65 percent of second- and third-or-more-generation Latinos who are often overlooked or neglected. These youth are the ones most at risk of gang violence, teenage pregnancy, and drug and alcohol abuse. Religious leaders need to be more proactive about capacity building, developing after-school youth programs, educational and tutoring programs, big brother and big sister mentoring programs, and spiritual formation groups. In light of the growing number of Latino youth ending up in the prison system, all organizations need to be more proactive and vigilant about addressing the legal system and correctional facility industry.

Fifth, Latino Catholics and Protestants need to work more aggressively at ecumenical and interdenominational cooperation and coalition building on issues like education, housing, youth violence, political representation, and other related matters. While respecting one another's differences on matters of faith, theology, and church polity, there is no reason why religious leaders cannot work together for the betterment of the Latino community on many political, civic, educational, and social issues. Furthermore, Latino Catholics and Mainline Protestants need to be more open about sharing power, authority, and influence with their Pentecostal, Evangelical, Mormon, and Jehovah's Witnesses counterparts. If they do not, they may find themselves competing for funds and wasting valuable staff, money, and resources duplicating programs already in existence. It is not enough to simply invite these groups to an already established agenda. Leaders may want to be more proactive and open about adjusting, modifying, and even changing their existing plans and programs to accommodate the new insights of hitherto doubly marginalized yet growing communities.

Sixth, Latinos need to build coalitions with blacks, Asians, Native Americans, and Anglo-Americans across denominational, theological, and political divides in order to address the political, civic, educational, and social needs of their constituents in urban centers and rural communities. The growth of these communities necessitates mutual cooperation, dialogue, and resource sharing to address the common maladies. In particular, Latinos need to partner and share resources with black civil rights and faith-based social and civic groups. Communities need to work quite intentionally to avoid competing for limited resources and, instead, work together to expand government, state, and city funding. Broad-based coalitions will be the key to future success and capacity building.

Seventh, Latinos need to create faith-based Washington, D.C., lobbying offices that can address the needs and concerns of the Latino faith community—regardless of their denominational or religious heritage. Although some denominations will want to have their own lobbying groups in Washington, there should also be several Hispanic-serving organizations, centers, or institutes that are interdenominational in scope to help shape and give voice to key educational, political, civic, social, and public policy issues. It cannot be assumed that secular Latino civil rights organizations have the personnel, resources, political will, or desire to address key issues on behalf of the Latino faith community; when possible, however, this lobbying organization should network with these organizations to build strategic alliances. Furthermore, it should sponsor its own workshops and seminars on how to empower Latino religious leaders and laity to engage in lobbying at all levels of national, state, and city government.

Eighth, U.S. Latinos need to be more proactive about transnational cooperation with their counterparts in Mexico, Puerto Rico, Cuba, the Dominican Republic, El Salvador, Guatemala, and other key Latin American–sending countries to the United States. This is important to better understand the sociocultural complexion of the increasingly diverse Latino community and to find creative ways to address issues that affect Latinos both before and after they arrive in the United States.

Ninth, Latino men need to be more proactive about sharing power and authority with women. As we have seen, women have done much of the behind the scenes work and yet received very little credit. It is not only important to empower women to lead because they make up a majority of grassroots activism and faith-based ministries, but also because Latinos need to avoid perpetuating sexism and gender-based discrimination. Justice demands no less than full gender equality in Latino political, civic, and social activist organizations and programs. This kind of discrimination not only weakens the Latino community's ability to tap into the tremendous insights and power of Latinas but also cripples the Latino community's ability to offer a united front. Doing anything less also undermines one's moral authority and larger struggle for empowerment.

Tenth, Latinos need to work on capacity and institutional building. Although much has been written about the negative side of institutions and organizations, this may be truer for the Anglo-American community because it may have an overabundance of them. The Latino faith community, however, is underserved by these kinds of resources. Because of its seismic growth, the Latino community needs new institutions and organizations like the Mexican American Cultural Center (MACC) in San Antonio, Resurrection House in Chicago, the Latino Pastoral Action Center (LPAC) in New York City, the Alianza de Ministerio Evangélicos Nacionales (AMEN) in southern California, and Nueva Esperanza in Philadelphia. The Latino community grew from 22.4 million in 1990 to 40 million in 2004. There is simply no way that a handful of such organizations, be they national, state, or regional, can met the growing demands of the Latino community. For this reason, Latino leaders need to proactively encourage the formation and development of new grassroots initiatives, especially among second- and third-or-more-generation Latinos who tend to be underserved by some of the above organizations. Rather than see the development of these new organizations, institutes, and centers as a threat, present organizations should help to birth these endeavors and see them as filling a particular niche in the community. Having said this, it is important that people think strategically and sensitively about them, lest they unnecessarily compete with existing organizations.

Eleventh, Latino clergy, churches, and religious organizations need to capitalize on their high levels of support in the Latino community and among civic leaders. Right now Latino clergy, churches, and religious organizations are highly valued resources but sorely underutilized by political, educational, and civic leaders. By parterning together, they can join forces with these leaders to have the kind of transforming impact on their communities they all desire. Latino religious leaders should proactively seek to build ties with American presidents and key politicians at all levels of city, state, and national politics in order to fight for badly needed funding for social services and education.

Twelfth, Latino political, civic, and religious leaders must be prophetic. They need to be counted on, when necessary, to protest, fast, or picket to defend the rights, honor, and dignity of millions of Latinos and all Americans across the United States. This may mean challenging existing laws, policies, and decisions on a wide range of issues from public school education to housing to gang violence to immigration reform. This will also mean continuing the fight against racism, discrimination, sexism, segregation, and injustice on behalf of the poor, marginalized, and oppressed.

The future of Latino political, civic, and social activism looks bright. In order to ensure this future, it is critical that Latino leaders encourage and empower the next generation of youth to pursue professional careers in politics and public life. Furthermore, the Latino community has to be willing to learn not only from its successes but also from its failures. To do this, it will need to uncover and critically analyze its past. Only through a process of self-criticism and self-discovery can Latinos draw on their intellectual and spiritual ancestors to draw strength and courage for the difficult journey ahead.

These seventeen essays only scratch the surface of more than 150 years of faith-based political, civic, and social action in the United States and Puerto Rico. It is our hope that they will spur on a new generation of scholars and students to explore this vitally important topic. We also hope that they will empower scholars, politicians, clergy, and activists to chart new courses for the Latino community in the twenty-first century.

NOTE

1. Robert Wuthnow and John H. Evans, eds., *The Quiet Hand of God: Faith-Based Activism and the Public Role of Mainline Protestantism* (Berkeley: University of California Press, 2002).

Chronology

1835–1836	Texas-Mexico War takes place; Texas becomes a Republic
1845	Texas is annexed by the United States
1846–1848	United States–Mexico War and Treaty of Guadalupe Hidalgo; Mexico loses Southwest
1847	New Mexicans try to expel Anglos in Taos Revolt
1850	Father Antonio José Martínez is elected to the New Mexican Constitutional Convention
1851	Bishop Jean Baptiste Lamy arrives in Santa Fe, New Mexico; opposes native clergy like Father Martínez
1853	Father Ramón Ortiz rides out from El Paso to confront New Mexican Anglo governor
1855	Tejano Catholics defeat anti-Catholic "Know Nothing" Party in San Antonio elections
1856	Pablo de la Guerra defends Californios in "Strangers in Their Own Land" speech A thousand Catholics rise up to protest removal of Santa Barbara priest to Mexico
1862	Bishop Thaddeus Amat of Los Angeles forbids Mexican Catholic faith statements
1875	Bishop Dominic Manucy forbids nuns to serve Mexican Catholics in Brownsville
1878	New Mexican Catholic politician Rafael Romero criticizes Anglo treatment of Hispanos

1889–1891	Gorras Blancas raid Anglo-American ranchers and railroads in New Mexico
1894	La Alianza Hispano-Americana forms in response to an anti-Mexican nativist threat at Tucson, Arizona
1898	Spanish-American War takes place; Puerto Rico and Cuba become U.S. colonies
1903	Mexican American Catholics build a "basement church" in Florence, Arizona
1906–1920s	Pentecostal leader Susie Villa Valdez conducts social work in Los Angeles and in migrant labor camps
1910–1917	Mexican Revolution takes place; second wave of immigrants floods across the border
1917	"First Great Puerto Rican Migration" to United States; islanders granted citizenship
1925	U.S. government sets up Border Patrol to control Mexican immigration
1926	César Chávez is born near Yuma, Arizona
1926–1928	Cristero Rebellion in Mexico fights to defend Catholic Church
1930s	Great Depression occurs; United States deports more than 500,000 Mexicans to Mexico Francisco Olazábal feeds poor in Spanish Harlem
1939	Francis J. Spellman creates the "integrated church" in New York Mama Leo co-leads Damascus Christian Church (Bronx)
1942	César Chávez leaves school to work full time to help his family financially Henry B. Cisneros and San Antonio Archdiocese protest segregation in Texas Juana García Peraza founds the Congregation Mita in Puerto Rico with social vision
1942–1964	U.S.-sponsored Bracero Program invites contract labor from Mexico
1952	U.S. Congress declares all actions protecting undocumented immigrants illegal
1954	Operation Wetback begins; it seeks to deport 1 million Mexicans to Mexico

1957	Mama Leo founds Pentecostal Damascus Youth Crusade (Bronx)
1960s	Presbyterian Church USA Latinos found La Raza Churchmen organization
1961	Cuban government nationalizes all church schools and expels foreign clergy
1961–1963	Operation Pedro Pan smuggles over 14,000 children from Cuba to the United States.
1962–1965	Vatican Council II emphasize role of laity and renewal in the church
1964	Juan Romero is ordained and assigned to St. Francis Church in East Los Angeles
1964–1969	Texas Council of Churches employs Leo Nieto to minister to farmworkers
1965	Chávez organizes the UFW strike in Our Lady of Guadalupe Church, Delano, CA
1965–1975	Mexican American civil rights (Chicano) movement
1966	Farmworkers' pilgrimage/march from Delano to Sacramento Reies López Tijerina and Alianza Federal de Mercedes Reales reclaim 500,000 acres and occupy the Echo Amphitheater campground Hispanic American Institute established at Austin Presbyterian Theological Seminary General Assembly of the PCUSA takes a more proactive stance on Latino issues Rosa Martha Zárate immigrates from Mexico with Sisters of the Blessed Sacrament Latino Methodist clergy support the farm workers' march from San Juan to Austin, Texas
1966–1972	Latino Methodists endorse farmworkers' rights for collective bargaining, just wages, and just working conditions
1967	Sonny Arguíuzoni founds Victory Outreach International and targets social outcasts
1968	Latin American Conference of Catholic Bishops, Medellín, Colombia César Chávez commits to his first of three public fasts Latino United Methodists form Latin American Methodist Action Group

1969	Virgilio Elizondo and Juan Romero organize PADRES in San Antonio, Texas
	Academia de la Nueva Raza, a nonprofit corporation for educational and research purposes, is founded in New Mexico
	Católicos por la Raza students protest shoddy treatment outside St. Basil's Cathedral in Los Angeles
	Institute for Cuban Studies founded
1970	The Presbyterian Church U.S.A. allocates $200,000 for *Academia de la Nueva Raza*
1970s	Joel Martínez and Leo Nieto serve on the National Farm Workers Ministry Board
	National Chicano Anti-War Moratorium March in East Los Angeles
1971	Sister Gloria Gallardo organizes Las Hermanas in Houston, Texas
	Cuban exiles denounce archbishop for discrimination in Miami
1972	Methodist Council on Hispanic American Ministries (COHAM) established
	Latino activists enter COHAM banquet calling for solidarity with oppressed
	José Mendiola criticizes the Río Grande Conference UMC for lack of social action
	First National *Encuentro* for Latino Catholics at Trinity College, Washington, D.C.
	PADRES and Las Hermanas plan first national *Encuentro* in Santa Fe, New Mexico
	Father Virgilio Elizondo cofounds Mexican American Cultural Center (MACC) in San Antonio
1973	Father Juan Romero and protestors arrested near Fresno after defending farmworkers
1970s	Communities Organized for Public Service (COPS) is formed in San Antonio
1970s	Chávez and UFW boycott nonunion grapes, lettuce, and Gallo wines
1974	Perkins School of Theology establishes the Mexican-American Program
1970s	The charismatic Latino Pastoral Action Center (LPAC) founded in New York City as Acción Civica Evangélica de las Iglesias Hispanas de Nueva York

1975–1978	Tesse Browne serves as the National Farmworkers Service Center Director
1976	Faith-based United Neighborhoods Organization (UNO) formed Zaraté organizes twenty-seven charity-based centers for the San Diego diocese
1977	PADRES and Las Hermanas hold second national *Encuentro*
1981	UFW appoints Sisters Tess Browne and Carol Ann Messina as citizen advocates, and they successfully lobby for legislation to abolish *el cortito* in Texas Quaker Jim Corbett begins Sanctuary movement to assist refugees in Tucson, Arizona The Cuban Institute for Religion and Democracy is founded in Washington, D.C.
1982	Aimee García Cortese founds Crossroads Christian Center (Bronx) and leads with a social vision Justice Department begins its surveillance of the Sanctuary movement Rev. Minerva Carcaño leads El Redentor UMC to join Valley Interfaith organization
1983	Father Virgilio Elizondo is appointed rector of San Fernando Cathedral in San Antonio
1984	Rev. Elias Galván is elected first Hispanic Bishop of the United Methodist Church
1986	Bishop Phillip Straling accuses Zaraté and Guillén of being "Marxists" and "Communists" Pentecostal evangelist Rosa Caraballo begins social ministry in New York City
1987	Catholic National Pastoral Plan for Latino Ministry is published
1990s	Border Patrol launches "Operation Hold the Line" in El Paso and "Operation Gatekeeper" in California
1991	Exilic Christian Democratic Party of Cuba is formed María Antionette Berriozábal wins San Antonio mayoral race
1992	Rev. Joel Martínez is elected United Methodist bishop Rev. Raymond Rivera reestablishes the Latino Pastoral Action Center (LPAC)
1993	César Chávez dies

1994	Bishop Gabino Zavala of Los Angeles protests Proposition 187
1997	Sister Tess Browne launches a UFW statewide rally in Watsonville, California
1999	David Sanes is killed in an accident at the U.S. Naval base in Vieques, Puerto Rico
	Comisión de Vieques of Puerto Rico issues its report to the U.S. Navy and President Bill Clinton
	Elián González is found floating on a piece of wood off the coast of Florida
	Juan Miguel González, Elián's father, demands Elián's return to Cuba
	Pew Charitable Trusts funds the ecumenical Hispanic Churches in American Public Life research project on Latino religions, politics, and civic activism
2000	Hispanic Churches in American Public Life Conference is held at U.C. Santa Barbara
	Puerto Rican governor capitulates to the presidential directives imposed by the Clinton administration
	Denominations form the Ecumenical Coalition of Churches (EEC) in Puerto Rico
	Pentecostal Wilfredo Estrada leads the EEC protest march
	The EEC meets with Governor Pedro Rosselló
	Dozens of people pray for Elián at the Shrine of Our Lady of Charity in Miami
	Ecumenical Coalition of Churches for Vieques (ECCV) conducts peaceful campaign and contributes to the defeat of the current pro-statehood administration in local elections in Puerto Rico
	Gov. Gray Davis declares Chávez's birthday an official state holiday in California
	About 150 undocumented immigrants die in the Arizona desert trying to cross into the United States
2001	Border Patrol captures 13,000 undocumented immigrants in the Arizona desert
	President George W. Bush meets with Latino Protestant and Catholic leaders at the White House to discuss Charitable Choice and Faith-Based Initiatives
	Faith-based Grupo Beta smuggles 15,600 undocumented immigrants into the United States
2002	The Ecumenical Center for Emerging Female Leadership Conference is held in New York City

President George W. Bush and Senator Joseph Lieberman speak at the first National Hispanic Presidential Prayer Breakfast in Washington, D.C.

Latinas in Ministry Focus Group is held at Alliance Theological Seminary

Hispanic Churches in American Public Life National Conference is held on Capitol Hill in Washington, D.C.

2003 Latino population in the United States hits 37 million and surpasses African-Americans

President George W. Bush closes U.S. Naval base in Vieques, Puerto Rico

2004 Latino population reaches 40 million

Fifty-three percent of Latinos vote for John Kerry, forty-four percent vote for George W. Bush

Bibliography

Actas Oficiales de la Conferencia Anual Río Grande de la Iglesia Metodista Unida. Kerrville, Texas, June 1970.

Acuña, Rodolfo. *Occupied America: A History of Chicanos.* San Francisco: Canfield Press, 1972.

______. *Occupied America: A History of Chicanos.* New York: Harper & Row, 1988.

Archdiocese of New York. *Hispanics in New York: Religious, Cultural, and Social Experience,* Vols. 1 & 2. New York: Archdiocese of New York Office of Pastoral Research, 1982.

Alba, John. "Heritage: Longstanding Leadership of Hispanics in Tucson Contrast Sharply with Their Development in Phoenix." *Metro Phoenix* (1988): 58.

Anzaldúa, Gloria. *Borderlands/La Frontera: The New Mestiza.* San Francisco: Aunt Lute Books, 1999.

Arnal, Oscar L. *Priests in Working-Class Blue: The History of the Worker-Priests, 1943–1954.* New York: Paulist Press, 1986.

Assmann, Hugo. "Justiça, paz e integridade da criação e o 'deus quente' do mercado Total." *Revista Eclesiástica Brasileira* 50 (June 1990).

Atkinson, Ernest E. "Hispanic Baptists in Texas: A Glorious and Threatened History." *Apuntes: Reflexiones Teológicas desde el Márgen Hispano* 17 (1997): 41–44.

Balderrama, Francisco E. and Raymond Rodríguez. *Decade of Betrayal: Mexican Repatriation in the 1930s.* Albuquerque: University of New Mexico Press, 1995.

Barrett, David B. ed. *World Christian Encyclopedia: A Comparative Survey of Churches and Religions in the Modern World.* New York: Oxford University Press, 1980.

Bellah, Robert N. *The Broken Covenant: American Civil Religion in Time of Trial.* Chicago: University of Chicago Press, [1975] 1992.

______. "Civil Religion in America." *Daedalus* 96 (Winter 1967): 1–21.

Benavides, Gustavo and M. W. Daly, eds. *Religion and Political Power*. Albany: State University of New York, 1989.

Bennett, Spencer. "Civil Religion in a New Context: The Mexican-American Faith of César Chávez." In *Religion and Political Power*, ed. Gustavo Benavides and M. W. Daly. Albany: State University of New York, 1989.

Berger, Rose Marie, and Susannah Hunter. "Between the Lines: Raising the Roof." *Sojourners Magazine* (September–October, 2001.)

Berryman, Phillip. Religion in the Megacity. Maryknoll, NY: Orbis Books, 1996.

Billingsley, Andrew. *Mighty Like A River: The Black Church and Social Reform*. New York: Oxford University Press, 1999.

Boccella, Kathy. "Controversial Priest Ousted in Hempstead." *Newsday* (May 29, 1988): 2.

Boff, Clodovis. "Pastoral de clase média na perspectiva da libertação." *Revista Eclesiástica Brasileira* 51 (March 1991).

Bourdieu, Pierre. *Distinction: A Social Critique of the Judgment of Taste*. Cambridge, MA: Harvard University Press, 1984.

Bowman, John S., ed. *Cambridge Dictionary of American Biography*. Cambridge: Cambridge University Press, 1995.

Brackenridge, R. Douglas, and Francisco O. García-Treto. *Iglesia Presbiteriana: A History of Presbyterianism and Mexican-Americans in the Southwest*. 2nd ed. San Antonio, TX: Trinity University Press, 1987.

Branch, Karen. "Adult Exiles Recall Cuban Childhoods." *Miami Herald* (April 15, 2000).

______. "Crowds Target Reno's Home." *Miami Herald* (April 6, 2000).

Brewer, William H. *Up and Down California in 1860–1864: The Journal of William H. Brewer, Professor of Agriculture in the Sheffield Scientific School from 1864 to 1903*. Ed. Francis P. Farquhar. Berkeley: University of California Press, 1966.

Brackenridge, Douglas, and Francisco García-Treto. *Iglesia Presbyteriana: A History of Presbyterianism and Mexican Americans in the Southwest*. San Antonio, TX: Trinity University Press, 1987.

Brinkley-Rogers, Paul. "Exiles Tearful over Boy's Future." *Miami Herald* (April 8, 2000).

______. "Protestors from Abroad Flock to Home." *Miami Herald* (April 19, 2000).

Brinkley-Rogers, Paul, Curtis Morgan, Elaine Dreviewle, and Audra D. S. Burch. "Case Provokes Harsh Feelings, Hope." *Miami Herald* (April 5, 2000).

Brinkley-Rogers, Paul Curtis Morgan, and Eunice Ponce. "For Most in Miami, Ruling Draws Restrained Reaction." *Miami Herald* (June 2, 2000).

Brooks, Karen. "Hispanics Note Conflicting Laws." *Fort-Worth Star Telegram* (June 7, 2001): 9

Brusco, Elizabeth. *The Reformation of Machismo: Evangelical Conversion in Colombia*. Austin: University of Texas Press, 1995.

Büntig, Aldo J. "The Church in Cuba: Toward a New Frontier." In *Religion in Cuba Today*, ed. Alice Hageman and Philip E. Weaton, III. New York: Association Press, 1971.

Bunting, Glenn F., and Paul Feldman. "Assessor Threatens Tax Status of Churches That Provide Asylum." *Los Angeles Times* (February 1988): 3.

Burdick, John. *Blessed Anastacia: Women, Race and Popular Christianity in Brazil*. New York: Routledge, 1998.

______. *Looking For God in Brazil*. Berkeley: University of California Press, 1993.

Burns, Jeffrey M. "The Mexican Catholic Community in California." In *Mexican-Americans and the Catholic Church, 1900–1965*, ed. Jay P. Dolan and Gilberto M. Hinojosa. Notre Dame, IN: University of Notre Dame Press, 1994.

Buroway, Michael. *Ethnography Unbound: Power Resistance in the Modern Metropolis.* Berkeley: University of California Press, 1991.

Busto, Rudy V. *King Tiger: The Religious Vision of Reies López Tijerina.* Albuquerque: University of New Mexico, 2005.

Cadena, Gilbert R. "Chicanos and the Catholic Church: Liberation Theology as a Form of Empowerment." Ph.D. diss., University of California, Riverside, 1987.

______. "Religious Ethnic Identity: A Socio-religious Portrait of Latina/os and Latinas in the Catholic Church." In *Old Masks New Faces: Religion and Latina/o Identities,* ed. Anthony M. Stevens-Arroyo and Gilbert R. Cadena, 33–59. Vol. 2 of PARAL Studies Series. New York: Bildner Center Books, 1995.

Cadena, Gilbert R., and Lara Medina. "Liberation Theology and Social Change: Chicanas and Chicanos in the Catholic Church." In *Chicanas and Chicanos in Contemporary Society,* ed. Roberto M. DeAnda. Needham Heights, MA: Allyn & Bacon, 2001.

Camarillo, Albert. *Chicanos in a Changing Society: From Mexican Pueblos to American Barrios in Santa Barbara and Southern California, 1848–1930.* Cambridge, MA: Harvard University Press, 1979.

Campos, Leonilda Silveira. "Teatro, templo e mercado: a igreja universal do reino de deus e as mutações no campo religioso protestante." *VII Jornadas sobre Alternativas Religiosas na América Latina* (São Paulo, September 22–25, 1998). Available: http://www.sociologia-usp.br/jornadas/index.htm. [1999].

Carlo, Luis A. "Let Us Overturn the Tables: Toward a New York Puerto Rican Pedagogy of Liberation." Ph.D. diss., Teachers College/Columbia University, 2002.

Carpentier, Alejo. *Viaje a la semilla.* Havana, Cuba: Úcar García, 1944.

Castañeda, Socorro. "El Catolicismo en la frontera: una fe perfumada de flor, canto, y cambio social." *El Mensajero de San Antonio* 7–8 (July–August, 1999): 10–11.

CELAM. *Iglesia y Liberación Humana: Los documentos de Medellín.* Barcelona: Editorial Nova Terra, 1969.

Chardy, Alfonso. "Family Ties Spurred Rafters on Elián Trip." *Miami Herald* (June 23, 2000).

Chávez, César. "Letter to the National Council of Churches." In *César Chávez: Rhetoric of Nonviolence,* ed. Winthrop Yinger. Hicksville, NY: Exposition Press, [1968] 1975.

______. "The Mexican American and the Church." *El Grito* 4 (Summer 1968).

______. "Non-Violence Still Works." *Look* (April 1, 1969).

______. "Our Best Hope." *Engage* 2 (November 11, 1969): 5.

______. "Love Thy Neighbor." *U.S. Catholic* 50 (October 1985): 10.

Chesnut, R. Andrew. *Born Again in Brazil.* New Brunswick, NJ: Rutgers University Press, 1997.

Claridad. "La marcha mas grande en nuestra historia." (February 25, 2000).

Christian Jr., William A. *Local Religion in Sixteenth-Century Spain.* Princeton, NJ: Princeton University Press, 1981.

Clifford, James, and George Marcu, eds. *Writing Culture: The Poetics and Politics of Ethnography.* Berkeley: University of California Press, 1986.

Collins, David R. *Farmworker's Friend: The Story of César Chávez.* Minneapolis: Carolrhoda Books, 1996.

Colton, Walter. *Three Years in California*. Stanford, CA: Stanford University Press, 1949.

Concepción, Juan, ed. *Ecos de vida: selección especial de himnos y canciones espirituales por compositores hispanos*. Brooklyn, NY: Editorial Ebenezer, n.d.

Cone, James H. *Black Theology and Black Power*. New York: Seabury, 1969.

Conord, Bruce. *César Chávez: Union Leader*. Broomall, PA: Chelsea House, 1992.

Corley, Julie A. "Conflict and Community: St. Mary's Parish, Phoenix, Arizona." M.A. thesis, Arizona State University, 1992.

Coutin, Susan Bibler. *The Culture of Protest: Religious Activism and the U.S. Sanctuary Movement*. Boulder, CO: Westview Press, 1993.

Cox, Harvey. *Fire From Heaven: The Rise of Pentecostal Spirituality and the Reshaping of Religion in the Twenty-first Century*. Reading, MA: Addison-Wesley, 1995.

Crittenden, Ann. *Sanctuary: A Story of American Conscience and the Law in Collision*. New York: Weidenfeld & Nicolson, 1988.

Cunningham, Hilary. *God and Caesar at the Río Grande: Sanctuary and the Politics of Religion*. Minneapolis: University of Minnesota Press, 1995.

Dalton, Frederick John. *The Moral Vision of César Chávez*. Maryknoll, NY: Orbis Books, 2003.

———. "The Moral Vision of César E. Chávez: An Examination of His Public Life from an Ethical Perspective." Ph.D. diss., Graduate Theological Union, Berkeley, 1998.

Davidson, Miriam. *Convictions of the Heart: Jim Corbett and the Sanctuary Movement*. Tucson: University of Arizona Press, 1988.

Davis, Kenneth G., Eduardo C. Fernández, and Veronica Méndez. *United States Hispanic Catholics: Trends and Works 1990–2000*. Scranton, PA: University of Scranton Press, 2002.

Day, Dorothy. *Forty Acres: César Chávez and the Farm Workers*. New York: Praeger, 1971.

DeAnda, Roberto M., ed. *Chicanas and Chicanos in Contemporary Society*. Needham Heights, MA: Allyn & Bacon, 2001.

Dear, John. "César Chávez on Voting in the Marketplace." *Pax Christi USA* (Winter 1992): 21.

de la Garza, Rodolfo. *Ethnic Ironies: Latino Politics in the 1992 Elections*. Boulder, CO: Westview Press, 1996.

de la Garza, Rodolfo, and Louis DeSipio. "Overview: The Link Between Individuals and Electoral Institutions in Five Latino Neighborhoods." In *Barrio Ballots: Latino Politics in the 1990 Elections*, ed. Rodolfo O. de la Garza, Martha Menchaca, and Louis DeSipio. Boulder, CO: Westview Press, 1993.

de la Garza, Rodolfo, Martha Menchaca, and Louis DeSipio, eds. *Barrio Ballots: Latino Politics in the 1990 Elections*. Boulder, CO: Westview Press, 1993.

de la Garza, Rodolfo, Louis DeSipio, F. Chris García, John A. García, and Angelo Falcón. *Latino Voices: Mexican, Puerto Rican, and Cuban Perspectives on American Politics*. Boulder, CO: Westview Press, 1992.

de la Guerra, Pablo. Speech to the California Legislature. *El Grito: A Journal of Contemporary Mexican-American Thought* 5 (Fall 1977).

De La Torre, Miguel A. "Miami and the Babylonian Captivity." In *Sacred Text, Secular Times: The Hebrew Bible in the Modern World*, ed. Leonard Jay Greenspoon and Bryan F. Le Beau, 269. Bronx, NY: Fordham University Press, 2000.

De León, Arnoldo. *The Tejano Community, 1836–1900*. Albuquerque: University of New Mexico Press, [1982] 1997.

Delgado, Gary. *Beyond the Politics of Place: New Directions in Community Organizing in the 1990s*. Oakland, CA: Applied Research Center, n.d. [circa 1993].
d'Epinay, Lalive. *Haven of the Masses: A Study of the Pentecostal Movement in Chile.* London: Lutterworth, 1969.
de Schmidt, Aurora Camacho. "U.S. Refugee Policy and Central America." *Christianity and Crisis* 49 (September 25, 1989): 283.
Díaz-Stevens, Ana María. "Latinas and the Church." In *Hispanic Catholic Culture in the U.S.: Issues and Concerns,* ed. Jay P. Dolan and Allan Figueroa Deck S.J. Notre Dame, IN: University of Notre Dame, 1994.
______. "The Saving Grace: The Matriarchal Core of Latino Catholicism." *Latino Studies Journal* 4 (September 1993): 60–78.
Díaz-Stevens, Ana María, and Anthony M. Stevens-Arroyo. *Recognizing the Latina/o Resurgence in U.S. Religion: The Emmaus Paradigm.* Boulder, CO: Westview Press, 1998.
Dietrich, Laura. "Political Asylum: Who Is Eligible and Who Is Not." *New York Times* (October 2, 1985): A-26
Dodd, D. Aileen. "Catholic Leaders Low-Profile." *Miami Herald* (April 15, 2000).
______. "Elián a Bridge Linking Rival Faiths." *Miami Herald* (April 10, 2000).
Dolan, Jay P,. and Allan Figueroa Deck, eds. *Hispanic Catholic Culture in the U.S.: Issues and Concerns,* S.J. Notre Dame, IN: University of Notre Dame, 1994.
Driggs, Howard R., and Sarah S. King, eds. *Rise of the Lone Star: A Story of Texas Told by Its Pioneers.* New York: Frederick A. Stokes, 1936.
Driscoll, Amy, and Sandra Marquez-García. "Thousands Join Glowing Prayer Vigil." *Miami Herald* (March 30, 2000).
Dudley, Carl S., Carroll, Jackson W., and Wind, James P. *Carriers of Faith.* Louisville, KY: Westminster/John Knox Press, 1983.
Dunne, John Gregory. *Delano: Revised and Updated.* New York: Farrar, Straus & Giroux, 1971.
Durand, Jorge. *Más allá de la línea: patrones migratorios entre México y Estados Unidos.* México City: Consejo Nacional para la Cultura y las Artes, 1994.
Durand, Jorge, and Douglas S. Massey. *Miracles on the Border: Retablos of Mexican Migrants to the United States.* Tucson: University of Arizona Press, 1995.
Dussel, Enrique. *A History of the Church in Latin America: Colonialism to Liberation. 1492–1979.* Grand Rapids, MI: Eerdmans, 1981.
______. *The Underside of Modernity: Apel, Ricoeur, Rorty, Taylor, and the Philosophy of Liberation,* trans. Eduardo Mendieta. Atlantic Highlands, NJ: Humanities Press International, 1996.
El Mundo. "Vieques vital para la defensa nacional" (April 25, 1999).
El Mundo. "Vieques reconoce haber usado balas de uranio" (May 28, 1999).
El Mundo. "Toman ímpetu los compamentos en zona restringida" (November 7, 1999).
El Mundo. "Obispo Álvqaro Corrada se une a la desobediencia civil" (January 31, 2000).
El Mundo. "Religiosos convocan marcha multitudinaria pro-Vieques" (February 23, 2000).
El Nueva Día. "Condena total por tragedia Vieques: voces unanimes" (April 21, 1999).
El Nueva Día. "Rosselló accede a la nueva politica y rechaza ser un triador" (February 1, 2000).
El Nueva Día. "Acuerdo final con Casa Blanca sobre Vieques" (February 23, 2000).
El Nueva Día. "Mar humano por Vieques" (February 27, 2000).

El Nueva Día. "Secretario Richard Danzig sin garantias traspaso tierras" (August 27, 2000).

El Nueva Día. "Continuan los arrestos en Vieques" (June 28, 2003).

Eliade, Mircea. *The Sacred and the Profane: The Nature of Religion,* trans. Willard R. Trask. New York: Harcourt, Brace & World, 1957.

———. *Patterns in Comparative Religion,* trans. Rosemary Sheed. New York: Meridian Books, 1963.

Elizondo, Virgilio P. *Christianity and Culture.* San Antonio, TX: Mexican American Cultural Center, 1999.

———. *The Future is Mestizo: Life Where Cultures Meet.* Rev. ed. Boulder: University Press of Colorado, 2000.

———. *Galilean Journey: The Mexican-American Experience.* 2nd ed. Maryknoll, NY: Orbis Books, 2000.

———. "The Mexican American Cultural Center Story." In *Listening: Journal of Religion and Culture* Vol. 32, no.3 (Fall 1997).

Elizondo, Virgilio P., and Timothy Matovina. *Mestizo Worship: A Pastoral Approach to Liturgical Ministry.* Collegeville, MN: Liturgical Press, 1998.

———. *San Fernando Cathedral: Soul of the City.* Maryknoll, NY: Orbis Books, 1998.

Ellingwood, Ken. "Humanitarians Test the Law in Aiding Border Crossers." *Los Angeles Times* (December 19, 2000): A-1.

Engh, Michael E. "From *Frontera* Faith to to Roman Rubrics: Altering Hispanic Religious Customs in Los Angeles, 1855–1884." *U.S. Catholic Historian* 12 (Fall 1994): 90–95.

———. *Frontier Faiths: Church, Temple, and Synagogue in Los Angeles, 1846–1888.* Albuquerque: University of New Mexico Press, 1992.

Erlmann, Veit. *Nightsong: Performance, Power, and Practice in South Africa.* Chicago: University of Chicago Press, 1996.

Eschbach, Karl, Jacqueline Hagan, Nestor Rodríguez, Rubén Hernández-León, and Stanley Bailey. "Death at the Border." *International Migration Review* 33 (Summer 1999): 430–454.

Espín, Orlando O. *The Faith of the People: Theological Reflections of Popular Catholicism.* Maryknoll, NY: Orbis Books, 1997.

Espinosa, Gastón. "Borderland Religion: Los Angeles and the Origins of the Latino Pentecostal Movement in the U.S., Mexico and Puerto Rico, 1900–1945." Ph.D. diss., University of California, Santa Barbara, 1999.

———. "*El Azteca:* Francisco Olazábal and Latino Pentecostal Charisma, Power, and Faith Healing in the Borderlands." *Journal of the American Academy of Religion* 67 (September 1999): 597–616.

———. " 'Your Daughters Shall Prophesy': A History of Women in Ministry in the Latino Pentecostal Movement in the United States." In *Women and Twentieth-Century Protestantism,* ed. Margaret Lamberts Bendroth and Virginia Lieson Brereton, 25–48. Urbana: University of Illinois Press, 2002.

———. 2004. "Changements démographiques et religieux chez les hispaniques des Etats-Unis." *Social Compass,* 51 (2004): 303–320.

———. 2004. "The Pentecostalization of Latin American and U.S. Latino Christianity." *Pneuma,* 26:2 (Fall 2004).

Espinosa, Gastón, Virgilio Elizondo, and Jesse Miranda. *Hispanic Churches in American Public Life: Summary of Finding,* 2nd ed. Notre Dame, IN: Institute for Latino Studies at the University of Notre Dame, 2003.

Espinosa, J. Manuel. "The Origins of the Penitentes of New Mexico: Separating Fact from Fiction." *Catholic Historical Review* 79 (July 1993): 454–477.
Espinosa, Victor M. *El dilemma del retorno: migración, género y pertenencia en un contexto transnacional.* Zamora: Colegio de Michoacán, 1998.
Fahlgren, Sue. "Elder Gets 150 Days in Halfway House." *Corpus Christi Times,* (March 28, 1985): A-1, A-4.
Falstein, Mark. *César Chávez.* Paramus, NJ: Globe Feron, 1994.
Ferreira, Rui. "Vigilia permanente en casa de Elián." *El Nuevo Herald* (April 5, 2000).
Ferriss, Susan. "Mexicans Pursue Survival Training for Migrants." Cox News Service (May 18, 2001).
______. "Mexico Group Aids Migrants Crossing Desert into U.S." *Austin American Statesman* (August 19, 2001): A-21.
Ferris, Susan, and Ricardo Sandoval. *The Fight in the Fields: César Chávez and the Farmworkers' Movement.* New York: Harcourt Brace, 1997.
Filho, Rev. José Bitenncourt. *Alternativos dos desperados: como se pode ler o pentecostalismo autônomo.* Río de Janeiro: Centro Ecumênico de Documentação e Informação, 1991.
Fishlow, David M. "Poncho Flores Is Dead." *Texas Observer* 63 (1971).
Fitzpatrick, Joseph P. *Puerto Rican Americans: The Meaning of Migration to the Mainland.* Englewood: Prentice-Hall, 1971.
Flores, William V. and Rina Benmayor. "Constructing Cultural Citizenship." In *Latino Cultural Citizenship: Claiming Identity, Space and Rights,* ed. William V. Flores and Rina Benmayor. Boston: Beacon Press, 1997.
Forbes, James. *The Holy Spirit and Preaching.* Nashville, TN: Abingdon Press, 1989.
Franco, Juan A. "Vieques, las iglesias y el 'kairos boricua.' " *Claridad* (February 25, 2000).
Franklin, John Hope, and Alfred A. Moss. *From Slavery to Freedom.* New York: Knopf, 1994.
Freire, Paulo. *Pedagogy of the Oppressed,* trans. Myra Bergman Ramos. New York: Herder and Herder, 1970.
Froehle, Bryan T., and Mary L. Gautier. *Catholicism USA: A Portrait of the Catholic Church in the United States.* Maryknoll, NY: Orbis Books, 2000.
______. *Ministry in a Church of Increasing Diversity: A Profile of Diocesan Hisapnic/Latino Ministry.* Washington, DC: Georgetown University: Center for Applied Research in the Apostolate, 2002.
Fulop, Timothy E., and Albert J. Raboteau, eds. *African-American Religion: Interpretive Essays in History and Culture.* New York: Routledge, 1997.
Galarza, Ernesto. *Farm Workers and Agri-Business in California, 1947–1960.* Notre Dame, IN: University of Notre Dame Press, 1977.
García, Ignacio M. *Chicanismo: The Forging of a Militant Ethos among Mexican-Americans.* Tucson: University of Arizona Press, 1997.
García, Mario T. "Catholic Social Doctrine and Mexican American Political Thought." In *El Cuerpo de Cristo: The Hispanic Presence in the U.S. Catholic Church,* ed. Peter Casarella and Raul Gómez, 292–311. New York: Crossroad, 1998.
______. *Desert Immigrants.* New Haven, CT: Yale University Press, 1980.
______. "Fray Angélico Chávez, Religiosity, and New Mexican Oppositional Historical Narrative." In *Fray Angélico Chávez: Poet, Priest, and Artist,* ed. Ellen McCracken, 25–36. Albuquerque: University of New Mexico Press, 2000.
______. *Luis Leal: An Auto/Biography.* Austin: University of Texas Press, 2000.

———. *The Making of a Mexican American Mayor: Raymond L. Telles of El Paso*. El Paso, TX: Texas Western Press, 1998.

———. *Memories of Chicano History: The Life and Narrative of Bert Corona*. Berkeley: University of California Press, 1994.

———. *Mexican Americans: Leadership, Ideology & Identity*. New Haven, CT: Yale University Press, 1981.

———. Interview with Father Juan Romero. Los Angeles (1998).

———. Interview with Father Luís Quihuis. Santa Barbara (1999).

———. Interview with Father Virgilio Elizondo. Santa Barbara (1997, 1998).

García, Mario T., and Frances Esquibel Tywoniak. *Migrant Daughter: Coming of Age as a Mexican American Woman*. Berkeley: University of California Press, 2000.

Gardner, Robert. *¡Grito!: Reies Tijerina and the New Mexico Land Grant War of 1967*. Indianapolis: Bobbs-Merrill, 1970.

Garma, Carlos. "Poder, conflicto y reelaboración simbólica: protestantismo en una comunidad totenaca." México, D.F.: Licenciado Thesis, Escuela Nacional de Antropología e Historia, 1983.

Gill, Lesley. *Precarious Dependencies: Gender, Class and Domestic Service in Bolivia*. New York: Columbia University Press, 1994.

Glover, Lloyd. "Methodists Hear Details on Church 'Reconciliation' Project in Valley." *Pharr News* (February 17, 1972): 1.

Goizueta, Roberto. *Caminemos con Jesus: Towards a Hispanic/Latino Theology of Accompaniment*. Maryknoll, NY: Orbis Books, 1998.

Golden, Renny and Michael McConnell. *Sanctuary: The New Underground Railroad*. Maryknoll, NY: Orbis Books, 1986.

Gómez-Quiñones, Juan. *Chicano Politics: Reality and Promise, 1940–1990*. Albuquerque: University of New Mexico Press, 1990.

Gonzáles, Doreen. *César Chávez: Leader for Migrant Farm Workers*. Springfield, NJ: Enslow Publishers, 1996.

Gonzáles, Manuel G. *Mexicanos: A History of Mexicans in the United States*. Bloomington: Indiana University Press, 1999.

Gonzáles, Manuel G. and Cynthia M. Gonzáles, eds. *En Aquel Entonces: Readings in Mexican-American History*. Bloomington: Indiana University Press, 2000.

González, Justo L., ed. *Each in Our Own Tongue: A History of Hispanic United Methodism*. Nashville, TN: Abingdon Press, 1991.

Gonzalez-Wippler, Migene. *Santería: The Religion*. New York: Harmony Books, 1989.

Goodwin, David. *César Chávez: Hope for the People*. New York: Ballantine, 1991.

Gramsci, Antonio. *Selections from the Prison Notebooks*. New York: International Publishers, 1999.

Granjon, Henry. *Along the Río Grande: A Pastoral Visit to Southwest New Mexico in 1902*, ed. Michael Romero Taylor, trans. Mary W. de López. Albuquerque: University of New Mexico Press, 1986.

Grech, Daniel A. "Pastors Join Criticism, But Appeal for Calm." *Miami Herald* (April 23, 2000).

Greenspoon, Leonard Jay, and Bryan F. Le Beau, eds. *Sacred Text, Secular Times: The Hebrew Bible in the Modern World*. Bronx, NY: Fordham University Press, 2000.

Grenier, Guillermo J., and Hugh Gladwin. FIU 1997 CUBA POLL, Institute of Public Opinion Research (IPOR) of Florida International University and *The Miami Herald*. http://www.fiu.edu/orgs/ipor/cubapoll/index.html, #28.

Grijalva, Joshua. *A History of Mexican Baptists in Texas 1881–1981: Comprising an Account of the Genesis, the Progress, and the Accomplishments of the People Called "Los Bautistas de Texas."* Dallas: Office of Language Missions, Baptist General Convention of Texas, in cooperation with the Mexican Baptist Convention of Texas, 1982.

Griswold del Castillo, Richard. *The Treaty of Guadalupe Hidalgo: A Legacy of Conflict.* Norman: University of Oklahoma Press, 1990.

Griswold del Castillo, Richard and Richard A. García. *César Chávez: A Triumph of Spirit.* Norman: University of Oklahoma Press, 1995.

Guerrero, Andrés. *Chicano Theology.* Maryknoll, NY: Orbis Books, 1987.

Gutiérrez, David G. *Walls and Mirrors: Mexican Americans, Mexican Immigrants, and the Politics of Ethnicity.* Berkeley: University of California Press, 1995.

Gutiérrez, Félix. "The Western Jurisdiction." In *Each in Our Own Tongue,* ed. Justo L. González. Nashville, TN: Abingdon Press, 1991.

Gutiérrez, José Angel. *The Making of a Chicano Militant: Lessons from Crystal.* Madison: University of Wisconsin Press, 1998.

Hageman, Alice, and Philip E. Weaton, eds. *Religion in Cuba Today.* New York: Association Press, 1971.

Hall, Thomas D. *Social Change in the Southwest, 1350–1880.* Lawrence: University Press of Kansas, 1989.

Hamm, Ron. "Sanctuary Movement Raises Hard Political Questions." *National Catholic Register* (February 12, 1984): 1, 7.

Hammerback, John C, and Richard J. Jensen. *The Rhetorical Career of César Chávez.* College Station: Texas A&M University Press, 1998.

Hart, Stephen. *Cultural Dilemmas of Progressive Politics.* Chicago: University of Chicago Press, 2001.

Harris, Fredrick C. Something Within: Religion in African-American Political Activism. New York: Oxford University Press, 1999.

Hartmire, Chris. In *Chávez and the Farm Workers,* ed. Ronald B. Taylor. Boston: Beacon Press, 1975.

Haslip-Vieran, Gabriel. "The Evolution of the Latino Community in New York City: Early Nineteenth Century to the Present." In *Latinos in New York: Communities in Transition,* ed. Gabriel Haslip-Viera and Sherrie L. Baver, 3–30. Notre Dame, IN: University of Notre Dame Press, 1996.

Haslip-Viera, Gabriel, and Sherrie L. Baver. eds., *Latinos in New York: Communities in Transition.* Notre Dame, IN: University of Notre Dame Press, 1996.

Hernández, Edwin I. "Moving from the Cathedral to Storefront Churches: Understanding Religious Growth and Decline among Latino Protestants." In *Protestantes/Protestants: Hispanic Christianity within Mainline Traditions,* ed. David Maldonado Jr. Nashville, TN: Abingdon Press, 1999.

Hernández Castillo, Aída. "Identidades colectivas en los márgenes de la nación: etnicidad y cambio religioso entre los mames de Chiapas." *Nueva Antropología* 45 (Abril 1994): 83–106.

Hernández Hernández, Alberto. "Sociedades religiosas protestantes en la frontera norte: estudio sociográfico en tres localidades urbanas." *Frontera Norte* 8 (enero–junio 1996): 107–132.

______. "El desarrollo de las alternatives religiosas en la Frontera Norte." El Colegio de la Frontera Norte. Unpublished paper, 1999.

Hernández Madrid, Miguel J. "Los movimientos religiosos poscristianos en perspectiva global y regional." *Relaciones: estudios de historia y sociedad* 18 (Aug. 1997): 157–178.

Herrera-Sobek, María. *Northward Bound: The Mexican Immigrant Experience in Ballad and Song.* Bloomington: Indiana University Press, 1993.

Hochschild, Arlie Russell. *The Second Shift.* New York: Avon, 1989.

Hoffman, Patricia. *The Ministry of the Dispossessed.* Los Angeles: Wallace Press, 1987.

———. *The Pentecostals.* Minneapolis: Augsburg Publishing House, 1977.

Holmes, Burnham. *César Chávez: Farm Worker Activist.* Austin, TX: Raintree Steck Vaugn, 1994.

Hollenweger, Walter J. "The Critical Tradition of Pentecostalism." *Journal of Pentecostal Theology* 1 (1992): 7–17.

Horwitt, Sanford. *Let Them Call Me Rebel: Saul Alinsky-His Life and Legacy.* Knopf, 1989.

Hribar, Paul Anthony. "The Social Facts of César Chávez." Ph.D. diss., University of Southern California, 1978.

Iglesia Apostólica de la Fe en Cristo Jesús. *Himnario de Suprema Alabanza a Jesús.* Guadalajara, México: Iglesia Apostólica de la Fe en Cristo Jesús, 1996, 6th edition.

Isasi-Díaz, Ada María. *En la Lucha: Elaborating a Mujerista Theology.* Minneapolis: Fortress, 1993.

———. *Mujerista Theology.* Maryknoll, NY: Orbis Books, 1996.

———. "Roundtable Discussion: *Mujeristas* Who We Are and What We Are About." *Journal of Feminist Studies in Religion,* Vol. 8 (1) (Spring 1992).

Isasi-Díaz, Ada María, and Yolanda Tarango. *Hispanic Women: Prophetic Voice in the Church.* San Francisco: Harper & Row, 1988.

James, William. *The Varieties of Religious Experience.* New York: Simon & Schuster, 1997.

Jones, Arthur. "Millions Reaped What César Chávez Sowed." *National Catholic Reporter* (May 7, 1993).

Jorge, Antonio, Jaime Suchlicki, and Adolfo Leyva de Varuna. eds., *Cuban Exiles in Florida: Their Presence and Contribution.* Coral Gables, FL: University of Miami Press, 1991.

Joseph, James A. *Remaking America.* San Francisco: Jossey-Bass, 1995.

Juárez, José Roberto. "La iglesia Católica y el Chicano en sud Texas, 1836–1911." *Aztlán* 4 (Fall 1973): 230–232.

Katz, Steven. *Mysticism and Philosophical Analysis.* New York: Oxford University Press, 1978.

King, Wayne. "Church Members Will Press Sanctuary Movement." *New York Times* (January 23, 1985): A-24.

———. "Trial Opening in Arizona in Alien Sanctuary Case." *New York Times* (October 21, 1985): A-10.

———. "Use of Informers Questioned in Inquiry on Aliens." *New York Times* (March 2, 1985): 6.

Kirk, John. *Between God and the Party: Religion and Politics in Revolutionary Cuba.* Tampa: University Presses of Florida, 1988.

Knight, Henry H. III. "God's Faithful and God's Freedom: A Comparison of Contemporary Theologies of Healing." *Journal of Pentecostal Theology* 2 (1993).

Kowalewski, David. "The Historical Structuring of a Dissident Movement: The Sanctuary Case." *Research in Social Movements, Conflicts, and Change* 12 (1990): 95.

Lara-Braud, Jorge. "Hispanic-Americans and the Crisis in the Nation." *Theology Today* 26, no. 3 (1969): 334–338.

Laughlin, Meg. "Prayer Vigil Lifts Elián Fervor to New High." *The Miami Herald* (March 31, 2000).

León, Luis D. *La Llorona's Children: Religion, Life and Death in the U.S.-Mexican Borderlands*. Berkeley: University of California Press, 2004.

Levitt, Peggy. "Two Nations under God? Latino Religious Life in the United States," in *Latinos Remaking America*, ed. Marcelo M. Suárez-Orozco and Mariela M. Páez. Berkeley: University of California Press, 2002.

Levy, Jacques E. *César Chávez: Autobiography of La Causa*. New York: Norton, 1975.

Limón, José. *Dancing with the Devil: Society and Cultural Poetics in Mexican-American South Texas*. Madison: University of Wisconsin Press, 1994.

Lincoln, C. Eric, and Lawrence H. Mamiya. *The Black Church in the African-American Experience*. Durham, NC: Duke University Press, 1990.

Lindstrom, Naomi. *Twentieth-Century Spanish American Fiction*. Austin: University of Texas Press, 1994.

Linthicum, Robert C. *City of God, City of Satan: A Biblical Theology of the Church*. Grand Rapids, MI: Zondervan, 1991.

López Cortés, Eliseo. *Último cielo en la cruz: cambio sociocultural y estructuras de poder en Los Altos de Jalisco*. Zapopan: El Colegio de Jalisco, 1999.

López Torres, Samuel. *Historia de la Iglesia Apostólica de la fé en Cristo Jesús en Tijuana: 1927–1997*. Tijuana: Samuel López Torres, 1999.

Lorentzen, Robin. *Women in the Sanctuary Movement*. Philadelphia, PA: Temple University Press, 1991.

Loret de Mola, Patricia Fortuny, ed. *Creyentes y creencias en Guadalajara*. México, D.F.: Instituto Nacional de Antropología e Historia, 1999.

Lucas, Isidro. *The Browning of America: The Hispanic Revolution in the American Church*. Chicago: Fides/Claretian, 1981.

Lummis, Charles F. *The Land of Poco Tiempo*. New York: C. Scribner's Sons, 1893.

Macedo, Edir. *Nos Passos de Jesus*. Río de Janeiro: Editora Grafica Universal, 1986.

MacEoin, Gary, ed. *Sanctuary: A Resource Guide for Understanding and Participating in the Central American Refugees' Struggle*. San Francisco: Harper and Row, 1985.

Maldonado, Jr., David, ed. *Protestantes/Protestants: Hispanic Christianity Within Mainline Traditions*. Nashville, TN: Abingdon Press, 1999.

Mann, Michael. *The Sources of Social Power*, vol. 1. Cambridge: Cambridge University Press, 1986.

Manza, Jeff and Clem Brooks. *Social Cleavages and Political Change: Voter Alignments and U.S. Party Conditions*. New York: Oxford University Press, 1999.

Mariz, Cecília Loreto. *Coping with Poverty*. Philadelphia, PA: Temple University Press, 1994.

Marsden, George. *Fundamentalism and American Culture: The Shaping of Twentieth-Century Evangelicalism, 1870–1925*. New York: Oxford University Press, 1980.

Martínez, Abelino. *Las sectas en Nicaragua: oferta y demanda de salvación*. San José, Costa Rica: Editorial Departmento Ecuménico de Investigaciones, 1989.

Martínez, Jesús. "Los Tigres del Norte en Silicon Valley." *Nexos* 16 (noviembre 1993): 191.

Martínez-Fernández, Luis. *Protestantism and Political Conflict in the Nineteenth-Century Hispanic Caribbean*. New Brunswick, NJ: Rutgers University Press, 2002.

Massey, Douglas S. and E. Parrado. "Migradollars: The Remittances and Savings of Mexican Migrants to the United States." *Population Research and Policy Review* 13 (1994): 3–30.

Massey, Douglas S. and Audrey Singer. "The Social Process of Undocumented Border Crossing Among Mexican Migrants." *International Migration Review* 3, vol. 32 (Fall 1998): 561–592.

Massey, Douglas S., Rafael Alarcón, Jorge Durand, and Humberto González. *Return to Aztlán: The Social Process of International Migration from Western Mexico.* Berkeley: University of California Press, 1987.

Matovina, Timothy. "Guadalupan Devotion in a Borderlands Community." *Journal of Hispanic/Latino Theology* 4 (August 1996): 10–18.

______. "Lay Initiatives in Worship on the Texas Frontera, 1830–1860." *U.S. Catholic Historian* 12 (Fall 1994): 108–111.

______. *Tejano Religion and Ethnicity: San Antonio, 1821–1860.* Austin: University of Texas Press, 1995.

______. ed. *Beyond Borders: Writings of Virgilio Elizondo and Friends.* Maryknoll, NY: Orbis Books, 2000.

Matovina, Timothy, and Gerald E. Poyo, eds. *¡Presente! U.S. Latino Catholics from Colonial Origins to the Present.* Maryknoll, NY: Orbis Books, 2000.

Matthiessen, Peter. *Sal Si Puedes: César Chávez and the New American Revolution.* New York: Harcourt-Brace, 1997.

Matus, Alejandra. "El fevor religioso aumenta entre los manifestantes frente a la casa de Elián." *El Nuevo Herald* (April 22, 2000).

Mays, Benjamin E., and J. W. Nicholson. *The Negro's Church.* New York: Institute for Social Research, 1933.

Maza, Manuel. "The Cuban Catholic Church: True Struggles and False Dilemmas." M.A. thesis, Georgetown University, 1982.

McAdam, Douglas. *Political Process and the Development of Black Insurgency, 1930–1970.* Chicago: University of Chicago Press, 1982.

McConnell, Dan. *The Promise of Health and Wealth.* London: Hodder and Stoughton, 1990.

McGinn, Barnard. *The Foundations of Mysticism: Origins to the Fifth Century.* New York: Crossroad, 1997.

Medina, Lara. "Calpulli: A Chicano Self-help Organization." *La Gente* (1990).

______. "Las Hermanas: Chicana/Latina Religious-Political Activism, 1971–1997." Ph.D. diss., Claremont Graduate University, 1998.

Meehan, Francis X. *A Contemporary Social Spirituality.* Maryknoll, NY: Orbis Books, 1982.

Meier, Matt S. *Mexican-American Biographies: A Historical Dictionary 1836–1987.* New York: Greenwood Press, 1988.

Meier, Matt S., and Feliciano Ribera. *The Chicanos: A History of Mexican-Americans.* New York: Hill & Wang, 1972.

Meier, Matt S., Conchita Franco Serri, and Richard García. *Notable Latino Americans: A Biographical Dictionary.* Westport, CT: Greenwood Press, 1997.

Merina, Victor. "Cities vs. INS." *Los Angeles Times* (November 17, 1985): 1.

Mora, Pat. *Nepantla: Essays from the Land in the Middle.* Albuquerque: University of New Mexico Press, 1993.

Morán Quiroz, Luis R. *Alternativa religiosa en Guadalajara: una aproximación al estudio de las iglesias evangélicas.* Guadalajara, México: Universidad de Guadalajara, 1990.

Morris, Aldon D. *The Origins of the Civil Rights Movement.* New York: Free Press, 1984.

Muñoz, Carlos Jr. *Youth, Identity and Power: The Chicano Movement.* New York: Verso Books, 1992.

Nabokov, Peter. *Tijerina and the Courthouse Raid.* Albuquerque: University of New Mexico Press, 1969.

Náñez, Alfredo. *History of the Río Grande Conference of the United Methodist Church.* Dallas, TX: Bridwell Library, Southern Methodist University, 1980.
National Catholic Reporter. "Hispanics Now Enter Desert, Hard Part of the Journey." *National Catholic Reporter* (September 5, 1985): 7.
National Conference of Catholic Bishops. "Economic Justice for All: Pastoral Letter on Catholic Social Teaching and the U.S. Economy." Washington, DC: National Conference of Catholic Bishops, 1986.
Navarro, José Antonio, ed. *Defending Mexican Valor in Texas: José Antonio Navarro's Historical Writings, 1853–1857.* Austin, TX: State House Printing, 1996.
Navarro, Mireya. "Puerto Rican Presence Wanes in New York." *New York Times* (February 28, 2000).
Nelsen, Hart M., and Anne Kusener Nelsen. *Black Church in the Sixties.* Lexington: University of Kentucky Press, 1975.
Nelson, Eugene. *Huelga.* Delano, CA: Farm Workers Press, 1966.
Neri, Michael Charles. *Hispanic Catholicism in Transitional California: The Life of José González Rubio, O.F.M. (1804–1875).* Berkeley, CA: Academy of American Franciscan History, 1997.
New York Post. "Vieques Awakens." *New York Post* (June 10, 2003): 8.
Niebuhr, G. Richard. *The Social Sources of Denominationalism.* New York: Henry Holt, 1929.
Nieto, Leo D. "The Chicano Movement and the Churches in the United States/El Movimiento Chicano y las Iglesias en Los Estados Unidos." *Perkins Journal* 29 (Fall 1975): 32–41; 76–85.
______. "The Chicano Movement and the Gospel: Historical Accounts of a Protestant Pastor." In *Hidden Stories: Unveiling the History of the Latino Church,* ed. Daniel R. Rodríguez-Díaz and David Cortés-Fuentes, 143–143–157. Decatur, GA: Asociación para la Educación teológica Hispana, 1994.
______. "Un martes inolvidable (otra versión)." *Texas Methodist, Río Grande Conference Edition* (March 10, 1972): 1.
Novas, Himilce. *The Hispanic 100: A Ranking of Latino Men and Woman Who Have Most Influenced American Thought and Culture.* New York: Citadel Press, 1995.
Oro, Ari Pedro. " 'Podem passar a sacolhina': um estudo sobre as representações do dinheiro no pentecostalismo autônomo brasileiro atual." *Revista Eclesiástica Brasileria* 53 (April 1992).
______. "Religões pentecostais e meios de comunicação de massa no sul de Brasil." *Revista Eclesiástica Brasileira* 50 (June 1990).
Ostrow, Ronald. "Clergy, Nuns Charged with Alien Smuggling." *New York Times* (January 15, 1985): A-1.
Overman, Stephanie. "Refugee Crisis Challenges U.S. Policy." *Florida Catholic* (January 25, 1985): 8.
Pardo, Mary S. *Mexican American Women Activists: Identity and Resistance in Two Los Angeles Communities.* Philadelphia, PA: Temple University Press, 1998.
Paredes, Américo. *Folklore and Culture on the Texas–Mexican Border.* Austin: Center for Mexican-American Studies, 1993.
______. *With a Pistol in His Hand.* Austin: University of Texas Press, 1958.
Peña, Manuel. *The Texas–Mexican Conjunto: History of a Working-Class Music.* Austin: University of Texas Press, 1985.
Piar, Carlos R. "César Chávez and La Causa: Toward an Hispanic Christian Social Ethic." *Annual of the Society of Christian Ethics* (1996).

Pinkerton, James. "Deportation Case Flood Is Predicted." *Houston Chronicle* (June 27, 2001): A-17.

Pitrone, Jean Maddern. *Chávez: Man of the Migrants.* New York: Pyramid Books, 1972.

Pitt, Leonard. *The Decline of the Californios: A Social History of the Spanish-Speaking Californians, 1846–1890.* Berkeley: University of California Press, 1966.

Ponce, Eunice and Elaine de Valle. "Mania over Elián Rising." *Miami Herald* (January 10, 2000).

Portes, Alejandro, and Rubén G. Rumbaut. *Immigrant America: A Portrait.* Berkeley: University of California Press, 1996.

Portes, Alejandro, and Alex Stepick. *City on the Edge: The Transformation of Miami.* Berkeley: University of California Press, 1993.

Primera Hora. "A negociar para limpiar el uranio." (January 8, 2000).

Primera Hora. "Guerrillas sin armas de desobediencia en Vieques" (March 18, 2000).

Pulido, Alberto L. "Are You an Emissary of Jesus Christ? Justice, the Catholic Church, and the Chicano Movement." *Explorationsin Ethnic Studies,* 14 (January 1991): 30.

———. "Mexican-American Catholicism in the Southwest: The Transformation of a Popular Religion." In *En Aquel Entonces: Readings in Mexican-American History,* ed. Manuel G. Gonzáles and Cynthia M. Gonzáles. Bloomington: Indiana University Press, 2000.

———. *The Sacred World of the Penitentes.* Washington, DC: Smithsonian Institution Press, 2000.

———. Interview with Adam Díaz. Phoenix, AZ (February 6, 1996).

———. Interview with Father Tony Sotello. Phoenix, AZ (July 20, 2000).

———. Interview with Francisco Navarette. Phoenix, AZ (August 3, 2000).

———. Interview with Annette Willis Smith. Phoenix, AZ (August 3, 2000).

———. Interview with Rev. Warren H. Stewart. Phoenix, AZ (July 22, 2000).

Ramírez, Daniel. "Proposition 187 and the Latino Church." *Pacific News Service.* San Francisco (February 13, 1995).

———. "Interview with Bishop Benjamin Cantú." Los Angeles (September 20, 1994).

Reed-Bouley, Jennifer. "Guiding Moral Action: A Study of the United Farm Workers' Use of Catholic Social Teaching and Religious Symbols." Ph.D. diss., Loyola University, Chicago, 1998.

Remy, Martha Caroline Mitchell. "Protestant Churches and Mexican-Americans in South Texas." Ph.D. diss., University of Texas at Austin, 1971.

Richman, Gary. "When the Topic Is the Universal Church of the Kingdom of God." Río de Janeiro: AP Worldstream (November 28, 1995).

Roberts, Donovan O. "Theory and Practice in the Life of César Chávez: Implications of a Social Ethic." Ph.D. diss., Boston University, 1979.

Roberts, J. Deotis. *A Black Political Theology.* Philadelphia: Westminster, 1974.

Roberts, Naurice. *César Chávez and La Causa.* Chicago: Children's Press, 1986.

Robinson, Andrea. "A Community Looks to Heal." *Miami Herald* (April 24, 2000).

Rodríguez, Consuelo. *César Chávez.* Broomall, PA: Chelsea House, 1991.

Rodríguez, Daniel R., and David Cortés-Fuentes, eds. *Hidden Stories: Unveiling the History of the Latino Church.* Decatur, GA: Asociación para la Educación teológica Hispana, 1994.

Rodríguez, Olga, ed. *The Politics of Chicano Liberation.* New York: Pathfinder, 1977.

Rogers, Mary Beth. *Cold Anger.* Dallas: University of North Texas Press, 1990.

Rojas, José Vincente. *José: God Found Me in Los Angeles.* Hagerstown, MD: Review and Herald Publishing Association, 1999.

Rolim, Francisco Cartaxo. *Pentecostais no Brasil*. Petrópolis: Vozes, 1985.

Romero, Juan. "Begetting the Mexican-American: Padre Martínez and the 1847 Rebellion." In *Seeds of Struggle/Harvest of Faith: The Papers of the Archdiocese of Santa Fe Catholic Cuarto Centennial Conference on the History of the Church in New Mexico,* ed. Thomas J. Steele S.J., Paul Rhetts, and Barbe Awalt. Albuquerque: LPD Press, 1998.

———. "Ministry to Farm Workers: Experiences in Advocacy." *Notre Dame Journal of Education,* 5 (Summer 1974): 186–187.

———. "Religiosidad Popular as Locus for Theological Reflection and Springboards for Pastoral Action." Unpublished paper.

———. "Usefulness of Hispanic Survey to Ministers of the Southwest." Unpublished paper.

Romero, Juan, and Moises Sandoval. *Reluctant Dawn: Historia del Padre A. J. Martínez, Cura de Taos.* San Antonio, TX: Mexican-American Cultural Center Press, 1976.

Rosaldo, Renato, and William V. Flores. "Identity, Conflict, and Evolving Communities: Cultural Citizenship in San Jose, California." In *Latino Cultural Citizenship: Claiming Identity, Space and Rights,* ed. William V. Flores and Rina Benmayor. Boston: Beacon Press, 1997.

Rosales, F. Arturo. *Chicano! The History of the Mexican American Civil Rights Movement.* Houston: Arte Público, 1997.

Roth, Daniel Shoer. "Los cubanos se ven reflejados en el niño balsero." *El Nuevo Herald* (January 7, 2000).

Rothstein, Arthur H. "New Faith Group Hopes to Place Water in Desert Areas to Help Migrants." Associated Press release (December 26, 2000).

Ruiz, Vicki. *From Out of the Shadows: Mexican Women in Twentieth-Century America.* New York: Oxford University Press, 1998.

Ruth, Anders. *Igreja Universal do Reino De Deus.* Stockholm: Almqvist & Wiskell International, 1995.

Sachs, Susan. "Hispanic New York Shifted in 1990's, Puerto Ricans Lost Their Plurality." *New York Times* (May 22, 2001).

Salazar, Carolyn, and Manny García. "Federal Agents Seize Elián in Predawn Raid." *Miami Herald* (April 22, 2000).

Samora, Julian. *Los Mojados: The Wetback Story.* Notre Dame, IN: University of Notre Dame Press, 1971.

Samora, Julian, and Patricia Vandel Simon. *A History of the Mexican-American People.* Rev. ed. Notre Dame, IN: University of Notre Dame Press, 1993.

San Bernardino and Riverside Newsletter. "Two Hispanic Centers Dedicated" (October 18, 1981): 6–7.

San Juan Star. "Vieques Bomb Error Leaves 1 Dead, 4 Hurt" (April 20, 1999).

San Juan Star. "EPA Agrees to Waste Clean-Up" (January 11, 2000).

San Juan Star. "Business As Usual in Vieques Civil Disobedience Camps" (February 6, 2000).

San Juan Star. "Grupos pro-Vieques se Apoderan de El Morro" (April 19, 2000).

San Juan Star. "Navy tags $3.5 million for pre-vote campaign" (September 8, 2001).

San Juan Star. "Navy resume training amid renewed protests" (August 3, 2001).

Sánchez, George J. *Becoming Mexican American.* New York: Oxford University Press, 1993.

Sandoval, Moises, ed. *Fronteras: A History of the Latin American Church in the USA Since 1513.* San Antonio: Mexican-American Cultural Center Press, 1983.

———. *On the Move: A History of the Hispanic Church in the United States.* Maryknoll, NY: Orbis Books, 1991.

———. "The Organization of a Hispanic Church." In *Hispanic Catholic Culture in the U.S.: Issues and Concerns,* ed. J. P. Dolan and Allan Figueroa Deck S.J. Notre Dame, IN: University of Notre Dame Press, 1994.

Scarry, Elaine. *The Body in Pain.* New York: Oxford University Press, 1985.

Schanche, Don and J. Michael Kennedy. "Pope Lauds Sanctuary for Central Americans." *Los Angeles Times* (September 14, 1987): A-6.

Schmidt, Steve. "3 decades after Chavez hunger strike, UFW wages old battles." *San Diego Union Tribune* (November 8, 1998): A1.

Scholem, Gershom. *Major Trends in Jewish Mysticism.* New York: Schocken, 1961.

———. *On the Kabbalah and Its Symbolism.* New York: Schocken, 1961.

Scott, Janny. "Master of the Mosaic That Is New York City: Expert Keeps Tabs on Changing Population." *New York Times* (September 1, 2001).

Shaull, Richard, and Waldo Cesar. *Pentecostalism and the Future of the Christian Churches: Promises, Limitations, Challenges.* Grand Rapids, MI: Eerdmans, 2000.

Sheridan, Thomas E. *Los Tucsonenses: The Mexican Community in Tucson, 1854–1941.* Tucson: University of Arizona Press, 1986.

Sherman, Amy. "The Community Serving Activities of Hispanic Protestant Congregations." Unpublished paper. Washington, DC: Hudson Institute Faith in Communities Initiative, 2003.

Sherry, Gerard E. "Symposium Focuses on Sanctuary for Refugees." *Our Sunday Visitor* (February 24, 1985): 4.

Silva Gotay, Samuel. *Protestantismo y política en Puerto Rico: 1898–1930.* San Juan: Editorial de la Universidad de Puerto Rico, 1997.

Skerry, Peter. *Mexican Americans: The Ambivalent Minority.* New York: Free Press, 1993.

Slater, Eugene. Eugene Slater-Personal Papers Box 360, Item 16, "Valley Ministry. Fund for Reconciliation," Bridwell Library, Perkins School of Theology, Dallas, Texas.

Smith, Christian. *The Emergence of Liberation Theology: Radical Religion and Social Movement Theory.* Chicago: University of Chicago Press, 1991.

Smith, R. Drew. *New Day Begun: African-American Churches and Civic Culture in Post-Civil Rights America.* Durham, NC: Duke University Press, 2003.

Soto, Antonio R. "The Chicano and the Church in Northern California, 1848–1978: A Study of an Ethnic Minority within the Roman Catholic Church." Ph.D. diss., University of California, Berkeley, 1978.

Steele, Thomas J., ed. *New Mexican Spanish Religious Oratory, 1800–1900.* Albuquerque: University of New Mexico Press, 1997.

Steele, Thomas J., Paul Rhetts, and Barbe Awalt, eds. *Seeds of Struggle/Harvest of Faith: The Papers of the Archdiocese of Santa Fe Catholic Cuarto Centennial Conference on the History of the Church in New Mexico.* Albuquerque: LPD Press, 1998.

Suárez-Orozco, Marcleo M., and Mariela M. Páez, eds., *Latinos Remaking America* Berkeley: University of California Press, 2002.

Sylvest, Jr., Edwin. "Hispanic American Protestantism in the United States." In *Fronteras: A History of the Latin American Church in the USA Since 1513,* ed. Moíses Sandoval. San Antonio, Texas: Mexican-American Cultural Center, 1983.

———. "The Mexican-American Program: Twenty-five Years of History." *Apuntes: Reflexiones Teológicas desde el Margen Hispano* 20, no. 2 (2000): 47–48.

Taylor, Mary D. "Cura de la Frontera, Ramón Ortiz." *U.S. Catholic Historian* 9 (Winter/Spring 1990): 78–79.

Taylor, Ronald B. *Chávez and the Farm Workers*. Boston: Beacon Press, 1977.

Terzian, James and Kathryn Cramer. *Mighty Hard Road: The Story of César Chávez*. Garden City, NY: Doubleday, 1970.

Teixeira, Ruy. *The Disappearing American Voter*. Washington, DC: The Brookings Institution, 1992.

Texas Methodist. "Activist Chicano Group Splits off from COHAM." *Texas Methodist Rio Grande Conference Edition* (March 10, 1972).

Tijerina, Reies López. *¿Hallará Fe en la Tierra?* Self-Published, 1954.

———. "The Spanish Land Grant Question Examined." Albuquerque: Alianza Federal de Pueblos Libres, 1966.

———. *Mi lucha por la tierra*. México: Fondo de Cultura Economica, 1978.

Tomsho, Robert. *The American Sanctuary Movement*. Austin, TX: Texas Monthly Press, 1987.

Tonin, Neylor, ed. *Nem anjos nem demônios: interpretações sociológicas do Pentecostalismo*. Petrópolis: Editora Vozes, 1994.

Triay, Victor Andres. *Fleeing Castro: Operation Pedro Pan and the Cuban Children's Program*. Miami: University Press of Florida, 2002.

Turner, Mark. "Sanctuary Evidence Suppression Sought." *Arizona Daily Star* (March 29, 1985): B-1.

U.S. Census Bureau, 2000 Census. Washington, D.C., 2000.

U.S. Controller General, Report to the Congress of the United States. "Central American/Refugees: Regional Conditions and Prospects and Potential Impact on the United States," Washington, D.C.: General Accounting Office (July 20, 1984).

United Farm Workers Organizing Committee, "Statement of the Fast for Non-Violence," February 25, 1968.

Utset, Joaquin. "Devotos de la Virgen dicen ver una señal contra el regreso del niño." *El Nuevo Herald* (March 26, 2000).

———. "Miles de personas participan en virilia en Miami." *El Nuevo Herald* (April 11, 2000).

Utset, Joaquin, and R. Ferreira. "De la protesta cívica al júbilo popular." *El Nuevo Herald* (January 9, 2000).

Valverde, Jaime. *Las sectas en Costa Rica: pentecostalismo y conflicto social*. San José, Costa Rica: Editorial Departamento Ecuménico de Investigaciones, 1990.

Vargas, Zaragosa, ed. *Major Problems in Mexican-American History*. Boston: Houghton Mifflin, 1999.

Vázquez, Lourdes Celina. *Identidad, cultura y religion en el sur de Jalisco*. Zapopan: El Colegio de Jalisco, 1993.

Vega, Santos C. "Pedagogy of Mexican-American Catholic Religious Practice as Based on Indicators of the Hispanic Ministry Encuentro Process, Historical Religious Experience, and in Relationship with the Treaty of Guadalupe Hidalgo, 1848." 1848/1898@TranshistoricThresholds Conference, file: D:\1848cd\papr.vega.html, a CDD–ROM. Arizona State University: Gary D. Keller and Cordelia Candelaria. Tempe, AZ: Bilingual Press/Editorial Bilingue, 2000.

Verba, Sidney, Kay Lehman Schlozman, and Henry E. Brady. *Voice and Equality: Civic Voluntarism in American Politics*. Cambridge, MA: Harvard University Press, 1995.

Vernon, Walter N., Robert W. Sledge, Robert C. Monk, and Norman W. Spellman. *The*

Methodist Excitement in Texas: A History. Dallas, Texas: Texas United Methodist Historical Society/Bridwell Library, Southern Methodist University, 1984.
Vervier, Jaques Hillaire. "Utopia cristã e racionalidade ecnômica." *Revista Eclesiástica Brasileira* 51 (September 1991).
Villafañe, Eldin. *The Liberating Spirit: Towards an Hispanic American Pentecostal Social Ethic*. Grand Rapids, MI: Eerdmans, 1993.
———. "A Spiritual Father and Spiritual Leader: Rev. Ricardo Tañon—An Apostle in the Bronx." *Catalyst, Magazine of the Latino Pastoral Action Center,* 1 (July–September 1998): 16.
Walter, Dan. "Courage in the Sanctuary; Nun Says She Must Aid Refugees." *Bergen Record* (April 1, 1986): A-19.
Ware, Timothy. *The Orthodox Church*. New York: Penguin, 1963.
Warren, Mark. *Dry Bones Rattling*. Princeton, NJ: Princeton University Press, 2001.
Whitaker, Matthew C. "In Search of Black Phoenicians: African-American Culture and Community in Phoenix, Arizona, 1869–1940." M.A. thesis, Arizona State University, 1997.
White, Florance. *César Chávez: Man of Courage*. Champlain, IL: Garrard, 1973.
Willems, Emilio. *Followers of the New Faith*. Nashville: University of Tennessee Press, 1967.
Wills, Kendall J. "Churches Debate Role as Sanctuary." *New York Times* (June 16, 1985): 35.
Wood, Richard L. *Faith in Action: Religion, Race, and Democratic Organizing in America*. Chicago: University of Chicago Press, 2002.
Wood, Richard L. and Mark. R. Warren. "A Different Face of Faith-Based Politics: Social Capital and Community Organizing in the Public Arena." *International Journal of Sociology and Social Policy*, 22: 11/12 (Fall 2002): 6–54.
Wright, Robert E. "Popular and Official Religiosity: A Theoretical Analysis and a Case Study of Laredo–Nuevo Laredo, 1755–1857." Ph.D. diss., Graduate Theological Union, Berkeley, CA, 1992.
Wuthnow, Robert, and John H. Evans, eds. *The Quiet Hand of God: Faith-Based Activism and the Public Role of Mainline Protestantism*. Berkeley: University of California Press, 2002.
Wuthnow, Robert, Martin E. Marty, Philip Gleason, and Deborah Dash Moore. "Sources of Personal Identity: Religion, Ethnicity, and the American Cultural Situation." *Religion and American Culture: A Journal of Interpretation* 2 (Winter 1992).
Yinger, Winthrop. *César Chávez: Rhetoric of Nonviolence*. Hicksville, NY: Exposition Press, 1975.
Yohn, Susan M. *A Contest of Faiths: Missionary Women and Pluralism in the American Southwest*. Ithaca, NY: Cornell University Press, 1995.
Young, Jan. *The Migrant Workers and César Chávez*. New York: Julian Messner, 1977.
Young, Richard A. *Carpentier: El Reino de Este Mundo*. London: Gran & Cutler, 1983.

Index